BIOMETRICS, COMPUTER SECURITY SYSTEMS

AND

ARTIFICIAL INTELLIGENCE APPLICATIONS

BIOMETRICS, COMPUTER SECURITY SYSTEMS AND ARTIFICIAL INTELLIGENCE APPLICATIONS

Edited by

Khalid Saeed
Bialystok Technical University, Poland

Jerzy Pejaś
Szczecin University of Technology, Poland

Romuald Mosdorf
Bialystok Higher School of Finance and Management, Poland

 Springer

Khalid Saeed
Bialystok Technical University
Faculty of Computer Science
Wiejska 45A
15-351 Bialystok
POLAND
Email: aida@ii.pb.bialystok.pl

Jerzy Pejaś
Szczecin University of Technology
Faculty of Computer Science
Zolnierska 49
71 210 Szczecin
POLAND
Email: jpejas@wi.ps.pl

Romuald Mosdorf
University of Finance and
Management in Bialystok
Ciepla 40
15 472 Bialystok
POLAND
Email: mosdorf@wsfiz.edu.pl

Biometrics, Computer Security Systems and Artificial Intelligence Applications
Edited by Khalid Saeed, Jerzy Pejaś, and Romuald Mosdorf

e-ISBN-13: 978-0-387-36503-9
e-ISBN-10: 0-387-36503-6

ISBN-13: 978-1-4419-4212-8

Printed on acid-free paper.

© 2010 Springer Science+Business Media, LLC
All rights reserved. This work may not be translated or copied in whole or in part without the written permission of the publisher (Springer Science+Business Media, LLC, 233 Spring Street, New York, NY 10013, USA), except for brief excerpts in connection with reviews or scholarly analysis. Use in connection with any form of information storage and retrieval, electronic adaptation, computer software, or by similar or dissimilar methodology now know or hereafter developed is forbidden.
The use in this publication of trade names, trademarks, service marks and similar terms, even if the are not identified as such, is not to be taken as an expression of opinion as to whether or not they are subject to proprietary rights.

9 8 7 6 5 4 3 2 1

springer.com

FOREWORD

The book to which I was asked by the editors to write a foreword is an interesting collection of contributions. It presents the extended versions of the authors' works already introduced at the International Multi-Conference on Advanced Computer Information and Security Systems ACS-CISIM 2005. These contributions had already been reviewed once before the conference for presentation at the conference while some of them passed another selection to be prepared in their current versions for this book.

I am convinced the book will be of help to the researchers in the field of Computer Methods in Biometrics, Security Systems and Artificial Intelligence. They would find the contributions of other researchers of real benefit to them.

I would encourage those who have the book in hands to read it.

Professor Andrzej Salwicki

Faculty of Mathematics,
Informatics and Mechanics
Warsaw University, Poland

ACKNOWLEDGEMENTS

The editors are thankful to all contributors whose works have proved to be of great interest to all participants of the International Conference ACS-CISIM, which was held in Elk, Poland in summer 2005.

We also are greatly indebted to the Invited Speakers for their really worth listening and reading keynote talks.

The book could not have appeared without the deep devotion and hard effort of the reviewers, to whom the editors and the contributors really feel grateful. Their reviews for both the Conference Proceedings and this Postconference Book were of great benefit especially to the young researchers whose work still needed others' professional expertise and comments despite the fact that their scientific research output was positively evaluated. Most of the reviewers did proofreading instead of refereeing. We really are proud of having the book contributions reviewed by them.

Therefore, our indebtedness is due to all the following Professors:

1) Abraham Ajith
2) Bagiński Czesław
3) Bartkowiak Anna
4) Bielecki Włodzimierz
5) Bobrowski Leon
6) Choraś Ryszard S.
7) Dańko Wiktor
8) Huntsinger Ralph
9) Jarmolik Vyacheslav
10) Kuriata Eugeniusz
11) Kompanets Leonid
12) Madani Kurosh
13) Mirkowska Grażyna
14) Ochin Evgeny
15) Petrovsky Alexander
16) Piegat Andrzej
17) Rakowski Waldemar
18) Rogoza Walery
19) Salwicki Andrzej
20) Skarbek Władysław
21) Akira Imada
22) Stepaniuk Jarosław
23) Stokłosa Janusz
24) Tadeusiewicz Ryszard
25) Wierzchoń Sławomir

Editors: Khalid Saeed, Jerzy Pejaś, Romuald Mosdorf

INTRODUCTION

This book presents the most recent achievements in the field of a very fast developing Computer Science. It is a very fascinating science, which still encompasses a number of uncovered areas of study with urgent problems to be solved. Therefore, thousands of scientists are dealing with it elaborating on more and more practical and efficient methods. It is likely that their work will soon result in construction of a very effective, artificial computer-brain.

All scientific works presented in this book have been partitioned in three topical groups:

1. Image Analysis and Biometrics,

2. Computer Security Systems,

3. Artificial Intelligence and Applications.

All papers in the book are noteworthy, but especially we would like to draw the reader's attention to some particular papers beginning from part 1.

Image analysis and biometrics is the branch of Computer Science, which deals with a very difficult task of artificial, visual perception of objects and surroundings and problems connected with it. To the most remarkable papers in this part certainly
belongs the invited paper of Anna Bartkowiak et al. where the authors present an interesting mathematical model showing their experience in visualization multivariate data. In his invited paper, Ryszard Choraś introduces a survey on Content-Based Image Retrieval showing his and others' last achievements in this field. Three innovative papers on Face Recognition are also given in the same part. The remaining papers outline their authors' contribution to Speech Analysis, Signature Recognition using Dynamic Time Warping algorithm and hybrid fused approaches for Speech and Speaker Identification.

Computer Security and Safety is at present a very important and intensively investigated branch of Computer Science because of the menacing activity of hackers, of computer viruses etc. To the most interesting papers in this chapter belongs the invited paper of Janusz Stokłosa et al. It contains an excellent overview of experiments in designing S-boxes based o nonlinear Boolean functions. The authors present also their new algorithm for random generation of perfect nonlinear function. Krzysztof Chmiel's paper concerns also S-boxes, but in contrast to the previous paper, the author discusses the problem of the differential and the linear approximations of two classes of S-box functions. Two other papers relate to PKI services, which can be used for sending sensitive information and for the public key certificate status validation.

The third part of the book **Artificial Intelligence** contains 15 absorbing papers, five of which are keynotes and invited papers. The keynotes and invited papers presented at or sent to the ACS-CISIM 2005 conference introduce the latest achievements of their authors W. Dańko, G. Facchinetti et al., A. Imada, K. Madani, G. Mirkowska with
A. Salwicki (their keynote paper is not included in this book on their request),
R. Tadeusiewicz et al. and S. Wierzchoń et al. The new approaches or notes they show in Computer Artificial Intelligence and its applications are really worth making use of. The remaining papers in this part demonstrate the latest scientific results in the works of their authors in different aspects and areas of Computer Science and its wide applications.

The works contained in the presented book will surely enable you, Dear Reader, to keep pace with significant developments in Computer Science.

We wish you a great satisfaction from reading it.

Professor Leon Bobrowski, Dean   **Professor Andrzej Piegat, Dean**
Faculty of Computer Science   *Faculty of Computer Science*
Bialystok Technical University   *Szczecin University of Technology,*
Poland   *Poland*

TABLE OF CONTENTS

PART I - IMAGE ANALYSIS AND BIOMETRICS

PART II - COMPUTER SECURITY SYSTEMS

PART III - ARTIFICIAL INTELLIGENCE AND APPLICATIONS

PART I

IMAGE ANALYSIS AND BIOMETRICS

Image Filtration and Feature Extraction for Face Recognition

Tomasz Andrysiak and Michał Choraś

Image Processing Group, Institute of Telecommunications,
University of Technology and Agriculture,
Kaliskiego 7, 85-796, Bydgoszcz, Poland.
[andrys][chorasm]@atr.bydgoszcz.pl

Abstract. In the article we propose Gabor Wavelets and the modified Discrete Symmetry Transform for face recognition. First face detection in the input image is performed. Then the face image is filtered with the bank of Gabor filters. Next in order to localize the face fiducial points we search for the highest symmetry points within the face image. Then in those points we calculate image features corresponding to Gabor filter responses. Our feature vectors consist of so called Gabor Jets applied to the selected fiducial points (points of the highest symmetry) as well as the statistical features calculated in those points neighborhood. Then feature vectors can be efficiently used in the classification step in different applications of face recognition.

1 Introduction

Effective and fast face feature extraction and reliable face feature representation is a key problem in many applications. The most important areas involved in implementing good solutions for that problem are: human-computer interaction, face biometrics, interpretation of face expression, face coding and face tracking. Even though there are many known methods of face detection in images, face feature extraction and representation, still the performance of real-time recognition systems, e.g. for biometrics human identification, is not satisfactory.

In general face feature extraction and representation can be appearance based, 2D geometry based or 3D model based. Since it is difficult to achieve reliable invariance to changing viewing conditions (rotation in depth, pose changes) while basing on 2D geometry [1][15] and 3D models techniques [4][10], currently most of the algorithms are appearance based and use PCA or its derivatives ICA and LDA [2][13] [19].

Another popular approach, which is based on Gabor Wavelets, is also appearance based, but local features are computed in the specified points as Gabor filtration coefficients (responses). Such approach relies on filtering the face image by the bank of Gabor filters. Then faces can be efficiently represented by the filter coefficients (so called Gabor Jets) calculated in the extracted fiducial (characteristic) points [12][14][20]. It is mainly because Gabor Wavelets are invariant to some degree to affine deformations and homogeneous illumination changes.

Moreover, Gabor Wavelets are good feature extractors and its responses give enough data for image recognition. The recognition performance of different types of features had been compared in literature and it is shown that Gabor Wavelet coefficients are much more powerful than geometric features [22].

In the article we propose to use Gabor Wavelets for face feature extraction and face feature representation. In section 2 face detection by the ellipse fitting is presented. Face image filtration by the set of Gabor filters is covered in details in the section 3. In section 4 we describe fiducial points extraction and we cover Discrete Symmetry Transform. We also describe the algorithm for determining only the most significant symmetry points within the face.

Face feature calculation in those selected symmetry points is performed next. In each point we compute the responses of Gabor filters for different filter parameters. Moreover, in order to improve the effectiveness of face recognition, we also calculate statistical features. Such algorithm of feature extraction together with the face feature representation is presented in the section 5. Then feature vectors are used in the classification step. Experiments, application to face recognition, discussion and conclusion is given in the next sections.

2 Face Detection

Face detection and extraction of the fiducial (characteristic) points of face are the crucial operations before calculating face features. Face detection is usually performed basing on the Hough Transform but other methods such as deformable templates and color skin models are also used [9][17].

We perform the face detection by the ellipse fitting on the input images. We also use color information and skin models to efficiently localize faces [5][9].

The ellipse fitting algorithm is not restricted to fit the face perpendicularly, therefore if the face is rotated under the angle α, the ellipse is also under the angle α towards the vertical axis (as shown in Figure 6). In our method the face detection stage is mainly used for fiducial points selection (Section 4.3).

3 Face Image Filtration

The Gabor Wavelets are used for image analysis because of their biological relevance and computational properties. The Gabor filter kernels model similar shapes as the receptive field of simple cells in the primary visual cortex [16].

Those are multi-scale and multi-orientation kernels and each kernel is a product of a Gaussian envelope and a complex plane wave.

We use Gabor Wavelets to extract the facial features as the set of filter responses with determined scale and orientation values.

The responses image of the Gabor filter can be written as a convolution of the input image $I(\vec{x})$, with the Gabor kernel $\psi_{\mu,\nu}(\vec{x})$ such as:

$$R_{\mu,v}(\vec{x}) = I(\vec{x}_o) * \psi_{\mu,v}(\vec{x} - \vec{x}_o),   \tag{1}$$

where vector coordinates $\vec{x}$ of the image $I(\vec{x})$ are equal to $\vec{x} = (x, y)$ and $*$ denotes the convolution operator.

Gabor filters $\psi_{\mu,v}$ (kernels) can be formulated as:

$$\psi_{\mu,v}(\vec{x}) = \frac{\vec{k}_{\mu,v}^{2}}{\sigma^2} \exp\left(\frac{\vec{k}_{\mu,v}^{2} \vec{x}^2}{2\sigma^2}\right) \left[\exp(i\vec{k}_{\mu,v}\vec{x}) - \exp\left(-\frac{\sigma^2}{2}\right)\right]   \tag{2}$$

The parameters μ and v define the orientation and scale of the Gabor kernels and $\sigma = 2\pi$.

The wave vector $k_{\mu,v}$ is defined as follows:

$$\vec{k}_{\mu,v} = \begin{pmatrix} k_{x_{\mu,v}} \\ k_{y_{\mu,v}} \end{pmatrix} = \begin{pmatrix} k_v \cos\phi_\mu \\ k_v \sin\phi_\mu \end{pmatrix}, \quad k_v = 2^{-\frac{v+2}{2}} \pi, \quad \phi_\mu = \frac{\pi}{8}\mu,   \tag{3}$$

where k_v is the spacing factor between kernels in the frequency domain.

In most cases Gabor wavelets are used at five different scales and eight orientations [20]. Sometimes other configurations e.g. six orientations are also deployed [22].

Hereby, we use eight orientations $\mu \in \{0,1,...,7\}$ and three scales $v \in \{0,1,2\}$ as presented in Figure 1 and 2.

In general, $\psi_{\mu,v}(\vec{x})$ is complex, however, in our approach, only the magnitudes are used since they vary slowly with the position while the phases are very sensitive. Graphical representation of Gabor wavelet kernels are shown in Fig. 1.

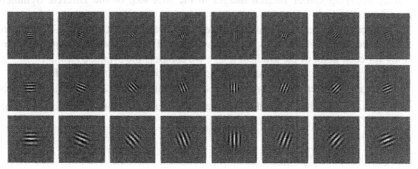

Fig. 1. The kernels of Gabor wavelets at three scales (top-down) and eight orientations (left to right).

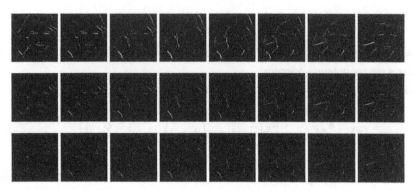

Fig. 2. Convolution outputs of example image (8 orientations and 3 resolutions).

4 Fiducial Points Extraction

In contrast to many methods which use manually selected fiducial points [22], we search for those points automatically. We use Discrete Symmetry Transform for choosing the points with the highest symmetry within the face. In contrast to a proposed method of DST [6][7], we apply DST onto combined image of Gabor directional filtration images.

Extraction of the High Symmetry Points

The face fiducial points extraction is based on the Discrete Symmetry Transform as presented in [6][7]. Hereby we modify the known method of symmetry points detection by applying Gabor filtered images in the first step of the Discrete Symmetry Transformation.

Our application to detect points of symmetry is developed in two steps. The first step is the Gabor Wavelet filtration for proper values of orientations and resolution. Secondly for each point of the gradient image we compute the symmetry value.

The algorithm to compute modified Discrete Symmetry Transform is following:

1. First we filter the image with the Gabor filters for 2 different orientations $(0, \pi/2)$. Then we add those images and in result of such filtering we obtain the combined image $O(x, y)$ such as:

$$O(x, y) = 1 - \sum_{\mu,v} R_{\mu,v}(x, y). \tag{4}$$

   The image $O(x, y)$ is presented in the Figure 4 (left).

2. Computation of the DST.

The Discrete Symmetry Transform is computed as the multiplication of the filter response image $O(x, y)$ with the image $M(x, y)$ such as:

$$DST(I(x, y)) = O(x, y) \times M(x, y),\tag{5}$$

where:

$$M(x, y) = \sqrt{\frac{1}{n}\sum_{k=0}^{n-1}(M_k(x, y))^2 - \frac{1}{n^2}\left(\sum_{k=0}^{n-1}(M_k(x, y))\right)^2},\tag{6}$$

and:

$$M_k(x, y) = \sum_{(p,q)\in\Pi_r}\left|(p-d)\sin\left(\frac{k\pi}{n}+\alpha\right) - (q-e)\cos\left(\frac{k\pi}{n}+\alpha\right)\right| \times I(x, y)\tag{7}$$

for the following parameters:
- (p, q) are the coefficients of each calculated symmetry point,
- (d, e) are the coefficients of the point belonging to the circle Π_r with the distance r from the point (p, q),
- Π_r is the circle centred in (p, q),
- r limits the size of the neighborhood of each point (p, q),
- n is the number of axial moments with the slope $k\pi/n$ with $k = 0, 1..., n$,
- and where α is the angle between the ellipse and the vertical axis of the image.

The final result of the modified DST computation is presented in Figure 5 (left).

Fig. 3. Results of directional Gabor filtration of for two orientations $(0, \pi/2)$.

Fig. 4. Images $O(x, y)$ (left) and $M(x, y)$ (right).

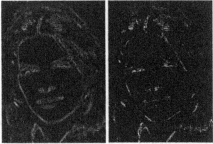

Fig. 5. Resulting image $DST(I(x, y))$ and image $ThreshDST(I(x, y))$.

Extracted Symmetry Points Thresholding

The computed $DST(I(x, y))$ gives the symmetry points on the $O(x, y)$ image, but not all the symmetry points become our fiducial points. In order to find the most significant of those points we perform the threshold operation according to the following rule [6]:

$$ThreshDST(I(x, y)) = \begin{cases} 1 & if \quad DST(I(x, y)) > mean + 3 * var \\ \\ 0 & otherwise \end{cases}, \quad (8)$$

where *mean* and var are the mean value and the standard deviation of $DST(I(x, y))$, respectively.

The resulting image $ThreshDST(I(x, y))$ is presented in Figure 5 (right).

Symmetry Points Selection

Moreover, in order to select only points within the faces, we take into account only those points which are localized within the area of the ellipse fitted into original input image as described in Section 2. The procedure of selecting fiducial points from the symmetry points is presented in the Figure 6.

Finally, we choose N points with the highest symmetry value within the detected ellipse and those points become our fiducial points. Usually we select 30 - 40 points of the highest value. Then in those points we calculate face features based on Gabor Wavelets responses (Gabor Jets) as presented in the next section.

Fig. 6. The consecutive steps of the fiducial points selection algorithm.

5 Face Feature Extraction and Representation

We calculate the face features only in the N extracted fiducial points. We usually choose 30-40 fiducial points. Moreover, we use Gabor filters responses for different orientations and scale as feature vector parameters (8 orientations × 3 scales). Therefore for each fiducial point we have a vector of 24 parameters. Such response vectors corresponding to face fiducial points are often called Gabor Jets [20]. The number of parameters in the final feature vector is given by:

$$F_{GJ} = \mu \times v \times N . \tag{9}$$

In order to enhance the effectiveness of standard Gabor Jets approach, we calculate the second feature vector in the extracted points neighborhood Ω *(k×k)*. Still we base on the Gabor-based filtration responses. Therefore the second feature vector consists of the following parameters:

1. mean value for $R_{\mu,v}^e(\vec{x})$ and $R_{\mu,v}^o(\vec{x})$:

$$sr_{\mu,v}^e(\vec{x}) = \mathop{E}_{\vec{x}\in\Omega}\left\{R_{\mu,v}^e(\vec{x})\right\}, \ sr_{\mu,v}^o(\vec{x}) = \mathop{E}_{\vec{x}\in\Omega}\left\{R_{\mu,v}^o(\vec{x})\right\} \tag{10}$$

2. variance for $R_{\mu,v}^e(\vec{x})$ and $R_{\mu,v}^o(\vec{x})$:

$$vr_{\mu,v}^e(\vec{x}) = \mathop{E}_{\vec{x}\in\Omega}\left\{R_{\mu,v}^e(\vec{x}) - sr_{\mu,v}^e(\vec{x})\right\}, \ vr_{\mu,v}^o(\vec{x}) = \mathop{E}_{\vec{x}\in\Omega}\left\{R_{\mu,v}^o(\vec{x}) - sr_{\mu,v}^o(\vec{x})\right\} \tag{11}$$

3. module and phase $R_{\mu,v}(\vec{x})$:

$$nr_{\mu,v}(\vec{x}) = \sqrt{\left(R_{\mu,v}^e(\vec{x})\right)^2 + \left(R_{\mu,v}^o(\vec{x})\right)^2}, \ pr_{\mu,v}(\vec{x}) = \arctan\left(\frac{R_{\mu,v}^e(\vec{x})}{R_{\mu,v}^o(\vec{x})}\right) \tag{12}$$

4. moments of order *p* and *q*:

$$mr_{\mu,v}^{(s,t)}(\vec{x}) = \mathop{E}_{\vec{x}\in\Omega}\left\{\vec{x}^{(s,t)} \cdot nr_{\mu,v}(\vec{x})\right\} \text{ for } (\vec{x})^{(s,t)} = \left(x^s, y^t\right) \tag{13}$$

where: $R_{\mu,v}^e(\vec{x})$ and $R_{\mu,v}^o(\vec{x})$ are the even and odd responses of Gabor Wavelets, respectively, and E is the averaging operator.

The second feature vector is given by:

$$F_S = \left[sr_{\mu,v}^e, \ldots, sr_{\mu,v}^o, \ldots, vr_{\mu,v}^e, \ldots, vr_{\mu,v}^o, \ldots, vr_{\mu,v}^e, \ldots, nr_{\mu,v}, \ldots, pr_{\mu,v}, \ldots, mr_{\mu,v}^{(s,t)} \ldots\right] \tag{14}$$

Such face feature vectors are used in the face recognition step. The recognition is based on simple comparison of the input image feature vector with all the vectors in the database. In the classification step we base on vector distances in feature space and we use City Block Classifier.

6 Experiments and Results

Reliable face feature extraction and representation depends on properly selected parameters in consecutive steps of our method. Firstly, the parameters of Gabor filters have to be properly tuned so that the effects of filtration can be further used in the calculation of the DST. Moreover, Gabor Wavelets also influence the face feature vector as it consists of the Gabor Wavelet responses.

We experimented with the number of scales and our conclusion is that 3 scales $v \in \{0,1,2\}$ are sufficient for reliable face representation. We can also add two more resolutions $v \in \{3,4\}$ but the filter responses are small and not distinctive within various images. Secondly, we experimented with the selection of parameters in the algorithm of the symmetry points calculation. Results for different selection of the radius value are presented in the Figure 7.

Another important factor in the symmetry points extraction algorithm is the number of symmetry axis. We use 2 axis: vertical and horizontal since in the case of faces such symmetries are most significant.

In our experiments we considered frontal view face images. For such dataset we obtained correct recognition ratio of 86% while comparing only Gabor Jets feature vector F_{GJ}, and 90% while comparing combined both vectors F_{GJ} and F_S.

Fig. 7. Points of the highest symmetry calculation for the radius value of 2 (left), 4 (middle) and 8 (right).

7 Conclusions

In the article we presented an efficient method of face recognition based on image filtering, novel method of automated fiducial points extraction and face feature representation. In our work we base on directional Gabor Wavelets and the modified Discrete Symmetry Transform for the extraction of the face fiducial points.

Then in those extracted points we apply parameterized bank of Gabor filters in order to calculate features needed for face representation and recognition. However, in contrast to many known methods, thanks to modified DST we extract the fiducial points automatically. The proposed method gives satisfactory results in comparison to other known implementations of EBGM and Gabor Jets approach to face recognition.

We obtain satisfactory correct recognition ratios while using combined both feature vectors F_{GJ} and F_S on frontal view face image databases for example FaDab [3].

Further work includes global features calculation and texture parameters calculation in fiducial points ROI neighborhoods.

References

1. Adini Y., Moses Y., Ullman S., *Face Recognition: the Problem of Compensating for Changes in Illumination Direction*, IEEE Trans. on PAMI, vol. 19, no. 7, 721-732, 1997.
2. Baek K., Draper B., Beveridge J., She K., *PCA vs. ICA: A Comparison on the FERET Data Set*, Proc. of Intl. Conf. on Computer Vision, Pattern Recognition and Image Processing, 2001.
3. Bobulski J., Face Identification Method Based on HMM, PhD Thesis (in polish), Czestochowa University of Technology, 2004.
4. Chang K., Bowyer K., Flynn P., *Face Recognition Using 2D and 3D Facial Data*, Proc. of Workshop on Multimodal User Authentication, 25-32, USA, 2003.
5. Choraś R.S., Choraś M, *Automatic face detection in 2D images* (in polish), Techniki Przetwarzania Obrazu, 262-267, Serock, 2002.
6. Gesu Di V., Valenti C., The Discrete Symmetry Transform in Computer Vision, Technical Report DMA 011 95.
7. Gesu Di V., Valenti C., Symmetry Operators in Computer Vision, Proc. CCMA Workshop on Vision Modeling and Information Coding, Nice, 1995.
8. Howell A.J., *Introduction to Face Recognition*, in Intelligent Biometric Techniques in Fingerprint and Face Recognition, CRC Press 1999.
9. Hsu R.L, Abdel-Mottaleb M., Jain A.K., *Face Detection in Color Images*, IEEE Trans. on PAMI, vol. 24, no 5, 696-706, 2002.
10. Kouzani A.Z., He F., Sammut K., *Towards Invariant Face Recognition*, Information Sciences 123, 75-101, Elsevier, 2000.
11. Kruger V., Potzsch M., Malsburg C.v.d., *Determination of Face Position and Pose with a Learned Representation Based on Labeled Graphs*, Technical Report 96-03, Ruhr-Universitat Bochum, 1996.
12. Kruger V., Sommer G., *Affine Real-time Face Tracking Using Gabor Wavelet Networks*, Proc. of ICPR, 141-150, Spain, 1999.
13. Liu C. Wechsler H., *Comparative Assesement of Independent Component Analysis (ICA) for Face Recognition*, Intl. Conf. AVBPA, 22-24, Washington DC, USA, 1999
14. Liu C. Wechsler H., *A Gabor Feature Classifier for Face Recognition*, Proc. of IEEE Intl. Conf. on Computer Vision, Canada, 2001.
15. Lee T., Ranganath S., Sanei S., *An Analytical Overwiev of New Trends in Face Recognition*, Proc. of IASTED Intl. Conf. on Signal Processing, Pattern Recognition and Applications, 202-206, Greece, 2002.
16. Marcelja S., *Mathematical description of the responses of simple cortical cells*, Journal of the Optical Society of America, 2(7), 1297-1300, 1980.
17. Pietrowcew A., *Face detection in colour images using fuzzy Hough transform*, Opto-Electronics Review 11(3), 247-251, 2003.
18. Reisfeld D., Yeshurun Y., *Robust Detection of Facial Features by Generalized Symmetry*, Proc. of ICPR, 1:117-120, The Netherlands, 1992.
19. Romdhani S., *Face Recognition Using Principal Component Analysis*, Technical Report, University of Glasgow, UK, 1996.
20. Wiskott L., Fellous J.M., Kruger N., Malsburg C.v.d., *Face Recognition by Elastic Bunch Graph Matching*, IEEE PAMI, vol. 19, 775-779, 1997.
21. Yang M.H., Kriegman D., Ahuja N., *Detecting Faces in Images: A Survey*, IEEE Trans. on PAMI, vol. 24, 34-58, 2002.
22. Zhang Z., Lyons M., Schuster M., Akamatsu S., *Comparison Between Geometry-Based and Gabor-Wavelets-Based Facial Expression Recognition Using Multi-Layer Perceptron*, Proc. of Intl. Conf. on Automatic Face- and Gesture- Recognition, Nara, Japan, 1998.

Visualization of Some Multi-Class Erosion Data Using GDA and Supervised SOM

Anna Bartkowiak[1], Niki Evelpidou[2]

[1] Institute of Computer Science, University of Wrocław,
Przesmyckiego 20, 51-151 Wrocław Poland, aba@ii.uni.wroc.pl
[2] Remote Sensing Laboratory, University of Athens
Panepistimiou Zoografou, Athens, Greece, evelpidou@geol.uoa.gr

Abstract. We present our experience in visualization multivariate data when the data vectors have class assignment. The goal is then to visualize the data in such a way that data vectors belonging to different classes (subgroups) appear differentiated as much as possible. We consider for this purpose the traditional CDA (Canonical Discriminant Functions), the GDA (Generalized Discriminant Analysis, Baudat and Anouar, 2000) and the Supervised SOM (Kohonen, Makivasara, Saramaki 1984). The methods are applied to a set of 3-dimensional erosion data containing N=3420 data vectors subdivided into 5 classes of erosion risk. By performing the mapping of these data to a plane, we hope to gain some experience how the mentioned methods work in practice and what kind of visualization is obtained. The final conclusion is that the traditional CDA is the best both in speed (time) of the calculations and in the ability of generalization.

1 Introduction

We consider the problem of multivariate data visualization when each data vector has a class (group) assignment. Generally, methods of data visualization perform linear or nonlinear mapping to a manifold of lower dimension. Say, this lower dimension is q. The most common visualization uses $q = 2$. Generally, it is expected that the projection gives us an idea on the shape of the data cloud. Here, we want more: Using the information about crisp group assignment ('crisp' is used here in the opposite meaning of 'soft'), we seek for such a projection (mapping), which shows distinctly differentiation between various groups of the data.

When intending a graphical visualization of the data, we should ask in first step about the intrinsic dimensionality of the data. It could happen that all the observed variables are generated by some unobserved variables, so called 'latent variables' located in a manifold of lower dimension – and we should know it. Thus, we should ask about the intrinsic dimensionality of the analyzed data. We will use for this purpose the correlation integral $C(r)$ and the correlation dimension D introduced by Grassberger and Procaccia [6], [4].

The next question is: What kind of projection or mapping should we use? The most simple method is the classical one using Fishers' criterion based on the between and within class variance and yielding so called 'canonical discriminant variates' or canonical discriminant functions [2], [5], [7], [12]. The method belongs to the class of linear methods and is referred to as CDA or Fisherian LDA. The method is extendable to the class of nonlinear methods – by use of appropriate transformation of the data. In particular one may use kernel transformations [8], [9], [5], [11].

Using the kernel approach, Baudat and Anouar [2] proposed a non trivial generalization of the canonical discriminant analysis. They called their algorithm GDA (generalized discriminant analysis). It represents the nonlinear discriminant functions.

As an alternative to the nonlinear GDA we will consider also quite a different algorithm, called SOM supervised (SOM_s) and based on a modification of Kohonens' self organizing map .

In the following, we will show how the mentioned methods work when analyzing a real data set of a considerable size, i.e. about 3 thousands of data vectors. The data set is subdivided into 5 erosion classes. We take for our illustration only 3 variables known as predictors for the erosion risk. In the case of 3 variables it is possible to visualize the data in a 3D plot. For the considered erosion data, the 3D plot shows plainly that the relations between the variables are highly nonlinear; thus nonlinear projection methods might show a more distinctive differentiation among the erosion classes.

The paper is organized as follows. In Sect. 2 we describe the data and their correlation dimension. Sect. 3 explains the accepted Fishers' criterion of separation between classes and the principles of building canonical discriminant functions (CDA alias LDA). Sect. 4 shows the nonlinear extension of LDA using the kernel approach proposed by Baudat and Anouar. In Sect. 5 we describe briefly the supervised SOM. Finally, Sect. 6 contains some concluding remarks.

2 The Erosion Data

Our interest in a trustful visualisation of subgroups of data originated from the research of erosion risk observed in the Greek island Kefallinia. The entire island was covered by a grid containing 3422 cells. The area covered by each cell of the grid was characterized by several variables. For our purpose, to illustrate some visualization concepts, we will consider in the following only 3 variables: drainage density, slope and vulnerability of the soil (rocks). The values of the variables were rescaled to belong to the interval [0, 1]. Thus, for our analysis, we got a data set containing N=3422 data vectors, each vector characterized by 3 variables. Using an expert GIS system, each data vector was assigned to one of five erosion classes: 1. very high (vH), 2. high (H), 3. medium (Me), 4. low (L) and 5. very low (vL). A 3D plot of the data is shown in Fig. 1. The data set contains a few outliers, which are strongly atypical observations. Two of them will be removed from further analysis.

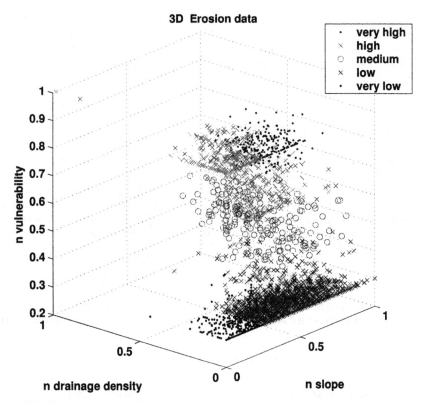

Fig.1. Visualization of the Kefallinia erosion data containing N=3422 data points, subdivided into 5 classes of progressing erosion risk. In some parts of the space the data points are much condensed. Two severe outliers are visible top left – they will be dropped in further analysis

The different classes of the data set are marked by different symbols and/or colours. Looking at the plot in Fig. 1 one may state that, generally, the distribution of the data is far from normality, also far from the ellipsoidal shape. The hierarchy of the classes exhibits a nonlinear pattern. Some parts of the space show a great concentration of the data points, while some other parts are sparsely populated.

The fractal correlation dimension calculated using the Grassberger-Proccacia index [6], [4] equals D = 1.6039. This is the estimate of the intrinsic dimension for the considered erosion data (For comparison, we have performed analogous calculations for two synthetic data sets of the same size, generated from the 3D and 5D normal distributions; as expected, we obtained the values D_3 = 3.0971 and D_5 = 4.9781 appropriately). Thus – the intrinsic dimension of the considered data set is less then 2 and a planar representation of the data is justified.

The data set contained two big outliers. To not confound the effects of the outliers and the effects of the methods, we have removed the outliers from the analyzed set. Next we subdivided the remaining 3400 data vectors into two parts (halves), each

counting N = 1710 data items. The first part (labelled samp1) was destined for learning (establishing the parameters of the models), and the second part (samp2) as test.
In the next three sections we will show mapping of the data to a 2D plane using three
different methods: canonical discriminant functions (CDA alias LDA), kernel discriminant functions (GDA) and the supervised SOM (SOM_s).

3   Canonical Discriminant Functions

We show now the canonical discriminant functions derived from Fishers' criterion.
The method is called sometimes also LDA [5], [2].
The case of *the two-class problem.* R. A. Fisher proposed to seek for the linear combination (**a**) of the variables, which separates the two indicated classes as much as
possible. The criterion of separateness, proposed by Fisher, is the ratio of between-
class to within-class variances. Formally, the criterion is defined as the ratio (see, e.g.
Duda [6] or Webb [11])

$$JF2 = [aT(m1-m2)]2 / [aTSw\ a],\quad \text{(2-class problem)}$$

where **a** is the sought linear form, m_1 and m_2 denote the sample group means, and S_w
is the pooled within-class sample covariance matrix, in its bias-corrected form given
by

$$S_w = (n_1 S_1 + n_2 S_2) / (n_1 + n_2 - 2).$$

Maximizing the J_{F2} criterion yields as solution the sought linear combination **a** for the
two-class problem.
In the case of *the multi-class problem,* – when we have k classes, k≥2, with sample
sizes $n_1, \ldots, n_k$ totaling N, and the overall mean m_* – the criterion J_{F2} is rewritten as
the criterion J_{Fk}, which accommodates the between class and within class variances:

$$J_{Fk} = \sum_j n_j a^T (m_j - m_*)^2 / [a^T S_w\ a],\ j=1,\ldots k\ \ (\textit{k-class problem})$$

where m_j denotes the mean of the j-th class and m_* stands for the overall sample
mean. The within class variance S_w is evaluated as (S_j denotes the covariance matrix
in the jth class, j=1, … ,k):

$$S_w = (\sum_j n_j S_j)/(N-k).$$

Maximizing the criterion J_{Fk} with respect to **a** we obtain, with accuracy to the sign, h
solutions, i.e. h vectors $a_1, \ldots, a_h$, h = min (k-1, rank of **X**), with **X** being the data
matrix. From these we obtain h canonical variates: $y_j = X a_j$, j = 1, … , h, called also
canonical discriminant functions. The separateness of the subgroups, attained when
considering the transformation yielded by subsequent canonical discriminant variates,
is measured by the criterion J_{Fk} evaluated as $J_{Fk}(a_j)$ and called also *lambda $_j$*. For each

vector a_j we obtain its corresponding value *lambda$_j$* = *lambda(a_j)* denoting the ratio of the between to the within class variance of the respective canonical variate derived from the vector a_j. Thus a big value of *lambda$_j$* indicates a high discriminative power of the derived canonical variate.

For the analyzed erosion data we got h=3 vectors a_1, a_2, a_3 and corresponding to them 3 values of *lambda* equal to [22.1995 0.7982 0.0003]. One may notice that the first canonical variate – compared to the remaining ones - has a very big discriminative power, while the contribution of the third canonical variate is practically none.

The projection of the data, when using the first two canonical variates, is shown in Fig. 2. One may notice that the subgroups are quite well separated. One may notice also that the second canonical variate, which – taken alone – has practically no discriminative power, however, when combined with the first variate, helps much in the display, i.e. in distinguishing the classes of erosion risk. We got very similar values of *lambda* and very similar displays both for the learning and the testing data sets (i.e. for samp1 and samp2) – thus the method has good generalization abilities.

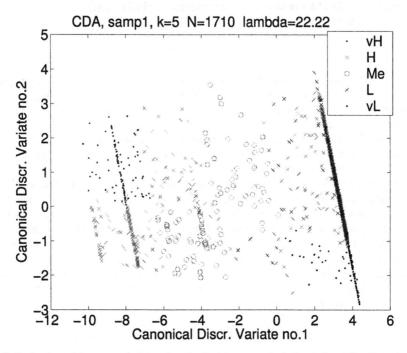

Fig.2. Projection of the samp1 data using the first two canonical discriminant functions derived from Fisher's criterion. The very low and very high erosion points keep opposite position, right and left, in the exhibit. The display for the samp2 data looks identical

4 Nonlinear Projection Using the Kernel Approach

The CDA, described in previous section, considers only linear functions of the variables and is proper when the groups (classes) are distributed elliptically. For our data this is not the case. Therefore, some nonlinear methods might be better for visualizing the class differentiation. A kind of non-linear discriminant analysis, called GDA (*Generalized Discriminant Analysis*) was proposed by Baudat and Anouar [2]. Their algorithm maps the input space into an extended high dimensional feature space. In the extended space, one can solve the original nonlinear problem in a classical way, e.g., using the CDA. Speaking in other words, the main idea is to map the input space into a convenient feature space in which variables are nonlinearly related to the input space. The fact of mapping original data in a nonlinear way into an extended feature space was met in the context of support vector machines (SVM) see e.g., [5], [8], [9], [11]. The mapping uses predominantly kernel functions. Direct coordinates – in the extended space – are not necessary, because the kernel approach needs only computations of so called 'dot products' formed from the original features.

Generally, the mapping reads

$$\Phi\colon X {\rightarrow} F,$$

with X denoting the input space (original data), and F the extended feature space, usually of higher dimensionality as the original data space. The mapping Φ transforms elements $\mathbf{x} \in X$ from the original data space into elements $\Phi(\mathbf{x}) \in F$, i.e. elements of the feature space.

Statistical and/or pattern recognition problems use extensively cross products (inner products), e.g. for obtaining the within and between group covariance. To calculate them, a special notation of kernel products was invented.

Let $\mathbf{x}_i$ and $\mathbf{x}_j$ denote two elements (row data vectors) of the input data matrix X. The *kernel function* $k(\mathbf{x}_i, \mathbf{x}_j)$ returns the inner product $\Phi^T(\mathbf{x}_i)\Phi(\mathbf{x}_j)$ between the images of these inputs (located in the feature space). It was proved that for kernel functions satisfying some general analytical conditions (possessing so called Mercer properties) the kernel functions $k(\mathbf{x}_i, \mathbf{x}_j)$ can be expressed as simple functions of the inner product $<\mathbf{x}_i, \mathbf{x}_j>$ of the original vectors. In such a case, we can compute the inner product between the projections of two points into the feature space *without evaluating explicitly* their coordinates (N denotes the number of data vectors, i.e. the number of rows in the data matrix $\mathbf{X}$):

$$k(\mathbf{x}_i, \mathbf{x}_j) = \Phi^T(\mathbf{x}_i)\Phi(\mathbf{x}_j) = k(<\mathbf{x}_i, \mathbf{x}_j>), \quad \text{for } i,j = 1, \dots, N.$$

The GDA algorithm operates on the kernel dot product matrix $\mathbf{K} = \{k(<\mathbf{x}_i, \mathbf{x}_j>\}$ of size N x N, evaluated from the learning data set. The most commonly used kernels are Gaussians (RBFs) and polynomials.

Let x, y be the two (row) input vectors. Let $d = x-y$. Using Gaussian kernels, the element $z = k(<\mathbf{x}_i, \mathbf{x}_j>)$ is evaluated as: $z = \exp\{-(d*d^T)/\sigma\}$. The constant σ, called kernel width, is a parameter of the model; its value has to be declared by the user.

Baudat and Anouar use as the index of separateness of the constructed projection a criterion, which they call **inertia**. This criterion is defined as the ratio of the between class to the total variance of the constructed discriminant variates. The inertia criterion takes values from the interval [0, 1]. High values of inertia indicate a good separation of the displayed classes.

For our evaluation we have used Matlab software implemented by Baudat and Anouar. For k = 5 classes we got 4 discriminative variates. The largest values of inertia were noted, as expected, for the first two GDA variates. What concerns the kernel width σ, we have tried several values: σ = 0.0005, 0.005, 0.05, 0.5, 1, 4, 6.5, 9, 14. For each value of σ, the system has been learning using the samp1 data, next the established model was tested using the samp2 data. Each run (i.e. calculations for one value of σ) needed about 12 minutes of computer time (PC, XPHome, Intel® Pentium® 4, Mobile CPU 1.80GHz, 512 MB RAM). The samp1 and samp2 data were of size [1710, 3]. Thus the computations were quite lengthy.

Generally, it was stated that for decreasing values of σ the classes appeared more and more separated (for values σ = 0.5 to 14, the displays were quite similar). As an exemplary exhibit we show here Fig. 3, obtained for σ = 1. The resulting inertias for variates no. 1-4 are: [0.968650 0.705236 0.550547 0.257248].

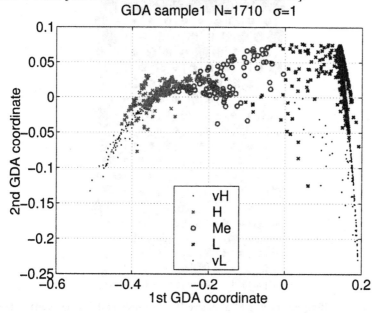

Fig. 3. GDA using Gaussian kernels with σ = 1 applied to the samp1 data. Horizontal and vertical axes denote first and second GDA coordinates. Five classes of data points corresponding to decreasing erosion risk – appearing from left (very high risk) to right (very low risk) – are marked differently. Generally, the topology of the subgroups is preserved and the groups appear fairly separated and condensed

The overall pattern of the point configuration in Fig. 3 is the same as in Fig. 2. From left to right we see groups of points corresponding to areas with very high (vH), high

(H), medium (Me), low (L), and very low (vL) erosion risk. Generally, the topology of the subgroups is preserved. Both variates contribute significantly to the differentiation of the risk classes. Unfortunately, the model when applied to the test set, yields projections appearing in quite different areas; thus it is not able to make the generalization.

5 Supervised SOM

Kohonen's self-organizing maps are a popular tool for visualization of multivariate data. The method was successfully applied to the Kefallinia erosion data [1].
The SOM method uses a general purpose methodology without accounting specially for the additional information on class membership of the data points. However, after constructing the map, we may indicate by so called 'hits', what is the distribution (location) of the different classes. Map with hits of the classes is shown in Fig. 4 below.

Sample1 Hits of 5 classes

Fig.4. Ordinary self-organizing map SOM of size 19 x 11 constructed from the samp1 learning data set using the Matlab SOM Toolbox by Vesanto *et al.* [10]. The erosion risk classes are neatly separated, with single overlapping hexagons. The erosion risk is progressing from the north (low risk) to the south (high risk)

Similarly as Fig. 3, also Fig. 4 was obtained using the data set samp1. When constructing the map, the class membership information was not used, The map was created and graphed using the Matlab SOM Toolbox [10]. The same toolbox contains also another procedure, called 'som_supervised' (SOM_s), and based on a proposal by Kohonen et al. [7], how to include during the process of training the information on class membership. The procedure was added to the Matlab SOM Toolbox by Juha Parhankangas, who keeps the copyright of that procedure [10].

We have applied the 'som_supervised' technique to our data with the hope that it will ameliorate the already good differentiation among the classes. The result was negative: we got even a deterioration of the display.

We considered the idea that perhaps we should normalize our data in a different way, say statistically, to have the data with mean=0 and variance=1. Result: We got even more mixed classes.

The **quality of a SOM** is usually measured by two indices: the quantization error q_e and the topographical error t_e [10]. They are:

	q_e	t_e
Ordinary map:	0.0362	0.0327
Supervised map:	0.0453	0.1544
Ordinary normalized:	0.2203	0.0246
Supervised normalized:	0.2247	0.0596

Thus our conclusion: the best **SOM quality** is attained for the ordinary SOM.

6 Concluding Remarks

We compared in detail three methods serving for visualization of multivariate data, whose intrinsic dimension - as evaluated by the correlation fractal dimension - equals 1.60. This justifies the mapping of the data to a plane. The data were subdivided into 5 erosion risk classes and we wanted the mapping algorithm to take into account the class membership.

From the 3 investigated methods, the first one uses classical canonical discriminant functions (CDA alias LDA), which provide linear projections. The other two applied methods were: Generalized Discriminant Analysis (GDA) based on Gaussian kernels, and the som supervised SOM (SOM_s), a variant of Kohonen's self-organizing map. All the 3 considered methods yielded similar results. In all projections, the erosion risk subgroups appeared fairly separated, as it should be. The GDA, by a proper tuning of the parameter 'sigma', yielded the classes more and more condensed and separated, however without generalization to other samples.

All the 3 methods preserved roughly the topology of the data, although the GDA has twisted sometimes the planar representation of the high and very high erosion group. The SOM_s appeared worse than the ordinary SOM, both in som quality and in differentiation of the risk classes. This is to a certain degree justified, because the ordinary SOM is trained to be optimal in the som quality, which means to be optimal in achieving both small quantization error and small topographic error. A change in conditions of the training may cause a deviation from optimality.

What concerns time of computing, the classical CDA and the SOM (also SOM_s) worked extremely fast (several seconds), while the kernel GDA needed about 12 minutes. This happens not only for the GDA. Let us mention that lengthy calculations do happen also for some other nonlinear methods, especially, when the complexity of calculations depends essentially from the cardinality of the analyzed data set.

References

1. Bartkowiak, A., Szustalewicz, A., Evelpidou, N., Vassilopoulos, A.: Choosing data vectors representing a huge data set: a comparison of Kohonen's maps and the neural gas method. Proc. of the First Int. Conf. on Environmental Research and Assessment, Bucharest, Romania, March 23–27, 2003. Ars Docendi Publishing House, Bucharest (2003) 5–20
2. Baudat, G., Anouar, F.: Generalized discriminant analysis using a kernel approach. Neural Computation 12 (2000) 2385–2404
3. Baudat G., Anouar F., Feature vector selection and projection using kernels. Neurocomputing 55 (2003) 21–38
4. Camastra, F., Vinciarelli, A.: Estimating the intrinsic dimension of data with a fractal-based method, IEEE Transactions on Pattern Analysis and Machine Intelligence, 24 (2002) 10 1404–1407
5. Duda, R.O., Hart, P.E., Stork D.E.: Pattern Classification, 2nd Edition, Wiley (2001)
6. Grassberger, P., Procaccia, I.: Measuring the strangeness of strange attractors. Physica D9 (1983) 189–208
7. Kohonen, T., Makisavara, K., Saramaki, T. :Phonetic maps – insightful representation of phonological features for speech recognition. ICPR Montreal, Canada (1984) 182–185
8. Shawe-Taylor, J., Christianini, N.: Kernel Methods for Pattern Recognition, Cambridge University Press (2004)
9. Scholkopf, B., Smola, A., Muller, K.R.: Nonlinear component analysis as a kernel eigenvalue problem. Neural Computation 10 (1998) 1291–1398
10. Vesanto, J., Himberg, J., Alhoniemi, E., Parhankangas, J. : SOM Toolbox for Matlab 5. Som Toolbox Team, Helsinki, HUT, Finland, Libella Oy, Espoo (2000), http://www.cis.hut.fi/projects/somtoolbox (2005)
11. Webb, A., Statistical Pattern Recognition. 2nd Edition, Wiley (2002) reprint (2004)
12. Yang, J., Jin, Z., et. al. : Essence of kernel Fisher discriminant: KPCA plus LDA. Pattern Recognition 37 (2004) 2097–2100

Wavelet Transform in Face Recognition

Janusz Bobulski

Czestochowa University of Technology
Institute of Computer and Information Science
Dabrowskiego Str. 73
42-200 Czestochowa, Poland
e-mail: januszb@icis.pcz.pl

Abstract: One of the parts person's identification systems is features extraction. This process is very important because effectiveness of system depend of it. Successful Wavelet Transform can be used in systems of persons' identification and pattern recognition.

Keywords: Face recognition, face identification, features extract, biometrics.

1 Introduction

A problem of person's identification is one of the main questions of many research centres at present. Interest of this discipline is a result of potential possibilities of practical application of new possibilities in person's identification in the systems demanding authorizations of person's access entitled to use potential resources.
One of the parts person's identification systems is features extraction. This process is very important because effectiveness of system depend of it. There are many difference way features extraction eigenface, Fourier Transform etc. This paper proposes in order to do this use Wavelet Transform (WT).
The features extraction has to get out information from a signal (image), which will be base for person identification. The separation of useful information from nose is very important, because this data will be used for identification and should clearly describe the face.

2 Wavelet Transform of Images

2.1 One-level Wavelet Transform

One major advantage afforded by wavelets is the ability to perform local analysis --
that is, to analyse a localized area of a larger signal. In wavelet analysis, we often
speak about approximations and details. The approximations are the high-scale, low-
frequency components of the signal. The details are the low-scale, high-frequency
components [1].

Using 2D WT (Fig. 1.), the face image is decomposed into four subimages via the
high-pass and low-pass filtering. The image is decomposed along column direction
into subimages to high-pass frequency band H and low-pass frequency band L. Assuming that the input image is a matrix of m x n pixels, the resulting subimages become $m/2$ x n matrices. At second step the images H and L are decomposed along row
vector direction and respectively produce the high and low frequency band HH and
HL for H, and LH and LL for L. The four output images become the matrices of $m/2$ x
$n/2$ pixels. Low frequency subimage LL (A_1) possesses high energy, and is a smallest
copy of original images (A_0). The remaining subimages LH, HL, and HH respectively
extract the changing components in horizontal (D_{11}), vertical (D_{12}), and diagonal
(D_{13}) direction [2].

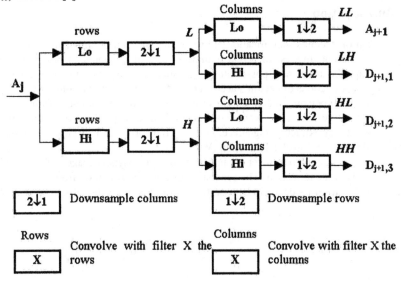

Fig.1. Scheme of one-level two-dimensional Wavelet Transform

The effect of use 2D WT on real image of face shown on Fig.2. The size of output
images is the same as the input image. It is result of down sampling that is rejection

of every second row and column. This operation don't increase amount of data and simultaneously don't cause loss of information.

2.2 Multi-level Wavelet Transform

The process of decomposition of image can be repeated by recurrence. The result of this is more detailed data about process information. After first level wavelet decomposition, the output images become input images of second level decomposition (Fig. 3) [3]. The results of two-level 2D WT are shown on Fig. 4.
Similarly can be made the multi-level WT. The tree of two-level decomposition is shown on Fig. 3.

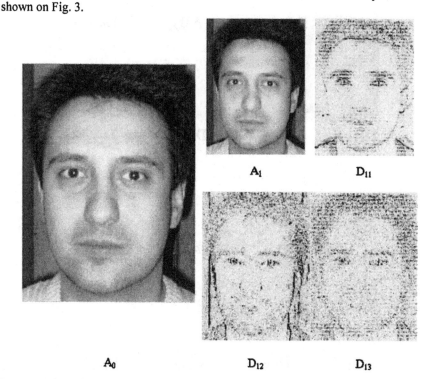

A_0 D_{12} D_{13}

Fig. 2. Result of one-level two-dimensional Wavelet Transform

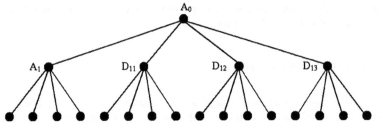

Fig. 3. The wavelet decomposition tree

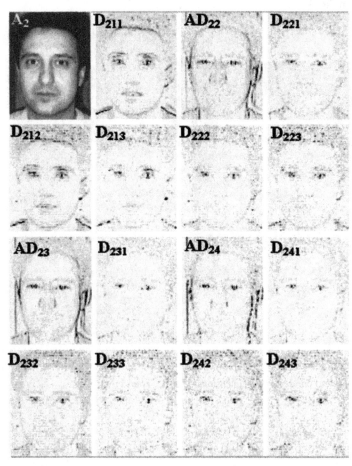

Fig. 4. Example of level 2 of the wavelet decomposition of image

2.3 Choice of Wavelet Function

The very important aspect of features extraction with WT is suitable choice of wavelet function [4,5,6]. The choice should adapt shape of wavelet to individual case and take into consideration the properties of the signal or image. The bad choice of wavelet will cause problems of analysis and identification processed signal [7,8].

In order to point the best wavelet function was used *FaMar* system of person's identification. This method is combination two mathematical tools, Wavelet Transform (WT) and Hidden Markov Model (HMM). Here, WT is used for features extraction, and HMM for identification [9]. The results of experiment are presented in Table 1. Experiment was carried out on the basis of the *BioID* face database in which there are 24 subjects. The best result achieve for function *Db1* from among accessible function of *Wavelet Toolbox* of set *MatLab*.

Analyse the result of Wavelet Transform (Fig. 6-9) we can see differences in contrast of fixed of boundary of face's elements. It is consequence of use different wavelet function (Fig. 5). Some of them (*Db1*) are better to features extraction because more clearly appoint contour of eyes and eyebrow.

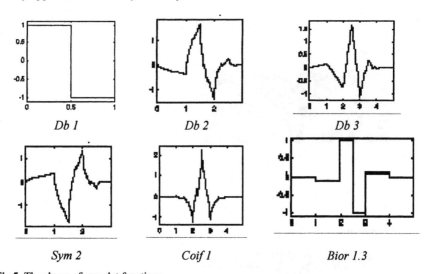

Fig.5. The shape of wavelet functions

Table 1. The result of experiment

Name of wavelet	Error rate [%]
Db1	**10**
Db2	30
Db3	35
Sym2	20
Coif1	40
Bior1.3	25

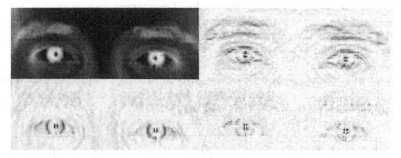

Fig. 6. Result of WT - *Db1*

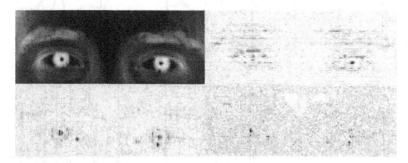

Fig. 7. Result of WT - *Db3*

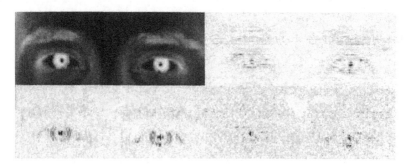

Fig. 8. Result of WT - *Coif1*

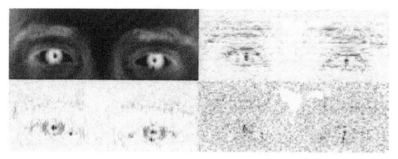

Fig. 9. Result of WT - *Sym2*

3 Conclusion

The choice of wavelet function is very important thing in features extraction. The effectiveness of recognition system depends on this selection. It guarantees a good recognition rate.

Successful Wavelet Transform can be used in systems of person's identification, pattern recognition and speech recognition also.

Unquestionable advantage of WT is possibility of suite wavelet function to processed signal.

References

1. Misiti M., Misiti Y., Oppenheim G., Poggi J.-M.: Wavelet Toolbox User's Guide, Math-Works (1998)
2. Chien J.T. Wu Ch.Ch., Discriminant Waveletface and Nearest Feature Classifiers for Face Recognition'. IEEE Transactions on Pattern Analysis and Machine Intelligence, Vol. 24 No. 12 (2002), pp. 1644–1649.
3. Garcia C., Zikos G., Tziritas G.: Wavelet Packet Analysis for Face Recognition, Image and Vision Computing 18 (2000) 289-297
4. Antoniadis A.; Oppenheim G.: Wavelets and Statistics, Lecture Notes in Statistics 103, Springer Verlag (1995)
5. Antoniadis A., Pham D.T.: Wavelet Regression for Random or Irregular Design, Comp. Stat. and Data Analysis 28 (1998) 353–369
6. Lavielle M.: Detection of Multiple Changes in a Sequence of Dependent Variables, Stoch. Proc. and their Applications, 83(2) (1999) 79–102
7. Mallet Y., Coomans D., Kautsky J., De Vel O.: Classification Using Adaptive Wavelets for Feature Extraction, IEEE Transaction on Pattern Analysis and Machine Intelligence, Vol. 19 No.10 (1997) 1058-1066
8. Laine A., Fan J.: Texture Classification by Wavelet Packet Signatures, IEEE Transaction on Pattern Analysis and Machine Intelligence, Vol. 15 No.11 (1993) 1186-1191
9. Bobulski J.: The Method of User's Identification Using the Fusion of the Wavelet Transform and Hidden Markov Models, Computing, Multimedia and Intelligent Technique, No 1(1), Czestochowa University of Technology, Institute of Computer and Information Science (2004)

Content-Based Image Retrieval – A Survey

Ryszard S. Choraś

Faculty of Telecommunications & Electrical Engineering
University of Technology & Agriculture
S. Kaliskiego 7, 85-796 Bydgoszcz

Email: choras@mail.atr.bydgoszcz.pl

Abstract: Current technology allows the acquisition, transmission, storing, and manipulation of large collections of images. Images are retrieved basing on similarity of features where features of the query specification are compared with features from the image database to determine which images match similarly with given features. Feature extraction is a crucial part for any of such retrieval systems. So far, the only way of searching these collections was based on keyword indexing, or simply by browsing. However nowadays digital images databases open the way to content-based efficient searching. In this paper we survey some technical aspects of current content-based image retrieval systems.

Keywords: Content Based Image Retrieval, Color histogram, Texture, Zernike moments.

1 Introduction

Content-Based Image Retrieval (CBIR) has received an intensive attention in the literature of multimedia information indexing and retrieval since this area started years ago, and consequently a broad range of techniques is proposed. Almost all kinds of image analysis techniques have been investigated in order to derive sets of meaningful features which could be useful for the description of pictorial information.

First-generation CBIR systems were based on manual textual annotation to represent image content. However, this technique can only be applied to small data volumes and is limited to very narrow visual domains.

In content-based image retrieval, images are automatically indexed by generating a feature vector (stored as an index in feature databases) describing the content of the image. The similarity of the feature vectors of the query and database images is measured to retrieve the image. Retrieval can be characterized in following queries: query-by-visual sample and/or linguistic queries. In a query by visual sample, a sample image is submitted to the system, and the system searches database to find the images most 'similar' to the sample image. The similarity measure is usually taken from image features such as color, texture and shape.

CBIR or Content Based Image Retrieval is the retrieval of images based on visual features such as color, texture and shape. In CBIR, each image that is stored in the database has its features extracted and compared to the features of the query image. It involves two steps:

- *Preprocessing*: The image is first processed in order to extract the features, which describe its contents. The processing involves filtering, normalization, segmentation, and object identification. The output of this stage is a set of significant regions and objects.

- *Feature Extraction*: The first step in the process is extracting image features to a distinguishable extent. Features such as shape, texture, color, etc. are used to describe the content of the image. Image features can be classified into primitives. We can extract features at various levels.

- *Matching:* The second step involves matching these features to yield a result that is visually similar.

The basic idea of the CBIR (Content-Based Image Retrieval) is to compactly describe an image by a feature vector and then match query images to the most resemblant image within the database according to the similarity of their features (Fig. 1).

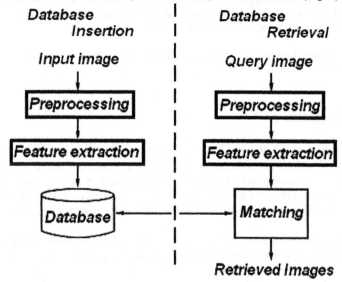

Fig.1. Feature extraction approach to image retrieval.

Let $F(x, y)$; $x, y = 1, 2, \ldots, N$ be a two-dimensional image pixel array. For color images $F(x, y)$ denotes the color value at pixel (x, y) i.e., $F(x, y) = \{F_R(x, y), F_G(x, y), F_B(x, y)\}$. For black and white images, $F(x, y)$ denotes the gray scale intensity value of pixel (x, y).

The problem of retrieval is following:

For a query image Q, we find image T from the image database, such that the distance between corresponding feature vectors is less than specified threshold, i.e., $D(Feature(Q), Feature(T)) \leq t$.

2 Representation of image content: feature extraction

The purpose of CBIR is to retrieve images from a database (collection), that are relevant to a query. Retrieval of images can be realized on the basis of automatically extracted features and finding images which are 'similar' to a query. Query describes the whole image or parts of an example image and similarity is based on either the whole image or parts of the image.

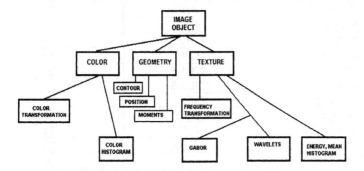

Fig. 2. Features which are used in CBIR.

CBIR systems include various levels of image description. Data which refer to the visual content of images – low intermediate features (color, texture, shape etc.) (Fig. 2) are known as content-dependent metadata. Data referring to content semantics are known as content-descriptive metadata.

In Content-Based Image Retrieval schemes we search for images by query by example:

- Select an example image,

- Extract features from the image (color, texture, shapes),

- Locate other images with similar colors, textures, and shapes,

- Match image.

Some of the best-known CBIR systems are included in Table 1.

To extract the color features, the image is transformed from RGB to HSV color space. This color space has a color representation closer to human perception than RGB. The first set of features are color histograms: three color histograms (one for

each color component). The color histograms are normalized, such that the sum of
the values for all bins of each color component sum to one. The color histogram values are included in the vector feature representation of the image. The fact that this
information is included in the vector feature representation solves the problem of the
combination of similarity measures from different approaches. The second set of
features are color moments: the first and second moments are found for each color
component.

Table 1. Current retrieval systems
(C=global color, R=color region, T=texture, S=shape, SR=spatial relationships).

Name	Queries	Ref.
Chabot	C	13
IRIS	C,T,S	14
MARS	C,T	15
NeTra	C,R,T,S	16
Photobook	S,T	17
PICASSO	C,R,S	18
PicToSeek	C,R	19
QBIC	C,R,T,S,SR	20
QuickLook	C,R,T,S	21
Surfimage	C,R,T	22
Virage	C,T,SR	23
Visual Retrievalware	C,T	24
VisualSEEk	R,S,SR	25
WebSEEk	C,R	26

Colors are commonly defined in three-dimensional color spaces. The color space
models can be differentiated as hardware-oriented and user-oriented. The hardware-
oriented color spaces, including RGB, CMY, and YIQ, are based on the three-color
stimuli theory. The user-oriented color spaces, including HLS, HCV, HSV, CIE-
LAB, and CIE-LUV, are based on the three human percepts of colors, i.e., hue, saturation, and brightness. The color space model can also be distinguished as uniform
and non-uniform depending on differences in color space as perceived by humans (in
fact, there is no truly uniform color space). The approximate uniform color spaces
include CIE-LAB, and CIE-LUV.
In the color space quantization, we reduce the color space of all possible colors to a
set of discrete colors. In fact, this process of quantization is the same as the process of
reducing colors.

2.1 Color histogram

Several methods for retrieving images on the basis of color similarity have been described. But most of them are variations on the same basic idea. Each image added to

the collection is analysed to compute a color histogram, which shows the proportion of pixels of each color within the image.

Color is one of the most widely used low-level feature in the context of indexing and retrieval based on image content. It is relatively robust to background complication and independent of image size and orientation. Typically, the color of an image is represented through some color model. A color model is specified in terms of 3-D coordinate system and a subspace within that system where each color is represented by a single point. The more commonly used color models are RGB (red, green, blue), HSV (hue, saturation, value) and YIQ (luminance and chrominance). Thus the color content is characterized by 3-channels from some color model. One representation of color content of the image is by using color histogram. For a three-channel image, we will have three such histograms. The histograms are normally divided into bins in an effort to coarsely represent the content and reduce dimensionality of subsequent matching phase. A feature vector is then formed by concatenating the three channel histograms into one vector. For image retrieval, histogram of query image is then matched against histogram of all images in the database using some similarity metric.

There are two types of color histograms, Global color histograms (GCH) and Local color histograms (LCH). A GCH represents one whole image with a single color histogram. An LCH divides an image into fixed blocks and takes the color histogram of each of those blocks. LCHs contain more information about an image but are computationally expensive when comparing images.

A color histogram H for a given image is defined as a vector $H = \{h[1], h[2], \ldots h[i], \ldots, h[N]\}$ where i represents a color in the color histogram, $h[i]$ is the number of pixels in color i in that image, and n is the number of bins in the color histogram, i.e., the number of colors in the adopted color model.

Typically, each pixel in an image will be assigned to a bin of a color histogram of that image, so for the color histogram of an image, the value of each bin is the number of pixels that has the same corresponding color. In order to compare images of different sizes, color histograms should be normalized. The normalized color histogram H' is defined for $h'[i] = \dfrac{h[i]}{P}$ where P is the total number of pixels in an image (the remaining variables are defined as before).

Among various low-level features, the color information has been extensively studied because of its invariance with respect to image scaling and orientation. Color is a very important cue in extracting information from images. Color histograms are commonly used in content-based retrieval systems [18, 19, 24] and have proven to be very useful though it lacks information about how the color is distributed spatially. It is important to group color in localized regions and to fuse color with textural properties. Color features used in image retrieval include global and local color histograms, the mean (i.e., average color), and higher order moments of the histogram [18]. The global color histogram provides a good approach to the retrieval of images that are similar in overall color content. There has been research to improve the performance of color-based extraction methods.

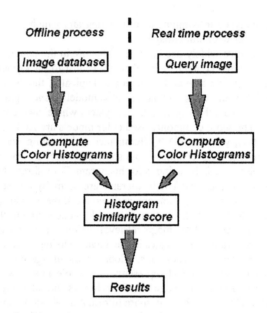

Fig. 3. Retrieval based on histograms.

Image search is done by matching *feature-vector* (here color histogram) for the sample image with feature-vector for images in the database. In CBIR, a color histogram is calculated for each target image as a preprocessing step, and then referenced in the database for each user query image.

The standard measure of similarity used for color histograms:

- A color histogram $H(i)$ is generated for each image i in the database (feature vector),
- The histogram is *normalized* so that its sum (now a double) equals unity (removes the *size* of the image),
- The histogram is then stored in the database,
- Now suppose we select a *model* image (the new image to match against all possible targets in the database).

We tried 3 kinds of histogram distance measures for a histogram $H(i)$, $i = 1,2,...,N$.

1) L-2 distance defined as:

$$d(Q,T) = \left[\sum_{m=1}^{N} \left(h_Q(m) - h_T(m) \right)^2 \right]^{\frac{1}{2}}. \qquad (1)$$

This metric is uniform in terms of the Eucledian distance between vectors in feature space, but the vectors are not normalized to unit length (in fact, they are on a hyper lane if the histogram is normalized).

2) Cosine Distance

If we normalize all vectors to unit length, and look at the angle between them, we have cosine distance, defined as:

$$d(Q,T) = \frac{2}{\pi}\cos^{-1}\left(\frac{\sum_{m=1}^{N} h_Q(m)h_T(m)}{\min(\| h_Q \|, \| h_T(m) \|)}\right). \tag{2}$$

Cosine Distance is more uniform in terms of the angle between the two vectors.

3) Histogram Intersection defined as:

$$d'_{Q,T} = 1 - \frac{\sum_{m=0}^{M-1} \min(h_Q(m), h_T(m))}{\min(\| h_Q \|, \| h_T \|)}. \tag{3}$$

The denominator term is needed for non-normalized histogram features (for example, edge histogram).

Color moments have been successfully used in many retrieval systems (like QBIC)[18],[10], especially when the image contains just the object. The first order (mean), the second (variance) and the third order (skewness) color moments have been proved to be efficient and effective in representing color distributions of images [19].

The first color moment of the k-th color component ($k = 1, 2, 3$) is defined by:

$$M_k^1 = \frac{1}{P}\sum_{j=1}^{P} f_{i,j},$$

where $f_{i,j}$ is the color value of the k-th color component of the j-th image pixel and P is the total number of pixels in the image. The h-th moment, $h = 2, 3, \ldots$, of k-th color component is then defined as:

$$M_k^h = \left(\frac{1}{P}\sum_{j=1}^{P}\left(f_{i,j} - M_k^1\right)^h\right)^{\frac{1}{h}}.$$

Take the first L moments of each color component in an image I to form a feature vector, CV, which is defined as

$$CV = [\alpha_1 M_1^1, \ldots, \alpha_1 M_1^L, \alpha_2 M_2^1, \ldots, \alpha_2 M_2^L, \alpha_3 M_3^1, \ldots, \alpha_3 M_3^L],$$

where $Z = L \cdot 3$ and $\alpha_1, \alpha_2, \alpha_3$ are the weights for the color components.

2.2 Texture

Texture models can be divided into following classes:
- statistical methods. Texture is defined in terms of the spatial distribution of gray values (e.g.. co-occurrence matrices, autocorrelation features). In the early 1970s, Haralick et al. proposed the co-occurrence matrix representation of texture features. This approach explored the gray level spatial dependence of texture. It first constructed co-occurrence matrix based on the orientation and distance between image pixels and then extracted meaningful statistics from the matrix as the texture representation.
- geometric methods,
- model based methods (e.g.. random field models and fractals),
- filtering methods – spatial and Fourier domain filtering, Gabor filtering and wavelet filtering.

Coarseness relates to distances of notable spatial variations of gray levels, that is, implicitly, to the size of the primitive elements (texels) forming the texture.
Contrast measures how gray levels vary in the image and to what extent their distribution is biased to black or white. The second- and fourth-order central moments of the gray level histogram, that is, the variance and kurtosis, are used in the definition of the

contrast: $F_{con} = \dfrac{\sigma}{(\alpha_4)^n}$ where $\alpha_4 = \dfrac{\mu_4}{\sigma^4}$ is the kurtosis, σ^2 is the variance

(second central moment of the gray level), and μ_4 is fourth central moment of the gray level distribution. The value $n=0.25$ is recommended as the best for discriminating the textures.
Degree of directionality is measured using the frequency distribution of oriented local edges against their directional angles.
Coarseness measures the texture scale, contrast measures the gray level variance, and directionality describes whether an image has a preferred direction.
The texture distance between two images (image i and image j) is computed as a weighted Euclidean distance in the 3d texture space:

$$d_{ij} = \frac{(O_i - O_j)^2}{\sigma_O^2} + \frac{(C_i - C_j)^2}{\sigma_C^2} + \frac{(D_i - D_j)^2}{\sigma_D^2}. \qquad (4)$$

At present, most promising for texture retrieval are multiresolution features obtained with orthogonal wavelet transforms or with Gabor filtering. These features describe spatial distributions of oriented edges in the image at multiple scales.
A 2D Gabor function is given by the following complex-valued function:

$$f(x, y) = \frac{1}{2\pi\sigma_x\sigma_y} \exp\left[-\frac{1}{2}\left(\frac{x^2}{\sigma_x^2}\right) + \left(\frac{y^2}{\sigma_y^2}\right)\right] \exp\left[2\pi\sqrt{-1}(ux + vy)\right]. \quad (5)$$

It minimises the joint 2D uncertainty in both spatial and frequency domain, and, by appropriate dilations and rotations of this function, a class of self-similar Gabor filters for orientation- and scale-tunable edge and line detection can be obtained. The Gabor texture features include the mean and the standard deviation of the energy distribution of the transform coefficients. The total number of Gabor filters is equal to the product of the numbers of scales and orientations.

The MPEG-7 ISO/IEC standard for *multimedia content description interface* is aimed, among a broad range of applications, at CBIR problems. It involves descriptors for color, texture, shape, and motion. For describing textures, it recommends two descriptors, namely *texture browsing descriptor* and *homogeneous texture descriptor* based on scale- and orientation-selective Gabor filtering. Both descriptors allow to represent homogeneous texture regions in images.

2.2.1 Texture Browsing Descriptor

This 12-bit descriptor relates to regularity, directionality, and coarseness (scale) of visual texture perception and can be used both for browsing and coarse classification of textures. First, the image is filtered with a bank of orientation- and scale-tuned Gabor filters in order to select and code two dominant texture orientations (3 bits per orientation). Then an analysis of filtered projections of the image along the dominant orientations specify the regularity (2 bits) and coarseness (2 bits per scale). The second dominant orientation and second scale features are optional.

2.2.2 Homogeneous Texture Descriptor

This descriptor uses 62 8-bit numbers per image or image region in order to allow for accurate search and retrieval. The image is filtered with Gabor filters, and the first and the second moments of the energy in the frequency domain in the corresponding subbands, that is, the means and the standard deviations of the filtered outputs in the spatial domain (5 scales × 6 orientations per scale) are used as the descriptor components.

2.3 Shape

In image retrieval, depending on the applications, shape representation is required to be invariant to translation, rotation, and scaling. In general, the shape representations can be divided into two categories, boundary-based and region-based. The most successful representations for these two categories are Fourier Descriptors and Moment Invariants. The main idea of Fourier Descriptors is to use the Fourier transformed boundary as the shape feature. The main idea of Moment Invariants is to use region based moments, which are invariant to transformation as the shape feature. Boundary/region based representations e.g. Zernike moments, pseudo-Zernike moments outperform the simple and efficient representations of shapes.

Zernike moments are the projections of the image function $f(x, y)$ onto the orthogonal basis functions $V_{nm}(x, y)$:

$$V_{nm}(x, y) = R_{nm}(x, y) \exp(jm \arctan(\frac{y}{x})) ,$$ (6)

where the radial polynomial is defined as:

$$R_{nm}(x, y) = \sum_{s=0}^{\frac{n-|m|}{2}} \frac{(-1)^s [(n-s)!] \, (x^2 + y^2)^{\frac{n-2s}{2}}}{s!(\frac{n+|m|}{2} - s)!(\frac{n-|m|}{2} - s)!} .$$ (7)

The Zernike moment of order n with repetition m is a complex number given by:

$$Z_{nm} = \frac{n+1}{\pi} \sum_{x=0}^{N-1} \sum_{y=0}^{M-1} f(x, y)[V_{nm}(x, y)]^* ,$$ (8)

with $x^2 + y^2 \leq 1$, and *denoting the complex conjugate.

Let $\rho = \sqrt{x^2 + y^2}$ be the length of the vector from the origin to the pixel (x, y), and $\theta = \arctan(\frac{y}{x})$ be the angle between that x-axis and that vector. $R_{nm}(\rho)$, the polar coordinate representation $(x = \rho\cos\theta, y = \rho\sin\theta)$ of $R_{nm}(x, y)$, is then a polynomial of degree n in ρ containing terms in $\rho^n, \rho^{n-2}, ..., \rho^{|m|}$. $R_{nm}(\rho)$ contains no power of ρ less than $|m|$.

The Zernike moment of the image $f(\rho, \theta)$ can be expressed in polar coordinates as:

$$Z_{nm} = \frac{n+1}{\pi} \int_0^{2\pi} \int_0^1 f(\rho, \theta)[V_{nm}(\rho, \theta)]^* \rho \, d\rho d\theta =$$
$$= \frac{n+1}{\pi} \int_0^{2\pi} \int_0^1 f(\rho, \theta) R_{nm}(\rho) \exp(-jm\theta) \rho \, d\rho d\theta .$$ (9)

$R_{nm}(\rho)$ is defined as follows:

$$R_{nm}(\rho) = \sum_{s=0}^{\frac{n-|m|}{2}} \frac{(-1)^s [(n-s)!] \rho^{\frac{n-2s}{2}}}{s!(\frac{n+|m|}{2}-s)!(\frac{n-|m|}{2}-s)!} . \qquad (10)$$

The reconstructed image $\hat{f}(x,y)$ can be computed from:

$$\hat{f}(x,y) = \sum_{n=0}^{n_{\max}} \sum_{m} Z_{nm} V_{nm}(x,y) , \qquad (11)$$

with $m \in N | (n-|m|)$ $even$ and $|m| \le n$.

$R_{nm}(\rho)$ is over the unit disc, $|R_{nm}(\rho)| \le 1$ and that $R_{nm}(1) = 1$ for any values of m and n.

We have $R_{nm}(\rho) = R_{m,-n}(\rho)$ and then $V_{nm}^*(\rho,\theta) = V_{m,-n}(\rho,\theta)$ and $Z_{nm}^* = Z_{m,-n}$.

For any order m, the number of Zernike moments is given by $m+1$, number of moments up to and including order m is $(\frac{m}{2}+1)(m+1)$.

The magnitude of Zernike moments has rotational invariance property. An image can be better described by a small set of its Zernike moments than any other type of moments such as geometric moments, Legendre moments, rotational moments, and complex moments in terms of mean-square error. Zernike moments do not have the properties of translation invariance and scaling invariance. The way to achieve such invariance is image translation and image normalization before calculation of Zernike moments.

Since the images are normalized with respect to scale and translation before the computation of Zernike moments, the rotation-invariant magnitudes of Zernike moments may be used as invariant features for the recognition of shapes (objects) in the retrieval process.

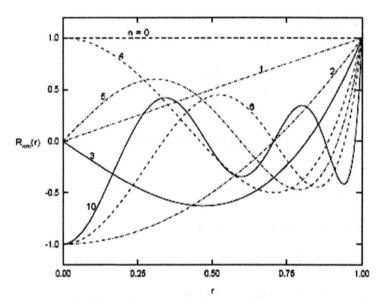

Fig.4. Radial polynomials $R_{nm}(\rho)$ of order $n = 0,\ldots,6,10$ and $m = 0$ or 1 corresponding respectively to an even or odd n.

3 Conclusion

It is widely recognized that most current content-based image retrieval systems work with low level features (color, texture, shape), and that next generation systems should operate at a higher semantic level. One way to achieve this is to let the system recognize objects and scenes.

The present and future trends are: indexing, search, query, and retrieval of multimedia data based on:

1. Video retrieval using video features: image color and object shape, video segmentation, video keyframes, scene analysis, structure of objects, motion vectors, optical flow (from Computer Vision), multispectral data, and so-called 'signatures' that summarize the data.
2. Use of the spatio-temporal queries, such as trajectories.
3. Semantic features; syntactic descriptors.
4. Use of relevance feedback, a well-known technique from information retrieval.
5. Retrieval using sound, especially spoken documents, e.g. using speaker information.
6. Multimedia database techniques, such as using relational databases of images.
7. Fusion of textual, visual, and speech cues.
8. Automatic and instant video manipulation; user-enabled editing of multimedia databases.

9. Multimedia security, hiding, and authentication techniques such as watermarking.

References

1. V. V. Gudivada, V. V. Raghavan, Guest Editors' Introduction: Content-Based Image Retrieval Systems, *IEEE Computer*, 28, 9, 1995.
2. IEEE Computer, special issue on Content Based Image Retrieval, 28, 9, 1995.
3. Niblak et al., The QBIC project: Querying images by content using color, texture, and shape, *Proceedings of the SPIE: Storage and Retrieval for Image and Video Databases*, vol. 1908, 1993.
4. M. Flickner et al., Query by Image and Video Content: The QBIC System, *IEEE Computer*, 28, 9, 1995.
5. Y. Gong and M. Sakauchi, Detection of regions matching specified chromatic features, *Computer vision and image understanding*, 61,2, 1995.
6. G. Wyszechi, W. S. Stiles, Color science: concepts and methods, quantitative data and formulas, Wiley, NewYork, 1982.
7. Y. Chen, J.Z. Wang, A region-Based Fuzzy Feature Matching Approach to Content-Based Image Retrieval, *IEEE Trans. on PAMI*, vol.24, no.9, pp.1252-1267,2002.
8. H. Wang, D. Suter, Color Image Segmentation Using Global Information and Local Homogeneity, *Proc. 7th Digital Computing Techniques and Applications (eds. C. Sun, H. Talbot, S. Ourselin, T. Adriaansen)*, pp. 89-98, Sydney,2003.
9. MPEG-7: Context and objectives (v.5) ISO/IEC JTC1/SC29/WG 11 N1920, MPEG97, Oct. 1997.
10. Jaimes, A., Tseng, B., Smith, J.: Modal keywords, ontologies, and reasoning for video understanding. In: International Conference on Image and Video Retrieval, Lecture Notes in Computer Science, vol. 2728, Springer (2003) 239–248.
11. Addis, M., Boniface, M., Goodall, S., Grimwood, P., Kim, S., Lewis, P. Martinez, K., Stevenson, A.: Integrated image content and metadata search and retrieval across multiple databases. In: International Conference on Image and Video Retrieval, Lecture Notes in Computer Science, vol. 2728, Springer (2003) 88–97.
12. M.S. Kankanhalli, B.M. Mehtre, H.Y. Huang, Color and spatial feature for content-based image retrieval, Pattern Recognition Lett. 20 (1) (1999) 109–118.
13. V.E. Ogle and M. Stonebraker, "Chabot: Retrieval from a Relational Database of Images," *IEEE Computer* 28(9):40–48, 1995.
14. P. Alshuth, T. Hermes, C. Klauck, J. Kreiss and M. Roper, "IRIS Image Retrieval for Images and Video," Proc First Int'l Workshop on Image Database and Multi-media Search, 1996.
15. T. Huang et al., "Multimedia Analysis and Retrieval System (MARS) Project," in *Digital Image Access and Retrieval*, P.B. Heidorn and B. Sandore eds., 1997.
16. W.-Y. Ma and B.S.Manjunath, "NeTra: A Toolbox for Navigating Large Image Databases," *Multimedia Systems* 7:184–198, 1999.
17. R. Picard, T.P. Minka and M. Szummer, "Modeling User Subjectivity in Image Libraries," in *Proc. IEEE Int'l Conf. on Image Processing*, 1996.
18. A. Del Bimbo, *Visual Information Retrieval*, Morgan Kaufmann, San Francisco, CA, 1999.
19. T. Gevers and A.W.M. Smeulders, "The PicToSeekWWWImage Search System," in *Proc. Int'l Conf. on Multimedia Computing and Systems*, 1999.

20. M. Flickner, H. Sawhney, W. Niblack, J. Ashley, Q. Huang, B. Dom, M. Gorkani, J. Hafner, D. Lee, D. Petkovic, D. Steele and P. Janker, "Query by Image and Video Content: the QBIC System," *IEEE Computer* 28(9):310–315,1995.
21. G. Ciocca, R. Schettini, "A Relevance Feedback Mechanism for Content- 35:605–632, 1999.
22. C. Nastar et al., "Surfimage: A Flexible Content-Based Image Retrieval System," in *Proc. ACM Multimedia*, 1998.
23. J.R. Bach, C. Fuller, A. Gupta, A. Hampapur, B. Horovitz, R. Humphrey and R. Jain, "The Virage Image Search Engine: an Open Framework for Image Management," in *Proc. SPIE Int'l Conf. on Storage and Retrieval for Still Image and Video Databases*, 1996.
24. J. Feder, "Towards Image Content-Based Retrieval for the World-Wide Web," *Advanced Imaging* 11(1):26–29, 1996.
25. J.R. Smith and S.-F. Chang, "Querying by Color Regions Using the VisualSEEk Content-Based Visual Query System," in *Intelligent Multimedia Information Retrieval*, M.T. Maybury, ed., 1997.
26. S.-F. Chang, J.R. Smith, M. Beigi and A. Benitez, " Visual Information Retrieval from Large Distributed Online Repositories," *Comm. of the ACM* 40(12):63–71, 1997.
27. F. Zernike, „Beugungstheorie des schneidenverfahrens und seiner verbesserten form, der phasenkontrastmethode", *Physica*, 1(8):689-704.
28. M.R. Teague, " Image analysis via the general theory of moments", *Journal of the Optical Society of America*, 70(8):920-930.
29. C.H. Teh, R.T. Chin, "On image analysis by the methods of moments", *IEEE Transactions on PAMI*, 10(4):496 -513.

Method of Speech Recognition and Speaker Identification using Audio-Visual of Polish Speech and Hidden Markov Models

Mariusz Kubanek

Czestochowa University of Technology,
Institute of Computer & Information Sciences
Dabrowskiego Street, 73, 42-200 Czestochowa, Poland
mariusz.kubanek@icis.pcz.pl

Abstract: Mainstream automatic speech recognition has focused almost exclusively on the acoustic signal. The performance of these systems degrades considerably in the real word in the presence of noise. It was needed novel approaches that use other orthogonal sources of information to the acoustic input that not only considerably improve the performance in severely degraded conditions, but also are independent to the type of noise and reverberation. Visual speech is one such source not perturbed by the acoustic environment and noise. In this paper, it was presented own approach to lip-tracking and fusion of signals audio and video for audio-visual speech and speaker recognition system. It was presented video analysis of visual speech for extraction visual features from a talking person in color video sequences. It was developed a method for automatically localization of face, eyes, region of mouth, corners and contour of mouth. It was proposed synchronous and two asynchronous of methods of fusion of signals audio and video. Finally, the paper will show results of lip-tracking depending on various factors (lighting, beard), results of speech and speaker recognition in noisy environments.

1 Generalized problem

Extensive use of the internet and advances in computational power and virtual reality has enabled researchers to develop different virtual reality systems in recent years. Some of these systems have been used to simulate human movements, such as human motion capture [1,4], virtual character positioning and balance control [2,4]. On the other hand, different lip-tracking algorithms have been developed and lip information is used in different areas such as audio-visual speech recognition [3,4].

It's well known that humans have the ability to lip-read. It was combined audio and visual information in deciding what has been spoken, especially in noisy environments. A dramatic example is the so-called McGurk effect, where a spoken in English language sound /ga/ is superimposed on the video of a person uttering /ba/ [5]. Most People perceive the speaker as uttering the sound /da/ [5,6]. In addition, the visual modality is well known to contain some complementary information to the audio modality [5,7]. For example in polish language, using visual cues to decide whether a person said /m/ rather than /n/ can be easier than making the decision based on audio cues, however deciding between /m/ and /p/ is more reliably done from the audio than from the video channel.

The above facts have recently motivated significant interest in the area of *Audio-Visual Speech Recognition* (AVSR), also known as *automatic lip-reading, speech-reading* [5,8]. Work in these field aims at improving automatic speech region by exploring the visual modality of the region of mouth of speaker, in addition to the traditional audio modality.

Automatic speech recognition by machine has been an active research area for several decades, but in spite of enormous efforts, the performance of current ASR system is far from the performance achieved by humans. Most state-of-the-art ASR systems make use of the acoustic speech signal only and ignore the visual speech cues. They are therefore susceptible to acoustic noise, and essentially all real-world applications are subject to some kind of noise. Although several audio-visual speech recognition systems have been proposed in the literature, most systems were dependent on constrained visual environments which prevents their use for real-word applications [17]. The aim of the speech-reading system described here is to perform speaker independent speech recognition for a large variety of speakers and without the use of visual aids.

Scheme of audio-visual speech recognition system was showed on Fig. 1.

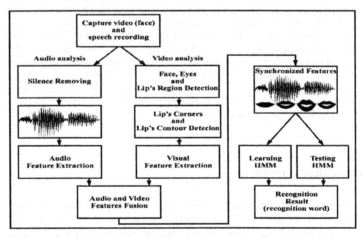

Fig. 1. Scheme of audio-visual speech recognition system

2 Hidden Markov Models modeling

Speech signals are slowly time varying signals. When examined over a sufficiently short period of time, the speech signal can be regarded as being stationary [18, 19]. Speech recognition systems generally assume that the speech signal is a realization of some message encoded as a sequence of one or more symbols. Speech recognition is the task of recognizing, the underlying symbol sequence given a spoken utterance. Hidden Markov Models (HMM) have been very widely used for speech recognition studies for the last few years because of its success to model speech signal. In the next sections, first a brief basic HMM theory is given and the developed HMM codes is discussed.

HMMs are stochastic models and are widely used for characterizing the spectral properties of frames of patterns [18, 19]. The underlying assumptions of using HMMs in speech recognition are that speech signals can be well characterized as a parametric random process, and that the parameters of the stochastic process can be determined (estimation) in a precise, well-defined manner (training) [18, 19].

A Hmm is characterized by: the number of states in the model N, the number of Gaussian mixtures per state M, the state transition probability distribution A, the observation symbol probability distribution B, and the initial state distribution π. The compact notation $\lambda = (A, B, \pi)$ is used to indicate the complete parameter set of an HMM model.

For speech recognition applications usually a left right HMM model is used because the underlying state sequence associated with the model has the property that as time increases, the state index increases (or stays the same). For this research left-right HMMs are used. For the developed of Matlab HMM code, the implementations for the first two problems of HMM were trivial. Forward backward and Viterbi algorithms were used to solve the first and second problems of HMM. For the most difficult HMM problem, namely training problem, Baum-Welch algorithm was used by talking into account the practical implementation issues, such as scaling, multiple observation sequences, initial parameter estimates, which are explained in [18, 19].

3 Speech coding with use MFCC and Lloyd algorithm

Speech processing applications require specific representations of speech information. A wide range of possibilities exists for parametrically representing the speech signal. Among these the most important parametric representation of speech is short time spectral envelope [18, 19]. Linear Predictive Coding (LPC) and Mel Frequency Cepstral Coefficients (MFCC) spectral analysis models have been used widely for speech recognition applications. Usually together with MFCC coefficients, first and second order derivatives are also used to take into account the dynamic evolution of the speech signal, which carries relevant information for speech recognition.

The term cepstrum was introduced by Bogert et al. in [20]. They observed that the logarithm of the power spectrum of a signal containing an echo had an additive periodic component due to echo. In general, voiced speech could be regarded as the response of the vocal track articulation equivalent filter driven by a pseudo periodic source [20].

The main difference between mel-cepstrum and cepstrum was that the spectrums were first passed through mel-frequency-bandpass-filters before they were transformed to the frequency domain. The characteristics of filters followed the characteristics old human auditory system. The filters had triangular band pass frequency responses. The bands of filters were spaced linearly for bandwidth below 1000 Hz and increased logarithmically after the 1000 Hz.

For acoustic speech recognition twenty dimensional MFCC was used as the standard audio features. It was applied Lloyd algorithm to vector quantization. For example, Tab. 1. shows vector of observation of audio speech for 37 codes of codebook, for polish word *recording*.

Table. 1. Vector of observation for 37 codes of codebook, for polish word recording

Word	Vector of observation
Recording	15 5 5 5 5 5 5 23 23 23 23 23 23 23 32 34 33 33 5 31 27 27 27 34 27 27 27 27 27 27 27 7 7 5 18 15 24 19 23 23 23 23 23 23 23 23 23 23 32 17 33 33 33 18 30 30 35 35 8 8 8 8 32 32 32 32 32 32 34 25 25 25 25 25 25 29 29 25

4 Tracking the facial features

For a lip-reading system, it's essential to track the region of mouth of the speaker. This can be achieved by tracking the lip-corners. Unfortunately, it's difficult to locate or track lip-corners alone. In order to find the lip-corners within a face, we might have to search other facial features using certain constraints and heuristics. Some facial features are easier to locate than lip-corners. For example, within a face, the pupils are two dark regions that satisfy certain geometric constraints, such as position inside the face, symmetry according to the facial symmetric axis and minimum and maximum width between each other. Once the eyes are located, the lip region can be predicted [9].

One should to record audio and video speech. Audio signals are sampled at 8 kHz with 16 bit resolution. Visual signals are represented by RGB video captured with frame rate of 15 frames/s, and each image has 640 x 480 pixel resolution. Lip-tracking is marked by video analysis (see Fig. 2.).

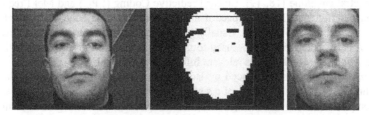

Fig. 2. Examples of face detection with use of property of skin's color

First, face of speaking person is detected. Before detection, one should to reduce the image size to 160 x 120, keeping the aspect ratio. The image is spreaded on three components RGB. Component B is subtracted from component R and area of color of human skin is received [10]. Then, a mask is put on in aim of qualification of face's area (see Fig. 2.).

It was been possible to search the pupils by looking for two dark regions lie within a certain area of the face. It is applied *Gradient Method and Integral Projection* (GMIP) [10] to finding horizontal (*h_line*) and vertical (*v_line*_1, *v_line*_2) line of eyes. Before, the image face is converted to the grayscale. Following equations (1, 2, 3) describe way of finding the pupils.

$$h\_line = MAX\left(\sum_{j=1}^{sixe\_x-1} \left| face\_image_{i,j} - face\_image_{i,j+1} \right|, \quad i = 1..size\_y \right) \tag{1}$$

$$v\_line\_1 = MAX\left(\sum_{i=h\_line-t}^{2t} \left| face\_image_{i,j} - face\_image_{i+1,j} \right|, \quad j = 1..\frac{size\_x}{2} \right) \tag{2}$$

$$v\_line\_2 = MAX\left(\sum_{i=h\_line-t}^{2t} \left| face\_image_{i,j} - face\_image_{i+1,j} \right|, \quad j = \frac{size\_x}{2} + 1..size\_x \right) \tag{3}$$

To search the lips initially, the approximate positions of the corners of mouth are predicted, using the positions of the eyes, the model of face and the assumption, therefore one should to have a near frontal view. Fig. 3. shows the search lip region.

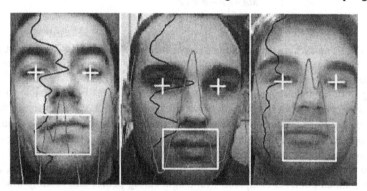

Fig. 3. Examples of mouth's area detection on basic of eyes position

5 The visual feature extraction

The position of the corners of mouth can be found by looking for the darkest pixel. This approach to search the horizontal line of corners of mouth using GMIP (1). The vertical boundaries of the lip can be found by applying gradient method to the refined search area and regarding the integral horizontal projection of this gradient method. Exact finding of corners of mouth is very most important because on basis of corners of mouth, edge of mouth will be defined.

Described above method of finding corners of mouth no always gives satisfactory results. If studied speaker has beard, and then gradient method can be ineffective. One should to introduce sure modifications. It was applied different method of finding corners of mouth. The corners of mouth are defined on basic of specific color of mouths and specific shape of mouths (*Color and Shape of Mouths*, CSM). First, position of mouths is found using specific color, and then corners of mouths are defined as extreme points of situated mouths. Fig. 4. shows difference among both methods.

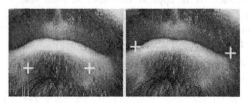

Fig. 4. Difference among GMIP (left images) and CSM (right images)

To qualification of specific color of mouth, video frame is spreaded on component RGB. Then, for color of mouth *MA* it's accepted area, in which:

$$MA = \begin{cases} B - G < T1 \\ R - B < T2 \\ R - G < T3 \end{cases} \qquad (4)$$

where *T1*, *T2* and *T3* are liminal values (experimental: $T1 \cong 20$, $T2 \cong 40$, $T3 \cong 40$).
Passed liminal values are dependent on from different factors: lightings, sometimes used lipstick, etc.
Having definite area of mouth and corners of mouth, it was been possible to mark external edges of mouth (*Lip Contour Detection*, LCD). On basis of corners of mouth resource of circle is defined, for which what α a ray is drawn, beginning from one from appointed corners of mouth. It's got $2\pi/\alpha$ of rays. Moving oneself along every from rays in direction of resource of circle, points are marked in which begins appointed earlier area of mouth *MA*. In aim of elimination of significant mistakes, every from appointed points is compared with neighbouring points, and suitably modified. In dependence from settle angle of jump α it's received $2\pi/\alpha$ points. One should α to accept experimental. It was accepted $\alpha = 2\pi/16$. Described method above was showed on Fig. 5.
On basic of characteristics points, defining external edges and corners of mouth, it were appointed codes as sum of relations of distance of all points from appointed line through corners of mouths. For all frames, it was created vector of observations for given word. For example, Tab. 2. shows vector of observation of visual speech for 37 codes of codebook, for polish word *recording*.

Table. 2. Vector of observation for 37 codes of codebook, for polish word *recording*

Word	Vector of observation
Recording	27 26 31 34 32 27 21 21 26 21 18 18 23 37 36 34 27 28 32 37 38 34 28 22 18

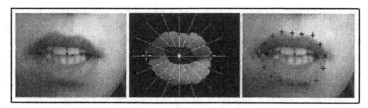

Fig. 5. Examples of detection of external edges of mouth with use CSM method

6 Fusion of signals audio and video

Mean of fusion of characters audio and video of speech, presented in form of vectors
of observations, it was realized onto three different methods.

In first proposed method *Sr*, it was applied synchronic approach, consisted on calculation of vector of resultants' observation, from vectors of observation of both entrance signals of given word.

In second proposed method *ASr_I*, both vectors of audio and video of speech were
given separately onto input of HMM. Peculiarity of this method depends on use vectors of observations of audio and video of speech as teaching data for the same
HMM.

In third proposed method *ASr_II*, it was applied approach, depending on creation of
separate HMMs for both vectors of observations. Every from models generated sequence of observation most probable to entrance, and the fusion of characters of
audio and visual was realized by sum of appointed probabilities.

7 Experimental results

In first experiment, two tests were moved. In first test, it was applied gradient method
and integral projection (GMIP). In second test, it was applied method using specific
color and shape of mouths (CSM). It was tested twenty different persons, speaking
individual word. Every recording contained about 50 frame/s, so it was tested near
1000 video frames. For every frame box corners mouth's were marked by hand, and
next this corners were compared with automatically situated corners mouth's received
at help of methods GMIP and CSM. Tab. 3. shows average mistakes committed
through both tested methods for all frames.

Table. 3. Average vertical and horizontal corners mouth's localization errors in pixel.

method	amount of frames	error$_x$ [pixels]	error$_y$ [pixels]
GMIP	1000	16,7	18,9
CSM	1000	4,8	5,7

In second experiment, methods GMIP and CSM were applied also. It was tested twenty different persons, spelling words with clear division onto phonems. Checking of effectiveness of both methods was assignment of this experiment in lip-tracking system. Every recorded frame box was checked, defining membership of recognized object to object mouth/non-mouth (+)/non-mouth (-). No-mouth (+) marks, that corners became recognized correctly and no-mouth (-) marks, that corners became recognized irregularly. Into this way lip-tracking in real-time was studied. Tab. 4. shows results of second experiment.

Table. 4. Result of lip-tracking in real-time

method	amount of frames	object mouth [%]	object non-mouth (+) [%]	object non-mouth (-) [%]
GMIP	1000	83,7	3,4	12,9
CSM	1000	94,2	1,2	4,6

These results show that we can track lip-corners in images with different speakers using method CSM. Method GAIP is less resistant onto disturbances. Large on proper lip-tracking has correct situating of corners mouth's. If only woman would be our speaker, then it was been possible to apply both methods, because how it results from our investigations, a largest disturbance introduces male beard.

In third experiment, it was tested level of mistakes of recognizing of audio speech in comparison with recognizing of audio-visual speech. Researches were made, using author base of statements of audio-visual speech. Ten users were tested, expressing seventy different commands (seven repetitions for every statement). It was tested 4900 expressing of audio and audio-visual speech. Researches were made for different degree of disturbance of signal audio (Signal to Noise Ratio, SNR = 0, 5, 10, 20 dB). It was accepted, that for SNR = 20 dB signal audio is clean. It was accepted, that signal of video is clean for different SNR of audio. All three method of fusion signals of audio and video were tested. Tab. 5. shows results of third experiment. Fig. 6. shows level of mistakes of recognizing of audio speech and audio-visual speech.

Table. 5. Result of audio and audio-visual speech recognition

Audio and audio-visual speech recognition								
signal	FRR [%]				FAR [%]			
	SNR 20dB	SNR 10dB	SNR 5dB	SNR 0dB	SNR 20dB	SNR 10dB	SNR 5dB	SNR 0dB
Audio	2,09	28,23	49,76	74,28	1,61	6,81	8,19	13,28
AV Sr	1,76	23,90	31,82	42,66	1,52	6,42	7,90	11,52
AV Sr_I	1,42	20,14	28,43	40,19	1,38	5,76	7,81	10,76
AV Sr_II	1,61	23,14	35,47	46,52	1,57	6,28	7,85	11,90

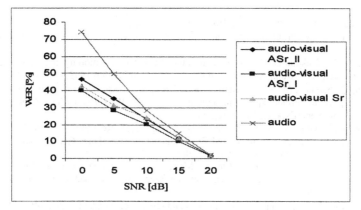

Fig. 6. Level of mistakes of recognizing of audio speech and audio-visual speech

8 Conclusion and future work

In this paper, it was presented a new approach to lip-tracking in real-time and audio-visual speech recognition in polish language. The basic idea is that not only the lips, but also other facial features such as eyes are tracked. It was also evaluated the robustness of the new approach. It was tested twenty different persons, speaking individual word. Every recording contained about 50 frame/s, so it was tested near 1000 video frames. These results show that it was been possible to track lip-corners in images with different speakers using method CSM. Method GAIP is less resistant onto disturbances. Large on proper lip-tracking has correct situating of corners mouth's. If only woman would be our speaker, then it was been possible to apply both methods, because how it results from our investigations, a largest disturbance introduces male beard.

The new approach was implemented in the lip-tracking module of our audio-video speech recognition system. The system was tested a database that contains image sequences of ten different speakers spelling seventy different commands steering

operating system in polish language. Audio-visual speech recognition gives better results than audio speech recognition, particularly in noisy environment.
It's known that human lip-readers rely on information about the presence/absence of the teeth and the tongue inside the lip contour [15,16]. For this reason it is likely that the best recognition system will ultimately be obtained from frontal view with this additional information extracted. In future we plan to consider internal edges of mouths as well as presence of language and teeth in our system.

References

1. Herda, L., Fua, P., Plankers, R., Boulic, R., Thalmann, D.: Skeleton-based motion capture for robust reconstruction of human motion. Proceedings Computer Animation 2000, pp. 77-83, 2000
2. Aydin, Y., Nakajama, H.: Realistic articulated character positioning and balance control in interactive environments. Proceedings Computer Animation 1999, pp. 160-168, 1999
3. Zhi, Q., Kaynak, M. N. N., Sengupta, K., Cheok, A. D., Ko, C. C.: A study of the modeling aspects in bimodal speech recognition. Proc. 2001 IEEE International Conference on Multimedia and Expo (ICME2001), 2001
4. Jian, Z., Kaynak, M. N. N., Cheok, A. D., Chung, K. C.: Real-time Lip-tracking For Virtual Lip Implementation in Virtual Environments and Computer Games. Proc. 2001 International Fuzzy Systems Conference, 2001
5. Neti, C., Potamianos, G., Luttin, J., Mattews, I., Glotin, H., Vergyri, D., Sison, J., Mashari, A., Zhou, J.: Audio Visual Speech-Recognition. Workshop 2000 Final Report, October 12, 2000
6. McGurk, H., MacDonald, J.: Hearing lips and seeing voices. Nature, 264:746-748, 1976
7. Massaro, D. W., Stork, D. G.: Speech recognition and sensory integration. American Scientist, 86(3):236-244, 1998
8. Hennecke, M. E., Stork, D. G., Prasad, K. V.: Visionary speech: Looking ahead to practical speechreading systems. In Stork and Hennecke [91], pages 331-349
9. Steifelhagen, R., Meier, U., Yang, J.: Real-Time Lip-Tranking for Lipreading.
10. Kuchariev, G., Kuźmiński, A.: Biometric technique. Part 1: Methods of face recognition. Departament of Computer Science, Szczecin University of Technology, 2003
11. Gee, A. H., Cipolla, R.: Fast visual tracking by temporal consensus. Technical Report CUED/F-INFENG/TR-207, University of Cambridge, February 1995
12. Basu, S., Oliver, N., Pentland, A.: 3D modeling and tracking of human lip motions. In Proc. International Conference on Computer Vision, 1998
13. Chan, M. T., Zhang, Y., Huang, T. S.: Real-time lip-tracking and bimodal continuous speech recognition. In Proc. IEEE 2nd Workshop on Multimedia Signal Processing, pages 65-70, Redondo Beach, 1988
14. Kubanek, M.: Method of edge EDGE to extraction of features of image of mouth in technique of integrated recognizing of speech audio-video. Information Sciences, Publisher of Czestochowa University of Technology, Czestochowa 2003, nr 4, s. 115-125
15. Kaucic, R., Dalton, B., Blake, A.: Real-Time Lip Tracking for Audio-Visual Speech Recognition Applications. In Proc. European Conf. Computer Vision, pp. 376-387, Cambridge, UK, 1996
16. Summerfield, Q., MacLeod, A., McGrath, M., Broke, M.: Lips, teeth and the benefits of lipreading. In A. W. Young and H. D. Ellis, editors, Handbook of Research on Face Processing, pp. 223-233, Elsevier Science Publishers, 1989

17. Luttein, J.: Visual Speech and Speaker Recognition. Dissertation submitted to the University of Sheffield for the degree of Doctor of Philosophy, May 1997
18. Rabiner, L., Yuang, B. H.: Fundamentals of Speech Recognition. Prentice Hall Signal Processing Series, 1993
19. Kaynak, M. N. N., Zhi, Q, Cheok, A. D., Sengupta, K., Chung, K. C.: Audio-Visual Modeling for Bimodal Speech Recognition. Proc. 2001 International Fuzzy Systems Conference, 2001
20. Bogert, B. P., Healy, M. J. R., Tukey, J. W.: The Frequency Analysis of Time-Series for Echoes. Proc. Symp. Time Series Analysis, 1963, Chap, pp. 209-243

Synthesis of Codebooks with Perceptually Monitored Structure for Multiband CELP-Coders

Michael Livshitz [1] and Alexander Petrovsky [2]

[1] Belarusian State University of Informatics and Radioelectronics, Computer Engineering Department, P.Brovky, 6, Minsk, Belarus, 220027, mlivshitz@tut.by
[2] University of Finance and Management in Bialystok branch in Elk, Grunwaldzka 1, Elk, Poland, palex@it.org.by

Abstract. The work is devoted to subband decomposition scheme and training set composition effect on quality of reconstructed speech when synthesising codebooks for multiband CELP-coders. Codebooks quality and its dependence on the codebooks structure are studied. The research work presents multiband codebook with multistage organization and reconfigurable structure optimized by SNR, Bark Spectrum Distortion (BSD), Modified Bark Spectrum Distortion (MBSD) and Noise-to-Mask Ratio (NMR) criteria for control by psychoacoustic model on the base of Warped Discrete-Fourier Transform (WDFT).

Keywords: Multiband CELP-coder, Codebook, Perceptually Monitored Structure, Psychoacoustics, WDFT

1 Multiband CELP-Coders Background

Wideband speech coding researches have been actively curried out lately. CELP-coders tend to prevail in the field because they provide high quality of the reconstructed speech at high compression ratio. Modern CELP-coders have made a long path of development. Last models allow transmitting not only acoustic environment around a speaker but also musical components and even music. The research work presents multiband codebook with multistage organization and reconfigurable structure optimized by SNR, Bark Spectrum Distortion (BSD) [1], Modified Bark Spectrum Distortion (MBSD) [1] and Noise-to-Mask Ratio (NMR) [2] criteria for control by psychoacoustic model on the base of Warped Discrete-Fourier Transform (WDFT) [3]. In some schemes, subband decomposition is performed by a filterbank and each of the subbands is encoded by a single CELP-encoder [4]. Such models generally suffer from degradation of speech quality in the frequency region where the responses of the filterbanks overlap and have moderate compression ratio.

Other schemes, examples of which can be found in [5-6], exploit an excitation signal generator using more than one source with different frequency ranges (multiband codebooks) to enable background music encoding. Such coders provide a several times better compression ratio than the coders described earlier, but have a drawback of fast bitrate growing when subband number and search depth in subband codebooks increase. Nevertheless, this drawback can be eliminated by using the codebooks with reconfigurable structure monitored by a psychoacoustic model.

2 Basics of Subband Decomposition and Codebooks Training in Multiband CELP-Coders

2.1 Subband Decomposition

The main principle of subband decomposition presumes reaching a trade-off among number of subbands, their bandwidth (each subband must contain approximately equal signal energy), coding gain maximum [7] and effective filterbank implementation. Moreover, it is necessary to divide the frequency range into non-uniform subbands to reflect properties of human auditory system [8] and formant structure of speech. Recently introduced CELP-coders with codebooks based on band-pass filtered vectors are being widely spread. Their popularity is connected with the reduction of computational complexity because the filterbank is used only at codebook training stage and can have a relatively high complexity. All modern transform coders encode signal in perceptual frequency domain. To exploit high compression ratio of linear prediction (LP) and perceptual capabilities of transform coders in CELP-coders with multiband excitation, it is necessary to use multiband codebooks that reflect non-uniform critical bands and provide an ability of structure tweaking according to perceptual properties of the encoded signal.

2.2 Subband Training sets and Codebook training

Subband training set is prepared by band-pass filtering of a wideband source material according to accepted scheme of subband decomposition. Usually, the original wideband source data are represented by original speech with duration from five to twenty minutes. Subband codebooks training can effectively be realized by well-known algorithms: K-means, Generalized Lloyd Algorithm (GLA), Linde-Buzo-Gray Algorithm, etc. [9-10].

2.3 Features of Quantization according to Multiband Codebooks

It is necessary to underline that filtered code vectors have final length (which equals subframe length). It leads to a "leakage" of spectral energy between adjacent subband codebooks. However, as code vectors of different codebooks are nearly orthogonal, a sequential search in each codebook provides almost the same quality as the optimal joint search in all subband codebooks with a significant complexity reduction. Moreover, the "leakage" of spectral energy of i-th subband can be compensated during quantization of $i+1$-th subband, thus leaving no need for a paraunitary filterbank.

Besides synthesis filter shapes noise-like excitation signal by spectrum envelope of
the currently encoded signal and allows correcting the spectrum of error.

2.4 Codebook Structuring

Fixed character of codebook structure can be changed by using subband codebooks with multistage organization and different detail level (number of code vectors). Such codebooks allow choosing the number of encoded subbands and limiting
search depth in subband codebooks to meet the requirements of coding bandwidth,
throughput capacity of communication channel and quality of the reconstructed
speech. In addition, their structure can be monitored by a psychoacoustic model to
reflect the perceptual characteristics of the encoded signal.

3 Codebook Implementation in Multiband CELP-Coders

Codebooks formed according to criteria listed in sections 3.1 and 3.2 are used in work
[5]. The coder proposed in this work is suitable for transmitting both speech and
music at 24 kbps (it is referred below as Coder 1). However, it has grave disadvantage – the fixed structure that does not reflect perceptual properties of the encoded
signal. Authors of Coder 1 refuse using a psychoacoustic model and accept a fixed
structure of codebook with the aim of reducing the computational complexity.
An improvement of approach presented in [5] is made in work [6]. This coder is referred below as Coder 2. In Coder 2 the number of subbands is successfully de-
creased from nine to eight (Table 1) and a psychoacoustic model based on MPEG-
standard [11] is included for retrieval the subband code vectors in order of their perceptual significance. To provide functioning of the coder at different bitrates, search
depth (number of stages) in the codebook is set by user. Coder 2 has several disadvantages: narrowing of the encoded frequency range from 7000 Hz down to 6500 Hz
and still fixed structure yet controlled by user in the presence of a psychoacoustic
model.
As it was mentioned earlier, one of the grave disadvantages of multiband CELP-
coders is a bitrate growth when increasing number of subbands and stages in subband
codebooks. Codebook information contributes considerably to the overall bitrate. To
avoid these problems, modification of multiband CELP-coder with variable search
depth multistage vector quantization was proposed in work [12], where frequency
range of encoded signal was widened up to 8000 Hz, while search depth control is
realized by a psychoacoustic model based on the WDFT [3]. It was also shown that
psychoacoustic model based on the WDFT provides better compression ratio against
MPEG based one [11], while having no perceptual differences in reconstructed
speech. Further improvement of the coder was proposed in [13], where a detailed
description of psychoacoustic model and reconfigurable structure codebook monitoring algorithm is implemented. Block diagram of the encoder is depicted in Fig.1 and
the scheme of subband decomposition is represented in Table 2. To obtain subband-

training sets, non-uniform cosine-modulated polyphase filterbank described in [14] is used. Scheme of speech model parameters quantization is shown in Table 3.

Table 1. Comparison of subband decomposition in coders

Subband	Coder 1	Coder 2	
	Freq. range, Hz	Freq. range, Hz	Barks
1	50-500	100-510	4
2	500-1000	510-1080	4
3	1000-1500	1080-1720	3
4	1500-2000	1720-2320	2
5	2000-2600	2320-3150	2
6	2600-3400	3150-4100	1.5
7	3400-4400	4100-5300	1.5
8	4400-5600	5300-6500	1
9	5600-7000	-	-

Such model allows taking into consideration and eliminating both statistical and perceptual redundancy while encoding source wideband speech. At the same time, the structure of the encoder (multiband codebook with multistage structure) is dynamically changed and is tuned to perceptual features of the currently encoded signal frame.

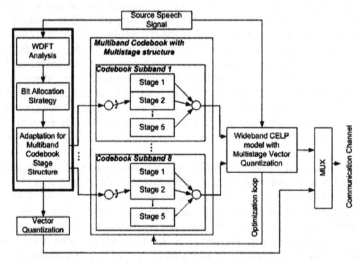

Fig. 1. Block diagram of the CELP-encoder with dynamic reconfigurable codebook structure

The scheme includes an additional procedure of LTP-filtering that results in a fine-tuned formant structure of speech in case the first two subbands are among the coding subbands. The procedure adds 2.6 kbps to a total bitrate (see Table 3, strings in italic). Comparative analysis of quality of this coder and MPEG1 Layer III coder [11] was implemented in work [15], where it was shown that the proposed coder signifi-

cantly exceeds the last one by perceptual quality based on BSD, MBSD and NMR.
However, as it will be shown later, the structure of the codebook in this coder is still
redundant and, consequently, needs to be optimized to fulfil the requirements formulated in section 3.1.

Table 2. Subband decomposition

Subband	Freq. range, Hz	Barks
1	100-510	4
2	510-1080	4
3	1080-1720	3
4	1720-2320	2
5	2320-3150	2
6	3150-4100	1.5
7	4100-5300	1.5
8	5300-8000	3

Table 3. Speech model parameters quantization scheme

Model parameter	Param./ frame	Bits/ param.	Bits/ frame	Frames/s	Bitrate, bps
LSF	16	1.6875	27		1350
Model Gain	1	7	7		350
LTP Delays	*4*	*8*	*32*		*1600*
LTP Gains	*4*	*5*	*20*	50	*1000*
Codebook Structure	1	1.25	10		500
Excitation Gains	0 – 32	4	0 – 128		0 – 6400
Book Indexes	0 – 32	4 – 8	0 – 256		0 – 12800
Peak bitrate, bps					24000

4 Techniques for Improving Codebook Quality and Structure Optimization

4.1 Choice of Codebook Training Set Composition by Analysis of Objective Quality of Reconstructed Speech

An influence of training set composition on the quality of the codebook is studied in
this subsection. The quality of codebook (as a part of wideband CELP-coder [15]) is
estimated at reconstructed speech. Three different training sets are used as a source
material:

- Wideband speech from the TIMIT database [16] with total duration of 5 minutes;

- Musical material (musical excerpts) with total duration of 5 minutes;
- Mixed training set (for subbands 1-6 – first training set is used, for subbands 7-6 – the second variant training set is used).

Multiband multistage codebooks with 5-stage structure (16, 32, 64, 128, 256 vectors per stage) was constructed for the abovementioned training sets composition. Comparison of quality is performed by two patterns of test material voice and music with 5 minutes length each. Average and total codebook bitrate values were evaluated along with SNRseg, BSD and MBSD [1]. Estimated parameters of quality for three training variants are shown in Table 4.

Table 4. Codebooks' quality comparison

Testing Material	Composition of training set	Avg. Codebook bitrate, bps	Peak Codebook bitrate, bps	SNRseg, dB	BSD	MBSD
Voices	Voice	5403	18700	10.94	0.093	0.042
	Voice+music			12.26	0.089	0.035
	Music			13.72	0.094	0.028
Music	Voice	10708	19200	9.18	0.097	0.045
	Voice+music			10.64	0.095	0.044
	music			11.48	0.087	0.032

Analysis of Table 4 shows that in general case training of the codebooks on excerpts of musical compositions (vocal with accompaniment) provides better quality of the reconstructed signal according either to objective or to subjective estimates of the quality. Psychoacoustically monitored structure of the codebook allows a three-time decrease of codebook bitrate for speech and provides almost a two-time decrease of codebook bitrate for music.

4.2 Analysis of the Subband Codebooks Contribution to Error Minimization

Reconstructed speech quality and its dependence on multiband codebook configuration in wideband CELP-coder [15] has been studied to determine an optimal structure of subband codebooks. Mixed data (voices+music) with total duration of 10 minutes composed from audio materials described in subsection 4.1 were used as a test material. Subband codebooks contribution to preceding stage error minimization for speech excerpts is shown in Fig. 2.

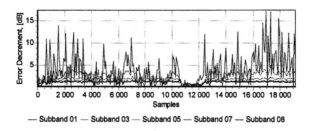

Fig. 2. Subband codebooks contribution to error minimization

Analysis of Fig. 2 shows that beginning from seventh subband error decrement reaches 1.5 dB, i.e. with further increase of subbands amount in codebook quantization error will insignificantly decrease. Relative contribution of subband codebooks with different quantity of stages to preceding stage error minimization averaged through the whole test material is depicted in Fig. 3. As it can be seen from Fig. 3, subbands 4 and 5 make the least contribution. The 5-th stage brings significant contribution in subbands from one to four, whereas the 3-rd stage - for others. Therefore, we can make conclusion that for subband codebooks (subbands from five to eight) a three-stage organization is the optimal one.

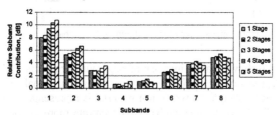

Fig. 3. Subband codebooks contribution to preceding stage error minimization (for all stages in each subband codebook)

SNRseg changing depending on subbands and stages amount in multiband codebook is illustrated in Fig. 4. Perceptual quality of reconstructed speech alterations according to multiband codebook configuration are depicted in Fig. 5. Changing BSD and MBSD criteria are shown in Fig. 6.

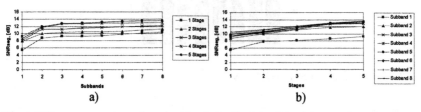

a)   b)

Fig. 4. SNRseg versus: a) number of subbands for fixed detail level (stages) in subband codebook; b) stages for fixed number of subbands

Analysis of Fig. 4a shows that starting with 2-nd subband the quality linearly improves and at the 5-th stage it reaches saturation. As it can be seen from Fig. 4b, SNRseg reaches saturation by the 8-th subband. Fig. 5 shows that perceptual quality of the reconstructed signal increases exponentially with subband amount, and number of stages in subband codebooks makes a moderate offset into characteristics.

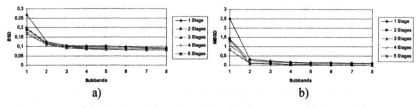

a)   b)

Fig. 5. Perceptual quality changing versus subbands with constant stage structure

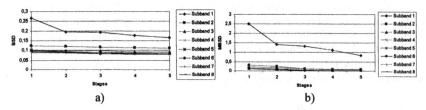

a)   b)

Fig. 6. Perceptual quality versus stages for fixed number of subbands

Analysis of Fig. 6 shows that an increase of stage number results in ill-defined linear growth of perceptual quality, excluding first two subbands. Signal energy in subbands (Table 2) averaged through the whole test material is represented in Fig. 7. It is evident from Fig. 7 that first three subbands concentrate more energy, but the others have practically equal level of energy.

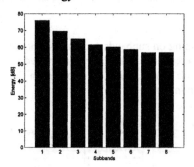

Fig. 7. Averaged signal energy in subbands

Table 5. Comparison of codebooks' configurations quality

Codebook Structure	NMRseg, dB	NMRtotal, dB	SNRseg, dB	SNRtotal, dB	BSD	MBSD
8 subbands with 5 stages each	-6.577	-6.364	13.442	12.498	0.0809	0.0211
8 subbands 1 – 4 (5 stages) 5 – 8 (3 stages)	-6.597	-6.501	13.439	12.483	0.0809	0.0184
Opt. Structure Coding Gain	0.02	0.137	-0.003	-0.015	0	-0.0027

All features mentioned above testify that multiband codebook with eight subband codebooks with five-stage organization for the first four subbands (16, 32, 64, 128, 256 vectors) and three-stage organization for the other three subbands (16, 32, 64 vectors) can be quite effective in multiband CELP-coders from the point of reaching the best quality. In this case, codebook bitrate (peak value) reduces from 12800 bps down to 11200 bps. Quality comparison results analysis of redundant and optimized codebooks shows (see Table 5) that the optimized structure of codebook allows reducing codebook information and even provides perceptual quality improvement at the cost of insignificant SNR impairment. Perceptual monitoring of the codebook structure can effectively be realized by using of psychoacoustic model based on WDFT [12-13]. As an example, outcomes of the proposed psychoacoustic model for subband masking thresholds ($MT_{Subbands}$) (Table 2) and masking thresholds in Barks (MT_{Barks}) estimation are shown in Fig. 8. Dynamic ranges of subband perceptual entropy (SPE) for the whole test material are depicted in Fig. 9. Analysis of Fig. 9 shows that perceptual significance of subbands (SPE max) evaluated by psychoacoustic model well correlates with relative contribution to error minimization data (Fig.3). Thus, psychoacoustic model is proved to be well balanced with accepted subband decomposition scheme in the coder.

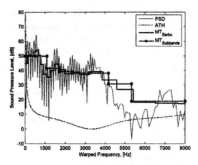

Fig. 8. Comparison of masking threshold in subbands and Barks

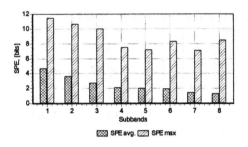

Fig. 9. SPE dynamic range estimation

5 Conclusions

Alteration of different parameters of multiband codebooks configuration is studied in the work. System approach for codebook synthesis in order to make a perceptually monitored structure of codebook is proposed. Synthesis is implemented by exploiting objective, subjective and perceptual quality criteria: SNR, BSD, MBSD, training set composition, etc. As a result, forming of the optimal (irredundant) structure of multiband codebook with multistage organization is reached and the control by psychoacoustic model based on the WDFT is done. Moreover, the new codebook structure provides quality improvement alongside with the codebook bitrate decrease.

References

1. W. Yang, M. Benbouchta, and R. Yantorno, "Performance of a modified bark spectral distortion measure as an objective speech quality measure,"// IEEE ICASSP, Seattle, (1998), pp.541-544
2. K. Brandenburg, T. Sporer: "NMR" and "Masking Flag": Evaluation of Quality Using Perceptual Criteria, // Proc. of the 11th Int. Conv. Aud. Eng. Soc., "Test and measurement", Portland, USA, May (1992), pp.169-179
3. M. Parfieniuk, A. Petrovsky: Warped DFT as the basis for psychoacoustic model // The proc. of the IEEE International conference on Acoustic, Speech, Signal processing, ICASSP, vol. IV, May (2004), Montreal, Canada, pp.185-188
4. P. Menardi, G.A. Mian, G.Riccardi: Dynamic Bit Allocation in Subband Coding of Wideband Audio with Multipulse LPC // Proc. of EUSIPCO, Edinburgh, September, (1994), pp.1453-1456
5. A. Ubale, A. Gersho: A Low-Delay Wideband Speech Coder at 24 kbps // Proc. of ICASSP, Seatle, (1998), pp.165-168
6. Alexis Bernard, Abeer Alwan: Perceptually Based and Embedded Wideband CELP Coding of Speech // Proc. of Eurospeech, (1999), pp.1543-1546
7. A. Makur: Derivation of Subband Coding Gain: The Most General Case, www.ntu.edu.sg/home/eamakur/codinggain.pdf
8. E. Zwicker, H. Fastl: Psychoacoustics Facts and Models, Springer-Verlag, Berlin Heidelberg, (1990)

9. Linde, Y., Buzo, A., and Gray, R.M.: An algorithm for vector quantizer design // IEEE
    Transactions on Communications, vol. COM-28, Jan. (1980), pp. 84 – 95
10. Gersho, A. and Gray, R.: Vector quantization and signal compression, Boston, Kluwer
    Academic Publishers, (1992)
11. ISO/IEC JTC1/SC29/WG11, MPEG, International Standard IS 13818-3 Information
    technology – Generic Coding of Moving Pictures and Associated Audio, (1994)
12. M.Z. Livshitz, M. Parfieniuk, A.A. Petrovsky: Multistage Vector Quantization with Vari-
    able Dimension in Perceptual Speech Encoders with Psychoacoustic Model Based on
    Warped DFT // Proc. of the 7th International Conference on Digital Signal Processing
    and its Applications, vol.VII-1, Moscow, Russia, (2005), pp.187-191
13. M.Z. Livshitz, M. Parfieniuk, A.A. Petrovsky: Wideband CELP-coder with Multiband
    Excitation and Multistage Quantization under Reconfigurable Structure Codebook //
    Digital Signal Processing, Moscow, Russia, vol.2, (2005), pp.20-35 (in Russian)
14. A. Petrovsky, M. Parfieniuk, K. Bielawski: Psychoacoustically Motivated Non-uniform
    Cosine Modulated Polyphase Filter Bank // 2nd International Workshop on Spectral
    Methods and Multirate Signal Processing (SMMSP 2002), Toulouse, France, September
    7-8, (2002), pp.95-101
15. Michael Livshitz and Alexander Petrovsky: Perceptually Constrained Variable Bitrate
    Wideband Speech Coder // The Proc. of EUROCON, Serbia & Montenegro, Belgrade,
    November 22-24, (2005), pp.1296-1299
16. DARPA TIMIT Acoustic-Phonetic Continuous Speech Corpus, Department of Com-
    merce, NIST, Springfield, Virginia, Oct. (1990)

The Color Information as a Feature for Postage Stamps Recognition

Mirosław Miciak

University of Technology and Agriculture, Institute of Telecommunications
and Electrical Engineering
ul. Kaliskiego 7, 85-791 Bydgoszcz, Poland
e-mail: miciak@mail.atr.bydgoszcz.pl

Abstract. This paper describes the method of postage stamps recognition and the experiments carried out with it. It represents the basic operations of the post mail image processing. The article contains basic processing of the stamps image and calculation of characteristic features, on basis of which it will be recognized. The main objective of this article is to use the color information to obtain a set of features which are invariant under translation and rotation. The proposed method of recognizing can be applied in checking the value of post payments. The value of a post stamp is connected with a picture. The picture is represented in the color space where classification is done. The today's systems of recognition often use classification on the basis of shape. Proposed method enables recognition of postal stamps from mail piece. Sources of errors as well as possible improvement of classification results will be discussed.

1 Introduction

Image recognition is important and difficult research area. Nonetheless, it still is an active area of research. No available solutions have been offered that solves the problem completely. Automatic image recognition is widely used for identification of people, objects, shapes, maps, etc. Image recognition can be realised by using various picture features such as information about pixels, histograms, colours, layers, shapes, patterns etc. The image recognition method depends on application. The image features on basis of recognition will be done, should be invariance from change scale, change orientation, skew transformation and change of intensity of lighting. Moreover features should be unaffected from errors from acquisition stage. Image recognition can be used for post stamps identification on envelopes to check postage as well as for identification of invalid ones. The basic invariant feature used for detection and identification of the post stamps on envelope or a postmail is color information. Analysis of the images for detection post stamps includes operations: image acquisition, segmentation, color transformation, features calculation as well as classification.

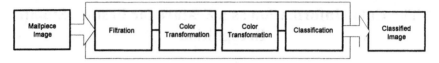

Fig. 1. Proposal of a method for recognition post stamps

Some countries, such as the Poland, are at an advantage in this because their amount of post stamps is relatively small, therefore the process of classification is easier. Recognition systems for the postal service could be enhanced to read the whole address and sort envelopes. Mail sorting is an ideal application for image processing because it has a wide variety of difficulty levels. The most simple case is recognizing post stamps situated without stamps and broken parts. In my paper this situation is chosen. The perception of human eye for information about color is independent from change lighting, scale, rotation and background. Possible is, to use color information as a feature for detecting interests area on envelope. The perception of human eye for information about color is independent from change lighting, scale, rotation and background. Possible is, to use color information as a feature for detecting interests area on envelope. The best way of use color as feature to distinction the post stamps, is take advantage of chrominance information.

2 Filtration

The first step of the postmails image processing is filtration. Filtration is used for improving the quality of the image, emphasize details and makes processing of the image easier. The filtration of digital images is obtained by convolution operation. The new value of point of image is counted on the basis of neighboring points value. Every value is classified and it has influence on new value of point of the image after filtration [5]. In the pre-processing part no-linear filtration was applied. The statistical filter separates the signal from the noise, but it does not destroy useful information. The applied filter is median filter, with mask 3x3.

$$A = \begin{bmatrix} f_{-1,-1} & f_{0,-1} & f_{1,-1} \\ f_{-1,0} & f_{0,0} & f_{1,0} \\ f_{-1,1} & f_{0,1} & f_{1,1} \end{bmatrix} \tag{1}$$

$$P = \left\{ b_{ij} \; ; 1 \le i \le M \quad 1 \le j \le N \right\} \tag{2}$$

$$\hat{b}_{ij} = \underset{A}{med}\left(f_{i+r,j+s}\right); (r,s) \in A \; ; (i,j) \in P \tag{3}$$

Where : A – the mask of filter, P – input image , M – height of the image, N – width of the image, b – point of the image. The median filter is sorting values of points of image and counting center value. The applying the filter to the whole image, allows to eliminate noise majority. This filter does not have a smooth effect, and has low computational complexity.

2 Color transformation

A color space is a way of representing colors and their relationship to each other. Human perception of color is a function of the response of three types of cones. There are numerous color spaces based on the tristimulus values. The YIQ color space is used in broadcast television. The XYZ space does not correspond to physical primaries but is used as a color standard. It is fairly easy to convert from XYZ to other color spaces with a matrix multiplication. Other color models include Lab, YUV, and UVW. All color space discussions will assume that all colors are normalized (values lie between 0 and 1.0). This is easily accomplished by dividing the color by its maximum value. For example, an 8-bit color is normalized by dividing by 255 [1]. In this approach color model (from acquisition stage) is RGB and can be expressed as 2D dimensional matrix of image points, where each point is represented by 3 coefficients. Let $\{F(x,y):x=1,2,...M, \quad y=1,2,...N\}$ will be a 2D dimensional matrix of image points about size MxN. $F(x,y)$ defines value of point color (x,y) $F(x,y)=\{Fr(x,y),Fg(x,y),Fb(x,y)\}$ [2]. Each point of the image can be expressed in 3 dimensional co-ordinates. The perception of human eye is independent from changing brightness, and kind of lighting source.

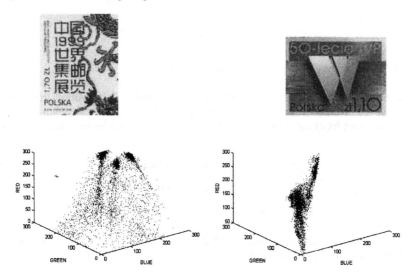

Fig. 2. The color images of post stamps and their RGB 3D representation

Perception of color is relatively constant in wide area of changes of lighting. The RGB model simplifies the design of computer graphics systems but is not ideal for all applications. The red, green, and blue color components are highly correlated. This makes it difficult to execute some image processing algorithms. These processes are easier implemented using another color models. Thus, YC_rC_b color space can be used for eliminating dependences from the image brightness information. The realisation of transformation from RGB color space to YC_rC_b color space is given by the following relationship:

$$\begin{bmatrix} Y \\ C_r \\ C_b \end{bmatrix} = \begin{bmatrix} 0,29900 & 0,58700 & 0,11400 \\ 0,50000 & -0,41866 & -0,08310 \\ -0,16874 & -0,33126 & 0,50000 \end{bmatrix} \begin{bmatrix} R \\ G \\ B \end{bmatrix} \tag{4}$$

There are several ways to convert to/from YC_bC_r. This is the CCIR (International Radi Consultive Committee) recommendation 601-1 and is the typical method used in JPEG compression. The received coefficients C_r and C_b for each point of the image, can be presented on 2D co-ordinates. The Y coefficient is not useful for next operations.

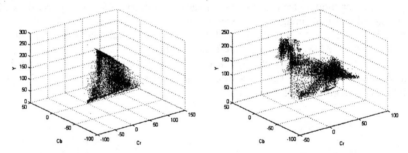

Fig. 3. YC_rC_b 3D representation of color images from Fig.2

Another representation of color space is CIEL*a*b* model. To transform from RGB to that space, it is necessary to use XYZ transformation first. The realisation of transformation from RGB color space to XYZ color space is given by the following relationship:

$$\begin{bmatrix} X \\ Y \\ Z \end{bmatrix} = \begin{bmatrix} 0,4412453 & 0,357580 & 0,180423 \\ 0,212671 & 0,715160 & 0,072169 \\ 0,019334 & 0,119193 & 0,950227 \end{bmatrix} \begin{bmatrix} R \\ G \\ B \end{bmatrix} \tag{5}$$

The realisation of transformation from XYZ color space to CIEL*a*b* color space is given by the following relationship:

$$L^* = 116 \left(\frac{Y}{Y_n} \right)^{\frac{1}{3}} - 16, \quad \left(\frac{Y}{Y_n} \right) > 0,008856 \tag{6}$$

$$L^* = 903 \left(\frac{Y}{Y_n} \right), \quad \left(\frac{Y}{Y_n} \right) \leq 0,008856 \tag{7}$$

$$a^* = 500 \left[f \left(\frac{X}{X_n} \right) - f \left(\frac{Y}{Y_n} \right) \right] \tag{8}$$

$$b^* = 500 \left[f \left(\frac{Y}{Y_n} \right) - f \left(\frac{Z}{Z_n} \right) \right] \tag{9}$$

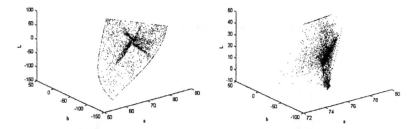

Fig. 4. The CIEL* a*b* 2D representation of color images from Fig.2

3 Color segmentation

The RGB color space 24bit image theoretically requires about 16,7Mb of memory. In reality, amount of memory is lower, it is depend from content of image.

To decrease application memory requirements, color segmentation should be done. The color segmentation from 24bit image (8bit for each coefficient) is realised by indirect addressing algorithm, as a result of that operation, 12bit image (4bits for each coefficient) is received. After this reduction, size of the color space is 64 times less than before. This decrease of amount of colors does not have a big influence on recognition rate. But it is important for amount of system recognition memory, size of database with patterns of images and for the speed of recognizing process.

4 Post stamps models

Two sets of data received from color transformation stage (C_r and C_b) are used to create model of post stamps. On basis of this information can be made 2D graph. The weakness of that solution is that we do not have any information about amount of pixels with the same color. Therefore while color transformations stage the histogram of color should be done. So histogram will be another factor of the post stamps model. As a result of this stage is a 3 - dimensional feature vector including coefficients C_r, C_b and color histogram.

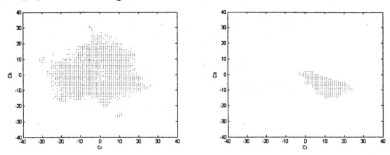

Fig. 5. The $C_r C_b$ representation of post stamp from Fig.2

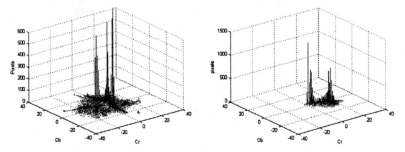

Fig. 6. The $C_r C_b$ and amount of pixels representation of color images from Fig.2

As a result of this stage is a 3 - dimensional feature vector including coefficients C_r, C_b and color histogram.

$$FV = \{\rho_0, \rho_1, ..., \rho_{4095}\} \tag{10}$$

Model of the post stamps *(FV)* contains amount of pixels for each chromination value on the color space Fig.6. This solution has additional problem which is connected with the feature vector. The coefficients C_r, C_b and color histogram are identical, for images from Fig.7.a.b and Fig.9.e.f. Therefore the feature vector should contain more information about color and their localization on image of the post stamp. Enhanced model of the post stamps contains values of centroid C_{r0}, C_{b0} for C_r, C_b representation and boundary points for 8-component neighbor in the form of distance $\rho_0, \rho_1,..., \rho_7$ from $C_{r0,}C_{b0}$.

$$FV = \{C_{r0}, C_{b0}, \rho_0, \rho_1,..., \rho_7\} \tag{11}$$

Taking into consideration only coefficients $C_{r0,}C_{b0}$ and $\rho_0, \rho_1,..., \rho_7$ from the special created database of 192 post stamps images, the upper limit of recognition rate is up to 70%. The recognition rate is to low for use in checking payment system therefore *(FV)* should additionally contain geometrical relationship. The points $\rho_0, \rho_1,..., \rho_7$ are described by chromination value of boundary point in each direction on the color space *Fig.8*. These values are reflecting many points on the geometrical plane of the input image Fig.10. So we can use those coordinates $x_{00}, y_{00}, x_{10}, y_{10},.., x_{70}, y_{70}$ for each point $\rho_0, \rho_1,..., \rho_7$ are defined as centroid of points with the same color values on the image Fig.9. as additional vector features (equation 12). In this way it can be possible to differentiate image Fig.7.a.b and Fig.8.e.f. As a result of this stage is a 18 - dimensional feature vector including coefficients from image of the post stamp.

$$FV = \{C_{r0}, C_{b0}, \rho_0, \rho_1,..., \rho_7, x_{00}, y_{00}, x_{10}, y_{10},..., x_{70}, y_{70}\} \tag{12}$$

This approach have better recognition rate, especially for broken and illegible intentionally prepared stamps, and so far the recognition rate increase to 81%.

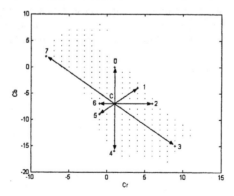
(a)   (b)

Fig. 7. The color images of post stamps (a) regular stamp (b) specially prepared stamp from testing set

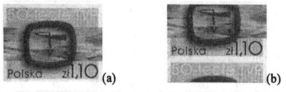

Fig. 8. The localization of ρ points on C_rC_b representation for the post stamps from Fig.7

Fig. 9 The samples of stamps from database (a-e) regular samples of stamps, (f) specially prepared stamp from testing set

In Table 1 we can observe how values obtain coefficients from feature vector for similar stamps from one stamp series. We can also notice that it is necessary to use geometrical plane values to build post stamp model vector (to differentiate images from Fig. 7.a.b and Fig. 9.e.f.).

Table 2. The values of feature vector for C_{r0}, C_{b0} and $\rho_0, \rho_1,..., \rho_7$ for images of the post stamps from Fig. 9.

Stamp	Cr0	Cb0	ρ0	ρ1	ρ2	ρ3	ρ4	ρ5	ρ6	ρ7
(a)	31	38	16	20	10	11	20	4	22	12
(b)	30	33	5	14	21	9	21	7	24	8
(c)	35	28	5	9	10	5	5	9	4	5
(d)	30	31	16	12	22	12	21	12	23	12
(e)	20	34	16	12	8	8	20	7	10	7
(f)	20	34	16	12	8	8	20	7	10	7

If similarity is suitably high it means that pattern is situated on the image. In this way are received patterns which are on the image. These data are enough to describe payment. The main sources of recognition error are acquisition stage processes and post stamp area detection algorithm. These areas of research must be improved to obtain better recognition rate.

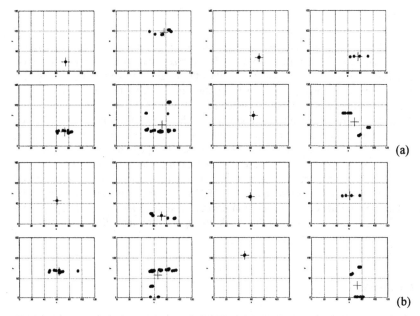

(a)

(b)

Fig. 10. The localization of ρ points on xy for the post stamps from (a)Fig.7.a and (b)Fig.7.b (dots – the points with the same color, cross – the centroid)

5 Classification

The classification module comparing features from the unknown image to model features sets obtained during the learning process. Based on the feature vector, the classification attempts to identify the image based on the calculation of Euclidean distance between the features of the image and of the image models [3]. The distance function is given by:

$$D(C_i, C_r) = \sum_{j=1}^{N} [R(j) - A(j)]^2 \qquad (13)$$

where:
C_i - is the predefined image,
C_s - in the image to be recognized,
R - is the feature vector of the image to be recognized,
A - is the feature vector of the predefined image,
N - is the number of features,
The minimum distance D between unknown image feature and predefined class of the image is the criterion choice of the post stamp [4].

6 Summary

The selecting of the features for postage stamps recognition can be problematic. Moreover fact that the mail pieces have different sizes, shapes, layouts etc. this process is more complicated. The paper describes the often used image processing. The proposed method of recognizing can be applied in checking the value of post payments. The value of a post stamp is connected with a picture.

The picture is represented in the color space where classification is done. The recognition on basis of the color space representation has invariance property against image transformation including translation, scaling, skew, and rotation. Moreover it is invariant from changing type and intensity of lighting. The weakness of this method is that some post mails can include graphics similar to the post stamps. The research is continued in aim decrease the quantity of RGB coefficients in color transformation stage and their influence on recognition errors. As well as another color spaces will be tested too. In connection with this work, the application including discussed algorithms is in progress.

References

1. Luong Chi Mai.: Introduction to computer vision and image processing, Institute of Information Technology, Hanoi, Vietnam (2000)
2. Choraś R.S. ,Choraś M.: Automatyczne wykrywanie i lokalizacja ludzkich twarzy w 2D obrazach, Techniki Przetwarzania Obrazu , Serock, (2002)
3. Aissaoui A.: Normalised Fourier Coefficients for Cursive Arabic Script recognition, Universite Mohamed, Morocco (1999)
4. Dutkiewicz P., Kiełczewski M.: Sprzężenie wizyjne w sterowaniu grupą robotów mobilnych, Politechnika Poznańska (2003)
5. Bellili A., Giloux M.: An MLP-SVM combination architecture for handwritten digit recognition, International Journal on Document Analysis and Recognition (2003)

Iris Shape Evaluation in Face Image with Simple Background

Szymon Rydzek

Czestochowa University of Technology,
Institute of Computer and Information Sciences,
Dąbrowskiego 73, 42–200 Częstochowa, Poland
Szymon.rydzek@icis.pcz.pl

Abstract. In this paper algorithm of exact iris shape determination in a face image with simple background was described. This work is a part of face recognition method and will be base for developing face features extraction procedure. The aim was to locate circles circumscribed about irises (radius and centers of such circles) in frontal face image. Presented algorithm combines known image processing algorithms and developed procedures. Achieved results are satisfactory for purpose of use in face recognition method, which is being developed.

1 Motivation

Nowadays face and iris detection methods are widely used in many computer vision applications, such as systems of human-computer interaction [1, 2].
Considerable part of applications is used in systems for face recognition in access control [3] and model-based video coding [4–6].
Author is developing face recognition method in which exact features extraction in eyes' part of face plays a meaningful role.
In this method the primary quantity is the iris diameter. As a constant of human body the diameter was used to construct unit called *Muld* which allow to measure face features on images in different scale [7, 8].
The first step is to locate face area on image. This is done by algorithm combining skin-like color detection method [9], median filtering [10] and simple method of determining region boundaries. Once the face has been detected the next step is to locate area of both eyes. For purpose of detecting eyes the 3-stage gray-level image projection algorithm was applied. The thresholding of gray-level image (with automated threshold selection), median filtering, *Canny* edge detection [11] and procedure of finding circles in eye's edge-image was combined to accomplish iris detection.

2   Related Works

There are many known approaches to realization the task of face detection in images.
Turk and Pentland [12, 13] proposed application of *Principal Component Analysis*
(PCA) for face detection. This method was improved by Moghaddam and Pentland in
[14].
Good results of face detection were observed in skin-color detection methods [15].
Procedures based on color information allows to segment image regions easy, but can
be affected by skin-like color areas in background.
There are also known such approaches as: shape analysis [16, 17], template-based [4,
18] and neural network-based [19].
Known approaches of realization the task of iris localization can be divided in 3 main
groups:
– intrusive
– non intrusive active
– non intrusive passive
Our approach is based on skin-color detection and can be classified as non intrusive
passive.

3   Face Detection

As input of face recognition procedure we assume to have the *RGB* color space, frontal face image. For purpose of detecting face in input image the algorithm of thresholding in *I2* color space was applied [9]. The *I2* color space let us to detect skin-like
color regions in *RGB* image with satisfactory result.
To transform image to the *I2* color space, we have to subtract R and B components of
RGB space. Let I_R and I_B represent matrix containing R and B components respectively, for each pixel of input image. The output I_{RB} matrix is obtained after subtraction:

$$I_{RB}[i][j] = \sum_{i=0}^{w}\sum_{j=0}^{h} I_R[i][j] - I_B[i][j] \tag{1}$$

where:
w, h - width and height of input image.

Once we have the *I2* color space image the next step is to apply thresholding procedure which can be described by following formula:

$$I'[x][y] = \begin{cases} 255 & for \quad I_{RB}[x][y] > T \\ 0 & for \quad I_{RB}[x][y] \leq T \end{cases} \tag{2}$$

where:
$x = 0...w, y = 0...h$ - coordinates of the pixel,

w, h - width and height of the image,
I_{RB} - input $I2$ color space matrix,
I' - output, thresholded image,
T - threshold.

As far as now the value of threshold T is assigned as constant. For face database used for purpose of testing the procedure, value of the threshold equals *37*. On Fig. 1 are presented images before and after skin-like color detection procedure.

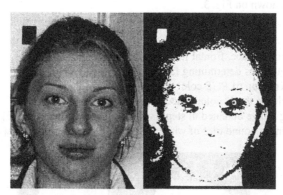

Fig. 1. Face image before and after I2 thresholding procedure with threshold value $T=37$

In order to eliminate noise around the face area and small objects in background the modified median filtering procedure was applied. In classic median filtering, values of pixels neighboring analyzed pixel (including analyzed pixel) are sorted from lowest to highest (or reverse). To analyzed pixel is assigned *median* value of surrounding pixels [10].

The filtration procedure after modification can be formulated as follows:

$$S(x,y) = \sum_{i=2}^{-2}\sum_{j=2}^{-2} I'[x+i][y+i] \qquad (3)$$

$$I''[x][y] = \begin{cases} 255 & for \ \ S(x,y) > 3315 \\ 0 & for \ \ S(x,y) \le 3315 \end{cases} \qquad (4)$$

where:
$x = 2...w - 2$, $y = 2...h - 2$ - coordinates of the pixel, w, h - width and height of the image, $S(x, y)$ - sum of *25* neighboring pixels (including analyzed), I' - input $I2$ thresholded image, I'' - output, filtered image.
Analyzed pixel is set to *white* if more than half of surrounding pixels is white (*sum* $S(x, y) > 3315$; $13 \cdot 255 = 3315$). In other case the pixel is set to *black*.

The result of modified median filtering is image with smoothed edges of face area. Also small background objects were eliminated. Fig. 2 shows example of median filtering of the image obtained after *I2* thresholding (procedure repeated *20* times). The boundaries of face region are acquired in simple procedure. The upper boundary is the row of image where number of white pixels (occurring continuously) exceeds given value. The lower boundary – the line where number of white pixels decreases below given value. Vertical boundaries are white pixels found most on left and right side of the image (in limits of horizontal boundaries). This procedure gives boundaries of region shown on Fig. 3.

The procedure of acquiring face area can be summarized in following algorithm:

Face area detection
IN: *RGB* color space, frontal face image
OUT: Boundaries determining face area
1. Transformation of *RGB* color space to *I2* according to (1)
2. Thresholding the *I2* color space image (2)
3. Filtering image obtained in step 2 with modified median filter (3) and (4)
4. Determining boundaries of white region in filtered image from step 3

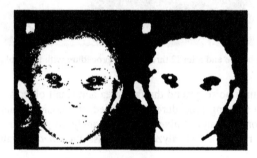

Fig. 2. Image before and after median filtering with *20* repeats

Fig. 3. Founded boundaries of the face area.

4 Eyes Localization

For purpose of accurate irises localization, we have to determine region of eyes – squares containing each eye. This has been accomplished in 3-stage gray-level image projection.

Stage 1 - Determining the line of eyes.

To find line where the eyes are located the gray-level image horizontal projection procedure was applied. Let I_{gray} be gray-level image obtained from RGB image according to following formula:

$$I_{gray}[x][y] = \frac{77 \cdot I_R[x][y] + 151 \cdot I_G[x][y] + 28 \cdot I_B[x][y]}{256} \tag{5}$$

where I_R, I_G, I_B are components of RGB color space.
The horizontal projection is defined as follows:

$$H_1[y] = \sum_{x=0}^{w-1} \left| I_{gray}[x][y] - I_{gray}[x+1][y] \right| \tag{6}$$

The line of eyes is determined by Maximum value H_I^{max}.

Stage 2 - Determining horizontal positions of eyes.

In this stage we consider zone $H_I^{max} - 20 \div H_I^{max} + 20$ and in this limits we calculate vertical projection according to:

$$V[x] = \sum_{y=H_1^{max}-20}^{H_1^{max}+20} \left| I_{gray}[x][y] - I_{gray}[x][y+1] \right| \tag{7}$$

Horizontal position of eyes is determined by two maximum values of $V[x]$.

Stage 3 - Correcting vertical position of each eye.

In case of inexact vertical position of head in image, determining the line of eyes' (by value of H_I^{max}) is not satisfactory for iris localization. To increase accurateness of eye localization the procedure of horizontal projection is repeated for both of eyes and in limits of ±20 pixels of maximums of vertical projection.

$$H_R[x] = \sum_{y=V_1^{max}-20}^{V_1^{max}+20} \left| I_{gray}[x][y] - I_{gray}[x+1][y] \right|$$

$$H_L[x] = \sum_{y=V_2^{max}-20}^{V_2^{max}+20} \left| I_{gray}[x][y] - I_{gray}[x+1][y] \right|$$

(8)

Area of eyes is square in size of *152x152* pixels with center in $(H_R(max),\ V_{max1})$ for right eye and $(H_L(max),\ V_{max2})$ for left. Fig. 4 presents sample results of eye localization procedure. Curves denotes values of horizontal and vertical projection, for each row/column, horizontal lines – limits the zone of eyes $(H_I^{max1} - 20 \div H_I^{max1} + 20)$ and boxes - areas of eyes. In further processing we will consider founded areas for both eyes separately.

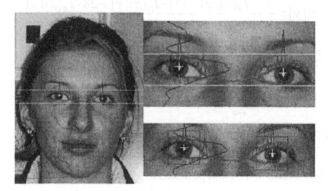

Fig. 4. Sample result of eye localization procedure

5 Iris Detection

Finally we have to find circle circumscribed about the iris on area of size *152x152* pixels containing image of the eye. This task will be completed in following steps.

1. Thresholding the gray-level image with automatically selected threshold and applying Canny edge detection procedure.
Many methods of analyzing histograms for purpose of estimating scene parameters can be found in literature [20–22]. In our procedure value of threshold is set as average value of pixels in analyzed image incremented by constant (*10*, this constant was determined experimentally). The threshold value is calculated using the relationship:

$$T = 10 + \frac{1}{w \cdot h} \sum_{x=0}^{w} \sum_{y=0}^{h} I[x][y]$$

(9)

After applying threshold, the median filtering procedure was used (see section 3). Fig. 5 shows result of above operations.

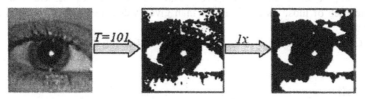

Fig. 5. Result of threshold with automatically selected threshold value ($T = 101$) and single course of median filtering

Next, the *Canny* edge detection procedure was applied [11]. Stage of Gaussian filtering was omitted due to reducing edge sharpness. Image of the eye after edge detection is shown on fig. 6.

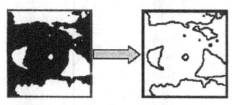

Fig. 6. Processed eye image before and after Canny edge detection procedure

2. Finding points on edge of the iris and determining best-fitted circle

In order to detect edge of the iris we use *10* rays with center in point of maximum projection (see section 3). The rays are inclined at angles of: *340°, 350°, 0°, 10°, 20°, 160°, 170°, 180°, 190°, 200°.*

In range of *20* to *65* pixels from the center, along each ray we find first occurrence of black pixel and set it as edge of the iris. This gives us set of *10* points – candidates for circle circumscribed about the iris. Result of above procedure is presented in Fig. 7.

Next step is to verify which points belongs to iris circle. To achieve that aim following algorithm was constructed:

Fig. 7. Result of finding point on edge of the iris

IN: Set of *10* points-candidates for edge of the iris.

OUT: Center and radius of a circle circumscribed about the iris.
1. Construct circles for points' triplets
2. Compare each circle with every other. If distance of centers and radius difference of those circles is lower than given value the *rank* of circle is incremented
3. Circle with maximum *rank* is accepted as best-fitting the iris.

6 Results

As shown on figures below, the procedure of determining circles circumscribed about irises gives satisfactory results, even in case of blurred images (Fig. 9).

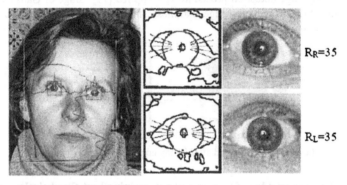

Fig. 8. Sample result of iris localization procedure

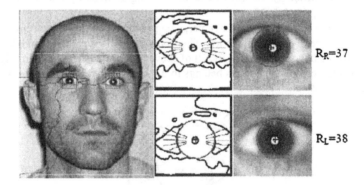

Fig. 9. Sample result of iris localization procedure - blurred image

7 Conclusions and Future Works

In this paper the procedure of iris detection was presented. Main aim was to find radius and center of circles circumscribed about both irises. Presented method of iris detection in image with simple background gives satisfactory results in aim of future processing in face recognition system. Major defect of this method is constant value of threshold in procedure of *I2* thresholding. The method will be improved by realization of automated threshold selection. This will be achieved by analyzing histogram of the *I2* color space image.

For purpose of further realization of the face recognition system the eyes feature extraction method will be developed.

References

1. L. Fan and K.K. Sung. Model-based varying pose face detection and facial feature registration in colour images. In *PRL*, 24, pages 237-249, January 2003.
2. T.J. Darrell, G.G. Gordon, J. Woodfill, and M. Harville. A virtual mirror interface using real-time robust face tracking. In *AFGR98*, pages 616–621, 1998.
3. K.M. Lam and H. Yan. An analytic to holistic approach for face recognition based on a single frontal view. *PAMI*, 20(7):673–686, July 1998.
4. C.J. Kuo, R.S. Huang, and T.G. Lin. 3-d facial model estimation from single front-view facial image. *CirSysVideo*, 12(3):183–192, March 2002.
5. P. Eisert, T. Wiegand, and B. Girod. Model-aided coding: A new approach to incorporate facial animation into motion-compensated video coding. *CirSysVideo*, 10(3):344–358, April 2000.
6. D.E. Pearson. Developments in model-based video coding. *PIEEE*, 83(6):892–906, June 1995.
7. L. Kompanets, M. Kubanek, and Rydzek Sz. Czestochowas precise model of a face based on the facial asymmetry, ophthalmogeometry, and brain asymmetry phenomena: the idea and algorithm sketch. In *ACS 03*, 2003.
8. L. Kompanets, M. Kubanek, and Rydzek Sz. Czetochowa-faces and biometrics of asymmetrical face. In *ICAISC 2004*, pages 742–747, 2004.
9. G. Kukharev and Kuzminski A. Techniki biometryczne czesc I - metody rozpoznawania twarzy. Politechnika Szczecinska, Wydzial Informatyki, 2003.
10. G.R. Arce and M.P. McLoughlin. Theoretical analysis of the max/median filter. *T-ASSP*, 35:60–69, 1987.
11. L. Ding and A. Goshtasby. On the canny edge detector. *PR*, 34(3):721–725, March 2001.
12. M. Turk and A.P. Pentland. Eigenfaces for recognition. *CogNeuro*, 3(1):71–96, 1991.
13. M. Turk and A.P. Pentland. Face recognition using eigenfaces. In *CVPR91*, pages 586–591, 1991.
14. B. Moghaddam and A.P. Pentland. Probabilistic visual learning for object representation. *PAMI*, 19(7):696–710, July 1997.
15. W. Skarbek and A. Koschan. Colour image segmentation — a survey. Technical report, Institute for Technical Informatics, Technical University of Berlin, October 1994.

16. Y. Suzuki and S. Saito, H. Ozawa. Extraction of the human face from the natural background using gas. In *IEEE TENCON, Digital Signal Processing Applications*, pages 221–226, 1996.
17. Y. Yokoo and M. Hagiwara. Human faces detection method using genetic algorithm. In *International Conference on Evolutionary Computation*, pages 113–118, 1996.
18. J. Miao, B. Yin, K. Wang, L. Shen, and X. Chen. A hierarchical multiscale and multiangle system for human face detection in a complex background using gravitycenter template. *PR*, 32(7):1237–1248, July 1999.
19. Q. Gu and S.Z. Li. Combining feature optimization into neural network based face detection. In *ICPR00*, pages Vol II: 814–817, 2000.
20. L. Wang and J. Bai. Threshold selection by clustering gray levels of boundary. *Pattern Recogn. Lett.*, 24(12):1983–1999, 2003.
21. N. Bonnet, J. Cutrona, and M. Herbin. A 'no-threshold' histogram-based image segmentation method. *Pattern Recognition*, 35(10):2319–2322, 2002.
22. C.L. Novak and S. Shafer. Method for estimating scene parameters from color histograms. *Journal of the Optical Society of America*, 11(11):3020 – 3036, June 1994.

Experimental Algorithm for Characteristic Points Evaluation in Static Images of Signatures

Khalid Saeed[1], Marcin Adamski[2]

Faculty of Computer Science, Bialystok Technical University
Wiejska 45A, 15-351 Bialystok, Poland*
<aida>[1],<adams>[2] @ii.pb.bialystok.pl
http://aragorn.pb.bialystok.pl/~zspinfo/

Abstract. The paper presents experimental method for the extraction of hand-written signature features with the aim of incorporating them in the offline signature recognition system. The algorithm uses view-based approach and searches for the extreme values with the threshold value being applied. This investigation is a continuation of previous work extended with experiments on classification of resulted feature vectors. The classification of feature vectors is conducted by means of Dynamic Time Warping (DTW) algorithm. Experiments were carried out with the standard DTW algorithm with window and slope constraints.

1 Introduction

The study reported in this paper is a continuation and extension of previous work [1], where an experimental method for extraction of handwritten signature features was presented. The proposed method is examined in order to evaluate its usefulness as a part of the signature recognition system.

There are two main approaches for the signature recognition: offline and online. The offline methods analyze the static picture of the signature, whilst the online algorithms consider the dynamics of the writing process [2], [3], [4], [5] as well. The algorithms that consider only the static image are less resistant to forgeries but in many cases the static image of the signature is the only available form of information. This paper focuses on the analysis of static features in a handwritten signature.

The image of the signature is a special type of object when looked at as the subject of recognition process. One of the problems which is likely to arise is that the signatures of a particular person are not exactly the same. Of course, during the application of the recognition system we may require that the signatures should be made carefully but there are always some differences we must deal with. This requires that the identification system should be flexible and allow certain variations

---

* This work is supported by the Rector of Bialystok University of Technology (grant number W/WI/3/04).

within the set of the signatures put down by one person. The type of error we want to reduce at this moment is the rejection of the genuine signatures.

On the other hand, in order to reduce misclassification and improve forgery resistance we must require that certain important features should be exactly recurrent and we must strictly demand their presence. The errors we are trying to minimize in this case are: acceptance of a fake signature and classifying one person's signature as belonging to another one.

Incorporating those two aspects – acceptance of the variance and the requirement for exactness of certain features in one system is a very difficult task and still there is no perfect solution. The techniques developed so far give good results but they still have a relatively significant error.

The alternative approach is to split those two aspects into separate tasks and then combine the results of both into one hybrid system. When human being attempts to handle signature recognition task it seems that the overall appearance or the general shape is the thing of highest importance. Only then, the particular features are examined in greater detail in order to make the correct judgment.

Following the above considerations, this paper focuses on the general shape of the signatures in order to prepare data for the first recognition step. Information acquired at this stage should enable differentiation between the signatures given by different people and be general enough to reduce influence of the variations among different occurrences of the same signature. This stage should be supplemented by more precise local investigations to form the complete recognition system

2 Signature Acquisition

The images of signatures (Fig. 1) stored as Portable Network Graphics (*.png) files are used as a source of data for further processing. This particular format of storing images provides lossless compression, which is important because it doesn't add artifacts and provides relatively small footprint.

The images can be obtained from documents by means of scanning devices. This approach can be applied to gather data from a variety of available sources in the form of signed forms because the signing on a paper form is still the most common authentication procedure.

Fig. 1. Examples of images of signatures given by different people

3 Selection of characteristic points

In [1] an experimental method to select signature characteristic points was presented.
Its main purpose was to reduce the dimensionality of data, whilst preserving the features necessary for distinguishing between different classes of signatures. The other
goal was to improve the separation of the classes. By the class of a signature we mean
the group of signatures signed by a particular person.
The first stage of the method uses the view-based approach [1], [6], [7], [8].
The algorithm chooses only those points with minimal and maximal values of y
coordinate. Points with minimal values form what is called the upper view, whilst
points with minimal values form the down view. The process is illustrated
in Fig. 2.

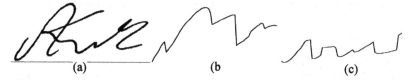

(a)   (b   (c)

Fig. 1. Signature (a) with its upper (b) and down (c) views

As a result the two vectors for each of the signatures are obtained (Eq. 1). The normalization (Eq. 2) is applied to get values ranging in $< 0,1 >$.

$$Y = \left\langle y_1, y_2, ..., y_{n-1}, y_n \right\rangle \tag{1}$$

$$y_i^{'} = \frac{y_i - y_{min}}{y_{max} - y_{min}} \tag{2}$$

During the next step extreme values from coordinates of vector Y are selected. This
operation reduces the influence of the variance among signatures of
a particular person. Equations 3 and 4 represent the conditions which were tested to
find the maximum and the minimum values accordingly.   In addition,
the threshold T value is applied in order to eliminate disturbances created by
roughness of the ink trace and minor artifacts which mostly are conducive to inaccuracy of the signing individual. If the difference between most recently acquired
extreme and the currently examined one does not exceed the threshold value (Eq. 5) it
is discarded from the final feature vector (Eq. 6).

$$y_i < y_{i+1}, \quad y_{i+k} > y_{i+k+1}, \quad y_{i+1} = y_{i+2} = ... = y_{i+k} \tag{3}$$

$$y_i > y_{i+1}, \quad y_{i+k} < y_{i+k+1}, \quad y_{i+1} = y_{i+2} = ... = y_{i+k} \tag{4}$$

$$\left| y_j^e - y^e \right| > T \tag{5}$$

$$Y^e = \left\langle y_1^e, y_2^e, ..., y_k^e, y_m^e \right\rangle \tag{6}$$

In this study, in order to compare the proposed method with other approaches, two additional ways for selection of characteristic points are introduced.

The first is the classic view-based approach described in detail in works [6], [7]. This method is also used here as the first stage of the examined experimental algorithm as described earlier in this section. Additionally, to proceed further with the reduction of data we select N equally spaced points from the resulted outline where the value of N depends on the height of the particular view.

The second approach is based on contour tracing technique [8]. The algorithm follows the outer boundary of each separate object comprising the signature image and collects y coordinates of its consecutive points. For each contour the upper part is separated from the down. Then all the upper parts and the down parts are concatenated separately (Fig. 3). In order to reduce the number of points a simple sampling is used by selecting every M-th value from the acquired sequences to form feature vectors, where M denotes the step length in the sampling process.

(a)   (b   (c)

Fig. 1. Signature (b) with its upper (a) and down (c) views

4 Classification

In [1] the results, achieved from the new method, were illustrated graphically. Feature vectors representing each of the signatures were shown on graphs (Fig. 4, 5, 6, 7 in the next section), and evaluated visually. Although they clearly showed that the new method gave good results, a new research was carried out to see how well the new method describes the signatures for the task of classification.

In the process of classification we used a measure based on Dynamic Time Warping (DTW) algorithm. This method was chosen due to its flexibility to compensate for the variations occur in handwritten signatures. Experiments showed that during signing process individuals often stretch and shrink local parts of the signature. Additionally, there is an increasing variance towards the end of the signature denoting decreasing accuracy of writing. DTW algorithm with its ability to eliminate the influence of such nonlinear fluctuations seems to be an appropriate tool for this kind of classification task [4], [8], [9], [10].

DTW algorithm defines a measure between two sequences $x_1, x_2, ..., x_{k-1}, x_k$ and

$y_1, y_2, ..., y_{l-1}, y_l$ as a recursive function (7):

$$D(i, j) + \min \left\{ \begin{array}{c} D(i, j-1) \\ D(i-1, j) \\ D(i-1, j-1) \end{array} \right\} + d(x_i, y_j) \qquad (7)$$

The distance measure $d(a_i, b_j)$ can be chosen in various ways depending on the application. In our case the square of Euclidean distance was used. The calculations are carried out using dynamic programming. The key part of this algorithm is the computation of cumulative distance $g(i, j)$ as the sum of distance $d(i, j)$ and one of the cumulative distances found in earlier iterations (Eq. 8):

$$g(i, j) = d(a_i, b_j) + \min\{g(i-1, j), g(i, j-1), g(i-1, j-1)\} \qquad (8)$$

In this study two modifications of the basic DTW algorithm were used. The first used a window which constrained possible paths in the matrix of $g(i, j)$ [9]. The second used a slope constraint allowing warping path to follow only particular directions [9]. The applied slop constraint can be expressed by the following equation (Eq. 9):

$$g(i, j) = \min \left\{ \begin{array}{c} g(i-1, j-2) + 2 * d(i, j-1) + d(i, j) \\ g(i-1, j-1) + 2 * d(i, j) \\ g(i-2, j-1) + 2 * d(i-1, j) + d(i, j) \end{array} \right\} \qquad (9)$$

5 Results

The objective of this investigation was to evaluate effectiveness of the proposed method for characteristic points selection from handwritten signatures. The database used in this experiment consisted of 60 signatures taken from 20 individuals, each repeated three times. For each person, each of the three repetitions was used as a reference pattern and the remaining two were utilized as subjects of the classification process. Therefore $20 \times 3 \times 2 = 120$ tests were conducted in each variant of the experiment. To simplify the comparison, only the upper views or contours were considered during those tests.

The most important parameter in the proposed method is the threshold value T. It allows for excluding the extremes which are artifacts and don't repeat between different occurrences of the same signature. Table 1 contains results of the classification process in which the feature vectors where built using various threshold values. Two modifications of Dynamic Time Warping algorithm were used:

- DTW – Dynamic Time Warping algorithm with window constraint,
- DTWS – Dynamic Time Warping algorithm with window and slope constraints.

Table 1. Percentage of properly classified signatures using extremes with threshold

T	DTW	DTWS
0	65,83%	66,67%
0,01	69,17%	74,17%
0,02	70,83%	76,67%
0,03	70,83%	75,00%
0,04	70,00%	70,83%
0,05	70,00%	70,00%
0,1	68,33%	67,50%

Table 1 shows percentage of properly classified signatures depending on the threshold value. The threshold value of zero means acceptance of all extremes into the feature vector. As can be seen the threshold value affects the effectiveness of classification process. The experiment carried out without applying threshold ($T = 0$) gave the worst results, whilst the best classification rate was achieved with $T = 0.02$.

The next experiment compares the experimental method with view-based and contour tracing techniques. Table 2 summaries the classification rate achieved by using each of the methods.

Table 2. Comparison of the three methods for selection of characteristic points

	DTW	DTWS
view based	40,83%	58,33%
extremes with threshold	70,83%	76,67%
contour tracing	68,33%	80,83%

The sampling steps N for the view based algorithm and M for the contour tracing where selected in such a way that the average lengths of the resulted feature vectors were nearly the same as in the algorithm with extremes and threshold. The average vector size was 17 elements, with minimum 7 and maximum 36 depending on the size of the signature. The threshold value was chosen from previous experiment ($T = 0.02$). The results confirm that selection of extremes from views is more effi-cient than using the views themselves. This fact was illustrated in previous work [1] by showing views and extreme values of the signatures on graphs (Fig. 4, 5, 6, 7).

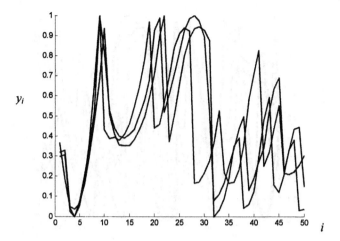

Fig. 4. The upper views of selected signature

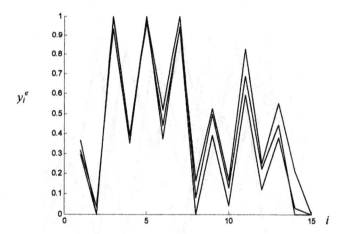

Fig. 5. Extreme values of the upper views of selected signature

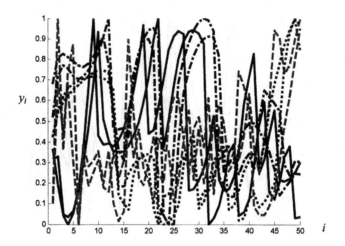

Fig. 6. The upper views of the signatures

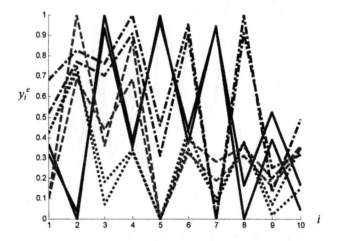

Fig. 7. Extreme values of the upper views

Fig. 4 represents the upper views of one of the signatures. Fig. 5 shows the results achieved after finding extreme values with the threshold for normalized data. As can be seen, the lines representing each version of the signature have similar characteristics, though, in the first graph the variance is significantly higher

Figs 6 and 7 present the results obtained for 4 signatures, each written twice. In Fig. 6 the number of extremes is constrained to the 10 first values.

The graphs of Figs 6 and 7 show that after applying the described algorithm to the original data, the separation of characteristics for each of the signatures is improved and the variance between different versions of the same signature is minimized. The results show that the contour tracing gave the best classification rate – 80%. It is also important to mention that the aim of this experiment was not to achieve the highest classification rate but to verify effectiveness and compare the proposed algorithm with other approaches. The classification rate could be easily improved by considering other information like down views or contours, internal contours and using more than one signature in each class as a reference pattern.

6 Conclusions and Future Work

The results of the presented method seem to be promising and hence encouraging to further work to incorporate them in the complete offline signature recognition system. The classification of the feature vectors using DTW algorithm confirmed effectiveness of the developed algorithm. It is also obvious that such a system should be supplemented by additional data from local features like placement and size of internal loops, number of segments, their positions and so on. The future research will be focused on incorporating all those features in one hybrid solution. As a part of authors' future work, it is planned to extend contour tracing technique by calculation of extremes with threshold value.

References

1. K. Saeed, M. Adamski, *"Extraction of Global Features for Offline Signature Recognition,"* Image Analysis, Computer Graphics, Security Systems and Artificial Intelligence Applications, WSFiZ Press, Bialystok 2005, pp. 429-436.
2. L. Lee, T. Berger, and E. Aviczer, *"Reliable on-line Human Signature Verifiaction Systems"*, IEEE Transactions on Pattern Analysis and Machine Intelligence, vol. 18, no. 6, June 1996, pp. 643-647.
3. K. Saeed, *"Efficient Method for On-Line Signature Verification"* Proceedings of the International Conference on Computer Vision and Graphics - ICCVG'02, vol. 2, Zakopane, 25-29 September 2002, pp. 635-640.
4. R. Martens; L. Claesen, *"On-line signature verification by dynamic time-warping"*, Proceedings of the 13th International Conference on Pattern Recognition, vol. 3, Vienna , Austria, August 1996, pp. 38-42.
5. G. Rigoll, A. Kosmala, *"A systematic comparison between on-line and off-line methods for signature verification with hidden Markov models"*, Proceedings of the 14th International Conference on Pattern Recognition, vol. 2, Brisbane, Australia, August 1998, pp. 1755-1757.
6. K. Saeed, M. Tabędzki, M. Adamski, *„A New Approach for Object-Feature Extract and Recognition"*, 9th International Conference on Advanced Computer Systems – ACS'02, Miedzyzdroje, 23-25 October 2002, pp. 389-397.

7. K. Saeed, M. Tabędzki, *"A New Hybrid System for Recognition of Handwritten-Script"*, International Scientific Journal of Computing, Institute of Computer Information Technologies, vol. 3, issue 1, Ternopil, Ukraine 2004, pp. 50-57.
8. C. Parisse, *"Global Word Shape Processing in Off-Line Recognition of Handwritting"*, IEEE Transactions on Pattern Analysis and Machine Intelligence, vol. 18, no. 5, April 1996, pp. 460-464.
9. H. Sakoe, S. Chiba: „Dynamic Programming Algorithm Optimization for Spoken Word Recognition", IEEE Transactions on Acoustics, Speech, and Signal Processing, vol. ASSP-26, no. 1, luty 1978, pp. 43-49.
10. K. Saeed, M. Adamski, "Klasyfikacja podpisu offline z wykorzystaniem metody DTW," XIV Krajowa Konferencja Naukowa - KBIB'05, vol I - Systemy Informatyczne i Telemedyczne, Czestochowa, pp. 455-460.

PART II

COMPUTER SECURITY SYSTEMS

Parallelization of Standard Modes of Operation for Symmetric Key Block Ciphers

Wlodzimierz Bielecki, Dariusz Burak

Faculty of Computer Science & Information Systems, Technical University of Szczecin, 49,
Żołnierska St., 71210 Szczecin, Poland
{wbielecki, dburak}@wi.ps.pl

Abstract. In this paper we present the parallelization process of standard modes of operation for symmetric key block ciphers: ECB, CBC, CFB, OFB and CTR along with the description of exploited parallelization tools. The data dependencies analysis of loops and loop transformations were applied in order to parallelize sequential algorithms. The OpenMP standard was chosen for representing parallelism of the standard modes of operation for block ciphers. The speed-up measurements for parallel programs are presented.

1 Introduction

In addition to security level, the cipher speed is one of the most important features of cryptographic algorithms. It is well known that by the same security level even a little difference of speed may cause the choice of the faster cipher. Therefore, it is so important and useful to enable the use of Shared Memory Parallel Computers for cryptographic algorithms processing. We propose a software approach based on the transformations of a source code representing a sequential algorithm. The creation of parallel algorithms is important not only for multiprocessors but also is connected with the current world tendency towards the hardware implementation of cryptographic algorithms, because we need parallel algorithms in this case. The major purpose of this paper is to present a parallelization process of the standard modes of operation for the symmetric key block ciphers along with the description of exploited parallelization tools.

2 Standard modes of operation for symmetric key block ciphers

There are the following standard modes of operation for the symmetric key block ciphers: ECB, CBC, CFB, OFB and CTR [1], [2].

2.1 Electronic Codebook (ECB) mode

The ECB mode is the simplest, most popular, and the least secure mode of operation for the block ciphers [1], [2].

It is defined as follows:

ECB Encryption: $c_j = E_K(x_j)$ for j=1 ...n.

ECB Decryption: $x_j = E_K^{-1}(c_j)$ for j=1 ...n.

In this mode, the message is divided into blocks of an equal size and each block is encrypted / decrypted separately and independently of each other. Regarding the above features, the ECB mode is fully parallelizable, because all blocks are independent.

2.2 Cipher Block Chaining (CBC) mode

The Cipher Block Chaining (CBC) mode is represented as follows [1], [2]:

CBC Encryption: $c_0 = IV$; $c_j = E_K(c_{j-1} \oplus x_j)$ for j=1 ... n.

CBC Decryption: $c_0 = IV$; $x_j = c_{j-1} \oplus E_K^{-1}(c_j)$ for j=1 ... n.

In the CBC encryption, the input block to each forward cipher operation (except the first one, which depends on an initialization vector (IV)) depends on the result of the previous forward cipher operation, therefore the forward cipher operations cannot be performed in parallel. In the CBC decryption, the ciphertext blocks are available without any dependencies, so multiple inverse cipher operations can be parallelized.

2.3 Cipher Feedback (CFB) mode

The Cipher Feedback (CFB) mode is defined as follows [1], [2]:

CFB Encryption: $c_0 = IV$; $c_j = x_j \oplus E_K(c_{j-1})$ for j=1 ... n.

CFB Decryption: $c_0 = IV$; $x_j = c_j \oplus E_K(c_{j-1})$ for j=1 ... n.

Similarly to the CBC mode, in the CFB encryption, the input block to each forward cipher function (except the first one) depends on the result of the previous forward cipher function and therefore multiple forward cipher operations cannot be performed in parallel. In the CFB decryption, the required forward cipher operations can be parallelized, because input blocks are available without any dependencies.

2.4 Output Feedback (OFB) mode

The formula of the Output Feedback (OFB) mode is the following [1], [2]:

OFB Encryption: $op_0 = IV$; $op_j = E_K(op_{j-1})$; $c_j = x_j \oplus op_j$ for j=1 ... n.

OFB Decryption: $op_0 = IV$; $op_j = E_K(op_{j-1})$; $x_j = c_j \oplus op_j$ for j=1 ... n.

In both the OFB encryption and OFB decryption, each forward cipher function (except the first one) depends on the result that yields the previous forward cipher function, therefore required forward cipher functions cannot be performed in parallel.

2.5 Counter (CTR) mode

The Counter (CTR) mode is defined as follows [1], [2]:

CTR Encryption: $c_j = E_K(L_j) \oplus x_j$ for j=1 ... n.

CTR Decryption: $x_j = E_K(L_j) \oplus c_j$ for j=1 ... n.

In both the CTR encryption and the CTR decryption, each forward cipher function depends on the following counter block, therefore the forward cipher function can be parallelized.

3 OpenMP API and Data Dependencies

In order to parallelize loops contained in cipher algorithms and to present parallel algorithms we have performed data dependencies analysis and have applied the OpenMP API.

3.1 OpenMP API

The OpenMP Application Program Interface (API) supports multi-platform shared memory parallel programming in C/C++ and Fortran on all architectures including Unix and Windows NT platforms. OpenMP is a collection of compiler directives, library routines and environment variables that can be used to specify shared memory parallelism. OpenMP directives extend a sequential programming language with Single Program Multiple Data (SPMD) constructs, work-sharing constructs and synchronization constructs and enable us to operate on private data. To build a correct parallel code, it is necessary to eliminate all blocking constructs in the source code [3], [4].

3.2 Data Dependencies

There are the following types of data dependencies blocking parallelism in "for" loops [5], [6]:

- Data Flow Dependence indicates that a write-before-read ordering must be satisfied for parallel computing.
- Antidependence indicates that a read-before-write ordering should not be violated for parallel computing.
- Output Dependence indicates a write-before-write ordering for parallel processing.

4   Parallelization process of the standard modes of operation for block ciphers

We applied the following parallelization strategy:
a) Parallelization of the loops included in functions that are responsible for data block encryption and decryption in the ECB mode of operation.
b) Separation of the above functions from the loops that are responsible for data block encryption and decryption in the CBC, CFB, OFB and CTR modes of operation (when possible).
c) Data dependence analysis of the most time-consuming loops included in the ECB, CBC, CFB, OFB and CTR modes of operation.
d) Parallelization of the parallelizable loops included in the ECB, CBC, CFB, OFB and CTR modes of operation.

4.1   The ECB mode

We adopted, presented in [1], the source codes of popular block ciphers: DES, Triple DES and IDEA in the ECB mode of operation. The parallelization process of the block ciphers in the ECB mode relies on parallelization of the most time-consuming loops. The parallelization degree of these loops has the fundamental meaning for the parallelization degree of the whole algorithm. For example, in the case of the DES algorithm such the neuralgic loops are situated in the des_enc() and the des_dec() functions, for the IDEA algorithm- the idea_enc() and the idea_dec(). In general, we will call such functions as the ecb_encryption() and the ecb_decryption(), respectively, for the encryption and decryption processes.

The papers [7], [8] show that the parallelization of block ciphers in the ECB mode is possible and effective..

4.2   The CTR mode

In the case of the CTR mode we have to examine separately the encryption and decryption processes.

Encryption. The following loop is responsible for 64-bit data blocks in the CTR mode encryption:

```
for(int i=0;i<total;i+=8) {
        ecb_encryption(&c,counter+i,1);
        for(int j=0;j<8;j++)
            enc_ctr[i+j] = data[i+j] ^ counter[i+j];
        } .
```

According to the presented parallelization strategy, this loop may be rewritten in the following form:

```
ecb_encryption(&c,counter,total/8);
```

```
for(int i=0;i<total;i++)
    enc_ctr[i] = data[i] ^ counter[i];
```

The ecb_encryption() function is parallelizable as it was presented in [7], [8]. Considering the fact that there is no data dependencies in the succeeding loop, the parallel form of this loop in accordance with the OpenMP standard is the following:

```
#pragma omp parallel
#pragma omp   for
for(int i<total;i++)
    enc_ctr[i] = data[i] ^ counter[i];
```

Decryption. The following loop code is responsible for 64-bit data blocks in the CTR mode decryption:

```
for(int i=0;i<total;i+=8) {
    ecb_encryption(&c,counter+i,1);
    for(int j=0;j<8;j++)
        dec_ctr[i+j] = enc_ctr[i+j] ^ counter[i+j];
    } .
```

This loop may be rewritten in the following form:

```
ecb_encryption(&c,counter,total/8);
for(int i=0;i<total;i++)
    dec_ctr[i] = enc_ctr[i] ^ counter[i];
```

The ecb_encryption() function is parallelizable.
Regarding the fact that there are no data dependencies in the succeeding loop, the parallel form of this loop is the following:

```
#pragma omp parallel
#pragma omp   for
for(int i<total;i++)
    dec_ctr[i] = enc_ctr[i] ^ counter[i];
```

4.3 The CBC mode

In the case of the CBC mode, we have to analyze separately the encryption and decrypytion processes.

Encryption. The following source code is responsible for 64-bit data blocks in the CBC mode encryption:

```
for(int i=0; i<8; i++)
    data_iv[i] = data[i] ^ iv[i];
ecb_encryption(&c data_iv,1);
for(i=0; i<8; i++)
    data_iv_enc[i] = data_iv[i];
for(i=8; i<total; i+=8) {
    for(int j=0; j<8; j++)
```

```
            data_iv[i+j] = data[i+j] ^ data_iv_enc[i+j-8];
        ecb_encryption(&c,data_iv+i,1);
        for(int k=0; k<8; k++)
            data_iv_enc[i+k] = data_iv[i+k];
    } .
```

Taking into account the fact, that the ecb_encryption() function is situated between nested loops and there are data flow dependencies, it is impossible to find equivalent code containing the ecb_encryption() function placed out of the main loop. However, the first loop is parallelizable, because there are no data dependencies.
The parallel loop is as follows:

```
#pragma omp parallel
#pragma omp  for
for(int i=0; i<8; i++)
    data_iv[i] = data[i] ^ iv[i];
```

Decryption. The following source code is responsible for 64-bit data blocks in the CBC mode decryption:

```
ecb_decryption(&c data_iv,1);
for(int i=0; i<8; i++)
    data_iv_dec[i] = data_iv[i] ^ iv[i];
for(i=8; i<total; i+=8) {
    ecb_decryption(&c,data_iv+i,1);
    for (int j=0; j<8; j++)
        data_iv_dec[i+j]=data_iv[i+j]^data_iv_enc[i+j-8];
} .
```

This loop may be rewritten in the following form:

```
ecb_decryption(&c,data_iv,total/8);
for(i=0; i<8; i++)
    data_iv_dec[i] = data_iv1[i] ^ iv[i];
for(i=8; i<total; i++)
    data_iv_dec [i]=data_iv[i]^data_iv_enc[i-8];
```

The ecb_decryption() function is parallelizable as it was presented in [7], [8].
Considering the fact that there are no data dependencies in the next loops, the parallel form of these loops is the following:

```
#pragma omp parallel
#pragma omp for
for(i=0; i<8; i++)
    data_iv_dec[i] = data_iv1[i] ^ iv[i];
#pragma omp parallel
#pragma omp for
for(i=8; i<total; i++)
    data_iv_dec [i] = data_iv[i] ^ data_iv_enc[i-8];
```

4.4 The CFB mode

In the case of the CFB mode we have to examine separately the encryption and decryption processes.

Encryption. The following source code is responsible for 64-bit data blocks in the CFB mode encryption:

```
for(int i=0; i<8; i++)
    data_xored[i] = iv[i];
ecb_encryption(&c, data_xored,1);
for(i=8; i<total; i+=8) {
    for(int j=0; j<8; j++)
        data_xored[i+j]=data[i+j-8]^data_xored[i+j-8];
    for(int k=0; k<8; k++)
        data_enc[i+k-8] = data_xored[i+k];
    ecb_encryption(&c, data_xored+i,1);
    } .
```

The ecb_encryption() is situated after nested loops and there are data flow dependencies, thus it is impossible to find equivalent code containing the ecb_encryption() function placed out of the main loop. However, the first loop is parallelizable, because there are no data dependencies:

```
#pragma omp parallel
#pragma omp  for
for(int i=0; i<8; i++)
    data_xored[i] = iv[i];
```

Decryption. The following source code is responsible for 64-bit data blocks in the CFB mode decryption:

```
for(int i=0; i<8; i++)
    data_xored[i] = iv[i];
ecb_encryption(&c, data_xored,1);
for(i=8; i<total; i+=8) {
    for(int j=0; j<8; j++)
        data_xored[i+j]=data[i+j-8]^data_xored[i+j-8];
    for(int k=0; k<8; k++)
        data_enc[i+k-8] = data_xored[i+k];
    ecb_encryption(&c, data_xored+i,1);
    } .
```

This loop may be rewritten as follows:

```
for(int i=0; i<8; i++)
    data_xored[i] = iv[i];
ecb_encryption(&c, data_xored, total/8);
for(i=0; i<total; i++)
    data_dec[i] = data_xored[i] ^ data_enc[i];
```

The ecb_encryption() function is parallelizable.

There are no data dependencies in the remaining loops, thus the parallel form is as follows:

```
#pragma omp parallel
#pragma omp  for
for(int i=0; i<8; i++)
    data_xored[i] = iv[i];

#pragma omp parallel
#pragma omp  for
for(i=0; i<total; i++)
    data_dec[i] = data_xored[i] ^ data_enc[i];
```

4.5 The OFB mode

In the case of the OFB mode we analyse separately the encryption and decryption processes.

Encryption. The following source code is responsible for 64-bit data blocks in the OFB mode encryption:

```
for(int i=0; i<8; i++)
    data_xored[i] = iv[i];
for(i=0; i<total; i+=8) {
    ecb_encryption(&c,data_xored,1);
    for(int j=0; j<8; j++)
        data_enc[i+j] = data[i+j] ^ data_xored[j];
} .
```

In view of the fact, that the ecb_encryption() is situated before nested loops and there are data flow dependencies, it is impossible to find equivalent code containing the ecb_encryption() function placed out of the main loop. However, the first loop is parallelizable, because there are no data dependencies:

```
#pragma omp parallel
#pragma omp  for
for(i=0; i<8; i++)
    data_xored[i] = iv[i];
```

Decryption. The following source code is responsible for 64-bit data blocks in the OFB mode decryption:

```
for(i=0; i<8; i++)
    data_xored[i] = iv[i];
for(i=0; i<total; i+=8) {
    ecb_encryption(&c,data_xored,1);
    for(j=0; j<8; j++)
        data_dec[i+j]= data_enc[i+j] ^ data_xored[j];
}
```

The ecb_encryption() is situated before nested loops and there are data flow dependencies, thus it is impossible to find equivalent code containing the ecb_encryption() function placed out of the main loop. However, the first loop is parallelizable.

5 Speed-up measurements

In order to study the efficiency of the parallelization proposed, the Omni OpenMP compiler has been used to run sequential and parallel algorithms. The results received for a 5 megabytes input file using a PC computer with two processors Xeon, has shown in Table 1.

Table 3. Speed-ups of the standard modes of operation for various block ciphers

Block Cipher	Mode of operation	ECB	CTR	CBC	CFB	OFB
DES	Encryption	1.65	1.65	1.00	1.00	1.00
	Decryption	1.65	1.65	1.65	1.65	1.00
	Total	1.60	1.60	1.25	1.25	1.00
Triple DES	Encryption	1.70	1.65	1.00	1.00	1.00
	Decryption	1.70	1.70	1.70	1.70	1.00
	Total	1.60	1.60	1.30	1.30	1.00
IDEA	Encryption	1.65	1.65	1.00	1.00	1.00
	Decryption	1.70	1.65	1.65	1.65	1.00
	Total	1.60	1.60	1.30	1.30	1.00

The total running time of each algorithm consists of the following operations:

− receiving data from an input file,
− data encryption,
− data decryption,
− writing data to an output file (both encrypted text and decrypted text).
The total speed up of the parallel algorithms depends heavily on the four factors:

− the degree of the ecb_encrypt() and ecb_decrypt() functions parallelization,
− the method of reading data from an input file,
− the method of writing data to an output file,
− the existence of data flow dependencies in the most consuming-time loops.
The block method of reading data from an input file and writing data to an output file was used. The following C functions and block sizes were applied:

− the fread() function and 10-bytes blocks for reading data,
− the fwrite() function and 512-bytes blocks for writing data.
The results confirm that algorithms based on the ECB and the CTR modes of operation have satisfactory speed-ups. Algorithms based on the CBC and the CFB modes of operation have satisfactory speed-ups for the decryption process.

6 Conclusions

In this paper, we described the parallelization process of the standard modes of operation for block ciphers. Each algorithm can be divided into parallelizable and unparallelizable parts. We have shown, that the most profitable modes for parallelization process are the ECB and CTR ones, because speed-ups are satisfactory in those cases (see Table 1). The decryption processes of the CBC and the CFB modes also have been parallelized with a relatively high value of speed-up. Unfortunately, the CBC and the CFB data encryption and the OFB mode processes are in the high range unparalleizable considering the existence of irremovable data flow dependencies in the most consuming-time functions. The experiments carried out on a two processor computer have shown that the application of parallel algorithms for multiprocessor computers can considerably boost the time of the ECB and CTR modes processing and the CBC and CFB data decryption. Parallel algorithms may be also helpful for hardware implementations of these algorithms. The hardware synthesis of algorithms will depend on the appropriate adjustment of the data transmission capacity and the computational power of applied hardware.

References

1. Schneier, B.: Applied Cryptography: Protocols, Algorithms, and Source Code in C, John Wiley & Sons, 2 edition (1995)
2. Dworkin, M.: Recommendation for Block Cipher Modes of Operation. Methods and Techniques., NIST Special Publication, 2001 Edition
3. OpenMP C and C++ Application Program Interface. Ver.2.0. (2002)
4. http://www.openmp.org
5. Allen, R., Kennedy, K.: Optimizing compilers for modern architectures: A Dependence-based Approach, Morgan Kaufmann Publishers, Inc. (2001)
6. Bielecki, W.: Essentials of Parallel and Distributed Computing, Informa (2002)
7. Beletskyy, V., Burak, D.: Parallelization of the IDEA Algorithm, Lecture Notes in Computer Science, Computational Science - ICCS 2004: 4th International Conference, Kraków, Poland, Proceedings, Part I, pp.635-638, Springer-Verlag Heidelberg (2004)
8. Beletskyy, V., Burak, D.: Parallelization of the Data Encryption Standard (DES) Algorithm, Enhanced Methods in Computer Security, Biometric and Artificial Intelligence Systems, pp.23-33, Kluwer Academic Publishers (2005)

On Differential and Linear Approximation
of S-box Functions

Krzysztof Chmiel

Poznań University of Technology,
pl. Skłodowskiej-Curie 5,
60-965 Poznań, Poland
Chmiel@sk-kari.put.poznan.pl

Abstract. In the paper the differential and the linear approximations of two classes of S-box functions are considered. The classes are the permutations and arbitrary functions with n binary inputs and m binary outputs, where $1 \leq n=m \leq 10$. For randomly chosen functions from each of the classes, the distribution of the best nonzero approximations is investigated. The based on the definitions of differential and linear approximation algorithms to compute a single element of the approximation tables, are of exponential complexity. The presented in the paper fast algorithms compute the best nonzero approximations in at worst linear time for a single element, without memory needed for storage of the whole table.

1 Introduction

Differential and linear cryptanalysis belong to main topics in cryptology since they were introduced and successfully applied to the Data Encryption Standard. Unlike the differential cryptanalysis, which is essentially a chosen-plaintext attack [1], [6], the linear cryptanalysis is essentially a known-plaintext attack and moreover is applicable to an only-ciphertext attack under some circumstances [2], [3], [4], [5], [6], [7].

The basic idea of differential cryptanalysis is to analyze the effect of particular differences in plaintext pairs on the differences of the resultant ciphertext pairs. The differences are usually calculated as a result of XOR operation. Input XOR of a cipher algorithm causes a specified output XOR with some probability. The appropriate, approximate expression will be called the differential approximation.

By the *differential approximation* of function $Y = f(X)$: $\{0,1\}^n \rightarrow \{0,1\}^m$ we mean an arbitrary equation of the form:

$$f(X) \oplus f(X \oplus X') = Y', \qquad (1)$$

fulfilled with approximation probability $p = N(X', Y') / 2^n$, where $X' \in \{0, 1, ..., 2^n-1\}$, $Y' \in \{0, 1, ..., 2^m-1\}$ and $N(X', Y')$ denotes the number of input pairs $(X, X \oplus X')$ for which the equation holds.

The numbers X', Y' are called input and output *difference* respectively and the function $N(X', Y')$ is called the *counting function* of the approximation. The magnitude of *p* represents the *effectiveness* of the approximation. Among approximations we distinguish the *zero differential approximation* with $X' = Y' = 0$, which probability *p* is equal to 1 for arbitrary function *f*.

The basic idea of linear cryptanalysis is to describe a given cipher algorithm by a linear approximate expression, so-called linear approximation. In general, the *linear approximation* of function $Y = f(X): \{0,1\}^n \rightarrow \{0,1\}^m$ is defined as an arbitrary equation of the form:

$$\bigoplus_{i \in Y'} y_i = \bigoplus_{j \in X'} x_j, \tag{2}$$

fulfilled with approximation probability $p = N(X', Y') / 2^n$, where $X' \subseteq \{1, 2, ..., n\}$, $Y' \subseteq \{1, 2, ..., m\}$ and $N(X', Y')$ denotes the number of pairs (X, Y) for which the equation holds. For simplicity the above equation is written in the following form:

$$Y[Y'] = X[X'] . \tag{3}$$

The sets of indexes X', Y' are called input and output *mask* respectively and the function $N(X', Y')$ is called the *counting function* of the approximation. The *effectiveness* of the approximation is represented by magnitude of $|\Delta p| = |p - 1/2|$. By the *zero linear approximation* we mean approximation with $X' = Y' = \Phi$, which probability *p* is equal to 1 for arbitrary function *f*. Masks X', Y' are often denoted by numbers, corresponding to the zero-one representation of sets.

2 Approximation Tables

The set of all differential approximations of function *f* can be described in the form of the *approximation table TDf*, called in [1] the *difference distribution table*. The element $TDf[X', Y']$ of the table, is defined as follows:

$$TDf[X', Y'] = N(X', Y') . \tag{4}$$

The maximum value of *TDf*, that corresponds to the best, i.e. most effective, nonzero differential approximation, is denoted by *maxTD* and is defined by formula:

$$maxTD = max\{TDf[X', Y'] : X' \neq 0 \vee Y' \neq 0\} . \tag{5}$$

Similarly, the set of all linear approximations of function *f* is represented in the form of the *approximation table TAf*. The element $TAf[X', Y']$ of the table, is defined in the following way:

$$TAf[X', Y'] = \Delta N(X', Y') = N(X', Y') - 2^{n-1} . \tag{6}$$

The maximum absolute value of *TAf* that corresponds to the best nonzero linear approximation, is denoted by *maxTA* and is defined as follows:

$$maxTA = max\{ |TAf[X', Y']| : X' \neq \Phi \vee Y' \neq \Phi\} . \tag{7}$$

Table 1. An example function f and its approximation tables TDf and TAf ($n=4$, $m=2$)

X	$Y=f(X)$
0	3
1	3
2	3
3	0
4	1
5	3
6	1
7	1
8	0
9	0
10	3
11	3
12	1
13	2
14	2
15	2

(f)

X'	Y'			
	0	1	2	3
0	16	0	0	0
1	10	0	2	4
2	6	0	2	8
3	6	0	2	8
4	2	8	6	0
5	2	8	6	0
6	0	2	12	2
7	2	4	10	0
8	4	2	0	10
9	2	0	2	12
10	8	2	0	6
11	8	2	0	6
12	0	6	8	2
13	0	6	8	2
14	2	8	6	0
15	2	12	2	0

(TDf)

X'	Y'			
	0	1	2	3
0	8	−2	−1	1
1	0	−2	1	−1
2	0	0	1	1
3	0	0	3	−1
4	0	0	−1	7
5	0	0	−3	1
6	0	2	1	−1
7	0	2	−1	1
8	0	−4	1	1
9	0	0	−1	−1
10	0	−2	−5	1
11	0	2	1	−1
12	0	2	−3	−1
13	0	−2	−1	1
14	0	−4	−1	−1
15	0	0	1	1

(TAf)

The approximation tables of an example function f are presented in table 1. There exist many effective approximations of the function, identified by nonzero values of the tables. The best nonzero differential approximations have $maxTD = 12$ and probability $p = 12/16$, while the best nonzero linear approximation has $maxTA = 7$ and probability $|\Delta p| = 7/16$.

```
TD-F(X', Y', f, n, m)
    1.  N(X', Y', f, n, m)
    2.    w ← 0
    3.    for X ← 0 to 2ⁿ – 1 do
    4.       if f(X) ⊕ f(X ⊕ X') = Y' then w ← w + 1
    5.    return w
    6.  return N(X', Y', f, n, m)
```

Fig. 1. Basic algorithm, computing a single element of the approximation table TDf

For clarity, in figure 1 is presented the basic algorithm computing a single element of the approximation table TDf. Function N(...) is the counting function of the approximation. The main function TD-F(...) returns the value of this function. The time complexity of the algorithm is $O(2^n)$.

In figure 2 is presented the basic algorithm computing a single element of the approximation table TAf. Auxiliary function BIT-XOR(...) computes the XOR of the n least significant bits of parameter X. Function N(...) is the counting function of the approximation. The main function TA-F(...) returns the value of ΔN. The time complexity of the algorithm is $O((n+m) \cdot 2^n)$.

TA-F(X', Y', f, n, m)
1.   BIT-XOR(X, n)
2. $w \leftarrow 0$
3.   **for** $i \leftarrow 0$ **to** $n - 1$ **do** $w \leftarrow w \oplus X_i$
4.   **return** w
5.   N(X', Y', f, n, m)
6. $w \leftarrow 0$
7.   **for** $X \leftarrow 0$ **to** $2^n - 1$ **do**
8. $Y \leftarrow f(X)$
9.   **if** BIT-XOR(X **and** X', n) = BIT-XOR(Y **and** Y', m)
10.   **then** $w \leftarrow w + 1$
11.   **return** w
12.   **return** N(X', Y', f, n, m) $- 2^{n-1}$

Fig. 2. Basic algorithm, computing a single element of the approximation table *TAf*

The size of the approximation tables *TDf* and *TAf* of function f is equal to 2^{n+m} and the basic algorithms compute a single element of the tables in exponential time. The presented in the next chapter fast algorithms compute the approximation tables in time at worst linear for a single element.

3 Fast Algorithms

The fast computation of approximation table *TDf*, for an arbitrary function $Y = f(X)$: $\{0,1\}^n \rightarrow \{0,1\}^m$, where n, $m \geq 1$, is suggested in [1]. Each row of *TDf* contains in fact the distribution of output differences Y' for all input pairs with difference X'. By examination of all input pairs $(X, X \oplus X')$ the whole row of *TDf* can be computed instead of a single element. The appropriate procedure is shown in figure 3.

CALC-TDR(*TDR*, X', f, n, m)
1. **for** $Y' \leftarrow 0$ **to** $2^m - 1$ **do** $TDR[Y'] \leftarrow 0$
2. **for** $X \leftarrow 0$ **to** $2^n - 1$ **do**
3. $Y' \leftarrow f[X] \oplus f[X \oplus X']$
4. $TDR[Y'] \leftarrow TDR[Y'] + 1$
5. **return**

Fig. 3. Procedure computing the row of the approximation table *TDf* for X'

Procedure CALC-TDR(...) computes the row of *TDf* for X' in time $O(2^{n-m})$ for a single element. If $n - m$ is limited by a constant, in particular for $n = m$, then the computation time is $O(1)$ for a single element.

The fast algorithm maxTD(...) presented in figure 4, computes the value of *maxTD*, that corresponds to the best nonzero differential approximation of function *f*. The computation is carried out row by row of *TDf*, in time $O(1)$ for a single element if $n - m$ is limited by a constant.

maxTD(*f*, *n*, *m*)
1. max := 0
2. **for** $X' \leftarrow 0$ **to** 2^n-1 **do**
3.   CALC-TDR(*TDR*, X', *f*, *n*, *m*)
4.   **for** $Y' \leftarrow 0$ **to** 2^m-1 **do**
5.   **if** $X' \neq 0$ **or** $Y' \neq 0$ **then**
6.   **if** max < *TDR*[*Y'*] **then** max $\leftarrow$ *TDR*[*Y'*]
7. **return** max

Fig. 4. Fast algorithm computing the value of *maxTD* for function *f*

The fast algorithm computing approximation table *TAf*, first described in [4], is composed of two main steps. In the first step the initial value of *TAf* is computed. The initial *TAf* contains elementary approximation tables of all residual functions of *f*, dependent on one variable X_0. In the second step the final value of *TAf* is computed, as a result of addition and subtraction of these elementary tables for consecutive variables. An important feature of the fast algorithm is, that the computation of *TAf* can be carried out column by column, without keeping the whole *TAf* in memory.

INI-TAC(*TAC*, Y', *f*, *n*, *m*, *TP*)
1. **for** $X' \leftarrow 0$ **to** 2^n-1 **do**
2.   *TAC*[*X'*] $\leftarrow$ BIT-XOR(*f*[*X'*] and Y', *m*)
3. **for** $X' \leftarrow 0$ **to** 2^n-2 **step 2 do**
4.   (*TAC*[*X'*], *TAC*[*X'*+1]) $\leftarrow$ *TP*[*TAC*[*X'*], *TAC*[*X'*+1]]
5. **return**

Fig. 5. Procedure computing the initial value of *TAf* column for Y'

The initial value of *TAf* column for Y' is computed by procedure INI-TAC(...) presented in figure 5. First, in steps 1-2, for each mask X', is calculated the value $Y[Y']$ with use of the auxiliary function BIT-XOR(...) from figure 2. Then, in steps 3-4, each pair of adjacent values, corresponding to the value 0 and 1 of variable X_0, is replaced by a pair stored in so called table of pairs *TP*.

Table 2. Table TP of pairs

v_0	v_1	$TP[v_0, v_1]$
0	0	(1, 0)
0	1	(0, 1)
1	0	(0,–1)
1	1	(–1, 0)

Table TP of pairs is presented in table 2. For each function of one variable, defined by the values of v_0 and v_1, it contains a pair of values from the right column of the appropriate elementary approximation table.

CALC-TAC(TAC, i, j)
1. **if** $j - i > 2$ **then**
2. $k \leftarrow (i + j)$ **div** 2
3.   CALC-TAC(TAC, i, k)
4.   CALC-TAC($TAC, k+1, j$)
5.   SUMSUB-TAC($TAC, i, k, k+1, j$)
6. **return**

Fig. 6. Procedure computing the final value of TAf column for Y', first call: CALC-TAC($TAC, 0, 2^n - 1$)

The final value of TAf column for Y' is computed by the recursive procedure CALC-TAC(...) presented in figure 6. In the first call of the procedure the initial value of TAf column must be used and the range of rows is from $i = 0$ to $j = 2^n - 1$. For the range greater than 2, the problem is solved by solution of two half-subproblems. Having solved the subproblems, the approximation table column of the problem is computed by the auxiliary procedure SUMSUB-TAC(...) from figure 7.

SUMSUB-TAC(TAC, i_1, j_1, i_2, j_2)
1. **for** $i \leftarrow 0$ **to** $j_1 - i_1$ **do**
2. $(TAC[i_1 + i], TAC[i_2 + i]) \leftarrow (TAC[i_1 + i] + TAC[i_2 + i],$
3. $TAC[i_1 + i] - TAC[i_2 + i])$
4. **return**

Fig. 7. Procedure SUMSUB-TAC(...)

Procedure SUMSUB-TAC(...), for two parts of TAf column that correspond to the subproblems, replaces first of them by their sum and the second by their difference.

maxTA(f, n, m)
1. max := 0
2. **for** $Y' \leftarrow 0$ **to** $2^m - 1$ **do**
3.   INI-TAC(TAC, Y', f, n, m, TP)
3.   CALC-TAC(TAC, 0, $2^n - 1$)
4.   **for** $X' \leftarrow 0$ **to** $2^n - 1$ **do**
5.   **if** $X' \neq 0$ **or** $Y' \neq 0$ **then**
6.   **if** max $< |TAC[X']|$ **then** max $\leftarrow |TAC[X']|$
7. **return** max

Fig. 8. Fast algorithm computing the value of *maxTA* for function f

It can be shown, that procedures INI-TAC(...) and CALC-TAC(...) compute the column of TAf for Y' in linear time $O(n + m)$ for a single element [4].

The fast algorithm maxTA(...) presented in figure 8, computes the value of *maxTA*, that corresponds to the best nonzero linear approximation of function f. The computation is carried out column by column of TAf, in time $O(n + m)$ for a single element.

4 Results

The presented in this chapter results of experiments concern the distribution of the best nonzero differential and linear approximations of two classes of S-box functions $Y = f(X)$. The classes are the permutations and arbitrary functions of the type $f:\{0,1\}^n \rightarrow \{0,1\}^m$, for $1 \leq n = m \leq 10$.

Table 3. Summarized results of experiments for permutations

(n, m)	Range of		Distribution maximum	
	maxTD	*maxTA*	value (%)	for (*maxTD*, *maxTA*)
(1,1)	2 - 2	1 - 1	100	(2, 1)
(2,2)	4 - 4	2 - 2	100	(4, 2)
(3,3)	2 - 8	2 - 4	45,3	(4, 4)
(4,4)	4 - 12	4 - 8	55,2	(6, 6)
(5,5)	6 - 16	8 - 14	39,0	(8, 10)
(6,6)	6 - 14	12 - 20	31,7	(8, 14)
(7,7)	8 - 16	20 - 30	33,8	(10, 24)
(8,8)	10 - 16	30 - 44	19,0	(12, 34)
(9,9)	10 - 16	46 - 72	21,7	(12, 52)
(10,10)	12 - 18	72 - 100	13,9	(14, 80)

Table 4. Summarized results of experiments for arbitrary functions

(n, m)	Range of		Distribution maximum	
	maxTD	maxTA	value (%)	for (maxTD, maxTA)
(1,1)	2 - 2	1 - 1	100	(2, 1)
(2,2)	2 - 4	2 - 2	73,6	(2, 2)
(3,3)	2 - 8	2 - 4	56,7	(4, 3)
(4,4)	4 - 10	4 - 8	40,5	(6, 6)
(5,5)	6 - 12	8 - 13	24,7	(8, 9)
(6,6)	6 - 16	12 - 21	20,6	(8, 14)
(7,7)	8 - 16	20 - 30	20,0	(10, 22)
(8,8)	10 - 16	30 - 47	9,5	(10, 35)
(9,9)	10 - 16	47 - 69	12,0	(12, 52)
(10,10)	12 - 16	70 - 97	7,8	(14, 79)

For each value of n, the investigation was carried out for 1000 randomly chosen functions from the class. For each function, with use of the presented in the previous chapter fast algorithms, were calculated values of $maxTD$ and $maxTA$. Distribution of pairs ($maxTD$, $maxTA$) was the goal of the computation. The obtained results, in a synthetic form, are presented in tables 3 and 4.

The first observation is, that the significant for distributions ranges of $maxTD$ and $maxTA$ as well as the values of pairs ($maxTD$, $maxTA$) for which are obtained maxima of distributions, are about the same for permutations and arbitrary functions. The values of maxima are greater for permutations. It follows from the fact, that for $n > 2$, the values of $maxTA$ are even for permutations and for arbitrary functions are odd as well.

Table 5. Results of experiments for permutations ($n=10$, $m=10$)

maxTD	maxTA												Total
	72	74	76	78	80	82	84	86	88	90	92	100	
12	1	17	55	86	81	46	26	21	10	6	4	0	353
14	3	37	93	127	139	83	52	29	11	7	4	1	586
16	0	1	11	7	15	10	5	5	1	0	1	0	56
18	0	1	0	1	1	0	2	0	0	0	0	0	5
Total	4	56	159	221	236	139	85	55	22	13	9	1	1000

The results in detail, obtained for permutations with 10 input bits and 10 output bits, are presented in table 5 and illustrated in figure 9.

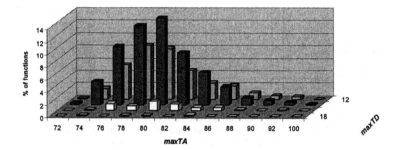

Fig. 9. Proportional distribution for permutations (n=10, m=10)

The obtained results indicate, that with the increase of n=m the values of *maxTA* rise much faster than the values of *maxTD*. It means that linear approximation of S-box functions becomes much more effective than differential approximation. This is probably the most important conclusion that results from the investigation.

5 Conclusion

The basic algorithms to compute a single element of the approximation tables TDf and TAf are of exponential complexity. The presented in the paper fast algorithms compute the values of *maxTD* and *maxTA* in at worst linear time for a single element, without memory needed for storage of the whole table. The fast algorithms were used to calculate the distribution of pairs (*maxTD*, *maxTA*) for randomly chosen permutations and arbitrary functions with n binary inputs and m binary outputs, where $1 \leq n$=$m \leq 10$. The main conclusion is, that starting from some value of n, linear approximation of S-box functions becomes much more effective than differential approximation. Moreover, this advantage of linear approximation rises with the increase of n.

References

1. Biham, E., Shamir, A.: Differential Cryptanalysis of the Data Encryption Standard. Springer-Verlag, Berlin Heidelberg New York (1993)
2. Chmiel, K.: Linear Approximation of some S-box Functions. Proceedings of the Regional Conference on Military Communication and Information Systems 2001, Vol. 1. WIŁ, Zegrze (2001) 211–218

3.   Chmiel, K.: Linear Approximation of Arithmetic Sum Function. In: Sołdek, J., Drobi-azgiewicz, L. (eds.): Artificial Intelligence and Security in Computing Systems. Kluwer Academic Publishers, Boston Dordrecht London (2003) 293–302

4.   Chmiel, K.: Fast Computation of Approximation Tables. In: Saeed, K., Pejaś, J. (eds.): Information Processing and Security Systems. Springer-Verlag, Berlin Heidelberg New York (2005) 125–134

5.   Chmiel, K.: On Arithmetic Subtraction Linear Approximation. In: Pejaś, J., Piegat, A. (eds.): Enhanced Methods in Computer Security, Biometric and Artificial Intelligence Systems. Kluwer Academic Publishers, New York (2005) 125–134

6.   Górska, A., Górski, K., Kotulski, Z., Paszkiewicz, A., Szczepański, J.: New Experimental Results in Differential – Linear Cryptanalysis of Reduced Variants of DES. Proceedings of the 8-th International Conference on Advanced Computer Systems ACS'2001, Vol. 1. Szczecin (2001) 333–346

7.   Matsui, M.: Linear Cryptanalysis Method for DES Cipher. In: Helleseth, T. (ed.): Advances in Cryptology Eurocrypt'93 (1993) 386–397

Random Generation of S-Boxes
for Block Ciphers

Anna Grocholewska-Czuryło[1] and Janusz Stokłosa
Poznań University of Technology, Institute of Control and Information Engineering, pl.
Skłodowskiej-Curie 5, 60-965 Poznań, Poland

Abstract: In the paper results of experiments in designing S-boxes and
nonlinear Boolean functions as their components are presented. We discuss deterministic algorithms for the construction of bent functions and we formulate
our algorithm for random generation of perfect nonlinear functions. We present
results of experiments performed on S-boxes and we compare them with results
obtained using deterministic methods.

1 Introduction

Symmetric key encryption is used in a large variety of applications: transmitted and
stored data files, e-mail messages, ATM PINs, video transmissions (e.g. pay-per-view
movies), UMTS communications, etc. Strong symmetric ciphers have properly designed S-boxes. Each cryptographic attack that is more effective than exhaustive
search explores some weaknesses in S-boxes.

In the paper we present results of our experiments on designing S-boxes and nonlinear Boolean functions as their components. We present design criteria for Boolean
functions and S-boxes. We discuss deterministic algorithms for the construction of
bent functions and we formulate our algorithm for random generation of perfect
nonlinear functions. We present results of experiments done on S-boxes and we compare them with results obtained using deterministic methods.

The results presented in the paper indicate that random generated perfect nonlinear
functions offer an interesting alternative to constructed methods. Not only nonlinear
characteristics are at least as good as those of constructed perfect nonlinear functions
but also generated functions have a very compact form which can be used for efficient storage and fast cryptographic routines.

---

[1] This research carried out by the first author was supported by the Polish Ministry of Education and Science as a 2004–2006 research project.

2 S-Boxes

An S-box is a component used in most block ciphers. S-boxes vary in both input size and output size, and can be created either deterministically or randomly. S-boxes were probably first used in Lucifer, then DES, and afterwards in many encryption algorithms.

S-boxes can either be large tables (like in DES), or derived algebraically (like in Safer, IDEA, or AES). The advantage of the former is that there is no simple mathematical structure that can be potentially used for cryptanalysis. The advantage of the latter is that the S-boxes are more compact, and can be more easily implemented in applications.

Essential S-box design criteria include: completeness, balancedness, nonlinearity, propagation criteria and good cryptoanalitycal profile [18]. However, in this paper we focus our attention especially on the nonlinearity and propagation criteria of Boolean functions and S-boxes composed of Boolean functions. We skip the problem of completeness because it is, for a given S-box, the question about the design of suitable round permutation and of how many rounds are necessary to build up the cipher. If we consider an S-box as the sequence of Boolean functions then we should also take into consideration such properties of Boolean functions as algebraic degree and order of correlation immunity [20].

3 Preliminaries

Throughout the paper F_2 is the finite field of order 2, or simply the set $\{0,1\}$, and F_2^j is j-dimensional vector space over the finite field F_2. The definitions and results presented below can be found (may be in an alternative form) in [1, 3–6, 12, 14–16, 18, 21, 23].

A substitution operation or an s×t S-box (or S-box of the size s×t) is a mapping

$$S : F_2^s \rightarrow F_2^t,$$

where s and t are fixed positive integers, $2 \leq t \leq s$.

An s-argument Boolean function is a mapping

$$f : F_2^s \rightarrow F_2.$$

An S-box $S : F_2^s \rightarrow F_2^t$ can be decomposed into the sequence,

$$S = (f_1, f_2, \ldots, f_t)$$

of Boolean functions such that

$$S(x_1, x_2, \ldots, x_s) = (f_1(x_1, x_2, \ldots, x_s), f_2(x_1, x_2, \ldots, x_s), \ldots, f_t(x_1, x_2, \ldots, x_s)).$$

We say that the functions $f_1, f_2, \ldots, f_t$ are component functions of S.

Let for an s-argument Boolean function $f_i : F_2^s \rightarrow F_2$, $i = 1, 2, \ldots, t$, the integer z be the decimal representation of its arguments $(x_1, x_2, \ldots, x_s)$. Let us denote $f(x_1, x_2, \ldots, x_s)$ as y_z. A truth table of the function f is denoted as $[y_0, y_1, \ldots, y_{2^s-1}]$.

In the sequel when we use f there is always an s-argument Boolean function.

A Boolean function can also be represented as a maximum of 2^s coefficients of the Algebraic Normal Form (ANF). These coefficients provide a formula for the evaluation of the function for any given argument $x = (x_1, x_2, \ldots, x_s)$:

$$f(x) = a_0 \oplus \sum_{i=1}^{s} a_i x_i \oplus \sum_{1 \le i < j \le s} a_{ij} x_i x_j \oplus \ldots \oplus a_{12\ldots s} x_1 x_2 \ldots x_s$$

where Σ denotes the modulo 2 summation.

The order of nonlinearity (denoted as $ord(f)$) of a Boolean function $f(x)$ is a maximum number of variables in a product term with non-zero coefficient a_J, where J is a subset of $\{1, 2, \ldots, s\}$. In the case where J is an empty set, the coefficient is denoted as a_0 and it is called a zero order coefficient. Coefficients of order 1 are a_1, a_2, ..., a_s, coefficients of order 2 are a_{12}, $a_{13}, \ldots, a_{(s-1)s}$, coefficient of order s is $a_{12\ldots s}$. The number of all ANF coefficients equals 2^s.

Let us denote the number of all (zero and non-zero) coefficients of order i of the function f as $\sigma_i(f)$. For s-argument function f there are as many coefficients of a given order as there are i-element combinations in s-element set,

$$\sigma_i(f) = \binom{s}{i}.$$

An s-argument Boolean function f is affine if it can be represented in the following form:

$$f(x_1, x_2, \ldots, x_s) = a_0 \oplus a_1 x_1 \oplus a_2 x_2 \oplus \ldots \oplus a_s x_s, \quad a_i \in F_2.$$

A Boolean function

$$f : F_2^s \rightarrow F_2$$

that is not affine is called a nonlinear Boolean function.

Hamming weight of a binary vector $x \in F_2^s$, denoted as $hwt(x)$, is the number of 1's in that vector. Hamming distance between two Boolean functions f, $g \colon F_2^s \rightarrow F_2$ is defined as:

$$d(f, g) = \sum_{x \in \{0,1\}^s} f(x) \oplus g(x).$$

The distance of a Boolean function f from a set X_s of s-argument Boolean functions

$$\delta(f) = min_{g \in X_s} d(f, g).$$

The distance of a function f from a set A_s of affine functions is the distance of function f from the nearest function $g \in A_s$. The distance of function f from a set of all affine functions is called the nonlinearity of function f and is denoted by N_f,

$$N_f = min_{g \in A_s} d(f, g),$$

It is known that $N_f \leq 2^{s-1} - 2^{s/2-1}$. If s is even then there exist functions with $N_f = 2^{s-1} - 2^{s/2-1}$. We call them bent functions. The function is bent if and only if the absolute value of its Walsh transform is constant for all w,

$$\left| F_{\bar{f}}(w) \right| = \left| \sum_{x \in V_2^s} \bar{f}(x)(-1)^{(x,w)} \right| = 2^{s/2},$$

where $\bar{f}(x) = g(f(x)) = (-1)^{f(x)}$ and $(x, w) = x_1 w_1 \oplus x_2 w_2 \oplus ... \oplus x_s w_s$.

For bent functions their correlation to any affine function is consistently bad.

Let $\#_0[y_0, y_1, ..., y_{2^s-1}]$ be a number of 0's in the truth table $[y_0, y_1, ..., y_{2^s-1}]$ of the function f, and $\#_1[y_0, y_1, ..., y_{2^s-1}]$ be number of 1's. A Boolean function f is balanced if $\#_0[y_0, y_1, ..., y_{2^s-1}] = \#_1[y_0, y_1, ..., y_{2^s-1}]$.

Let $f : F_2^s \rightarrow F_2$, where $s \geq 3$, be balanced. Then

$$N_f \leq \begin{cases} 2^{s-1} - 2^{s/2-1} - 2 & \text{for } s \text{ even} \\ \lfloor\lfloor 2^{s-1} - 2^{s/2-1} \rfloor\rfloor & \text{for } s \text{ odd} \end{cases}$$

where $\lfloor\lfloor x \rfloor\rfloor$ denotes the maximum even integer less than or equal to x.

The function f satisfies SAC if complementing any single input bit changes the output bit with the probability equal to ½. f satisfies SAC if $f(x) \oplus f(x \oplus \alpha)$ is balanced for any $\alpha \in F_2^s$ such that $hwt(\alpha) = 1$.

A generalization of the SAC property where the number of input changes is greater than one, is called the higher order SAC. Both the SAC and the higher order SAC are collectively called propagation criteria.

A function $f : F_2^s \rightarrow F_2$ is said to fulfill the Strict Avalanche Criterion of order 1 if and only if:

- f fulfills the SAC,
- every function obtained from f by keeping the i-th input bit constant and equal to c fulfills the SAC as well (for every $i \in \{1, 2, ..., s\}$, and for $c = 0$ and $c = 1$).

A function $f : F_2^s \rightarrow F_2$ satisfies SAC(v), $1 \leq v \leq s-2$, if and only if
- f satisfies SAC($v-1$),
- any function obtained from f by keeping any v input bits constant satisfies SAC.

A Boolean function $f : F_2^s \rightarrow F_2$ is perfect nonlinear if and only if $f(x) \oplus f(x \oplus \alpha)$ is balanced for any $\alpha \in F_2^s$ such that $1 \leq hwt(\alpha) \leq s$. For a perfect nonlinear Boolean function, any change of inputs causes the change of outputs with probability equal to ½.

Meier and Staffelbach [12] proved that if s is even then the set of perfect nonlinear Boolean functions is the same as the set of bent functions defined by Rothaus [19].

Perfect nonlinear functions are not balanced. This property prohibits their direct application as components in S-box construction. However, there exists a number of methods for modifying perfect nonlinear function in such a way that the resulting function is balanced and still maintains the good cryptographic properties of a (almost perfect) nonlinear function.

Bent functions exist only for even s. Their nonlinear order is bounded from above by $s/2$ for $s > 2$. The number of Boolean bent functions for $s > 6$ remains an open problem. Currently, for $s = 6$ (i.e., in the input dimension of the DES S-boxes) it is impossible to find perfect nonlinear functions either by exhaustive search or by pure random search.

4 Algorithms for Bent Functions' Generation

4.1 Determinictic Algorithms

There exist a number of algorithms for constructing bent functions. Such constructions have been given by Rothaus, Kam and Davida, Maiorana, Adams and Tavares, and others [1, 8, 10, 17, 19, 22].

Let B_s denote a set of s-argument perfect nonlinear functions with s even.

Algorithm 1
INPUT: $a, b \in B_6, a \neq b$.
OUTPUT: bent functions in the set B_8 of 8-argument bent functions.
METHOD: the function $g : F_2^8 \rightarrow F_2$ defined by:

$$g(x_0...x_7) = \begin{cases} a(x_0...x_5), & x_6 = 0, x_7 = 0 \\ a(x_0...x_5), & x_6 = 0, x_7 = 1 \\ b(x_0...x_5), & x_6 = 1, x_7 = 0 \\ b(x_0...x_5) \oplus 1, & x_6 = 1, x_7 = 1 \end{cases}$$

is bent [8].
Permutations of the arguments in the expression also result in bent functions.
The method given in Algorithm 1 can be extended [3].

Algorithm 2 (Rothaus)

INPUT: s-argument bent functions $a(x)$, $b(x)$ and $c(x)$ such that $a(x) \oplus b(x) \oplus c(x)$ is bent.

OUTPUT: $(s+2)$-argument bent function g.

METHOD: $g(x, x_{s+1}, x_{s+2}) =$
$a(x)b(x) \oplus b(x)c(x) \oplus c(x)a(x) \oplus [a(x) \oplus b(x)]x_{s+1} \oplus [a(x) \oplus c(x)]x_{s+2} \oplus x_{s+1}x_{s+2}$.

Most of the known perfect nonlinear (or bent) function constructions take s-argument perfect nonlinear functions as their input and generate perfect nonlinear functions of $s+2$ arguments. A major drawback of these methods is the fact that they are deterministic. Only perfect nonlinear functions of 4 or 6 arguments are selected at random and the resulting function is obtained using the same, deterministic formula every time. Even if there is some "random" element in such generation (like adding a linear term to the resulting function) it does not bring any new quality to the generated function.

Algorithm 3 (Maiorana functions)

INPUT: bijective mapping $\pi : F_2^{s/2} \rightarrow F_2^{s/2}$, function $g : F_2^{s/2} \rightarrow F_2$, s – even.

OUTPUT: bent function $f_M : F_2^s \rightarrow F_2$ called Maiorana function.

METHOD:
$$f_M(x\|y) = \pi(x) \cdot y \oplus g(x),$$
where $x, y \in F_2^{s/2}$, $\|$ is the concatenation and $(a_{s/2-1}, a_{s/2-2}, ..., a_0) \cdot (b_{s/2-1}, b_{s/2-2}, ..., b_0) = a_{s/2-1}b_{s/2-1} \oplus a_{s/2-2}b_{s/2-2} \oplus ... \oplus a_0b_0$.

Let $(a_0, a_1, ..., a_7)$ be a permutation of $\{0,1,...,7\}$. The function

$$\hat{f}(x_0, x_1 ..., x_7) = f_M(x_{a_0}, x_{a_1}, ..., x_{a_7}),$$

where f_M is a Maiorana function, is bent. We will refer to these functions as Maiorana functions with permuted inputs [14].

4.2   Random Generation of Bent Functions

It would be of special interest if we could generate bent functions at random, and not only via some deterministic constructs, as presented above. The reason for this interest is the fact that constructed bent functions have some inherent properties that are induced by the method of their construction. And that is obviously not desired, as such properties may be used to design a cryptanalitic attacks.

However, it is impossible to find all bent functions by a pure random search for 6-argument Boolean functions. ANF representation of Boolean functions opens up some possibilities for random search. We have used that representation to generate successfully random bent functions of up to 16-argument functions.

Operating on ANF representation gives a great control over the nonlinear characteristics of generated functions. Basic properties of bent function can then be used to tremendously narrow search space which makes generation of bent functions feasible for $s \geq 8$ even on a standard PC machine.

The algorithm for the generation of bent functions in ANF domain takes as its input the minimum and maximum number of ANF coefficients of every order that the resulting functions are allowed to have. Since the nonlinear order of bent functions is less or equal to $s/2$, clearly in ANF of a bent function there can not be any ANF coefficient of order higher then $s/2$. This restriction is the major reason for random generation feasibility, since it considerably reduces the possible search space.

The number of ANF coefficients of orders less or equal to $s/2$ can be fixed or randomly selected within allowed range. If the number of coefficients for a given order i is fixed then all generated functions will have the same number of coefficients of that order, but the coefficients themselves will be different in each generated function. If the number of coefficients for a given order i is randomly selected then all generated functions will not only have different coefficients but also the number of coefficients of order i will vary from function to function.

It is of course possible to fix the number of coefficients for some orders and obtain varied number of coefficients for other orders.

An important consequence of this approach is the possibility of prohibiting the generation of bent functions which are merely linear transformations of other bent functions. This is easily achieved by setting the number of coefficients of order 0 and 1 to 0. So in the ANF of the resulting functions there will be no linear part. Bent functions of any order can be generated with this method, simply by setting any higher order coefficients to 0.

An drawback of the method results from the fact that it does not guarantee the generation of bent functions without repetitions, although the chance of generating two identical bent functions is minimal with any reasonably selected ranges of number of ANF coefficients. However, if avoiding repetitions is an absolute requirement, the set of generated bent functions must be checked for duplicates.

The limitations of this approach are twofold. First, there is a feasibility limit. Number of possible functions grows with the number of coefficients of higher orders ($i > 2$) and generating a bent function quickly becomes infeasible. So the algorithm works good with the low number of higher order coefficients (e.g., less than 6 for $s = 8$, $i = 3$ and 4).

Due to the above limitation, this method does not generate all possible bent functions with equal probability. In principle, it would be possible but is not feasible for the reason described above. One has to limit the number of higher order coefficients and at the same time prohibit the generation of some bent functions.

Algorithm 4 (Randomly generated bent functions)
INPUT:
- the number s of arguments such that s is even,
- for each order ord such that $0 \le ord \le s/2$ define minimum (denoted as $cmin_{ord}$) and maximum (denoted as $cmax_{ord}$) number of coefficients of ANF,

$$0 \le cmin_{ord} \le cmax_{ord} \le \binom{s}{ord}.$$

OUTPUT:
- randomly generated perfect nonlinear function f_{ANF} in ANF,

–   randomly generated perfect nonlinear function f_{TT} in the form of the truth table.

METHOD:
  (1)   Repeat steps (1.1) and (1.2) for each order ord such that $0 \leq ord \leq s/2$:
        (1.1)   generate randomly the number of coefficients c_{ord} of ANF for a given order ord such that $cmin_{ord} \leq c_{ord} \leq cmax_{ord}$,
        (1.2)   for f_{ANF} fix randomly the value 1 for coefficients of order ord.
  (2)   Transform f_{ANF} to f_{TT} .
  (3)   Calculate the distance of f_{TT} from the set of affine functions.
  (4)   If the distance calculated in the step (3) is equal to $2^{s-1} - 2^{s/2-1}$, then f_{TT} (and f_{ANF}) is bent – stop; otherwise go to (1).

If the first input of Algorithm 4 is dropped (allowing s to be even or odd) then the algorithm can be used to obtain highly nonlinear functions even for odd number of arguments (in the sequel we will refer to it as to **Algorithm 4'**). These functions are not bent (as these do not exist for odd arument number) so step (4) of the algorithm is not perfomed – the algorithm should be used in a loop that generates random functions, many of which are highly nonlinear.

5   Nonlinearity of S-boxes

The nonlinearity of an S-box, meant as a function $S : F_2^s \rightarrow F_2^t$ such that $S(x_1,x_2,...,x_s)$ = $(f_1(x_1,x_2,...,x_s), f_2(x_1,x_2,...,x_s),..., f_t(x_1,x_2,...,x_s))$, is calculated as minimal nonlinearity of all linear combinations of S's component functions. The nonlinearity of a S-box is then defined as follows:

$$N_S = \min\{N_{f_J} \mid f_J = \sum_{i \in J} f_i, \ J \subseteq (1,2,...,t)\} .$$

To calculate a nonlinearity of a single S-box $2t$ linear combinations have to be constructed and their distance to affine functions calculated. The lowest of all calculated nonlinearities is the nonlinearity of the S-box.

In Fig.1 to Fig.4 the distributions of nonlinearities of 8×6 S-boxes are depicted (each S-box is constructed of six 8-argument functions). By comparing Fig.1 and Fig.2 one can see that balanced Boolean functions are better for building S-boxes than pure random Boolean functions, as there are more S-boxes of relatively high nonlinearity (98 and 100).

Just slightly better than S-boxes built from random balanced Boolean functions are S-boxes built from constructed bent functions (Algorithm 2) (see Fig.3). Only for the high nonlinearity equal to 98 there are a little more S-boxes built using constructed bent functions.

Quite different distribution of nonlinearity characterizes S-boxes built from randomly generated bent functions (depicted in Fig.4). In this group there exist S-boxes of the highest found nonlinearity of 112, for c.a. 5% of all generated S-boxes (note that 5% is still too little to be visible on the graph in Fig.4 hence the highest value of nonlinearity on the graph is 104). There is also about 20 times more S-boxes of very high nonlinearity of 100 than in case of S-boxes built from constructed bent functions or random balanced functions.

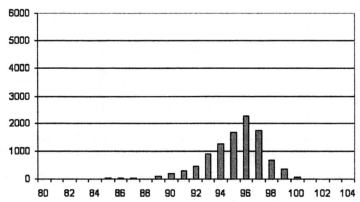

Fig.1. Number of S-boxes built of random Boolean functions with respect to their nonlinearity

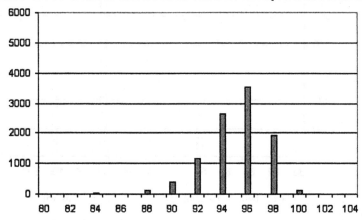

Fig.2. Number of S-boxes built of random balanced Boolean functions with respect to their nonlinearity

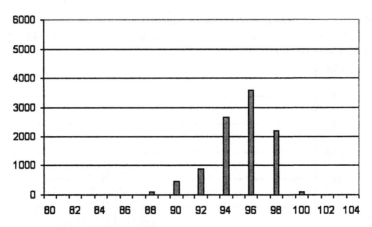

Fig.3. Number of S-boxes built of constructed bent functions (Algorithm 2) with respect to their nonlinearity

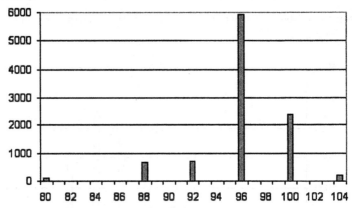

Fig.4. Number of S-boxes built of randomly generated bent functions with respect to their nonlinearity

This means that using randomly generated bent functions may lead to constructing S-boxes of better cryptographic qualities in shorter time.

However, it should be noted that in case of randomly generated bent functions there are also S-boxes of relatively poor nonlinearity (like 80). So building S-boxes from these functions requires (more than in other cases) careful checking the resulting S-boxes for possibly low nonlinearity.

6 Strict Avalanche Criterion for S-Boxes

The generalization of SAC(v) to vector output Boolean functions (S-boxes) has been proposed by Kurosawa and Satoh [9] as a step toward the security of block ciphers against attacks which keep some input bits constant. We say that $S = (f_1, f_2, ..., f_t)$ is an (s, t)-SAC(v) function if all nonzero linear combinations of $f_1, f_2, ..., f_t$ satisfy SAC(v). As mentioned earlier, S-boxes are not usually built directly from bent functions, as it is one of the fundamental cryptographic requirements for Boolean functions (building blocks of an S-box) to be balanced. Balancing bent randomly generated bent functions will be covered in the next section. However, for the purpose of comparing constructed and generated bent functions we decided to test S-boxes built directly from bent functions. These S-boxes were not necessarily chosen to fit any particular application but to clearly show the differences between constructed bent functions (Algorithm 2) and randomly generated bent functions. Such an S-box in its simplest form would be just a pair of two Boolean functions (S-box of the size 8×2). The number of 10000 S-boxes has been tested during each of the experiments mentioned below.

For 8×2 S-boxes (pairs of bent functions) there also has not been a single S-box found that would satisfy SAC for constructed bent functions (Algorithm 2). For randomly generated bent functions the proportions of SAC fulfilling S-boxes were shown in Table 1.

Table 1. (8,2)-SAC(v) fulfilling S-boxes

v	Percentage of S-boxes
0	26.80
1	33.00
2	15.60
3	2.40
4	0.20

Table 2. (6,2)-SAC(v) fulfilling S-boxes

v	Percentage of S-boxes
0	37.80
1	19.60
2	3.90
3	0.30
4	0.00

Similarly, for S-boxes of the size 6×4, there were no SAC S-boxes built from constructed bent functions while there where about 3% of (6,4)-SAC(0) S-boxes built from randomly generated bent functions.

For S-boxes of the size 6×2 (pairs of 6-argument bent functions) there were ca. 3% of (6,2)-SAC(0) S-boxes built from constructed bent functions (Algorithm 2), and results for randomly generated bent functions are given in Table 2.

Another set of S-boxes tested were S-boxes of the size 8×4 built from constructed bent functions (Algorithm 2). There is not a single S-box found that would satisfy even the original SAC ((8,4)-SAC(0)), while among the same size S-boxes built from randomly generated bent functions there is ca. 71,5% of non-SAC fulfilling S-boxes, 28,2% of (8,4)-SAC(0) fulfilling S-boxes and the remaining 0,3% of (8,4)-SAC(1) S-boxes.

As one can easily see from the results presented above, randomly generated bent functions have some interesting cryptographic qualities, quite distinct from those of constructed bent functions. Generation time for randomly generated bent functions are up to 40 times shorter then time required for the constructing a bent function (using Rothaus algorithm for 8-argument bent functions). This opens new possibilities for designing fast algorithms for strong S-box constructions.

7 Balancing Bent Functions

As bent functions achieve maximum possible nonlinearity they are often used as a foundation for constructing highly nonlinear balanced functions that could be used directly in S-boxes. In recent years some methods have been proposed that transform bent functions to balanced Boolean functions with minimal loss in nonlinearity [10, 11]. For the purpose of this research none of these methods has been implemented. Instead the adopted approach was to balance generated bent functions randomly, without any sort of optimization and then to test the nonlinearity of resulting balanced functions. Thus balancing is performed as follows. A bent function is randomly generated. Depending on whether bent function's Hamming weight is $2^{s-1} - 2^{s/2-1}$ or $2^{s-1} + 2^{s/2-1}$ "missing" 1's or 0's are added at random positions.

Table 3 summarizes the obtained results. It shows the nonlinearity of balanced Boolean functions achieved by the best currently known techniques with best theoretical upper bounds and the best currently known examples. The table contains values for Boolean functions of 8 up to 12 arguments. Results for lower number of arguments are the same for all algorithms and are in fact maximum achievable.

Table 3. Conjectured upper bounds and attained values for nonlinearity of balanced functions of given number (8–12) of arguments

	8	9	10	11	12
LUB	**118**	**244**	**494**	**1000**	**2014**
BK	**116**	**240**	**492**	**992**	**2010**
BC	112	240	480	992	1984
R	112	230	472	962	1955
RHC	114	236	476	968	1961
GA	116	236	484	980	1976
DNL	114	236	480	974	1972
NLT	116	238	486	984	1992
ACT	116	238	484	982	1986
GEN	**116**	**240**	**488**	**992**	**2002**

Abbreviations: LUB – Lowest upper bound, BK – Best known example [7], BC – Bent concatenation, R – Random, RHC – Random & Hill-Climb [2], GA – Genetic algorithms [13], DNL – Direct nonlinearity [2], NLT – Nonlinearity targeted [2],

ACT – Auto-correlation targeted [2], GEN – balanced randomly generated functions (see Algorithm 4 and Algorithm 4')

As it can be clearly seen from Table 3, a random generation algorithm presented in this paper gives the same results of nonlinearity of balanced functions only for $s = 8$, and is better then any of other methods for all higher number of arguments, and most profoundly so in case of 11 and 12 arguments. It is also worth noting, that for $s = 9$ and $s = 11$ random generation method yields results equal to the best known examples of highly nonlinear balanced Boolean functions.

Other interesting results are presented in Table 4. The number of 200000 12-argument bent functions were randomly generated and then randomly balanced. Table 4 shows the nonlinearity of the resulting balanced functions. The majority (more than 97%) of balanced Boolean functions in Table 4 has nonlinearity between 1994 and 2000, which is very high (see Table 3).

Table 4. Nonlinearities of balanced 12-argument functions obtained by random balancing generated bent functions

Nonlinearity	Number of functions
1986	3
1988	41
1990	543
1992	3979
1994	22458
1996	76492
1998	87004
2000	9474
2002	6

8 Concluding Remarks

From the results presented in the paper it seems that random generated bent (and in general highly nonlinear) functions offer an interesting alternative to constructed methods. Not only nonlinear characteristics of these functions are equal or better than those of constructed perfect nonlinear functions but also generated functions have a very compact (small) ANF which can be used for efficient storage and fast cryptographic routines.

Perfect nonlinear functions with relatively small number of arguments (i.e., for $s \leq 10$) generated with a combined method of ANF generation and then used as an input for deterministic constructions can indeed yield interesting results. Such functions should be further tested to verify their possibly superior cryptographic qualities.

References

1. Adams, C.M., Tavares, S.E.: Generating and Counting Binary Bent Sequences. IEEE Transactions on Information Theory, IT-36 (1990) 1170–1173
2. Clark, J.A., Jacob, J.L., Stepney, S.: Searching for cost functions. In: International Conference on Evolutionary Computation, IEEE, Portland, OR, USA (2004) 1517–1524
3. Dawson, M., Tavares, S. E,: An Expanded Set of S-Box Design Criteria Based on Information Theory and its Relation to Differential-Like Attacks. In: Davies, D.W. (ed.), Advances in Cryptology – Eurocrypt '91. Lecture Notes in Computer Science, Vol. 547. Springer-Verlag, Berlin (1991) 352–367
4. Dillon, J.F.: A Survey of Bent Functions. NSA Technical Journal, Special Issue (1972) 191–215
5. Forré, R.: The strict avalanche criterion: spectral properties of Boolean functions with high nonlinearity. In: Goldwasser, S. (ed.), Advances in Cryptology – CRYPTO '88. Lecture Notes in Computer Science, Vol. 403. Springer-Verlag, Berlin (1990) 450–468
6. Grocholewska-Czuryło, A., Stokłosa, J.: Generating Bent Functions. In: Sołdek, J., Pejaś, J. (eds.): Advanced Computer Systems, Kluwer, Boston (2002) 361–370
7. Hou, X.D.: On the norm and covering radius of first order Reed-Muller codes. IEEE Transactions of Information Theory IT-43(1997) 1025–1027
8. Kam, J.B., Davida, G.: Structured Design of Substitution-Permutation Encryption Networks. IEEE Transactions on Computers C-28(1979) 747–753
9. Kurosawa, K., Satoh, T.: Generalization of higher order SAC to vector output Boolean functions. IEICE Transactions, E90 1(1998)
10. Maiorana, J.A.: A Class of Bent Functions., R41 Technical Paper (1971)
11. Maity, S., Maitra, S.: Minimum distance between bent and 1-resilient Boolean functions. In: Roy, B., Meier, W. (eds.): Fast Software Encryption. Lecture Notes in Computer Science, Vol. 3017. Springer-Verlag, Berlin (2004) 143–160
12. Meier, W., Staffelbach, O.: Nonlinearity criteria for cryptographic functions. In: Brassard, G. (ed.): Advances in Cryptology – EUROCRYPT '89. Lecture Notes in Computer Science, Vol. 434. Springer-Verlag, Berlin (1990) 549–562
13. Millan, W., Clark, A., Dawson, E.: Heuristic design of cryptographically strong balanced Boolean functions. In: Nyberg, K. (ed.): Advances in Cryptology EUROCRYPT '98. Lecture Notes in Computer Science, Vol. 1403. Springer-Verlag, Berlin (1998) 489–499
14. Mister, S., Adams, C.: Practical S-Box Design. In: Workshop on Selected Areas in Cryptography (SAC '96) Workshop Record. Queens University (1996) 61–76
15. Nyberg, K.: Constructions of bent functions and difference sets. In: Damgård, I.B. (ed.): Advances in Cryptology – EUROCRYPT '90. Lecture Notes in Computer Science, Vol. 473. Springer-Verlag, Berlin (1991) 151–160
16. Nyberg, K.: Perfect nonlinear S-boxes, Davies. In: D.W. (ed.): Advances of Cryptology – EUROCRYPT '91. Lecture Notes in Computer Science, Vol. 547. Springer-Verlag, Berlin (1991) 378–386
17. O'Connor, L.J.: An analysis of a class of algorithms for S-box construction. Journal of Cryptology 3(1994) 133–152
18. Pieprzyk, J., Hardjono, T., Seberry, J.: Fundamentals of Computer Security. Springer-Verlag, Berlin (2003)
19. Preneel, B, Van Leekwijck, W, Van Linden, L, Govaerts, R, Vandewalle, J.: Propagation characteristics of Boolean functions. In: Damgård, I.B. (ed.): Advances in Cryptology – EUROCRYPT '90. Lecture Notes in Computer Science, Vol. 473, Springer-Verlag, Berlin (1991) 161–173
20. Rothaus, O.S.: On bent functions. Journal of Combinatorial Theory, 20(1976) 300–305

21. Seberry, J., Zhang, X.M., Zheng, Y.: Systematic generation of cryptographically robust S-boxes. In: Proceedings of the 1st ACM Conference on Computer and Communication Security (1993)
22. Webster, A.F., Tavares, S.E.: On the Design of S-Boxes. In: Williams, H.C. (ed.): Advances in Cryptology – CRYPTO '85. Lecture Notes in Computer Science, Vol. 218. Springer-Verlag, Berlin (1986) 523–534
23. Yarlagadda, R., Hershey, J.E.: Analysis and synthesis of bent sequences. In: Proceedings of the IEE, vol.136 (1989) 112–123

Problems of Sending Sensitive Information

Eugeniusz Kuriata

University of Zielona Góra,
Institute of Control and Computation Engineering,
ul. Podgórna 50, 65-246 Zielona Góra,Poland,
e-mail:E.Kuriata@issi.uz.zgora.pl

Abstract: This paper addresses the problem of an electronic document generation in the case when sensitive information is proceded. Proposed schemes based on two-phase procedure of the message ciphering. It guarantees the required security level. In addition, all attributes of the physical carrier are satisfied. Furthermore, schemes are presented to illustrate clearly the proposed methodology of generating and deciphering the electronic document containing sensitive information.

Keywords: Generating of electronic document, public key infrastructure, sensitive information.

1 Introduction

The first countries that step in an information society will gain the greatest profits. Obviously, the countries that put such a decision aside or decide to apply only partial solutions may have economic problems like a decrease in the investment, competitiveness along with reduction of the work market [1,2].

It is well-known fact that telecommunications infrastructure improvement, especially development of new technologies in the teleinformation branch, gives an effect similar to the increase in the innovativeness of the economy. An economic growth and facilitate access to information conducive to an increase of many dangers, e.g. expose people to loss of their privacy. Appearance of such a kind of dangers necessities development of information security which fulfills the specification of privacy and security of network users. This should conducive to the fast development of electronic economy.

Developing information processing algorithms that contribute to the rise of the electronic document that is equivalent-in-law to the physically existing document is an element that dynamizes a common application of the teleinformatic infrastructure in the economy.

2 Circumstances and the legislative state of the electronic document

One of the most important tasks faced by governments of all countries in the World is the establishing such a law and technical conditions so as to ensure that the electronic information can be treated as a rightful document [1].

Development of mechanism ensuring that the features of electronic documents will be identical like that of physical ones will conducive, in particular, to the introduction of the electronic mail as an information circulation standard. In the light of the above statement, this will contribute to the development of the secure network. Such solutions are particularly expected by public administration as well as in business structures. Such a state will allow to connect internal networks of the departments, containing qualified information. This means that this is necessary to "acceptance of legislative procedures of establishing document validity and authenticity as well as digital signatures, original sanctity, conditions of copy preparation and modification, a lack of the possibility of signature withdrawing or forging and determining when saving entails legislative results" [2]. Works in this direction are led in many EU countries.

It is obvious that putting into practice new computer science technologies will cause an increase in the number of computer crimes and, in particular, teleinformatic crimes. More and more often, in the networks there appears illegal and harmful information pertaining pornography, materials of terror organizations, and nationalist groups as well as information conducive to the functioning of the organized crime including international one. Such information may result in serious economical losses of separate countries as well as in a global scale.

3 Generation of electronic document

In [2] there are defined features that must be possessed by the electronic information that can be treated as an electronic document. It has to possess features that are guarantied for the physical document, in particular

- guarantying confidentiality,
- guarantying possibility of authenticity checking,
- to make impossible to deny of electronic document preparation and sending by the sender (non-repudiation of sending) ,
- to make impossible to deny of electronic document receipt by the receiver (accountability of receipt) ,
- assurance of the moment (time) of document preparation,
- leading the evidence (saving), i.e. who had an access to information,
- leading the evidence (saving), i.e. when receiver got a given information,
- denoting who has an electronic document in a given moment.

Guarantying confidentiality for the electronic document may be optional [8] but in the case of sensitive information this requirement is absolutely necessary. Checking the authenticity of the electronic document containing sensitive information should be possible to do and it has to be realizable. Ensuring this feature makes it impossible to introduce any modification into the document both in the preparation process by the sender, transmission as well as the receipt by the receiver. All the changes appearing in the electronic document, after its preparation, should be detectable.

Non-repudiation of preparing an electronic document means that the sender of information cannot deny the fact that the document has been generated by himself and then send to the declared receiver. Such a mechanism make its impossible to withdrawn the generated and sent document.

Receiving accountability of the electronic document allows unambiguously establish who received a document and in the same way it makes it impossible that user declared by the sender will deny that he has received a document that has been meant for him. If forgery of the document happened during the transmission of the document then there exist the possibility to establish which of the participants taking part in the exchange of the information allow himself to forge the electronic document. In the case of sensitive documents, and in particular not public information, it is important to lead the registry with such information like: who had an access to the information, when a given user received a given information, as well as where presently is a document with a given information.

An electronic document, like any other document, should be accompanied with a time of its preparation. Till now there is no time signing standard of the electronic information. In [6, 8] as a time of preparing an electronic document the moment when the server signs the time pattern of the hash functions of the ciphered file is assumed.

Ensuring all features characteristic of information saved on a physical material will make more flexible the process of sending sensitive information in the form of electronic documents to specific, previously declared users.

In [8] electronic documents is formed by ciphered information, ciphered key of the symmetrical cryptographic system as well as timestamp concerning preparation of the document. Taking into account the necessity of guarantying additional features characteristic of sensitive information, it is necessary to apply additional mechanisms allowing an uninhibited distribution in the Internet, particularly classified information.

It is obvious that the lack of any of the previously described features of the electronic document or distortion of it discredit such information and it cannot be perceived as a document. In the case of not public information written on a physical material we can easily determine if it (the document) satisfies all the features specific of the document. The copy of such a document is not a document. If there is a prohibition of making copies from a document then possessing, by anybody, a copy of such a document is a proof for illegal leak of information. Thus, possessing an electronic document is not the same as possessing an information contained in an electronic document. An electronic document has a specified form and shape while the information contained in it may be in an arbitrarily form. In the case of not public information document circulation, including an electronic form, is rationed, but spreading the information around not entitled people both in oral or by other ways, is forbidden.

Nowadays, transmitting not public information is realized through special, separate corporation teleinformatic networks. It is allowed to transmit it through the open Internet network after doing the previously – described security procedures, e.g. ciphering. In the case when the information exchange takes places in the corporation network then transmission of sensitive information is allowed after previous authentication of the participants. If one of the addressees of such a information is the participant that is not a member of a given corporation then using of such a network or an access to its equipment is difficult (if not impossible).

The subsequent part of this paper presents an exchange information system that allows transmitting sensitive information through the open Internet network. It ensures all the features of the electronic document along with receipt confirmation (acquainting with the document by the receiver).

In order to ensure saving who had an access to a given information, when a given user got this information who has the document with the information it is necessary to accompany an electronic document by not public information, apart from ciphered information, a ciphered key, timestamp, additional information received from the corporation server.

An access management regarding sensitive information is the task of the corporation server.

The message sender declares a list of people who can acquaint with a given document as well as he defines the laws of the receivers with respect to the redistribution of this document. During the document generation, the part of the cipher key employed to ciphering the message, along with a list of people authorized to read this message, is sent to the corporation server that stores this data. In order to decipher the electronic document, the receiver of the message gets a key from the corporation server that transmits the message through the time server to the sender confirming the time in which the receiver acquaints with the document.

It is assumed in the system that the cipher key of the symmetrical cryptographic system is a sum of the hash function of the ciphered message and the hash function of the message identifier introduced by the message sender. Moreover the value of the hash function of the message identifier is sent to the corporation server. This means that the receiver cannot decipher a received message until getting the hash function of the message identifier. The corporation server notifies the fact of getting the message identifier as well as it sends a confirmation message to the sender notifying him that the receiver read the information addressed to him.

Checking if a given receiver may get an message identifier, may distribute sensitive information etc. is a function of the corporation server.

Figure 1 shows the algorithm of generating an electronic document of sensitive information.

Plain text M is sent to the coder of the symmetrical cryptographic system in order to cipher it as well as to determine its shortcut WSP which is summed in the summator with the hash function of the massage identifier.

$$WSP \oplus WSID = WSK.$$

WSK is announced to the coder of the symmetrical cryptographic system as a cipher key of message M. It should be strongly underlined that the cipher key is divided – one part of it is introduced by the message sender (ID) while the second one is functionally related with the message itself (*WSP*). As a ciphering result of file *M* we get a cryptogram *ZP*.

$$ZP = ((WSP \oplus WSID)M).$$

The hash function of file *WSP* is ciphered with the public key of the receiver E_O.

$$A = E_O(WSP)$$

and then with the private key of the sender D_N

$$B = D_N(A)$$

and it is added to the ciphered file *ZP*

$$Z = ZP\|B.$$

In order to signify the time of creating the electronic document the sender of the message calculates the value of the hash function ciphered file *WSZP* which is ciphered with his private key D_N

$$D = D_N(WSZP)$$

and then to the signed value of the ciphered file *D*, the sender includes his certificate *CN*

$$E = D\|CN$$

and then it is ciphered with the public key of the time server public key E_S

$$F = E_S(D\|CN)$$

and then it is sent to the time server.
The time server ciphers the received *F* with its private key D_S

$$F_S = D_S(F) = D\|CN$$

and then F_S separates the certificate of sender *CN*.
The time server accompanies *D* with the timestamp *ZCN*

$$U_S = D\|ZCN$$

and then U_S is ciphered with its private key D_S

$$H = D_S(U_S)$$

as well as with the public key of the sender EN

$$L = E_N(H).$$

L ciphered in such a way is sent by the time server to the sender of the message. All parameters that are necessary to determine the sender in order to send L to him are contained in the certificate obtained allow with F_S.

After receiving L the sender of the message performs its ciphering with his private key D_N

$$N = D_N(L)$$

and then N is ciphered with the public key of the server E_S

$$P = E_S(N).$$

From resulting P

$$P = D\|ZCN$$

one can get timestamp ZCN, while D is ciphered with the public key of the sender E_N

$$G = E_N(D),$$

and then it is compared in comparator ZC with the ciphered with the private key of the sender D_N of the hash function of the ciphered file $WSZP$.

If

$$G = D,$$

then it is assumed that timestamp ZCN has been included to the transmitted message, while the sender ciphers N with the public key of the receiver E_O

$$Q = E_O(N)$$

And he includes it to the ciphered file ZP as well as to the ciphered key B

$$W = Z\|Q = ZP\|B\|Q.$$

In the case when these quantities are different then receiver repeats his request for getting an improved timestamp.

The presented scheme is similar to the algorithm of generating an electronic document [6, 8].

In the case of sensitive information, and in particular in the case of not public information it is required, apart from the features ensured for the electronic document, to save who had an access to a given information, giving the possibility of the information receipt time as well as where is the information in a given moment. Such requirements may be fulfilled by introducing the corporation server whose task, in particular, storing the message identifier being part of the cipher key of the message M as well as it defines means which may have access to the information. People who will have an access to a given information are declared by the sender through detailing receiver certificates of this information. Each of the receivers, possessing appropriating rights, may redistribute this information but in this case he will be its sender and in the same way he will be responsible for its distribution.

The sender of the message sends to the corporation server the hash function of the ciphered message $WSZP$ along with the ciphered, with the public key of the receiver E_O, hash function of the message identifier $WSID$

$$ZWSID = E_O(WSID).$$

The certificate of receiver CO and its certificate

$$X = WSZP\|WSID\|CO\|CN$$

crypted previously value of X with the public key of the corporation server E_{SL}

$$U = E_{SL}(X)$$

and then crypted again with its private key D_N

$$Y = D_N(U).$$

After receiving Y, the corporation server is ciphering it with the public key of the sender E_N

$$V = E_N(Y)$$

and then with its private key D_{SL}

$$V_B = D_{SL}(V).$$

The triple: the hash function of the file *OWSZP*, the hash function of the identifier *OWSID* and the certificate (certificates) of the receiver *CO* is saved into the database in the corporation server. The certificate *CN* of the sender is saved in this database as well.

The resulting hash function of the ciphered file *OWSZP*, the corporation server is ciphering with the public key of the receiver E_O

$$R = E_O(OWSZP)$$

and then with its private key D_{SL}

$$S = D_{SL}(R).$$

After receiving from the corporate server, the ciphered message *S*, the sender of the message is deciphering it with the public key of the corporation server E_{SL}

$$T = E_{SL}(S) = R.$$

This message is compared in the comparator *NI* with the ciphered with the public key of the receiver E_O, of the hash function of file *WSZP*

$$TT = E_O(WSZP).$$

When the values

$$T = TT$$

then the server is appending the value of *S* to the value of *W*

$$ZD = W\|S$$

and then is sending to the receiver of the message. On the other hand, if

$$T \neq TT$$

then the sender renews the attempt to get the correct value of *S* form the corporation server.

Figure 2 shows the algorithm of deciphering an electronic document of sensitive information.

After obtaining the ciphered message *OZP*, the ciphered key *OB*, the ciphered time-stamp *OQ* and signed through corporation server ciphered with public key of the receiver E_O ciphered the hash function of the OS the receiver is separating these values.

Such a received hash function of the file $OWSZP$, ciphered with the public key of the receiver E_O and then with the private key of corporation server D_{SL}

$$OS = D_{SL}\left(E_o\left(OWSZP\right)\right)$$

then receiver is ciphering it with the public key of the corporation server E_{SL}

$$OR = E_{SL}\left(OS\right)$$

and then with its private key D_O

$$DD = D_O\left(OR\right).$$

The resulted value of DD is compared in the comparator ZCR with the hash function of the ciphered file $WSOZP$ and if the following condition holds

$$WSOZP = DD.$$

It means, that received document was registered in the corporation server and to deciphering process it is essential to get the hash function of the identifier $WSID$ from the server.

Without the hash function of the identifier $WSID$, the receiver of the message is not able to decipher the file M, because its ciphered key is a sum of the hash function $WSID$ and the hash function of the file WSP

$$WSK = WSID \oplus WSP,$$

In the value of B there occurs only the hash function of WSP in the sent package ZD distinct from the scheme of generating the electronic document presented in [6, 8].

In order to obtain the hash function of the identifier $WSID$, the receiver of the message appends the certificate of the sender CN and its certificate CO to the hash function of the file

$$PP = WSOZP\|CO\|CN$$

and then the value PP is ciphered with the public key of the corporation server E_{SL}

$$OA = E_{SL}\left(WSOZP\right)$$

and then with its private key D_O

$$OB = D_O(OA)$$

finally, it is sent to the corporation server.

The received message OB is ciphered in the corporation server with the public key of the receiver E_O

$$OC = E_O(OB)$$

and then with its private key D_{SL}

$$OD = D_{SL}(OC) = WSOZP\|CO\|CN .$$

In the comparator KZ value of the hash function of the ciphered file $WSOZP$ is compared with the received hash function of the ciphered file $OWSZP$ stored in the database in the corporation server.

In the comparator KO certificate of the receiver CO is compared with certificate of the receiver CO stored in the database in the corporation server.

In the comparator KN certificate of the sender CN is compared with certificate of the sender CN stored in the database in the corporation server.

If the following condition holds

$$WSOZP = OWSZP \text{ and } CO = CO(Database) \text{ and}$$
$$CN = CN(Database)$$

then the corporation server appends the certificate of the sender CN and its certificate CC to the ciphered file $WSOZP$

$$ON = WSOZP\|CN\|CC$$

and is ciphering message ON with the public key of the time server E_S

$$GF = E_S(ON)$$

and is sending it to the time server in order to forward to the sender and storing into the time database the timer pointer of receiving message M by the receiver. Moreover, the corporation server is ciphering with its private key D_{SL} the received ciphered hash function of the identifier $OZWSID$, which is stored in the database

$$OE = D_{SL}(OZWSID)$$

and is sending it to the receiver of the electronic document.

After receiving the message OE, the receiver is ciphering it with the public key of the corporation server E_{SL}

$$OH = E_{SL}(OE).$$

And this resulted message is ciphered with the private key of the receiver D_O

$$OF = D_O(OH)$$

in the next step, it is summed with the receives hash function of $OWSP$. $OWSP$ is obtained by deciphering the ciphered key OB i.e. with the sender's public key E_N

$$OL = E_N(OB)$$

and next, with the receiver's private key D_O

$$OWSP = D_O(OK).$$

OH and $OWSP$ are summed

$$OK = OH \oplus OWSP$$

and if $OH = WSID$, then OK is the symmetric ciphering key for the cryptographic system, in which the ciphered file OZP can be deciphered. For the obtained message OM, the hash function OWS is determined. OWS is compared with $OWSP$ (obtained due to the deciphering the key OB) in the comparator I.
If $OWSP$ and OWS are equal, then it is assumed that received file is genuine

$$OWSP = OWS,$$

then we assume that obtained file OM is an authentic.
After determining the hash function of the received file $WSOZ$, the receiver of the message is ciphering the received pointer of the time OQ signed by the server, with its private key D_O

$$SS = D_O(OQ)$$

and then with the server of time public key E_S

$$SP = E_S(SS) = U_S$$

where

$$U_S = D\|ZCN.$$

The time pointer *ZCN* got during generation of the electronic document is extracted form *SP* and *D* is ciphered with the public key of the sender E_N

$$SU = E_N(D).$$

SU is compared with the hash function of the ciphered file *WSOZP* in the comparator *T*.
If

$$SU = WSOZP$$

then the time pointer *ZCN* has been appended to the received message *M*.
After receiving message *GF* the time sever is deciphering it with its private key D_S

$$PR = D_S(GF).$$

The certificate of the sender *CN* and the certificate of the corporation server *CC* are extracted from *PR*

$$HH = WSOZP$$

and then the pointer of time of the received electronic document *ZCO* is appended to the value *HH*

$$HT = HH\|ZCO = WSOZP\|ZCO$$

and the value HT is sent to the sender of the electronic document. Simultaneously, the time server ciphers *HT* with the public key of the sender E_N

$$HL = E_N(HT)$$

and then with its private key D_S

$$HN = D_S(HL),$$

which is send through server into the receiver of electronic document. At the same time, the time server is ciphering the value of *HT* with its private key D_S

$$HP = D_S(HT)$$

and then with public key of the corporation server E_{SL}

$$HR = E_{SL}(HP)$$

which the server send to the corporation server.

After receiving the message *HR*, the corporation server is deciphering it with its private key D_{SL}

$$TK = D_{SL}(HR)$$

and then with the public key of the time server E_S

$$TE = E_S(TK) = HT,$$

where

$$HT = HH\|ZCO = WSOZP\|ZCO.$$

Size of *WSOZP* is compared with size of *OWSZP* from the database on the corporation server in the comparator *SL* and if

$$WSOZP = OWSZP$$

then for a given receiver (defined by the certificate *CO*) the time stamp of the access to electronic document *ZCO* is kept in the memory.

After receiving the time pointer HN from the time server, the sender of the message is deciphering it with the public key of the time server E_S

$$HS = E_S(HN)$$

and next with its private key D_N

$$FF = D_N(HS) = ON = WSOZP\|ZCO.$$

The sender extracts the time stamp *ZCO* from *ON*, which points the time of the access to the electronic document by the receiver and the obtained size of *WSOZP* is compared with size of *WSZP* in the comparator *OD*.

If the following holds

$$WSOZP = WSZP,$$

then the sender of the message, assumes that receiver received the message and acquainted the content sent to it electronic document.

The receiver of the electronic document ciphers the obtained time stamp OQ with its private key D_O

$$Q = E_O\left(D_N\left(E_N\left(D_S\left(D\|ZCN\right)\right)\right)\right) = E_O\left(D_S\left(D\|ZCN\right)\right)$$

ciphered its private key D_O

$$RR = D_O\left(OQ\right)$$

and then with the public key of the time server E_S

$$RT = E_S\left(RR\right) = D\|ZCN$$

it extracts the time stamp ZCN from RT.

The receiver ciphers the value D with the public key of the sender E_N

$$RG = E_N\left(D\right)$$

in the comparator T, the value of RG is compared with the hash function of the received file $WSOZP$.

If values

$$RG = WSOZP$$

then it is assumed that the time stamp ZCN has been appended to the received OM. On the contrary, if

$$RG \neq WSOZP$$

then the receiver questions the received electronic document, suspecting that the time stamp has been appended to another file.

It is obvious, that there exists a possibility of committing the forgery in such a way, that for a given file, the time stamp can be obtained earlier and use it at the moment of generation of the document. Such a operation would cause, that the time of the creating the document would be earlier than the real time of the generating the document. In the case, when the time of accessing the document is considered simultaneously, so the last one is the real time.

4 Conclusions

Presented in the paper framework of generating the electronic document for the sensitive information requires the detailed procedure. For the information stored on the physical carrier, the procedure allowing the secure exchange of the information has been developed. Presented way of securing the information causes, that it characterize all features for the information stored on the physical carrier

Advantages of the presented procedure can be itemized as follows:
- the owner (sender) of the message specifies the set of entitled for the accessing to the content of it persons,
- the corporation server limits possibilities of the information redistribution, by unauthorized persons (the sender gives the rights for the accessing the message),
- the existence of the corporation server prevents redistribution of the sensitive information (this is the analogical case to copying the not public document – it is allowed to read it and is not to make a copy),
- the sender gets the confirmation with the time stamp, that the receiver has read the content of the electronic document,
- forcing users of the sensitive information to apply the security rules due to organization,
- confirmation of the accessing to the document (the time stamp) is done by the time server and the corporation server initializes such a procedure,
- possibility of the not public information distribution in Internet,
- possibility of downloading the sensitive data without necessity of physical accessing to selected networks,
- there exists a possibility to specify entities entitled to accessing the sensitive information.

The drawbacks of the presented procedures are:
- there is no explicit possibility removing the owner of the sensitive information at the receiver's side
- the fact of removing the electronic document, containing sensitive information relies on the statement of the receiver
- complex database in the corporation server
- a monitoring of the corporation server can be the possible point of failure
- the security of the distribution the electronic documents is depends on the proper working of the corporation server database

Beside the drawbacks, the presented procedure can be applied to more dynamical distribution of the sensitive information.

References

1. Aims and directions of informatics society developing in Poland Act of polish Government about the process of building the informatics society. (Stanowisko Rady Ministrów w sprawie uchwały Sejmu RP z dnia 14 lipca 2000r. W sprawie budowania podstaw społeczeństwa informacyjnego w Polsce, druk sejmowy nr 2435). (in polish)
2. Document of Polish Government about the electronic documents interchange. (Propozycje legislacyjne w zakresie uznania elektronicznej wymiany dokumentów (EDI) jako równoważnej obiegowi dokumentów papierowych, Raport Zespołu ds. Dokumentu Elektronicznego, Rada Koordynacyjna ds. Teleinformatyki przy Radzie Ministrów, Warszawa), September 1996. (in polish)

3. Document of Polish Government about the national security and public order. (Rozporzą-
    dzenie Ministra Infrastruktury z dnia 24 stycznia 2003 r. w sprawie wykonywania przez
    operatorów zadań na rzecz obronności, bezpieczeństwa państwa oraz bezpieczeństwa i
    porządku publicznego (Dz.U.2003 nr 19 poz.166)). (in polish)
4. E. Krouk. A new Public Key Cryptosystem. Proc. of Sixth Joint Swedish-Russian Intern.
    Workshop on Information Theory, 1993
5. E. Kuriata – Method of encryption keys generating. Patent submission no. P325317. (in
    polish)
6. E. Kuriata – Method of generation of electronic document with timestamp, Patent sub-
    mission no. P366965 (05.04.2004) (in polish)
7. E. Kuriata, M. Jędraszek, R. Barańczak. Risk of fabrication of electronic document. In:
    Zastosowania rozwiązań informatycznych w bankowości. Akademia Ekonomiczna we
    Wrocławiu. Wrocław 2000. (in polish)
8. E. Kuriata, P.B. Myszkowski - The Electronic Document, Computing, Multimedia and
    Intelligent Techniques – special issue: Live biometrics and security. – 2005, Vol. 1, no 1,
    s.163 - 171: Częstochowa.
9. E. Kuriata, T. Hebisz – Key Space in Cryptographic Systems based on Reed-Solomon
    Code, IEEE Transaction on Dependable and Secure Computing (in print)
10. E. Kuriata, T. Hebisz – Problems of fulfilling of accessibility of information in real-time
    systems. PAK, No 4 2005 (in polish)
11. Europe and the global information society: Recommendations to the European Council,
    Brussels 26 may 1994 – Report Bangemanna.
12. J. McNamara. Secrets of Computer Espionage, Wiley Publishing Inc. 2003.
13. PGP Homepage http://www.pgp.com/.
14. R. J. McEliece. A Public Key Cryptosystem Based on Algebraic Coding Theory.
    JPLDSN Progress Rept., 1978
15. Schneier B., "Applied Cryptography. Protocols, Algorithms, and Source Code in C".
    John Wiley & Sons, 1994

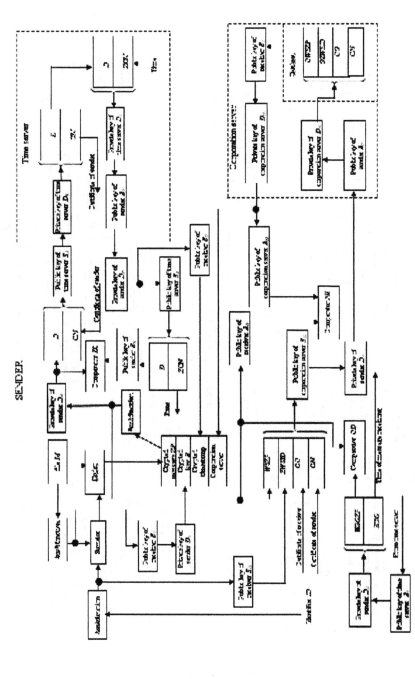

Fig. 1. Algorithm of generation of electronic document of sensitive information

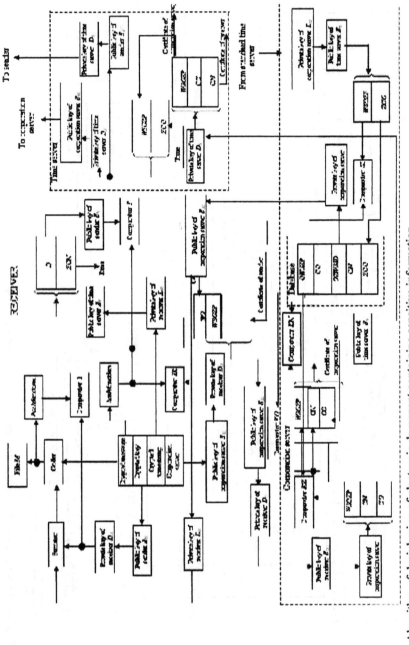

Fig. 2. Algorithm of deciphering of electronic document containing sensitive information

Hash Chaining for Authenticated Data Structures Freshness Checking

Eugeniusz Kuriata[1], Witold Maćków[2], and Paweł Sukiennik[2]

[1] University of Zielona Góra, Faculty of Electrical Engineering, Computer Science and Telecommunications, ul. Podgórna 50
65-246 Zielona Góra, Poland
E.Kuriata@issi.uz.zgora.pl
[2] Szczecin University of Technology, Faculty of Computer Sience and Information Systems, ul. Żołnierska 49
71-210 Szczecin, Poland
{wmackow, psukiennik}@wi.ps.pl

Abstract. In systems based on public key infrastructure in most cases we depend on trusted third party. Development of computer security systems and increase in popularity of public key infrastructure and its uses led to development of new data distribution methods – distribution based on untrusted publishers. It is possible to publish data by an untrusted publisher, however this data must contain authentication information in it. Validation of that information allows verification of information origin. Starting with certificate revocation list, certificate revocation trees we analyze these structures and find their strengths and weaknesses. By improving their strengths and eliminating their weaknesses we introduce a method for publishing data and their authentication information by an untrusted publisher. Basic concept of existing solutions is described in chapter 1. Chapter 2 introduced our method for publishing self authenticated data structures. Conclusions are described in chapter 3.

1 Authenticated structures

1.1 Basic concept

Data structure authentication was at first developed for Certification Revocation Lists (CRL's) used in Public Key Infrastructure. New group of efficient certificate revocation methods was based on authenticated structures, exactly on authenticated dictionaries. Dictionaries are common data structures that support search, insert and delete operations. Authenticated dictionaries are dictionaries that additionally contain authentication information. In this manner, data owner (O) may spread information by untrusted publishers (P). End entities – clients (C) – may verify correctness of received data. Schema of such a system is shown on Fig 1. The Merkle hash tree scheme was used to implement the simplest static authenticated dictionary – Certificate Revocation Tree (CRT) presented in [5]. Skip List [3] and 2-3 tree [10] were used for dynamic implementations of authenticated dictionaries. Interesting usage of cryptographic accumulators for data sets authentication was defined in [4].

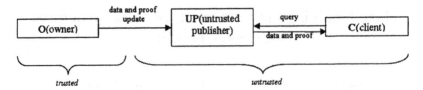

Fig. 1. Authenticated data flow between data owner, untrusted publisher and client

1.2 Structure definitions

We base our further considerations on a general model of authenticated data structures proposed in [7] and discussed in [11]. This structure consists of a directed acyclic graph G, an associated search procedure S and a proof of structure authenticity P. We denote the whole structure as (G, S, P).

Directed Acyclic Graph (G). Graph is defined as $G = (V, E)$, where V is a set of vertexes and E is a set of edges. We define function d to describe a degree of graph vertex $\forall v \in V : d(v) = d^+(v) + d^-(v) + d^o(v) + d^-(v)$. Because graph is acyclic and directed, only $d^+(v)$ and $d^-(v)$ parts may be different from 0. We call these parts outdegree and indegree of vertex v. We can define them as follows: $d^+(v) = \left|\Gamma^+(v)\right|$, where $\Gamma^+(v)$ is a set of vertex v successors, and $d^-(v) = \left|\Gamma^-(v)\right|$, where $\Gamma^-(v)$ is a set of vertex v predecessors. We can define a set R of nodes $\exists R \subset V : \forall r \in R : d^-(r) = 0$, further called *roots* and a set L of nodes $\exists L \subset V : \forall l \in L : d^+(l) = 0$, called *leafs*. We make assumption that graph is connected. There is exactly one root in our graph ($\left|R\right| = 1$) and there are many leafs ($\left|L\right| \geq 1$). Each vertex v posses: key information $\delta_k(v)$, successors information $\delta_s(v)$ and additional information $\delta_a(v)$. We will use notation $\delta(v)$ for whole information placed in vertex. In addition we assume, that all successors of v are arranged in a strict order (we can always find first one, second one and so on).

Search procedure (S). Owner should define deterministic search procedure S. Procedure takes as an input search key q and starting from the root node begins comparison of visited vertex keys. On the basis of this comparison procedure query q returns answer Q or continues searching one of successors of last visited vertex. Search procedure in BST is a classical example : if q value is equal to vertex key $\delta_k(v)$, this vertex is returned. If q is smaller then $\delta_k(v)$, the first (left) successor will be visited and searched, if q is greater then $\delta_k(v)$ the second (right) successor will be chosen for searching.

Proof of authenticity (P). Owner should chose collision-intractable hash function h. The authentication information α is associated with each node:

$$\alpha(v) = \begin{cases} h(\delta(v)) : v \in L \\ h(\delta(v), \alpha(v_1),...,\alpha(v_i)) : v \notin L \end{cases}$$

where $v_1, ..., v_i$ are ordered successors of v vertex ($\Gamma^+(v) = \{v_1,...,v_i\}$). In this manner we can compute general authentication information $\alpha(r)$, where r is a *root*. This value is obviously dependent on all other vertexes. There is a proof of authenticity P for whole graph prepared on the base of general authentication information. In classical solutions owner posses a pair of keys (a private and a public key) and in a final stage the general authentication information is signed by owners private key, where P is created as result. Use of this authentication information will be explained in the next section.

1.3 Actions

1.3.1 Owner data update

Owner updates his data set inserting or removing some data. Usually parts of data structure should be rebuild after such action. Update information should be sent to the untrusted publisher (1.3.2 Publisher data update). Moments, when data changes are collected in a set $TU = \{tu_0, tu_1, tu_2, ...\}$.

Insert operation. Owner wants to add a new data to the data structure in moment tu_i. There is an insertion procedure I defined for particular graph type. It takes as an input key value k and additional information associated with that key. Procedure can be divided into three stages: 1) search of predecessor for new vertex (based on search procedure S); 2) creation of new vertex and partial reconstruction of the graph (if any construction rules were violated); 3) update action described in *Update finalization* (for example partial reconstruction of authentication information).

Delete operation. Owner wants to remove data from structure. There is a deletion procedure D defined for particular graph type. It takes as an input key value k. Procedure can be divided into three stages: 1) search for vertex containing k key (based on search procedure S); 2) removal of located vertex and partial reconstruction of the graph (if any construction rules were violated); 3) update action described in *Update finalization* (for example partial reconstruction of authentication information).

Update finalization. All vertexes, which were changed during the second stage may be temporarily marked and only for these vertexes new value $\alpha(v)$ will be computed. Finally general authentication information $\alpha(v)$ is computed. Value $\alpha(v)$ is generated from updated graph in time tu_i and we mark it as $\alpha(r, tu_i)$. The owner O owns a pair of keys: *SO* (a secret key) and *PO* (a public key). He signs $\alpha(r,tu_i)$ with his private key and creates a proof $P(tu_i) = \{\ \alpha(r,tu_i),\ SIG_{SO}\ (\ \alpha(r,tu_i)\ )\}$. The process of creating a new graph is finished. In addition, owner O generates additional update information, which are send to untrusted publisher P instead of sending the entire graph. New update information consists of:

- removed subgraph U_R, defined as: $U_R(tu_i) = G(tu_{i-1})\setminus G(tu_i)$;

- added subgraph U_A, defined as: $U_A(tu_i) = G(tu_i)\setminus G(tu_{i-1})$.

Example on how to create update information was shown in Fig 2.

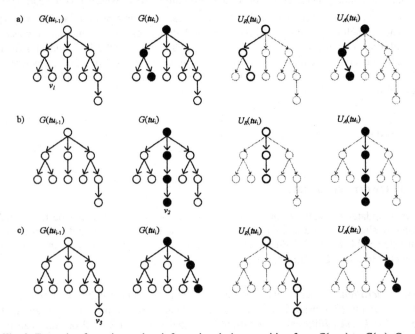

Fig. 2. Example of creating update information during transition from $G(tu_{i-1})$ to $G(t_{ui})$. Cases: a) value $\delta_a(v_1)$ was changed, b) vertex v_2 was deleted, c) vertex v_3 was added.

1.3.2 Publisher date update

Publisher data update may be initiated by publisher himself (active waiting) or by owner (updates broadcasting). After initiation, update data is transmitted to the publisher and necessary reconstruction is made. Moments of publisher data updates are collected in a set $TP = \{tp_0, tp_1, tp_2, ...\}$.

Data transmission. Owner (O) sends current update information $U(tu_i)$ and proof $P(tu_i)$ to untrusted publisher (UP) (tu_i denotes time of last owner data update).

O→UP: $\{\ U_R(tu_i),\ U_A(tu_i),\ P(tu_i)\}$

Structure update. Update begins at time tp_j ($tu_i \geq tp_j > tu_{i+1}$). If received proof $P(tu_i)$ differs from last local copy of a proof $P'(tp_{j-1})$, the data structure reconstruction is needed. Publisher prepares his copy of a graph $G'(tp_j)$, defined as: $G'(tp_j) = [G'(tp_{j-1}) \setminus U_R(tu_i)] \cup U_A(tu_i)$, where $G'(tp_j)$ is a publisher copy of $G(tu_i)$ and $G'(tp_{j-1})$ is a publisher copy of $G(tu_{i-1})$. New proof $P'(tp_j) = P(tu_i)$ is also published.

1.3.3 Client query

Client query. Client (C) sends query q to the untrusted publisher (UP). For simplicity we made assumption that q value is a key of needed vertex.

C→UP: { q }

Publisher response. Untrusted publisher starts search procedure S for value q. Finally vertex v_q is reached. The v_q is wanted vertex (if $\delta_k(v_q) = q$), or v_q is the last visited vertex (if key q was not found). All vertexes on the path from root to v_q create ordered set $p(v_q) = \{r, v_1, ..., v_q\}$. Successors of all vertexes from path create set $\Gamma_p^+(v_q) = \bigcup_{v \in p(v_q)} \Gamma^+(v)$. Publisher prepares set $\Delta(v_q) = \{\delta(v) : v \in p(v_q)\}$ and set $A(v_q) = \{\alpha(v) : v \in \Gamma_p^+(v_q) \setminus p\}$. Both sets are prepared on the bases of the last local copy of graph $G'(tp_j)$ and then send to the client along with last proof $P' = P'(tp_j)$.

UP→C: { $\Delta(v_q)$, $A(v_q)$, P' }

Response verification. Last element of $\Delta(v_q)$ is an answer for query q (value $\delta(v_q)$). Other information received from untrusted publisher (UP) are used for authenticity verification only. Authentication information $\alpha'(r)$ is calculated according to definition:

$$\alpha'(v) = \begin{cases} h(\delta(v)) : v \in p(v_q) \cap L \\ h(\delta(v), \alpha(v_1), ..., \alpha(v_i)) : v \in p(v_q) \setminus L \\ \alpha(v) : \Gamma_p^+(v_q) \setminus p(v_q) \end{cases}$$

In other words: $\alpha'(r)$ is computed on the basis of $\Delta(v_q)$ and $A(v_q)$. Client compares calculated $\alpha'(r)$ and original $\alpha(r, tu_i)$ (received in P') and verifies owner signature. We assume, that the client C is in possession of owners public key (PO) and can verify signature $SIG_{SO}(\alpha(r, tu_i))$, which is a part of the proof P'.

1.4 Possible publisher fraud

There is vulnerability in presented system. Untrusted publisher may be dishonest or just unreliable. Client has no possibility to verify freshness of untrusted publisher data, which were used to create an answer. We present such an example situation:

- there are two updates of owners data in moments tu_{i-1} and tu_i (where $tu_{i-1} < tu_i$); updated structures are denoted $G(tu_{i-1})$ and $G(tu_i)$, updated proofs $P(tu_{i-1})$ and $P(tu_i)$; second update concerns insertion of data associated with key q;
- dishonest untrusted publisher ignores last update ($G(tu_i)$ and $P(tu_i)$); his current local data are based on previous update: $G'(tp_j) = G(tu_{i-1})$ and $P'(tp_j) = P(tu_{i-1})$;
- client asks about element associated with key q at moment t_q ($t_q > tu_i$); answer from untrusted publisher is prepared on the basis of an obsolete data (there's no element associated with key q in $G'(tp_j)$); client correctly verifies an answer (whole path and signature) and he is sure that element he seek for wasn't located.

2 Protection schema

2.1 Existing solution

Solution was discussed in [7]. When publisher updates data, only $G(tu_{i-1})$ is sent from owner to untrusted publisher. Clients query is a little modified: proof of authenticity P' is received directly from owner O. In case of publisher fraud (usage of obsolete data) general authentication information $\alpha'(r)$ computed from publisher data will differ from signed proof P' received from owner. This solution clashes with main idea of authenticated structure usage – data distribution without owner activity.

2.2 Our proposal

2.2.1 First solution: asynchronous proof updates with proof signing

We separate publisher data update and publisher proof update processes (shown in Fig 3). Data structure update is the same as in base schema. Each change (e.g. adding new element) requires reconstruction of graph (optional) and preparation of new authentication value $\alpha(r, tu_i)$. Update subgraphs are generated similarly $U_{Rs}(tu_i)$ and $U_A (tu_i)$. Changes refer to method the proof $P(tu_i)$ is generated.

Generation of proof. The owner sets commonly known period of proof validity Δt. Succeeding proofs are generated in constant periods of time Δt. Proof $P(tu_i, n)$ (tu_i is a time of data structures update and n is a sequent proof number starting with tu_i) is defined as follow: $P(tu_i, n) = \{ \ \alpha(r, tu_i) , \ tu_i, \ n, \ SIG_{SO} (\ \alpha(r, tu_i) , \ tu_i, \ n) \}$

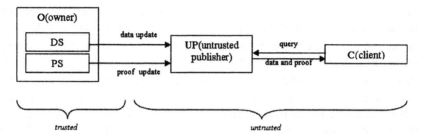

Fig. 3. Authenticated data flow between data owner, untrusted publisher and client with separation of data and proof updates. DS denotes data update service, PS denotes proofs update service.

It is obvious, that the moment when proof is generated is $tu_i + n*\Delta t$. Example is presented in Fig 4

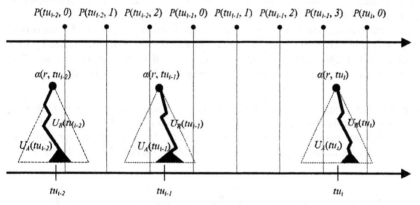

Fig. 4. Data and owner proofs update. Data update (lower axis) is set in tu_{i-2}, tu_{i-1} and tu_i. Proof update (upper axis) is set in constant periods of time.

Untrusted publisher local data update. The update is similar to the base schema, however, instead of { $U_R(tu_i)$, $U_A(tu_i)$, $P(tu_i)$}, set { $U_R(tu_i)$, $U_A(tu_i)$ } is send from owner to the untrusted publisher. Local data structure update is identical to the base schema, we just skip proof update.

$O\rightarrow UP$: { $U_R(tu_i)$, $U_A(tu_i)$ }

Untrusted publisher proof update. The update can be initialized by both: the publisher or by the owner. As an effect, the owner sends updated proof to publisher. Untrusted publisher stores local copy of the proof: $P'(tp_j) = P(tu_i, n)$.

$O\rightarrow UP$: { $P(tu_i, n)$}

Client query. Client C sends query to the untrusted publisher similar to the base schema. As an answer he receives $\{\ \Delta(v_q)$, $A(v_q)$, $P'\}$. Answer authenticity verification is also the same as the base schema, but only to the moment, where calculated values $\alpha'(r)$ are compared with $P'=\{\ \alpha(r,tu_i)$, tu_i, n, $SIG_{SO}(\alpha(r,tu_i)$, tu_i, $n)\}$. The client compares $\alpha'(r)$ and $\alpha(r,tu_i)$, verifies owner signature and makes the decision whether time of proof creation $tu_i + n*\Delta t$ satisfies him. This way untrusted publisher does not have to constantly update entire data but only proofs. If for some reason (e.g. fraud attempt) untrusted publisher does not own updated proof and will issue post dated proof, the client can make a decision whether to accept or reject it. The need to constantly generate proofs (which is signing authenticated data) will put big load of job on the owner. It is the major disadvantage of this method.

2.2.2 Second solution: asynchronous proof updates with hash chaining

The next solution is a modification of the previous proposition. It is based on schemas presented in [8] and [9]. It is commonly known, that making a hash from information is up to 10000 times faster then signing that information [9]. In proposed schema only first proof made after data update is signed. The remaining proofs are created by hash function. Owner data structure update is similar to the previous proposition. The changes are made in the way the proof is generated, updated and verified.

Generation of proof. The owner sets a commonly known proof validity period Δt. After data update he also generates secret value R in time tu_i and sets maximum number - d of proof updates generated from that proof. In next step, owner generates values: $R_0, R_1, R_2, \ldots, R_i, \ldots, R_{d-1}, R_d$, where $R_i = H^{d+1-i}(R)$, and H is a hash function.

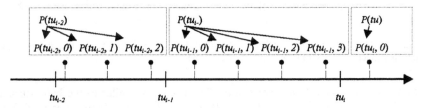

Fig 5. Periodic proof updates after data updates.

Base proof is defined as follow: $P(tu_i) = \{\ \alpha(r,tu_i)$, tu_i, R_0, d, $SIG_{SO}(\alpha(r,tu_i)$, tu_i, R_0, $d)\}$. Next proof update (generated in constant periods of time Δt) for $tu_i + n*\Delta t$ is defined as: $P(tu_i, n) = \{\ R_{d-n}, n\}$. Fig 5 presents an example of this operation.

Untrusted publisher proof update. The update can by initialized by publisher or by owner and is made of two stages:
- uploading base proof, distinctive for actual data update: O→UP: $\{\ P(tu_i)\}$
- uploading for distinctive base proof: O→UP: $\{\ P(tu_i, n)\ \}$.

Untrusted publisher stores local copy of proof $P'(tp_j) = \{\ P(tu_i), P(tu_i, n)\}$.

Client query. Client C sends a query to untrusted publisher the same as in the base schema. As an answer he also receives $\{\ \Delta(v_q)$, $A(v_q)$, P'$\}$. Answer authenticity

verification is also the same, up to the moment when computed $\alpha'(r)$ value is compared with P' data. P' also contains base proof of the last data update and last proof update (P(tu$_i$) and P(tu$_i$, n)), therefore: P' = { $\alpha(r, tu_i)$, tu$_i$, R$_0$, d, SIG$_{SO}$ ($\alpha(r, tu_i)$, tu$_i$, R$_0$, d), R$_{d-n}$, n }.
Client compares $\alpha'(r)$ and $\alpha(r, tu_i)$, verifies owner signature and makes a decision whether time of proof generation $tu_i + n*\Delta t$ satisfies him. Signature verification confirms only authenticity of base proof. The user verifies authenticity of proof update in a separated process. At first, value $R_x = H^{d-n}(R_{d-n})$ is calculated and after that, this value is compared with R$_0$ from base proof. If they are identical, update is authentic. Both values should be identical, because: $R_x = H^{d-n}(R_{d-n}) = H^{d-n}(H^{d-d+n+1}(R)) = H^{d-n}(H^{n+1}(R)) = H^{d+1}(R) = H^{d+0+1}(R) = R_0$.
Untrusted publisher is not able to generate false update, because he would need R value to do so, or one of the hashes from the chain used to generate future proofs updates (which in fact was not published before).

3 Conclusions

Trust is now a days a major problem when dealing with information security and authentication. Not every publisher or data server can be trusted when one would like to use information supplied by it. Proposed schema could be successfully used to publish data (e.g. certificate revocation lists) by untrusted publishers. Presented method is safe, efficient and reliable. It could be easily adapted to many branches of information systems, not only to public key infrastructure but data mining in general. Implementation of the method should be our next concern. More examination must be made to verify methods weaknesses and strengths.

References

1. Diestel R.: Graph Theory, Electronic Edition 2000, Springer-Verlag, New York (2000), pp.2-26
2. Even S., Goldreich O., Micali S.: On-Line/Off-Line Digital Signatures, Journal of Cryptology, Springer-Verlag, Vol. 9 (1996), pp. 35-67,
3. Goodrich M., Tamassia R., Schwerin A.: Implementation of an Authenticated Dictionary with Skip Lists and Commutative Hashing, Proc. DARPA Information Survivability Conference and Exposition (DISCEX '01), IEEE Press, vol. 2 (2001), pp. 68-82
4. Goodrich M., Tamassia R., Hasic J.: An Efficient Dynamic and Distributed Cryptographic Accumulator, Proc. Information Security Conference (ISC 2002) Lecture Notes in Computer Science, vol. 2433, Springer-Verlag (2002), pp. 372-388
5. Kocher P.: A Quick Introduction to Certificate Revocation Trees(CRTs), Technical report, ValiCert, (1999)
6. Maćków W.: Linked authenticated dictionaries for certificate status verification, Enhanced Methods in Computer Security, Biometric and Artificial Intelligence Systems, Springer (2005), pp.35-46,
7. Martel C., Nuckolls G., Devanbu P., Gertz M., Kwong A., Stubblebine S.: A General Model for Authentic Ddata Structures, Algorithmica (2001)
8. Micali S.: Efficient Certificate Revocation, Technical Memo MIT/LCS/TM-542b, (1996)

9.   Muñoz J., Forné J., Esparza O., Bernabe I., Soriano M.: Using OCSP to secure certifi-
     cate-using transactions in m-commerce, Applied Cryptography and Network Security,
     vol. 2846 of LNCS, Springer-Verlag (2003), pp. 280-292
10. Naor M., Nissim K.: Certificate Revocation and Certificate Update, Proceedings 7th
     USENIX Security Symposium, San Antonio, Texas, (1998)
11. Tamassia R., Triandopoulos N.: On the Cost of Authenticated data Structures, Technical
     Report, Brown University, (2003)
12. Tamassia R., Triandopoulos N.: Computational Bounds on Hierarchical Data Processing
     with Applications to Information Security, Technical Report, Brown University, (2004)

Stream Cipher Keys Generation with Low Power Consumption Based on LFSR

Miroslaw Puczko[1], Vyatcheslav Yarmolik[2]
Bialystok University of Technology, Computer Science Department
15-351 Bialystok, Wiejska 45A, Poland

[1]mpuczko@ii.pb.bialystok.pl
[2]yarmolik@ii.pb.bialystok.pl

Abstract. A method of stream cipher keys generation with low power consumption based on LFSR (Linear Feedback Shift Register) is presented in this paper. The idea of power consumption minimization by modifying the structure of main element of cipher keys generator (LFSR) have been proposed. In this paper some examples are included.

1 Introduction

Key generation is the main problem during designing a stream cipher. It generates a key which is as long as the plain message. Each binary digit in the message is encrypted through a function which reads a corresponding binary digit within the key, and also takes into account additional information contained in the plaintext.

The most common tool in generating such random series is the Linear Feedback Shift Register (LFSR), which is a described by its primitive polynomial. Some pseudo-random non linear pattern generators based on LFSR used in stream cipher cryptography are presented in [1]: the Geffe generator, the Jennings generator, the Beth-Piper stop-and-go generator, the Gollmann cascade stop-and-go generator. Stream ciphers can be used to encrypt the plaintext message to form the ciphertext.

2 Power consumption and switching activity

We assume that mentioned cipher keys generators are made in CMOS technology which guarantee low power consumption for keys generation. The average power consumption in conventional CMOS digital circuits can be expressed as the sum of three main components, namely, (1) the dynamic (switching) power consumption, (2) the short-circuit power consumption, and (3) the leakage power consumption. If the system or chip includes circuits other than conventional CMOS gates that have continuous current paths between the power supply and the ground, a fourth (static) power component should also be considered. Our calculations are based on a designing the structure which assure lower dynamic power consumption in CMOS.

Below is shown detailed description of switching power dissipation component which is used in our research. It represents the power dissipated during a event of switching, i.e., when the output node voltage of a CMOS logic gate makes a power consuming transition. Dynamic power is dissipated when energy is drawn from the power supply to charge up the output node capacitance. During this phase, the output node voltage makes a transition from 0 to VDD. Let us consider the example where a two-input NOR gate drives two NAND gates, through interconnection lines. The total capacitive load at the output of the NOR gate consists of (1) the output capacitance of the gate itself, (2) the total interconnect capacitance, and (3) the input capacitances of the driven gates.

The output capacitance of the gate consists mainly of the junction parasitic capacitances, which are due to the drain diffusion regions of the MOS transistors in the circuit. The interconnect lines between the gates contribute to the second component of the total capacitance. Any CMOS logic gate making an output voltage transition can thus be represented by its nMOS network, pMOS network, and the total load capacitance connected to its output node. The average power dissipation (1) of the CMOS logic gate, driven by a periodic input voltage waveform with ideally zero rise- and fall-times, can be calculated from the energy required to charge up the output node to VDD and charge down the total output load capacitance to ground level.

$$P_{avg} = \frac{1}{T}\left[\int_0^{T/2} V_{out}\left(-C_{load}\frac{dV_{out}}{dt}\right)dt + \int_{T/2}^{T}(V_{DD}-V_{out})\left(C_{load}\frac{dV_{out}}{dt}\right)dt\right] \tag{1}$$

Evaluating this integral yields the well-known expression for the average dynamic (switching) power consumption in CMOS logic circuits. Any CMOS logic gate making an output voltage transition can thus be represented by its nMOS network, pMOS network, and the total load capacitance connected to its output node. The average power dissipation of the CMOS logic

$$P_{avg} = \frac{1}{T}C_{load}V_{DD}^2 \tag{2}$$

or

$$P_{avg} = C_{load}V_{DD}^2 f \tag{3}$$

Equation (3) shows that the average dynamic power dissipation is proportional to the square of the power supply voltage, hence, any reduction of VDD will significantly reduce the power consumption. Another way to limit the dynamic power dissipation of a CMOS logic gate is to reduce the amount of switched capacitance at the output.

The analysis of switching power dissipation presented above is based on the assumption that the output node of a CMOS gate undergoes one power-consuming transition (0-to-VDD transition) in each clock cycle. This assumption, however, is not always correct; the node transition rate can be smaller than the clock rate, depending on the circuit topology, logic style and the input signal statistics. To better represent this behavior, we will introduce aT (node transition factor), which is the effective number of power-consuming voltage transitions experienced per clock cycle. Then, the average switching power consumption becomes

$$P_{avg} = a_T \, C_{load} V_{DD}{}^2 f_{CLK} \qquad (4)$$

In the most general case, the internal node voltage transitions can also be partial transitions, i.e., the node voltage swing may be only Vi which is smaller than the full voltage swing of VDD. Taking this possibility into account, the generalized expression for the average switching power dissipation can be written as

$$P_{avg} = \left(\sum_{i=1}^{\substack{number\ of\ nodes}} a_{Ti} \, C_i \, V_i \right) V_{DD} f_{CLK} \qquad (5)$$

where C_i represents the parasitic capacitance associated with each node and a_{Ti} represents the corresponding node transition factor associated with that node [2]. It is also called switching activity factor and researches presented in this paper are about reducing it during generation stream cipher keys.

Increased generator activity and hence power consumption can lead a generator to failure. A detailed description of these problems is proposed in [3]. A cryptographic key generators and other silicon devices affect power consumption in the rising of working frequencies, lowering of applied voltage and the tightening of timing constraints [4]. The main factors which are considering during designing System-On-Chip (SOC), which is also a cipher keys generator, are : energy, average power, peak power, instantaneous power and thermal overload [5]. In [6],[7], [8], [9], [10] are presented low power Test Pattern Generators (TPG) used in Built-In Self-Testing (BIST) which are designed to reduce switching activity, thus reducing power consumption.

2 Stream cipher key generators

Both secrecy as well as authenticity of a message can be achieved through cryptography with a cipher. A cipher encrypts a plaintext message (the message in its original form), to a ciphertext, i.e. the message which is incomprehensible and cannot be duplicated by an outsider. Stream ciphers divide the plaintext into characters, and encipher each character with a function which is dependent upon the current state. In this research, we consider secret-key stream ciphers, specifically one-time pads [11]. The key length for the one-time pad is equal to the length of the plaintext and this key is secret. To encrypt the message, the plaintext message is added modulo 2 (Exclusive-ORed) to the secret key. To decrypt the message, the ciphertext is Exclusive-ORed with the secret key again.

The problem with the one-time pad is the length of the key. Therefore, the key is often replaced with a Pseudo-Random Pattern Generator (PRPG) with a secret seed. A large pseudo-random sequence can now be produced and duplicated with a small length key.

Some pseudo-random non linear pattern generators used in stream cipher cryptography are presented in [11]: the Geffe generator, the Jennings generator, the Beth-Piper stop-and-go generator, the Gollmann cascade stop-and-go generator, the Massey-Rueppel multispeed generator, Rueppel's self-decimated sequence and Gollman's self-decimated sequence. Each of the generators use a combination of LFSR.

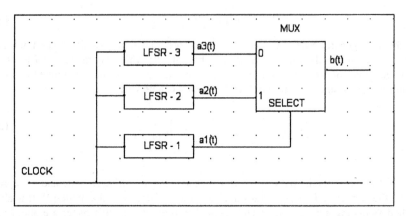

Fig. 1. The Geffe generator

In the Geffe generator, three LFSRs are used to create the output sequence (Fig.).
The Geffe generator uses a design technique which is classified as a non linear feedforward transformation. The bit generated by one LFSR selects either of the other two
sub-machines, and the corresponding bit from the selected machine is used in the
final output sequence. A 2-to-1 multiplexor (MUX)is used to make the selection and
creates the non linear transformation. The degree of the characteristic polynomial for
each of the three LFSRs can be different. Assuming a_1, a_2, a_3 are corresponding input
bits of LFSRs the output bit of the Geffe generator is equal:

$$b = (a_1 \& a_2) \oplus ((\overline{a_2}) \& a_3) \tag{6}$$

If the length of the LFSRa are equal n_1, n_2, n_3 then linear complexity of this generator
is equal:

$$(n_1 + 1)n_2 + n_1 n_3 \tag{7}$$

where $n_1 \Diamond n_2$ and $n_1 \Diamond n_3$ and $n_2 \Diamond n_3$.

3   Generation of new bits in LFSR

Mathematical description of standard LFSR which is used for stream cipher keys
generation is in the equation (8).

$$A(k+1) = V \times A(k) \tag{8}$$

where $A(k+1)$ is a vector with the next state of LFSR, the $A(k)$ vector of previous
state and V is the transition matrix. For example V for the primitive polynomial,
$F(x)=1+x^2+x^5$ is write as:

$$V = \begin{vmatrix} 0 & 1 & 0 & 0 & 1 \\ 1 & 0 & 0 & 0 & 0 \\ 0 & 1 & 0 & 0 & 0 \\ 0 & 0 & 1 & 0 & 0 \\ 0 & 0 & 0 & 1 & 0 \end{vmatrix} \tag{9}$$

New bits are described by equations (10), where $a(k+1)$-next state of bit $a(k)$

$$
\begin{aligned}
a_1(k+1) &= a_2(k) \oplus a_5(k) \\
a_2(k+1) &= a_1(k) \\
a_3(k+1) &= a_2(k) \\
a_4(k+1) &= a_3(k) \\
a_5(k+1) &= a_4(k)
\end{aligned} \tag{10}
$$

Disadvantage of this realization is that only one new bit is produced per each clock cycle of the circuit. By modifying (8) we are able to obtain more than one new bit. To realize it we will insert N which is the power of matrix V.

$$A(k+1) = V^N \times A(k) \tag{11}$$

Matrix V for N=3 is presented below.

$$V^3 = \begin{vmatrix} 0 & 1 & 1 & 0 & 1 \\ 1 & 0 & 0 & 1 & 0 \\ 0 & 1 & 0 & 0 & 1 \\ 1 & 0 & 0 & 0 & 0 \\ 0 & 1 & 0 & 0 & 0 \end{vmatrix} \tag{12}$$

V^3 was built by using below equation which describe generation of three new bits per one clock cycle.:

$$
\begin{aligned}
a_1(k+1) &= a_2(k) \oplus a_3(k) \oplus a_5(k) \\
a_2(k+1) &= a_1(k) \oplus a_4(k) \\
a_3(k+1) &= a_2(k) \oplus a_5(k) \\
a_4(k+1) &= a_2(k) \\
a_5(k+1) &= a_3(k)
\end{aligned} \tag{13}
$$

In the next section will be shown switching activity calculation for the modified structure of LFSR which is used for stream cipher keys generation.

4 Switching activity calculation

By modifying the standard structure of LFSR, what was presented in the previous section, it is possible to obtain more than 50% power reduction [12]. Using this technique it is possible to generate more than one new bit generated by *LFSR* per clock [13]. Let us calculate minimal, maximal and an average power consumption for stream keys cipher generator based on LFSR. Each LFSR is describe by its primitive polynomial. Let us calculate switching activity for LFSR of m-degree (for example for primitive polynomial $F(x)=1+x+x^4$, $m=4$) which will produce d new bits per one clock. Next we determine the number of switchings for the case of generation of all test patterns ($2^4=16$ clock pulses). All nodes of this circuit can be presented as 3 subsets $S1$-clock inputs of the flip-flops $(|S1|=8)$, $S2$-data flip-flops inputs $(|S2|=8$, $S3$-inputs of the feedback circuit constructed on the XOR gates $(|S3|=2)$. Let us designate switching activity of clock inputs, as SA_{S1}.The number of clock inputs equals 8. The number of clock pulses is equal 16 (each clock pulse twice changes a logical level). Thus, $SA_{S1}=8*16*2*5=1280$. The number of data inputs is equal 8. Thus, $SA_{S2}=8*(8*4+8*15)=1216$. Subset $S3$ consists of two inputs to XOR gate, that is $SA_{S3}=2*8*3=48$. As a results we receive $SA_{LFSR}=SA_{S1}+SA_{S2}+SA_{S3}=2544$. There are $4*16=64$ symbols of M – *sequence* applied on LFSR output. Weighted Switching Activity (number of switching for generating one new test bit) can be rewritten as $WSA_{LFSR}=2544/64=39,75$.

Our generator will be built from m memory elements (flip-flops) and will be divided into 7 nodes which allow us to calculate switching activity. $(S1=m, S2=m)$, feedback adder $(S3_{min}=2, S3_{max}=2m-2)$, output of the generator $(S4=1)$, $(S5=d-1)$, $(d-1)$-multi-input modulo 2 adder for copy of M-*sequence* $(S6_{min}=2(d-1), S6_{max}=(d-1)(2m-2))$ and output d-input modulo 2 adder $(S7=d)$.

Based on the above equations we will calculate switching activity for one clock of the generator. We assume that LFSR has two kind of inputs: logic inputs and synchronization inputs. In the synchronization inputs (subset S1) during one clock cycle logical level changes twice ($f_S=2$). Like it was proved in [14], probability than logical inputs changes its state is equal 0,5 ($f_L=0.5$).

$$WSA_{cl}=f_S S1+f_L(S2+S3+dS4+S5+S6+S7) \tag{14}$$

Now we will insert the coefficient k. Assuming optimal realization output adder on the two-input elements its switching activity will increase k times, where k is coefficient which describe increasing of the switching activity during realization on two-input elements:

$$k = \lfloor \log_2 d \rfloor + 4(1 - 2^{\log_2 d}/d) \tag{15}$$

Assuming optimal realization of generator on 2-input elements its switching activity will increase k-times comparing with non optimal realization. Now we will write an expressions for calculation minimal, maximal and an average switching activity of generator which generate d –new bits per one clock:

$$WSA_{Tmin}=(2.5m+2d+0.5kd-0.5)/d \tag{16}$$
$$WSA_{Tmax}=(2.5m+0.5kd+md-0.5)/d \tag{17}$$
$$WSA_{Tav}=(2.5m+0.5md+0.5kd+d-0.5)/d \tag{18}$$

Now we will calculate switching activity for the LFSR. $S1$ and $S2$ will not change. Output of the generator $S4$ has double switching activity. Subset $S3$ will divide into two subsets $SM1$ and $SM2$. Subset $S5$ is built from two elements E, and subset $S7$ is built from output adder.

Let us calculate switching activity per one new bit, where appropriate subsets have values: $S1=4$, $S2=4$, $S3=4$, $S4=1$, $S5=1$, $S7=2$:

$$WSA_{CL}=2S1+0.5(S2+S3+S5+S7)+S4=8+0.5(4+4+1+2)+1=14.5 \qquad (19)$$

Assuming that during one clock we get two new bits switching activity will be:

$$WSA_T= WSA_{CL} / 2 = 7.25 \qquad (20)$$

Now we will write an expression for the general case for generation of two new bits per one clock. For the primitive polynomial of m-degree $S1=m$, $S2=m$, $S4=1$, $S5=1$, $S7=2$:

$$WSA_T=(2S1+0.5(S2+S3+S5+S7)+S4)/2=1.25m+1.25+0.25S3 \qquad (21)$$

What is more, we will find maximal, minimal and an average value of WSA_T. Subset $S3$ consists of inputs of the adders so its switching activity will increase twice. Assuming optimal realization on two-input adders values of subset $S3$ can be from 4 to $4m-4$, then $S3_{min}=4$, $S3_{max}=4m-4$. Based on the above calculation now we will write an expressions for minimal, maximal and an average values of WSA_T:

$$WSA_{Tmin}=1.25m+2.25 \qquad (22)$$
$$WSA_{Tmax}=2.25m+0.25 \qquad (23)$$
$$WSA_{Tav}=1.75m+1.25 \qquad (24)$$

For the next step we will find equations which will calculate switching activity of the m-degree generator which will produce d-new bits per one clock. The generator will need m-elements of memory ($S1=m$, $S2=m$), d-feedback adders ($S3_{min}=2d$, $S3_{max}=(2m-2)d$), output of the generator ($S4=1$), $S5=(d-1)$, and output d-input modulo 2 adder ($S7=d$).

$$WSA_{Tmin}=(2.5m+2d+0.5kd-0.5)/d \qquad (25)$$
$$WSA_{Tmax}=(2.5m+md-0.5+0.5kd)/d \qquad (26)$$
$$WSA_{Tav}=(2.5m+d-0.5+0.5kd+0.5md)/d \qquad (27)$$

In the next section we will calculate switching activity of Geffe stream cipher keys generator.

5 Power reduction estimation for the Geffe generator

Let us now consider the case of pseudo-random pattern generation for the Geffe generator presented in Fig. . The switching activity was calculated using (26). We were taking into considerations number of new bits generating per one clock and a degree of LFSR's. As it was presented in Fig. accordingly $n1=10$, $n2=15$, $n3=20$ and the number of new bits $2..100$. The results are presented in the Fig. .

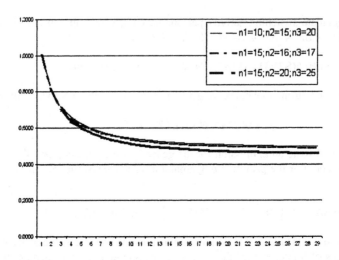

Fig. 2. WSA$_{average}$ for Geffe generator for n1=10, n2=15,n3=20 and n1=15,n2=20,n3=25 for the number of new bits 1-30

As we can observe the more new bits is generated the less value is *WSA$_{average}$* per one clock.

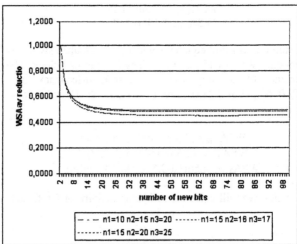

Fig. 3. WSAaverage reduction for Geffe generator for n1=10, n2=15,n3=20, n1=15, n2=16 n3=17 and n1=15 n2=20 n3=25 for the number of new bits 1-30

6 Results

Analyses of the presented results show the way of power reduction estimation for stream cipher keys generators. As it was showed in the *Fig.* when using *LFSRs* of higher degrees the Weighted Switching Activity is also higher. In the Fig. 3 there is presented Geffe generator with three different values of n1, n2, n3 suitably equal

10,15,20; 15,16,17; 15,20,25. During generating more than 20 new bits per one clock WSA_{av} differ only a little between these three series. As we can observe power reduction is about 45% for number of new bits equal 25..100.
In the next step we will try to decrease Weighted Switching Activity in other stream cipher keys generators.

References

1. Zeng K., Yang C., Wei D. and Rao T.R.N.. pseudo-random bit generators in stream-cipher cryptography. *Computer*, 1991.
2. Mlynek D., Design of VLSI systems, Webcourse, http://lsiwww.epfl.ch
3. Girard P., Low Power testing of VLSI circuits: Problems and Solutions // IEEE International Symposium on Quality of Electronic Design, March 2000, pp. 173-179
4. Pedram M., Power Minimization IC Design: Principles and Applications // ACM Trans. On Design Auto of Electronic Systems, 1996, Vol. 1, no. I, pp.3-56
5. Bonhomme Y., Girard P., Landrault C., Pravossoudovitch S., "Power conscious testing", Proceedings of East-West Design&Test Conference (EWDTC'03), Yalta Ukraine 2003, pp. 29-31
6. Wang S., Gupta S., „DS-LFSR : A New BIST TPG for Low Heat Dissipation", IEEE International Test Conference, November 1997, pp.848-857
7. Wang S., Gupta S., „LT-RTPG: A New Test-Per-Scan BIST TPG for Low Heat Dissipation", IEEE International Conference, September 1999, pp. 85-94
8. Zhang X., Roy K., Bhawmik S., "Powertest: A Tool for Energy Conscious weighted Random Pattern testing", IEEE International Conference on VLSI Design, 1999
9. Corno F., Rebaudengo M., Sonza Reorda M., Squillero G., Violente M., "Low Power BIST via Non-Linear Hybrid Cellular Automata", IEEE VLSI test Symposium, May 2000, pp.29-34
10. Gizapoulos D., Kranitis N., Paschalis A., Psarakis M., Zorian Y., "Low Power/Energy BIST scheme for Datapaths", IEEE VLSI Symposium, May 2000, pp.23-28
11. Zeng K., Yang C., Wie D. and Rao T.R.N., Pseudo-random bit generators in stream-cipher cryptography. Computer , 1991
12. Murashko I., Yarmolik V.N., Puczko M.: "The power consumption reducing technique of the pseudo-random test pattern generator and the signature analyzer for the built-in self-test", Proceedings of the VIIth International Conference of CAD Systems in Microelectronics 2003, Lviv-Slavske, Ukraine, pp.141-144
13. Puczko M., Yarmolik V.N.: „Low power design for two-pattern test sequence generator based on LFSR", in book Computer Information Systems and Applications vol. I, Białystok 2004, pp.246-253
14. Golomb S.W. Shift Register Sequences, Holden Day, 1967

The Quality of Obfuscation and Obfuscation Techniques

Joanna Witkowska

University of Finance and Management in Bialystok branch in Elk, Faculty of Engineering, Grunwaldzka 1, 19-300 Elk, Poland

Email: joannawitkowska@interia.pl

Abstract: This paper aims an overview of the obfuscation transformations like layout, data, control, preventative and stealthy obfuscation. Software obfuscation is the common way to prevent reverse engineering. Obfuscation is one of the software secrets technique protections and in general, describes a practice that is used intentionally to make something more difficult to understand. Obfuscation techniques convert program into another one with the same behavior that is more difficult to understand. Obfuscation cannot be mathematical analyze and it is very hard to predict the effectiveness of obfuscation transformations.

1 Introduction

Obfuscation is an old technique that has been used since programmers first started to worry about protecting their intellectual property from reverse engineering. The application of obfuscation was studied by Cohen in 1992. He was looking for a protection of the operating systems from hackers' attacks or viruses. Recently, obfuscation has gained a lot of interest with the appearance of Java, which bytecode binary executable format is very easy to decompile back into its original source. Obfuscation is one of the software secrets technique protection and in general, describes a practice that is used intentionally to make something more difficult to understand. In a programming context, it means that code will be harder to understand or read, generally for privacy or security purposes. A tool called an obfuscator is sometimes used to convert a straightforward program into this one, which works in the same way, but it is much harder to understand. Obfuscation automatically applies to any computation that can be expressed as a program. Level of security which gives by obfuscation techniques depend on the sophistication of the transformations employed by obfuscator, the power of available deobfuscation algorithms and the amount of resources (time and space) available to the deobfuscator.

2 The Quality of an Obfuscating Techniques

The quality of an obfuscating transformation is describing by three components: potency, resilience and cost.
We can classify software metrics:

- program length – the number of operators and operands,
- data flow complexity - the number of inter – block variable references,
- cyclomatic complexity – number of predicates in a function,
- nesting complexity – number of nesting level of conditionals in a program,
- data structure complexity - complexity of the static data structures in the program like variables, vectors, records,
- OO metrics: level of inheritance, coupling, number of methods triggered by another method.

The transformation is a potent obfuscating transformation if increase overall program size and introduce new classes and methods, introduce new predicates and increase the nesting level of conditional and looping constructs, increase the number of method arguments and inter – class instance variable dependencies, increase the height of the inheritance tree, increase long – range variable dependencies [1]. Potency defines to what degree the transformed code is more obscure than the original. Software complexity metrics define various complexity measures for software. The goal of obfuscation is to maximize complexity based on these parameters.

It is necessary to introduce the concept of resilience because of useless potent transformations. Resilience measures how well a transformation holds up under attack from an automatic deobfuscator and it can be seen as the combination of two measures: programmer and deobfuscator effort. Programmer effort is the time required to construct an automatic deobfuscator, which is able to reduce the potency of obfuscating transformation. Deobfuscator effort is the execution time and space required by such an automatic deobfuscator that is able to effectively reduce the potency of obfuscating transformation. A transformation is resilient when if it confuses an automatic deobfuscator. The highest degree of resilience is a one-way transformation that cannot be undone by a deobfuscator.

The cost of transformation is the execution time, space penalty that a transformation incurs on an obfuscated application. A transformation with no cost associated is free. Cost is also context-sensitive.

3 Obfuscation Techniques

The problem of obfuscation could be shown in following way. We are given a set of obfuscating transformations $T = \{T_1, ..., T_n\}$ and a program P consisting of source cod objects (classes, methods, statements, etc.) $\{S_1, ..., S_k\}$ and we should find a new program $P' = \{S'_j = T_i(S_j)\}$[2] such that

1) P' has the same observable behavior as P, i.e. the transformations are semantics – preserving.

2) The obscurity of P' maximized, i.e., understanding and reverse engineering P' will be strictly more time – consuming than understanding and reverse engineering P.

3) The resilience of each transformation $T_i(S_j)$ is maximized, i.e., it will either be difficult to construct an automatic tool to undo the transformations or executing such a tool will be extremely time – consuming.

4)   The stealth of each transformation $T_i(S_j)$ is maximized, i.e. the statistical properties of S_i are similar to those of S_j.

5)   The cost (the execution time, space penalty incurred by the transformations) of P' is minimized. [2]

There are many techniques of obfuscation. We can classified them in categories:
1)   Layout obfuscation
2)   Data obfuscation
3)   Control obfuscation
4)   Preventive obfuscation
5)   Stealthy obfuscation

3.1   Layout obfuscation

Layout obfuscation alters not necessary to the execution of the program information, such as variable names and comments. This is commonly referred to lexical transformations. Layout transformation is the simplest form of obfuscation (simple to apply and cheap in terms of added code size and execution time) but has low potency and it is not enough by itself. This is one-way transformation. Layout obfuscation removes comments and identifiers, scramble identifiers, limited format changes, use method overloading. Many obfuscators depend on layout transformations.

3.2   Data obfuscation

Data obfuscation obscures the data structures. These transformations can be classified into affecting storage, encoding, aggregation and ordering of data.

Obfuscating storage and encoding transformation attempts to choose unnatural ways to encode and store data items in a program. For example: changing encoding of primitive data types, promoting variables from more specialized forms (e.g. a primitive type) to more generalized ones (e.g. a class), splitting variables, and converting static to procedural data.

Aggregation is used to hide the data structures of a program by changing ways of data items are grouped together. We could use following ways to obfuscate the data structures: merging scalar variables, restructuring arrays, and modifying inheritance relations.

Ordering transformation is used in randomizing the order of declarations in a program (randomizing the declarations of methods and instance variables within classes, randomizing the order of parameters within methods, using a mapping function to reorder data within arrays).

3.3   Control obfuscation

Control obfuscation aimed at obfuscating the flow of execution (change the flow of the program, break the link between the original code and the obfuscated code). It can be classified into affecting the aggregation, ordering or computations of the flow of control.

Computational transformation inserts redundant or dead code into the program. That alter control of computational overhead will be unavoidable for obfuscation. For a developer it means that he have to choose between a highly efficient program and a highly obfuscated program. The biggest issue with control transformation is making them computationally cheap, yet hard to deobfuscate. [1] We can classify these transformations in three categories: hiding the real control flow, introducing cod sequences, removing real control flow abstractions or introducing superior one. We could achieve this for example by inserting dead or irrelevant code, using more complicated but equivalent loop conditions, using language breaking transformations that take advantage of constructs available in the binary code but not at the source level (e.g., goto's in Java), removing library calls and programming idioms, implementing a virtual machine with its own instruction set and semantics, adding redundant operands, and converting a sequential program into a multithreaded one by using automatic parallelization techniques or by creating dummy processes that do not perform anything relevant. [7]

Control aggregation transformations make code harder to understand by breaking the abstraction barriers represented by procedures and other control structures. It is one of the important procedures for obfuscator. We can classify them in following way: inlining subroutine calls and outlining sequences of statements (turning them into a subroutine), interleaving methods, cloning methods, and loop transformations. All of them have one idea to break up the code and scatter over the program, or aggregate the code into one method.

Control ordering transformation alters the order in which computations are carried out. These transformations change the order of statements, blocks, or methods, within the code, being careful to respect any data dependencies. They have low potency, but have high and one way resilience, too. In most cases, it is impossible for an automatic deobfuscator to restore the code ordering to its original form. Code ordering transformations have also been proposed as a method for software watermarking and fingerprinting software. [7]

3.4   Preventative obfuscation

Preventative obfuscation works by trying to break already known deobfuscation techniques. Preventative transformations are different from control and data transformations because of lack confuse a human reader only automatic deobfuscation difficult. We could classified them in following way

1. Inherent preventative transformations which include problems hard to solve with known automatic deobfuscation techniques, for example: adding variable dependencies to prevent program slicing, adding bogus data dependencies, using opaque predicates with side effects, making opaque predicates using difficult theorems.

2. Target preventative transformations that include knowledge of the specific weaknesses in existing deobfuscation programs.

3.5   Stealthy obfuscation techniques

The stealth of obfuscation is relay on similarity of obfuscating and original code and how well it fits in with the other code. The more stealthy obfuscation is the more reverse engineering aware of change.

Method inlining is technique that replaces a function call with the body of the called function. [11] In this body every occurrence of a method parameter is replaced with the actual parameter, some variable can be renamed too.

Opaque predicates are Boolean valued expressions. This values are well known to the obfuscator but difficult to determine for an automatic deobfuscator. Opaque it means difficult to understand.

Identifier switching we can classify to variable names, method names and class names. Variable names is a technique which switch the names. In this way reader believe that the code has not been obfuscate. Method names is a technique with re-names methods but it is important to take consideration that function might be called from outside the class and we should not rename inherited functions. Class names is similar to technique which rename methods. First all classes names are collected, a mapping between this class names is created and finally all occurrences of each class are replaced with it's mapping [11].

Writing out loops is an obfuscating technique, which depended on type of loop. There are two types of loops: with definite iterations and indefinite iterations. When we know the number of iterations we can replace the iteration with the code that would have been executed when the loop was iterated.

Variable outsourcing is a data obfuscating technique, which removes a group of variables from a class and place these variables in a separate class. These classes are equipped with set and get methods to read and write the "outsourced" variables [11].

Obfuscation is the process of transforming bytecode to a less human readable form with the purpose of complicating reverse engineering. It typically includes stripping out all the debug information, such as variable tables and line numbers, and renaming packages, classes, and methods of machine generated names. Obfuscation transform program not affecting what the program does. In a nutshell, obfuscating transformations are meant to destroy relationships that exist between the compiled and source-code versions of the code. Because of stealthy obfuscation techniques reverse engineer does not notice that the code has been obfuscated. The idea of making program code harder to understand is seen as a valuable component in computer security.

3 Tools

Nowadays, we have many programs, which use obfuscation techniques. Obfuscator must keep the specification of program and should transform automatically the program into harder to understand. The most general technique, which is used in obfuscation tools is symbol name transformation. Obfuscator has to make application more difficult for human and automated attacks. An obfuscation difficult for a human to understand is often easy for an automated tool to handle, and vice-versa. A quality obfuscator should use techniques difficult for both kinds of attacks. Collberg proposed to build obfuscator which applies all techniques and more over which analyzes the code and determine appropriate transformations to apply to different parts of code. The University of Arizona developed SandMark. It is a Java tool for software watermarking, temper – proofing and code obfuscation. The code obfuscation algorithms in SandMark take a Java – jar file as input and produce an obfuscated jar – file as output. SandMark supports 25 algorithms. Detailed explanations of these algorithms can be found in [13]. SandMark provides a GUI for a tool called Soot, an optimization tool that can also decompile bytecode. These tools together obfuscate Java code and then decompile it to see the effect of the obfuscations. If you apply the obfuscation algorithm to example [13] like this

```
public class IfElseDemo {
    public static void main(String[] args) {
        int testscore = 76;
        char grade;
        if (testscore >= 90) {
            grade = 'A';
        } else if (testscore >= 80) {
            grade = 'B';
        } else if (testscore >= 70) {
            grade = 'C';
        } else if (testscore >= 60) {
            grade = 'D';
        } else {
            grade = 'F';
        }
        System.out.println("Grade = " + grade);
    }
}
```

and decompiled by Soot we receive obfuscated source code like this

```
public class IfElseDemo
{
    public static void main(java.lang.String[] r0)
    {
        long l0, l7, l16;
        char c50;
        l0 = 1L;
        l7 = l0 ^ ((long) 76 ^ l0) & (- (1L)) >>> 32;
        if ((int) l7 < 90)
        {
            if ((int) l7 < 80)
            {
                if ((int) l7 < 70)
                {
                    if ((int) l7 < 60)
                    {
                        l16 = l7 ^ ((long) 70 << 32 ^
l7) & (- (1L)) << 32;
                    }
                    else
                    {
                        l16 = l7 ^ ((long) 68 << 32 ^
l7) & (- (1L)) << 32;
                    }
                }
                else
                {
                    l16 = l7 ^ ((long) 67 << 32 ^ l7) &
(- (1L)) << 32;
                }
            }
            else
```

```
                       {
                              116 = 17 ^ ((long) 66 << 32 ^ 17) & (-
         (1L)) << 32;
                       }
               }
               else
               {
                       116 = 17 ^ ((long) 65 << 32 ^ 17) & (-
         (1L)) << 32;
                       }

               c50 = (char) (int) (116 >> 32);
               System.out.println((new String-
         Buffer()).append("Grade = ").append(c50).toString());
               return;
         }
         public IfElseDemo()
         {
               super();
               return;
         }
}
```

Another interesting example of obfuscation tool is JHide. It is a tool kit for Java programs. JHide supports 30 obfuscation algorithms. What is interesting that 5 of them is new obfuscation algorithms based on composite function and known mathematical concepts of discrete logs and affine ciphers. Basis on the classification of obfuscation techniques, the algorithms supported by JHide use:

1) layout transformations which modify a program's formatting
2) control transformations which hide the flow of control using opaque predicates, one of this technique is modify If Else block
3) data transformations affect the data structures used by program
4) preventative transformations which intended to stop decompilers and deobfuscators from functioning correctly
5) merging transformations which merges all possible program constructs
6) reordering and miscellaneous transformations [14]

We have many commercial and popular obfuscation tools for example: Salamander.Net Obfuscator, ASP, ProGuard, Java Source Code Obfuscator (Semantic Designs), DotFuscator. Most of the them work by taking as input arbitrary program source code, and they output obfuscated binary or source code that is harder to reverse engineer.

4 Conclusions

Almost all obfuscating transformation have a deobfuscation transformation. There exist some transformations which are useful for reverse engineering obfuscated code. An obfuscation application is good as long as the deobfuscator have to be built. In this paper I was trying to overview obfuscation transformations with stealthy obfuscation techniques. Recently security of obfuscation was formally defined and examined theoretically, but not all software can be obfuscated. Obfuscation is the reasonably safe process that should preserve application functionality. However, in certain cases the transformations is performed by obfuscators, which can inadvertently break code that used to work. There are many advantages of using obfuscation techniques and nowadays they are very useful in obfuscator programs, but the main disadvantage of obfuscation is that it is not mathematically analyze and very hard to predict the effectiveness of the obfuscation transformations.

References

1. Collberg, C.; Thomborson, C.; Low D. "A Taxonomy of Obfuscating Transformations." Technical Report#, Department of Computer Science, University of Auckland, 1997.
2. Collberg C.; Thomborson C.; "Watermarking, Tamper – Proofing, and Obfuscation – Tools for Software Protection", University of Arizona Technical Report 2000-03, University of Auckland Technical Report #170, 2002
3. Collberg C., Thomborson C., Low D.; "Manufacturing Cheap, Resilient, and Stealthy Opaque Constructs" ACM SIGPLAN-SIGACT Symposium on Principles of Programming Languages (POPL98) , San Diego, California, 1998
4. Lynn B; Prabhakaran M;Sahai A. „Positive Results and Techniques for Obfuscation" Advances in Cryptology - EUROCRYPT 2004: International Conference on the Theory and Applications of Cryptographic Techniques, Interlaken, Switzerland, May 2-6, 2004. Proceedings http://eprint.iacr.org/2004/060.pdf
5. Eoff B.; Hamilton J.A.; "Vulnerability of Simulation Executables" Proceedings of the 2003 Military, Government, and Aerospace Simulation Symposium http://www.scs.org/scsarchive/getDoc.cfm?id=2111
6. B. Barak, O. Goldreich R. Impagliazzo, S. Rudich, A. Sahai, S. Vadhan and K. Yang," On the (Im)possibility of Obfuscating Programs", Advanced in Cryptology - CRYPTO 2001 Proceedings, Springer Verlag, 2001.
7. Luis F. G. Sarmenta "Protecting Programs from Hostile Environments: Encrypted Computation, Obfuscation, and Other Techniques" Area Exam Paper, Dept. of Electrical Engineering and Computer Science, MIT. July, 1999.
8. Just J.E.; Cornwell M.W., "Review and Analysis of Synthetic Diversity for Breaking Monocultures", Proceedings of the 2004 ACM workshop on Rapid malcode, October 2004, Washington DC, USA
9. Jacob M., Boneh D., Felten E., „ Attacking an obfuscated cipher by injecting faults" Proceedings of the 2002 ACM Workshop on Digital Rights Management, November 2002, Washington DC, USA. http://crypto.stanford.edu/~dabo/papers/obfuscate.pdf
10. Andrzej Siłuszek, „Przestępstwa komputerowe - nieznajomość prawa nie chroni przed odpowiedzialnością", PCKurier 8/2000
11. Arjan de Roo, Leon van den Oord, "Stealthy obfuscation techniques: misleading the pirates" Department of Computer Science University of Twente, http://wwwhome.cs.utwente.nl/~oord/paper.pdf
12. J. Witkowska, "A short overview of the Obfuscation Techniques and Solutions" ACS – CISIM International Multi – Conference on Advanced Computer Systems and Computer Information Systems and Industrial Management, WSFiZ Białystok 2005, Vol. 1, pp. 287-293.
13. Matthew Russell, "Protect your source code: Obfuscation 101" http://www.macdevcenter.com/pub/a/mac/2005/04/08/code.html?page=1
14. Lovent Ertaul, Suma Venkatesh, "JHide – A Tool Kit for Code Obfuscation" Proceedings of the Eight Lasted International Conference Software Engineering and Applications, November 9-11, 2004, Cambridge, USA

PART III

ARTIFICIAL INTELLIGENCE AND APPLICATIONS

Capability and Functionings:
A Fuzzy Way to Measure Interaction
between Father and Child

Tindara Addabbo[1], Gisella Facchinetti[1], Giovanni Mastroleo[2]

[1] University of Modena and Reggio Emilia, Faculty of Economics - Modena, Italy
addabbo.tindara@unimore.it; facchinetti.gisella@unimore.it
[2] University of Calabria, Faculty of Economics - Cosenza, Italy
mastroleo@unical.it

Abstract. This paper aims at analyzing the building of social interaction a relevant dimension in the description and conceptualization of child well being by using the capability approach. In this paper we deal with a special dimension of this capability that involves the capability of interaction between father and child. We will try to put in relation and to come to a measure of different factors that can affect its development. We propose a fuzzy expert system to measure this capability both at a theoretical and empirical level. In the applied part of the paper we use a data set based on a ISTAT (Italian National Statistical Office) multipurpose survey on family and on children condition in Italy to recover information on children's education, the socio-demographic structure of their families, child care provided by relatives and parents according to the type of activities in which the children are involved.

1 Introduction

This paper aims at analysing the building of social interaction a relevant dimension in the description and conceptualisation of child well being by using Sen's capability approach [10]. In this paper we deal with a special dimension of this capability that of interaction between father and child. The importance of father's role in child well being construction is well documented by evolutionary psychology and psychoanalysis, and it is an important element of social interaction a capability that has been considered as relevant in the list endorsed in [2]. This list of capabilities includes: Life and physical health, Mental Well being, Bodily Integrity, Education and knowledge, Leisure activities, Play and Social Interaction. Here we will try to put in relation and to measure different factors that can affect father's interaction with their children. How we can do it?

Measurement is at the heart of scientific work. Ever since Galileo the process of scientific discovery has gone hand-in-hand with the development of methods and techniques for measurement and analysis, influencing decisively the opportunities for scientific progress. However, science, business and government now present challenges to measurement, which are intrinsically more complex, problematic and subject to interpretation. Many phenomena of significant interest to contemporary science are intrinsically multidimensional and multi-disciplinary, with strong crossover between physical biological and social sciences. Products and services appeal to consumers according to parameters of quality, satisfaction, etc., which are mediated by human perception. Public authorities, private bodies such as schools, kindergarten, provide citizens with support and services whose performance is measured according to parameters of life quality, security or wellbeing. These parameters are described in an imprecise way as: sufficient wellbeing, good level of quality of life, etc. People have used imprecise information for thousands of years. But conventional mathematics enables processing of precise information. Because of this, the efficiency of many classical decision-making methods was considerably limited all the more, as in some systems imprecise information is the only accessible one. Thus, the practical challenge facing scientists is often to "measure the impossible" to go beyond the existing science of measurement, and the assumptions that surround it. The domain of mathematics dealing with imprecise information is named Fuzzy Set Theory. This theory in connection with conventional mathematics enables the processing and use of any information [9].

This paper wants to sign the beginning for the creation of new, interdisciplinary partnerships between researchers within the field of measurements and researchers in a range of psychologists, sociologists and economists, and cross-fertilisation of research relating to complex measurements across different fields of science, which involve complex issues of interpretation, and/or mediation by human perception, using emerging methodologies and techniques. We outline if and to what extent this fuzzy technique can be used to measure functionings with special reference to an important dimension of child wellbeing. Fuzzy set theory has been already used to measure functionings [5, 6]. However the idea followed is different from the one developed in this paper. They use data to build the slopes of fuzzy variables membership functions and then they aggregate them using different averages. We do not use data, but only experts' opinions to build a picture of interactions between several items involved. The power of Fuzzy Expert Systems comes from the ability to describe linguistically a particular phenomenon or process, and then to represent that description with a small number of very flexible rules. In a Fuzzy Expert System, the knowledge is contained both in its rules and in fuzzy sets, which hold general description of the properties of the phenomenon under consideration. For testing the system, we will use a data set based on a ISTAT (Italian National Statistical Office) multipurpose survey on family and on children condition in Italy to recover information on children's education, the socio-demographic structure of their families, child care provided by relatives and parents according to the type of activities in which the children are involved (Section 2). The system used to measure interaction between child and father is described in Section 3, while the first outcome is analysed with reference to the observed characteristics of fathers and area where the family lives in Section 4.

2 Elements of interaction

The importance of father's role in child well being construction is well documented by evolutionary psychology and psychoanalysis, and it is an important element of social interaction a capability that has been considered as relevant in the list endorsed in [2]. This list of capabilities includes: Life and physical health; Mental Well being; Bodily Integrity; Education and knowledge, Leisure activities, play and Social Interaction. Here we will try to put in relation and to measure different factors that can affect father's interaction with their children by using ISTAT (Italian National Statistical Office) multipurpose survey on family and on children condition in Italy (year 1998) and by applying a Fuzzy Expert System procedure. Istat multipurpose survey provides information on children's education, the socio-demographic structure of their families, childcare provided by relatives and parents according to the type of activities in which the children are involved. The source of data is going to affect the system developed in this paper, however our aim is to develop in a further step of analysis a larger system with more indicators than the ones currently available that can be collected in a further step of this research directly or by making use of different sources of data. This is a first step of a more complex system allowing for a richer set of indicators and of dimensions of child well being as well as for their interaction. The survey collects information on 20,153 families. The very definition of relevant functionings is bound to change with the age of children therefore we have decided to focus on a particular phase of children's life by analysing the interaction of children aged six to ten years old (in primary school age) with their fathers. We have analysed 3,251 families with at least one child aged from six to ten years old. Moreover in this first application we will focus only on those mononuclear families where both parents are present and there is only one child. This decision brought us a sample of 485 children (each one of them belongs to a single child-double parents household). The sample is made of 238 boys and 247 girls. We have attached information on their parents to each child's record. From a first analysis on parents' variables that can be related to the interaction between parents and children we can see that our sample confirms the disequilibrium in total working time by gender (Table 1) observed also in other studies, a disequilibrium that in Italy is higher than in other industrialized countries [1, 8].

Table 1. Parents' allocation of time

	father		mother	
	mean	*st.dev.*	*mean*	*st.dev.*
average hours of paid work	41,26	13,27	20,25	18,64
average hours of unpaid work	6,65	9,16	34,38	19,04

As we can see in Table 2, mothers do play more often with their child (54% of them play everyday) while fathers tend on average to play more than once a week (47% of them) or everyday (35% of them). Turning to fathers' level of education 44% of them have on average secondary high school education, 41% high school, 8% degree or higher level or education while 7% primary or no education. According to their employment condition, 94% are employed, fathers' job position is mainly blue collar (40% of them are in this position), 29% are white collar, 6% are in managerial position and 24% self employed (including also entrepreneurial positions). Looking at the average hours of work spent by fathers by their job position with the family (in unpaid working activities that include care) and in their job we can see that teachers work on average the lowest number of hours (27) whereas self employed work on average 47 hours a week. Teachers' contribution to unpaid working time is higher (10 hours on average a week) whereas the lowest contribution comes from self-employed, 5 hours a week.

Table 2. How often do parents play with the child

	father	mother
all days	35,05%	53,81%
more than once a week	47,22%	33,61%
once a week	7,42%	3,30%
some times monthly	5,77%	6,39%
sometimes yearly	2,68%	0,82%
never	1,86%	2,06%

3 The fuzzy model: a Fuzzy Expert System.

A Fuzzy Expert System (FES) utilizes fuzzy sets and fuzzy logic to overcome some of the problems that occur when the data provided by the user are vague or incomplete. The power of FES comes from the ability to describe linguistically a particular phenomenon or process, and then to represent that description with a small number of very flexible rules. In a FES, the knowledge is contained both in its rules and in fuzzy sets, which hold general description of the properties of the phenomenon under consideration. One of the major differences between a FES and another Expert System is that the first can infer multiple conclusions. In fact it provides all possible solutions whose truth is above a certain threshold, and the user or the application program can then choose the appropriate solution depending on the particular situation. This fact adds flexibility to the system and makes it more powerful. FES use fuzzy data, fuzzy rules, and fuzzy inference, in addition to the standard ones implemented in the ordinary Expert Systems. Functionally a fuzzy system can be described as a function approximator. More specifically it aims at performing an approximate implementation of an unknown mapping $f : A \subseteq R^n \to R^m$ where A is a compact of R^n. By means of variable knowledge relevant to the unknown mapping, it is possible to prove that that fuzzy systems are dense in the space of continuous functions on a compact domain and so can approximate arbitrarily well any continuous function on a compact domain [7, 11]. The following are the main phases of a FES design [3, 9]:

- identification of the problem and choice of the type of FES which best suits the problem requirement. A modular system can be designed. It consists of several fuzzy modules linked together. A modular approach may greatly simplify the design of the whole system, dramatically reducing its complexity and making it more comprehensible;
- definition of input and output variables, their linguistic attributes (fuzzy values) and their membership function (fuzzification of input and output);
- definition of the set of heuristic fuzzy rules. (IF-THEN rules);
- choice of the fuzzy inference method (selection of aggregation operators for precondition and conclusion);
- translation of the fuzzy output in a crisp value (defuzzification methods);
- test of the fuzzy system prototype, drawing of the goal function between input and output fuzzy variables, change of membership functions and fuzzy rules if necessary, tuning of the fuzzy system, validation of results.

In this section we will try to apply the logical system of indicators looking at useful
data and by proposing a fuzzy set scheme to measure them.

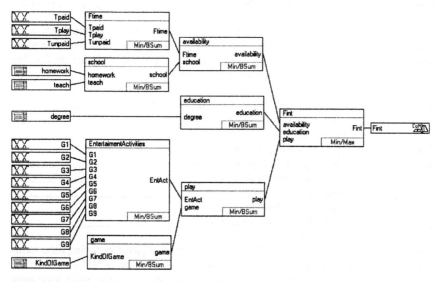

Fig. 1. Interaction with father: a fuzzy representation

The system we propose has: 16 input variables, 7 intermediate variables, 1 output
variable, 8 rule blocks, 155 rules, 82 membership functions. The variables are so
identified:

Degree	father's level of education	input
G1	He reads tales	input
G2	He invents tales	input
G3	He watches television with the child	input
G4	He watches videocassettes with the child	input
G5	He goes to the cinema with the child	input
G6	He goes to sport shows with the child	input
G7	He hears music with the child	input
G8	He goes to the park with the child	input
G9	He sings, dances, plays with the child	input
Homework	Father's assistance in doing homework	input
KindOfGame	Kind of games they do together	input
teach	Relations with teachers	input
Tpaid	Father's working hours	input
Tplay	Father's play frequency with the child	input
Tunpaid	Father's housework's hours	input
availability	Availability evaluation	intermediate variable
education	Education evaluation	intermediate variable
EntAct	Entertainment activities evaluation	intermediate variable
Ftime	Father availability	intermediate variable
play	Favourite game evaluation	intermediate variable

game	Game frequency evaluation	intermediate variable
school	Time for school activities availability	intermediate variable
Fint	Interaction with father	output

Some variables are described in a categorical way and other by a typical fuzzy input with a different number of granules described by fuzzy numbers with linear memberships. The categorical variables are used when the fuzzification is not useful. For example, a variable like "KindOfGame" has this structure:

fg1	They play with videogames/computers
fg2	They play with building toys/puzzles
fg3	They play with table games
fg4	They play with rule games
fg5	They play with movement plays
fg6	They build or repair objects
fg7	They draw/paint
fg8	They play making housework
fg9	They play with different toys

It assumes only discrete integer values, these values are equivalent to linguistic terms and each term can accept the membership degree 1 or 0 (true or false) only. When this type of variable enters the fuzzy system, the experts give a linguistic judgement to every term, like this:

Table 3.

IF: KindOfGame	THEN: game
fg1=They play with videogames/computers	low
fg9=They play with different toys	low
fg3=They play with table games	medium
fg4=They play with rule games	medium
fg6=They build or repair objects	medium
fg8=They play making housework	medium
fg2=They play with building toys/puzzles	high
fg5=They play with movement plays	high
fg7=They draw/paint	high

A judgement has also been given with regards to the type of activities father and child do together as follows:

G1	Reading tales	high
G2	story telling	high
G3	watching tv	low
G4	watching videotapes	low
G5	going to the movies	medium
G6	attending sport shows	medium
G7	listening to music	high
G8	going to a park	high
G9	singing, dancing and playing together	high

The two input variables can be fuzzified to provide the intermediate variable 'play' that gives a measure of the quality of playing and entertainment activities that father and child do together. We have inserted in the model as intermediate variable "father's education". This variable can be a proxy of family income (that is not directly available in this data set and that in a further step of this research will be imputed , a higher income can provide higher possibilities for the child to participate to activities with higher chances of interaction with other people. A higher level of education in this model leads also to a higher level of interaction under the hypothesis that a more educated parent can have more ability in engaging in certain activities or game with the child (like home-working, story telling or reading tales). We assume that, taking home-working into account, a more educated father is more productive in this activity. Taking the activity of listening to music, we assume that a more educated parent can have a wider musical knowledge and can transmit it to the child doing this activity together.

An example of a typical fuzzy input is "Tpaid". It provides, for difference, father's presence. It has this description:

Table 4. Tpaid variable: definition points

Term Name	Shape/Par.	Definition Points (x, y)		
low	Linear	(30, 1)	(38, 0)	(41, 0)
medium	Linear	(30, 0)	(38, 1)	(41, 0)
high	Linear	(30, 0)	(38, 0)	(41, 1)

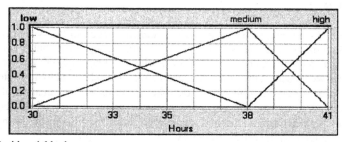

Fig. 2. Tpaid variable: layout

The intermediate variable 'school' in Figure 1 has to do with how much time the father spends with his child both in doing homework (input variable homework) and in the relationship with child's teachers (input variable teach). The intermediate variable 'availability' regards both directly or indirectly father's availability of time to be spent with his child: how often does the father play with his child (input variable Tplay), the time that he devotes to care and housework inside the family (input variable Tunpaid) (the assumption is that a higher number of hours in these activities increases the value of interaction) and his paid working hours (input variable Tpaid, a higher number of hours of work reduces the time available to play and interact with the child and it is considered as an indirect indicator of father's availability) and this is the rule block that we have fixed with experts' suggestions:

#.	Tpaid	Tplay	Tunpaid	Ftime
1	low	everyday	low	medium_high
2	low	everyday	medium v high	high
3	medium v high	everyday	low	medium_low
4	medium	everyday	medium	medium_high
5	medium	everyday	high	high
6	high	everyday v sometimes	medium	medium_low
7	high	everyday	high	medium_high
8	low v medium	sometimes	low	medium_low
9	low	sometimes	medium	medium_high
10	low	sometimes	high	high
11	medium	sometimes v never	medium	medium_low
12	medium	sometimes	high	medium_high
13	high	sometimes v never	low	low
14	high	sometimes v never	high	medium_low
15	low	never	low v medium	medium_low
16	low	never	high	medium_high
17	medium	never	low	low
18	medium	never	high	medium_low
19	high	never	medium	low

Fig. 3. Tpaid variable: its influence in Ftime rule block

4 Results

The source of data that we have used for the implementation of the system is ISTAT (Italian National Institute for Statistics) "1998 Famiglia, soggetti sociali e condizione dell'infanzia" survey on about 24,000 households and about 60,000 individuals. In this chapter we present some of the 485 records we have submitted to the system. The system produces very sensible results consistent with experts' evaluation of the records involved in the analysis. For a better understanding of the final results, for all the variables we describe in Table 4 range, type and if their linguistic attributes are allotted in an increasing or decreasing way.

Table 4.

#	Variable Name	Type	Min	Max	Monotonicity
1	degree		1	9	increasing
2	G1		1	6	decreasing
3	G2		1	6	decreasing
4	G3		1	6	decreasing
5	G4		1	6	decreasing
6	G5		1	6	decreasing
7	G6		1	6	decreasing
8	G7		1	6	decreasing
9	G8		1	6	decreasing
10	G9		1	6	decreasing
11	homework		0	1	increasing

#	Variable Name	Type	Min	Max	Monotonicity
12	KindOfGame	[icon]	1	9	non monotone
13	teach	[icon]	0	1	increasing
14	Tpaid	[icon]	30	41	decreasing
15	Tplay	[icon]	1	6	decreasing
16	Tunpaid	[icon]	3	18	increasing

In Table 5 we have listed all the variables, the intermediate variables defuzzified and in the last column the final output. The evaluation of the intermediate variables is very useful to understand how the different components affect the final result.

Table 5. Results

ID	homework	KindOfGame	G1	G2	G3	G4	G5	G6	G7	G8	G9	Tplay	Tpaid	Tunpaid	teach	degree	availability	game	EntAct	play	school	Ftime	education	Fint
11836	1	5	6	6	1	1	6	6	6	6	6	2	55	10	6	5	0.500	1.000	0.000	0.500	0.500	0.333	0.500	**0.500**
11848	1	7	6	6	5	5	6	6	6	5	6	2	38	10	6	5	0.500	1.000	0.013	0.506	0.500	0.370	0.500	**0.504**
11866	0	2	4	4	1	1	4	6	1	2	6	1	36	4	4	3	0.141	1.000	0.480	0.740	0.000	0.521	0.500	**0.494**
11876	0	5	5	4	1	2	6	6	6	2	4	4	36	8.5	6	5	0.000	1.000	0.389	0.694	0.000	0.308	0.500	**0.393**
11899	0	5	4	2	2	4	2	3	3	3	3	2	42	3	4	3	0.000	1.000	0.401	0.701	0.000	0.000	0.600	**0.395**
11910	1	7	2	2	1	4	5	6	1	4	4	1	40	5	4	3	0.500	1.000	0.660	0.830	0.500	0.417	0.500	**0.614**
11917	0	1	6	6	3	3	5	5	6	5	6	5	44	0	6	5	0.000	0.000	0.055	0.027	0.000	0.000	0.500	**0.167**
11928	1	2	2	2	1	2	4	4	4	3	2	1	48	0	6	5	0.500	1.000	0.583	0.792	0.500	0.333	0.500	**0.601**
11944	0	2	6	4	1	4	5	6	6	2	6	3	48	3	4	3	0.000	1.000	0.321	0.661	0.000	0.000	0.500	**0.370**
11952	1	5	6	6	1	6	6	6	1	6	1	2	30	14	2	1	1.000	1.000	0.667	0.833	1.000	0.852	1.000	**0.944**
11959	1	7	6	5	2	5	5	6	3	2	6	2	39	60	6	5	0.500	1.000	0.281	0.640	0.500	0.556	0.600	**0.544**
11979	0	5	4	4	3	5	5	4	3	4	2	2	10	4	4	3	0.042	1.000	0.282	0.641	0.000	0.389	0.500	**0.430**
12060	0	3	6	6	2	2	5	6	2	2	5	2	36	0	7	6	0.000	0.500	0.276	0.388	0.000	0.333	0.500	**0.204**
12100	0	7	6	6	1	2	2	2	1	6	6	2	60	5	4	3	0.000	1.000	0.409	0.705	0.000	0.111	0.500	**0.393**
12119	0	2	4	6	2	2	5	6	4	5	6	4	45	7	1	0	0.000	1.000	0.209	0.604	0.000	0.000	1.000	**0.362**
12139	0	0	6	6	2	3	5	6	6	3	6	1	36	10	6	5	0.347	0.000	0.099	0.050	0.000	0.795	0.500	**0.250**
12154	0	4	2	4	5	5	5	6	3	2	5	1	40	14	6	5	0.233	0.500	0.478	0.489	0.000	0.644	0.500	**0.408**
12157	0	2	6	6	1	4	6	6	6	4	6	2	40	5	5	4	0.000	1.000	0.111	0.556	0.000	0.200	0.500	**0.333**
12164	0	5	2	6	2	5	3	5	6	2	6	1	36	14	4	3	0.423	1.000	0.306	0.653	0.000	0.897	0.500	**0.472**

4.1 Modelling the outcomes

In this section we use econometric moelling to interpret the results obtained from the fuzzy expert system. If we analyze how different fathers' characteristics are going to affect the intermediate variable 'play' (an intermediate outcome of fuzzy expert system that measures the observed interaction of the father with the child in the types of games and activities they do together) we can see that amongst fathers who are employed, teachers and white collars tend to score better (and when we restrict the analysis to employees the effect of these job positions becomes more statistically significant), the level of interaction of fathers with girls is better and a positive effect of more hours of unpaid work directly performed by father emerges. The positive coefficient of variable 'girl' can be driven from the rules that we have included to define this intermediate variable. For instance in evaluating the type of entertainment activities they do together we gave a better score to story telling, and to reading tales, activities that probably fathers are more inclined to do with girls than with boys and this may drive the positive coefficient obtained by the variable 'girl' in the model estimated for playing activities. The effect of father's characteristics on the interaction with child in playing and other activities (all fathers working as employees) is showed in the Table 6.

Table 6.: Variables affecting playing and other activities of fathers with his child (all fathers working as employees)

	Coef.	Std. Err.	t
log father's age	0,014	0,08	0,18
log father's years of education	-0,024	0,04	-0,58
father teacher	0,138	0,08	1,83
father manager	0,043	0,05	0,93
father white collar	0,046	0,02	1,85
log father's paid hours of work	0,050	0,06	0,85
log father's unpaid working hours	0,011	0,01	1,13
North	-0,015	0,02	-0,69
Child is a girl	0,030	0,02	1,40
constant	0,371	0,37	1,00
number of observations	347		
F(9,337)	1,220		

As far as the interaction with child in schooling activities (homework and relation with school teachers), is concerned the most important variable affecting it is the number of hours devoted by the father to unpaid working activities.

We have then estimated the relation existing amongst the final outcome of the fuzzy expert system with a set of father's characteristics (his age, employment condition, type of job) not including the ones that we have entered the system, with the child's sex and with the area where the household lives, by estimating a regression model having as dependent variable father's interaction with the child. Interaction with child has been found to be higher for teachers and white collar fathers and it improves also with father's age.

Table 7. Father's interaction with child and father's characteristics (whole sample)

	Coef.	Std. Err.	t
father's age	0,002	0,001	1,62
father unemployed	0,030	0,033	0,91
father not in the labour force	-0,013	0,043	-0,29
father teacher	0,242	0,048	5,08
father manager	0,016	0,029	0,55
father white collar	0,043	0,016	2,75
father self employed	-0,007	0,016	-0,44
South	0,013	0,015	0,90
Centre	0,020	0,016	1,26
child is a girl	0,001	0,013	0,08
constant	0,319	0,046	6,90
number of observations	485		
F(10,474)	4,25		

5 Concluding remarks and future research

In this work we have focused on an application of Fuzzy Expert System to the evaluation of child well being by using the capability approach and measuring a component
of social interaction and child well being: the interaction of child with the father. We
are currently working to extend the model by including other dimensions of social
interaction and by defining a system also on mother's interaction with child. The latter
can be used to show how parents' interactions with their child combine to determine
child's well being and detect cases of poor interaction with both parents or cases
where one parent dominates in the interaction with the child. A more structured relation with psychologists and pedagogues is then needed to interpret these cases and call
for social policies to tackle them. The source of data affects the system developed in
this paper, however we will develop a larger system with more indicators than the
ones currently available that can be collected in a further step of this research directly
or by making use of different sources of data. This research is inserted in a wider
project that involves experts from other disciplines that can provide theoretical reasoning for the rules that we assume in the fuzzy scheme as well as on the implications
of the obtained results for the building of child well being and child's development.
The results we have obtained in this initial phase of our applied research encourage us
to go on in this line of research.

References

1. Addabbo, T.: Unpaid work by gender in Italy,Ch.2 in 'Unpaid work and the economy',
    A.Picchio (ed.) Routledge,London and New York (2003)
2. Addabbo, T., Di Tommaso, M.L. and Facchinetti, G.: To what extent fuzzy set theory and
    structural equation modelling can measure functionings? An application to child well
    being. Materiali di Discussione del Dipartimento di Economia Politica n.468, Modena
    (2004)
3. Altrock, C.: Fuzzy Logic & Neurofuzzy Applications in Business & Finance, Prentice
    Hall PTR, New Jersey, (1995)
4. Cerioli, Zani: A Fuzzy Approach to Measurement of Poverty, in C. Dagum & M. Zenga
    (eds.), Income and Wealth Distribution, Inequality and Poverty, Springer- Verlag, Berlin,
    (1990) 272-284
5. Cheli, B., Lemmi, A.: A totally fuzzy and relative approach to the multidimensional
    analysis of poverty, Economic Notes, 1 (1995) 115-134
6. Chiappero Martinetti,E.: Standard of living evaluation based on Sen's approach: some
    methodological suggestions, Notizie di Politeia 12 (43/44) (1996) 37-53
7. Kosko, B.: Fuzzy Systems as Universal Approximators. Proc. IEEE Int. Conf. On Fuzzy
    Systems (1992) 1153-1162
8. Picchio, A. (ed.): Unpaid work and the economy, Routledge, London and New York
    (2003)
9. Piegat A. Fuzzy Modelling and Control, Physica Verlag, New York (1999)
10. Sen, A.K.: Capability and Well-Being, in Nussbaum M., Sen A.K (Eds), The Quality of
    Life, Clarendon Press, Oxford (1993) 30-54
11. Wang, L.: Fuzzy systems are universal approximators, Proc. Of Int. Conf. On Fuzzy En-
    gineering (1992) 471-496

Concluding remarks and future research

References

Remarks on Computer Simulations [1]

Wiktor Dańko

Białystok Technical University,
Wiejska 45A, 15-351 Białystok, Poland

Abstract. In computer modeling of real stochastic processes, the fundamental mechanism of the simulation procedure is a pseudo-random object generator. In the paper it is discussed the case, where the Markov Chain model is used. For this model we can establish, in a theoretical way, many parameters (e.g., the average number of steps) and next compare with the results of a simulation. It is demonstrated that results of a simulation essentially depend on the quality of used generators and could essentially differ from theoretically determined parameters.

1 Introduction

In the paper we shall use the model of Iterative Probabilistic Algorithms interpreted in a finite structure (cf. [3]). Iterative probabilistic algorithms are equivalent (cf. [7]) to Finite Markov Chains, therefore one can use them in all those situations, where Markov Chain model is suitable.

Moreover, Iterative Probabilistic Algorithms are especially useful in the case, where the modeled process consists of several sub-processes related in a probabilistic and/or algorithmic manner. Using iterative probabilistic algorithms one can obtain an algorithm modeling the whole process as an (algorithmic) composition of algorithms corresponding to sub-processes.

On the other hand, a simulation model described in the form of an iterative probabilistic algorithm, is more convenient for computer implementation than a Markov chain model.

Similarly to the case of finite Markov chains, there is an effective procedure relating to an iterative probabilistic algorithm P the corresponding transition matrix P. This matrix contains total probabilities of passing from an initial state to a final state (cf. [1],[3]). Using the matrix P we can also determine, in a theoretical way, another parameters describing the properties of the algorithm P, like the average number of steps of computations (cf. [6]). We would like to stress that numerical errors do not have an essential effect on theoretically determined parameters.

On the other hand, we can organize a simulation procedure consisting in implementing and realizing many times the algorithm P and determine, in an experimental, statistical way, a matrix P' containing experimentally established probabilities of passing from initial to final states; the average number of steps, related to such an experiment is also easy to determine.

---

[1]This research was supported by Białystok University of Technology under grant S/WI/1/03.

A comparison of matrices P and P' and others, theoretically and experimentally de-termined parameters, enables us to speak about the quality of the simulation.
The presented paper contains an extremely simple example demonstrating that even for very small models, the differences between theoretically and experimentally de-termined parameters could be considerable.

2 Iterative Probabilistic Algorithms

To discuss iterative probabilistic algorithms in a formal way, we shall use an abstract programming language L_P (cf. [8], [3]) being an extension of a first order language L containing a countable set $X = \{x, y, z, ...\}$ of variables, a set $F = \{f, g, ...\}$ of function symbols, a set $R = \{ r, t, ...\}$ of relation symbols and a set $C = \{ c, d, ...\}$ of constant symbols.
The set ALG of iterative probabilistic algorithms of L_P is the least set of expressions, containing assignments

> $x := t$, where x is a variable and t is a term of L,
>
> $x := random$,

and such that

> if γ is an open formula of L, and K, M belong ALG, then the expressions
>> begin K ; M end,
>>
>> if γ then K else M,
>>
>> while γ do K ,
>
> belong to ALG.

We shall consider only finite interpretations of the language L. Let $\Im = \langle A; f_\Im, g_\Im, ...; r_\Im, t_\Im, ... ; c_\Im, d_\Im, ... \rangle$ be a structure for L, where A is a nonempty set, called the uni-verse of the structure. For a given function, relation or constant symbol s, $s_\Im$ will denote its interpretation; for example, for a function symbol f, the interpretation $f_\Im$ of the symbol f, is a function with arguments in A and with values in A.
Let $\{x_1, ..., x_k\} \subset X$ be a finite set of variables. By a valuation of variables $x_1, ..., x_k$ in A we shall understand any mapping ω: $\{x_1, ..., x_k\} \to A$. It is easy to note that the set of all valuations is finite and contains $n = m^k$ elements, where m denotes the number of elements in A. Each valuation ω can be represented as a table:

x_1	x_2	$\cdots$	x_k
a_1	a_2	$\cdots$	a_k

where $a_1, ..., a_k \in A$. The set of all valuation of variables $x_1, ..., x_k$ will be denoted by $Wx_1, ..., x_k$ or W if this does not lead to any misunderstanding. In the sequel we shall assume that there is a fixed enumeration of the elements of the set W;

$$W = Wx_1, ..., x_k = \{\omega_1, \omega_2, ..., \omega_n\}.$$

The interpretation of terms and formulas of the first order language L in the structure $\Im$ at a valuation ω is defined in a standard way (cf. [3], [8]). For a term t and a for-mula γ of L, having all variables among $x_1, ..., x_k$, their values at the valuation ω will be denoted by $t_\Im(\omega)$, $\gamma_\Im(\omega)$ respectively. Obviously $t_\Im(\omega)$ is an element of A, $\gamma_\Im(\omega)$ is true (1) or false (0). To stress that all variables of an expression θ of L_P belong to $\{x_1, ..., x_k\}$, we shall often write $\theta(x_1,...,x_k)$ instead of θ.

We shall now define the interpretation of algorithms from *ALG*.
To define the meaning of the operation *random* we shall assume that there is defined
a fixed probability distribution ρ on the set A:

$$\rho : A \rightarrow [0,1], \ \sum_{a \in A} \rho(a) = 1. \tag{1}$$

ρ(a) corresponds to the probability, that after the realization of an assignment of the
form $x := random$, the value of the variable x is equal to a.
By a probabilistic structure for the language L_p we shall understand the pair $< \Im,p >$.
To define the interpretation of an algorithm from *ALG*, having all variables in x_1, ...,
x_k, in the structure $< \Im,p >$ we need the notion of a sub-distribution of probabilities on
the set W of valuations of variables x_1, ..., x_k :
by a sub-distribution of probabilities on W we shall understand any mapping μ such
that:

$$\mu : W \rightarrow [0,1], \ \sum_{\omega \in W} \mu(\omega) \leq 1. \tag{2}$$

Obviously, μ can be treated as n –element vector, $\mu = [\mu_1, ..., \mu_n]$, where $\mu_i = \mu(\omega_i)$.

The main idea is to treat an algorithm P as a mapping transforming sub-distributions
into sub-distributions:

$$
\begin{array}{c}
\omega_1 \xrightarrow{\ \mu_1\ } \\
\cdots \\
\omega_n \xrightarrow{\ \mu_n\ }
\end{array}
\left[\quad P \quad \right]
\begin{array}{c}
\xrightarrow{\ \eta_1\ } \omega_1 \\
\cdots \\
\xrightarrow{\ \eta_n\ } \omega_n
\end{array}
\tag{3}
$$

In the above $\mu(\omega_i)$ $(\eta(\omega_i))$ is denoted shortly by μ_i $(\eta_i.)$.
The result sub-distribution after realization of an algorithm P at the initial sub-
distribution μ will be denoted by $P_{<\Im,\rho>}(\mu)$.

Remark 1. We shall use sub-distributions instead of distributions, because a program
could not finish computations. For instance, the output sub-distribution η for the program *while x=x do x:= x* satisfies $\eta(\omega) = 0$, for any valuation ω
The formal definition of the interpretation of an algorithm $P(x_1, ..., x_k)$ proceeds by
induction on the number of program construction and is omitted here (we refer the
reader to [3] for details). Instead of formal definition we shall use the following
Lemma (cf. [3]) that replaces, in some sense, this definition and describes the behavior of probabilistic algorithms in a manner typical for Markov chain theory. Valuations will play the role of states, and the initial distribution μ will correspond to the
initial vector of probabilities (at the time 0).

Lemma 1 (cf. [3])

Let $<\Im,\rho>$ be a probabilistic structure for L_p with a m –element universe A. For every
program $P(x_1, ..., x_k)$ we can construct, in an effective way, a n×n matrix P =

$[p_{ij}]_{i,j=1,...,n}$, where $n = m^k$, such that for every sub-distributions $\mu = [\mu_1,...,\mu_n]$, $\eta = [\eta_1, ..., \eta_n] = P_{\mathfrak{I},\wp}(\mu)$, the following holds:

$$[\eta_1,...,\eta_n] = [\mu_1,...,\mu_n] \times \begin{bmatrix} p_{11} & \cdots & p_{1n} \\ & \cdots & \\ p_{n1} & \cdots & p_{nn} \end{bmatrix} \qquad (4)$$

Moreover, an element p_{ij} of P corresponds to the probability that ω_j is the output valuation after realization of the program P, provided that the valuation ω_i appears as the input valuation with the probability 1.

The mentioned above construction of the transition matrix for a probabilistic algorithm is described in the Appendix (we restrict ourselves to the case of one-variable programs, which is sufficient for examples considered in the paper; a full version of the construction one can find in [3]).

Remark 2. Let us note, that the transition matrix of a Markov chain and the transition matrix of an algorithm describe different facts:
- if $M = [m_{ij}]_{i,j=1,...,n}$ is the transition matrix of a Markov chain, then m_{ij} denotes the probability of passing from the state i to the state j in one transition step,
- if $P = [p_{ij}]_{i,j=1,...,n}$ is the transition matrix of a probabilistic algorithm, then p_{ij} denotes the probability of passing from the (initial) valuation ω_i to the (final) valuation ω_j after any number of steps of computations, provided that the valuation ω_i appears at the initial sub-distribution with the probability 1 ($\mu(\omega_i) = 1$).

Roughly speaking, probabilistic algorithms correspond to absorbing Markov chains (cf. [7]) and the transition matrix of an algorithm corresponds to the total transition matrix of the corresponding Markov chain.

3 An Example

We start with a very simple example of an algorithm

        P: *while x≠3 do*
                 if x≠2 then x:=random else x:= 1

interpreted in a three element set {1,2,3}, where the random generation of elements is described in the following table containing the probabilities ρ_i of generating the element i, i = 1,2,3:

1	2	3
0.5	0.25	0.25

Speaking in a more formal way, the universe of the structure $\mathfrak{I}$ is the set {1,2,3}, the set of valuations $W = W_x$ contains three valuations (states) ω_1, ω_2, ω_3 satisfying

$\omega_1(x)=1$, $\omega_2(x)=2$, $\omega_3(x)=3$, respectively. The valuations ω_1, ω_2, ω_3 will be denoted simply by $(x=1)$, $(x=2)$, $(x=3)$.

This algorithm can be also viewed and analyzed in terms of a Markov chain. In the terminology of Markov chains the valuation $(x=3)$ is a *final state* and there is no other *absorbing states*.

3.1 Theoretical Analysis of the Algorithm

We shall first determine the transition matrix P for the above algorithm P. We recall that an element p_{ij} of the matrix P corresponds to the probability that ω_j is the output valuation after realization of the program P, provided that the valuation ω_i appears as the input valuation with the probability 1.

Using the method described in the Appendix we shall first construct transition matrices for the assignments $x:= random$ and $x:= 1$

$$\begin{bmatrix} 0.5 & 0.25 & 0.25 \\ 0.5 & 0.25 & 0.25 \\ 0.5 & 0.25 & 0.25 \end{bmatrix}, \begin{bmatrix} 1 & 0 & 0 \\ 1 & 0 & 0 \\ 1 & 0 & 0 \end{bmatrix}, \tag{5}$$

next for the subprogram M: *if $x\neq2$ then $x:=random$ else $x:= 1$*

$$M = \begin{bmatrix} 0.5 & 0.25 & 0.25 \\ 1 & 0 & 0 \\ 05 & 0.25 & 0.25 \end{bmatrix}, \tag{6}$$

and finally for the program P

$$P = \begin{bmatrix} 0 & 0 & 1 \\ 0 & 0 & 1 \\ 0 & 0 & 1 \end{bmatrix}. \tag{7}$$

To determine the average number of steps of the above algorithm we shall consider two cases: the algorithm starts with the state $(x=1)$ or the algorithm starts with $(x=2)$. Denote these numbers by m_1 and m_2, respectively. The vector

$$\mathbf{m} = \begin{bmatrix} m_1 \\ m_2 \end{bmatrix} \tag{8}$$

can be determined, according to the Appendix, as follows:

$$\mathbf{m} = (I - T)^{-1} \times \mathbf{e}, \tag{9}$$

where the matrix T is a part of the matrix M_γ constructed for the program *if γ then M*, and γ denotes the formula $x \neq 3$,

$$M_\gamma = I_\gamma \times M + I_{\neg\gamma} \times I = \begin{bmatrix} 0.5 & 0.25 & 0.25 \\ 1 & 0 & 0 \\ 0 & 0 & 1 \end{bmatrix}, \tag{10}$$

The following sub-matrix T of M_γ corresponds to non-final valuations $(x=1)$, $(x=2)$:

$$T = \begin{bmatrix} 0.5 & 0.25 \\ 1 & 0 \end{bmatrix}. \tag{11}$$

Next, we have

$$(I - T)^{-1} = \begin{bmatrix} 4 & 1 \\ 4 & 2 \end{bmatrix}, \tag{12}$$

and

$$\mathbf{m} = (I - T)^{-1} \times \mathbf{e} = \begin{bmatrix} m_1 \\ m_2 \end{bmatrix} = \begin{bmatrix} 4 & 1 \\ 4 & 2 \end{bmatrix} \times \begin{bmatrix} 1 \\ 1 \end{bmatrix} = \begin{bmatrix} 5 \\ 6 \end{bmatrix}. \tag{13}$$

Thus
- the average number of steps of the algorithm (starting with $x=1$) is 5; $m_1 = 5$,
- the average number of steps of the algorithm (starting with $x=2$) is 6; $m_2 = 6$.

3.1 The Simulation Procedure

We shall now describe an computer experiment related to the statistical estimation of the average number of steps during several realizations of the algorithm P considered above.

The (PASCAL) program, given below, implements the simulation procedure:
- the algorithm P is realized 10 000 times,
- for each realization of P, the number of steps of the computation is determined (the variable ns is used),
- the average number of steps (with respect to all realizations) is established (as the final value of the variable ans).

```
program Simulation;
      const max =10000;
    var i, ns, sns: integer;
              ans: real;
    function RandEl: integer;
        var y: integer;
        begin
            y:= random(4);
            if y=0 or y=1 then RandEl:= 1;
             if y=2 then RandEl:= 2;
```

```
            if y=3 then RandEl:= 3;
        end;
  begin {of the program}
      sns:= 0;
      for i:= 1 to max do
          begin (of the simulation of a realization
                  of the algorithm)
            ns:= 0;
            x:= 1; {the choice of the initial value
                      of the variable x}
            while x<>3 do
                begin
                    if x<>2 then x:= RandEl
                            else x:= 1;
                    ns := ns + 1;
                end;
              sns: = sns + ns;
        end (of the simulation of a realization
                of the algorithm);
        ans := sns / max;
        write('average number of steps');
        writeln('of the algorithm');
        write('(starting with x =', x, ') =  ');
        writeln(ans:2:5);
  end {of the program}.
```

The results of a realization of this program (Celeron 633, Borland PASCAL7.0) are
the following:

```
    average number of steps of the algorithm
    (starting with x = 1) = 3.9567.
```

Denote this value by m'_1; $m'_1 = 3.9567$.
If the instruction x:= 1 (marked by {the choice of the initial value
of the variable x}) is replaced by x:= 2 then the result is:

```
    average number of steps of     the     algorithm
    (starting with x = 2) = 5.0709.
```

Analogously, denote this value by m'_2; $m'_2 = 5.0709$.

4 Comparing Simulation Results with Theoretically Determined Parameters

In comparing the theoretical analysis of the algorithm with the results of the simulation procedure we restrict ourselves to the case of the average number of steps. We
recall that the theoretically determined values of the average number of steps for the
initial states $(x=1)$, $(x=2)$ are denoted by m_1 and m_2, respectively, and the experimental equivalents of m_1 and m_2 are denoted by m'_1 and m'_2. Thus we have:

-    for the initial state $(x=1)$: $m_1 = 5$, $m'_1 = 3.9567$,

-    for the initial state $(x=2)$:$m_2 = 6$, $m'_2 = 5.0709$.

It is easy to note that the difference exceeds 15% (this is for an algorithm operating
on 3 valuations only !).

Remark 3. In experiments with the above algorithm we also used another pseudorandom generator (regarded as very good), but the differences between the simulation results and the theoretically determined parameters were often essential.

5 Main Questions

As we have stated above, the difference between the average number of steps of an algorithm, operating on three states, determined in two ways, theoretical and experimental, may exceed 15%.

The question arises in a natural way:

How large difference is possible for algorithms operating on, e.g., 100 states ?

On the ground of our experience we can formulate (in an informal manner) the following observations:

> For a random variable X, denote by X' its equivalent received by means of a computer simulation procedure. Then
>
> - the values $E(X)$ and $E(X')$ may be often of the same order,
> - the values $Var(X)$ and $Var(X')$ may be often highly different.

This suggests that a pseudo-random generator, for our simulation procedure, should be chosen in a very careful way. Before-hand statistical tests are absolutely recommended!

Another possible solution is to construct another pseudo-random generator, appropriate only for investigations related to some fixed parameters of the Markov model. For such a generator we do not require to satisfy all possible tests verifying quality of pseudo-random generators. The idea of the construction of such a generator will be discussed in a separate paper.

References

1. Borowska A.: Determining Probabilities of Transitions in Probabilistic Algorithms, MSc Thesis, University of Białystok, 1999
2. Borowska A., Dańko W., Karbowska-Chilińska J.: Probabilistic Algorithms as a Tool for Modelling Stochastic Processes, Proceedings of CISIM'04, Ełk, 2004, (to appear in Springer-Verlag)
3. Dańko W.: The Set of Probabilistic Algorithmic Formulas Valid in a Finite Structure is Decidable with Respect to Its Diagram, Fundamenta Informaticae, vol. 19 (3-4), 1993 (417-431)
4. Dańko W.: Verification of Results of Computer Simulation, Image Analysis, Computer Graphics, Security Systems and Artificial Intelligence Applications, vol. II, , University of Finance and Management in Białystok, 2005, (39-45)
5. Feller W.: An Introduction to Probability Theory (Polish translation), vol.1, PWN, Warsaw, 1977
6. Josifescu M.: Finite Markov Processes and Their Applications, John Wiley & Sons, New York, London 1988

7. Koszelew J.: The Methods for Verification of Properties of Probabilistic Programs, (doctoral dissertation), ICS PAS, Warszawa, 2000;
8. Mirkowska G., Salwicki A.: Algorithmic Logic, D.Reidel Publ. Co. & PWN, Warsaw, 1987

Appendix: The Construction of The Transition Matrix for a Probabilistic Algorithm

We shall briefly describe the method of associating with each program P its transition matrix P (cf. [1], [3]). We shall restrict ourselves to the case of one variable programs, which simplifies the general method described in [1], [3].

Assume that the algorithm is interpreted in a set $A = \{a_1, ..., a_n\}$ and the probability of random generation of the element a_i is denoted by q_i, $i = 1, ..., n$.

We shall now describe how to assign to an algorithm P its transition matrix $P = [p_{ij}]_{i,j=1,...,n}$. We recall that p_{ij} denotes the probability of passing from the state $(x = a_i)$ to the state $(x = a_j)$, provided that P start from $(x = a_i)$, i.e., the probability that, the initial value of the variable x is a_i, is equal to 1.

(DA)   For an assignment P of the form $x := a_k$, the corresponding matrix $P = [p_{ij}]_{i,j=1,...,n}$ is defined as follows: if $j = k$ then $p_{ij} = 1$, otherwise $p_{ij} = 0$,

(RA)   For an assignment P of the form $x := random$, the corresponding matrix $P = [p_{ij}]_{i,j=1,...,n}$ is defined as follows: $p_{ij} = q_j$, $j = 1, ..., n$.

In the sequel, for a test γ, we shall denote by I_γ the diagonal $n \times n$ matrix $I_\gamma = [d_{ij}]_{i,j=1,...,n}$ satisfying:
    $d_{ij} = 1$ iff $i = j$ and the valuation $x = a_i$) satisfies the test γ, otherwise $d_{ij} = 0$.

(C)   If P is of the form $begin\ M_1;\ M_2\ end$, and the matrices M_1 and M_2 for the subprograms M_1 and M_2 are constructed, then the matrix P for the program P is defined as follows:

$$P = M_1 \times M_2, \qquad\qquad (14)$$

(B)   If P is of the form $if\ \gamma\ then\ M_1\ else\ M_2$, and the matrices M_1 and M_2 for the subprograms M_1 and M_2 are constructed, then the matrix P for the program P is defined as follows:

$$P = I_\gamma \times M_1 + I_{\neg\gamma} \times M_2, \qquad\qquad (15)$$

(L)   If P is of the form $while\ \gamma\ do\ M$, and the matrix M for the subprogram M is constructed, then the matrix P for the program P should satisfy the equation

$$P = I_{\neg\gamma} \times I + I_\gamma \times M \times P, \qquad\qquad (16)$$

motivated by the equivalence of the following two algorithms

while γ do M,
if not γ then {STOP} else begin M; while γ do M end.

This equation may be written as:

$$(I - I_\gamma \times M) \times P = I_{\neg\gamma}, \qquad\qquad (17)$$

where I denotes the unity n×n matrix.

To solve this equation it is sufficient to consider the sub-matrix of

$$(I - I_\gamma \times M) \tag{18}$$

obtained by rejecting all positions related to final and absorbing states. The determinant of this matrix differs from 0 (cf. [1], [3]).

We shall end this Appendix by describing the method of determining, for a given algorithm P of the form *while γ do M*, the average number of steps of repetitions of the sub-program M. Since this value depends on the initial state (valuation), we can speak about the vector of average numbers of steps of computations, with positions corresponding to initial (non-final) valuations. In the example considered in the paper this vector (denoted by **m**) has two positions: the first position corresponds to the valuation $(x=1)$, and the second one corresponds to the valuation $(x=2)$.

The method enables us to determine the vector of average numbers of repetitions of the subprogram M of the program P of the form *while γ do M* and can be only applied to the case, where P has does not contain other (non-final) absorbing states, i.e., all absorbing states are final.

For simplicity, assume that the valuations are numbered in the following way: numbers of non-final valuations are less than numbers of final valuations.

We start with the following partition of the matrix M_γ corresponding to the program *if γ then M*:

$$M_\gamma = \begin{bmatrix} T & R \\ '0' & I \end{bmatrix}, \tag{19}$$

where I is the identity k×k matrix (k denotes the number of final states, i.e. valuations satisfying the condition γ) and '0' denotes the k×(n-k) matrix with all positions equal to 0. The sub-matrix T of M_γ corresponds to transitions from non-final valuations to non-final valuations.

The matrix T will be used in order to determine the vector **m** of average numbers of repetitions of the subprogram M in computations of the program P. Namely,

$$\mathbf{m} = (I - T)^{-1} \times \mathbf{e}, \tag{20}$$

where **e** denotes the column vector with all positions equal to 1.

Analysis of E-learning System Dynamics

B. Ignatowska, R. Mosdorf

Higher School of Finance and Management in Bialystok; 1 Grunwaldzka
St., Elk, Poland

Abstract: In the paper the analysis of dynamics of e-learning system activity has been presented. The aim of analysis was the identification of dynamical properties of e-learning system. The changes in time of system users' logs (administration workers and teachers) and logs into web server (internet pages) have been analysed. The following methods: autocorrelation function, Fourier analysis, wavelet analysis, Hurst exponent, attractor reconstruction, correlation dimension and largest Lyapunov exponent have been used. It has been found that frequency analysis and non-linear analysis can be useful method for identification of activity of different kinds of users of e-learning system.

1 Introduction

One of the key problems, which should be solved during the construction and development of Learning Management System (LMS) of Higher School, is to define the system development strategy. The aim of the paper is to determine the methods of analysis helpful in evaluation and planning of development of LMS of Higher School.

One of methods which can be used to identify changes in time of behaviours of LMS users can be based on analysis of time series of users' logs to the system. Identification and understanding trends in users' behaviors can be useful method to optimize development of LMS from the economical and organizational point of view.

In academic year 2002/2003 the internet application 'Recto' was applied in University of Finance and Management in Bialystok in order to support the management of university administration and the learning process. This system is integrated with the university website and consists of such modules like: E-student, Candidate, Teacher and Dean's Office [1]. Teachers use their module to input syllabuses, marks, reports and materials for students. Technically 'Recto' is based on relational database and has been created using such tools like: Windows 2000 server, SQL server database and programming software Visual Studio .NET [2]. At present the 'Recto' system contains registered accounts of about 6 500 students, 480 teachers and 30 administrative users. There are also about 1500 syllabuses in the system.

The university server collects daily information about all requests made to the web server in one log file. The size of the log file was about 8,5 GB. To analyze this data the computer program Analog 5.91beta1 has been used. The Analog 5.91beta1 does not collect information in database files but creates HTML reports with determined parameters. The time series of number of requests per day come from such reports.

The dynamics of changes in time of logs to: www pages, administration module and teacher module have been analyzed. The following methods: autocorrelation function,

Fourier analysis, wavelet analysis, Hurst exponent, attractor reconstruction, correlation dimension and largest Lyapunov exponent has been used.

2 Data Analysis

The university web site is used by different groups of users like: students, teachers, administrative workers and also users who search for information about the university. For the evaluation of the activity of e-learning system we need to know the dynamic characteristic of different kinds of system users' behaviours. Obtaining the information about dynamics of users' activity requires application of sophisticated methods of nonlinear analysis [7], [8], [9].
We would like to answer the question which methods are useful to identify the behaviours of different groups of users. The analyzed data comes from two sources: logs into the Recto system (the system database) and logs into the web server, which were processed by the program Analog 5.91beta1 [4], [5], [6]. In Fig.1 the analyzed logs time series have been presented.

2.1 Frequency Analysis

The power spectrum [7] of time series of logs is shown in Fig.2. The results of frequency analysis presented in Fig.2 allow us to distinguish limited number of dominant frequencies.   The dominant five frequencies have been found out. The example of changes of number of logs into www pages has been shown in Fig.3, where the observed periods changes of the number of visited web pages have been schematically shown.
In all data series we can identify two dominant low frequencies connected with time periods equal to 375 and 125 days. It seems that these changes are connected with yearly and semester activity of system users.   The rest of identified dominate frequencies with time periods equal to 7, 3.5, 2.3 days appears in analyzed data series with different intensity. These frequencies can be clearly identified in the data series describing the activity of university administration (Fig.2b). The 7 days cycle seems to correspond with the weekly cycle of administration work, but remain 3.5 and 2.3 days cycles are connected with changing of logs numbers within the weeks. The examples of such changes are shown in Fig.3 where the decrease of number of logs within subsequent weeks can be observed.

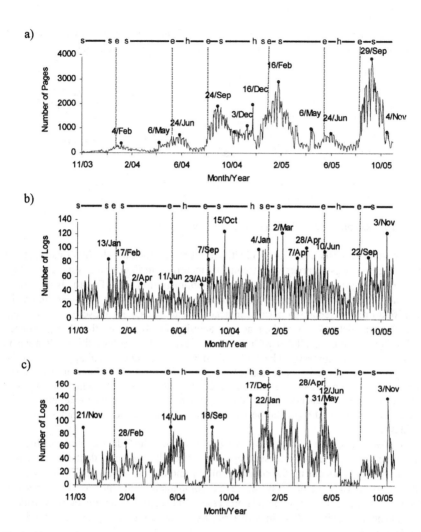

Fig.1. The logs into: www pages, administration module and teacher module. a) logs into the web server; processed by the program Analog 5.91beta1 [4], b) logs of the university administration into the Recto system (database), c) logs of teachers into the Recto system (database), e – exams, h – holidays, s – semester

The changes characterized by time periods equal to 7, 3.5 and 2.3 days are clearly visible also within logs into the www pages (Fig.2a), whereas the 7 days cycle disappears in teachers' logs data series. That can be driven by the fact that university teachers don't work as regular as administration. A lot of them have lectures on Sunday, Saturday, once in two weeks or once a month. The teachers like to cumulate their hours and come to have some time to carry out their research, prepare themselves to lectures and so on.

The changes of dominant frequencies in time can be analyzed with using the windowed Fourier transform [11]. The windowed Fourier transform is used for extraction of local-frequency information from a signal, but this is an inaccurate method of time–frequency localization. The wavelet analysis is free from this inaccuracy [10], [11]. The wavelet power spectrum of logs time series is shown in Fig.4.

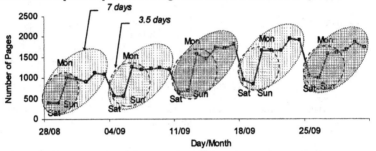

Fig.3. The examples of periodic changes of daily www logs

The wavelet analysis allow us to identify the time periods in which we can observe the changes of logs numbers with frequency identified in Fourier analysis. The 7 days cycle of changes of numbers of university administration logs (Fig.4b) is present in the whole analyzed time. The 3.5 days cycle appears in the whole first year but can be identified only in separated periods in second year. It happens close to terms of exams. The wavelet analysis of the teachers' activity (Fig.4c) shows that the appearance of 3.5 days cycle is correlated with the time of exams. Incidentally this cycle appears during the time of semester. The cycle of 7 days is not intensive and appears incidentally which shows the irregular usage of system by teachers. The intensity of appearance of 7 days cycle is similar with the intensity of 14 days cycle, which seems to be connected with the teachers' work during external study. The disappearance of the cycles shorter than 20 days can be observed during the periods of summer students' holidays.

In the power spectrum of logs into www pages (Fig.4a) the 7 days cycle is visible too. The intensity of appearance of such cycle increases during the students' examination time and disappears during the summer holiday and during semesters. The increase in intensity of appearance of 7 days cycle is accompanied by the increase in intensity of 3.5 and 2.3 cycles. It seems that this process is connected with administration workers and teachers' activities. Activities of other users cause the disappearance of 3.5 and 2.3 days cycles.

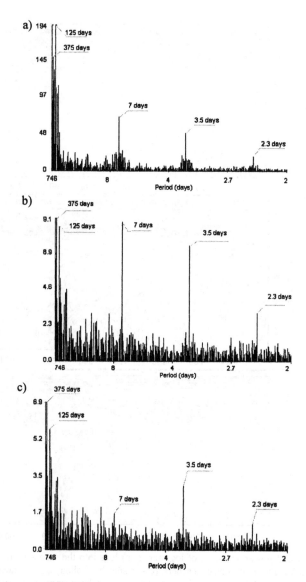

Fig.2. The power spectrum of logs time series: a) logs into the web server, b) logs of the university administration, c) logs of teachers.

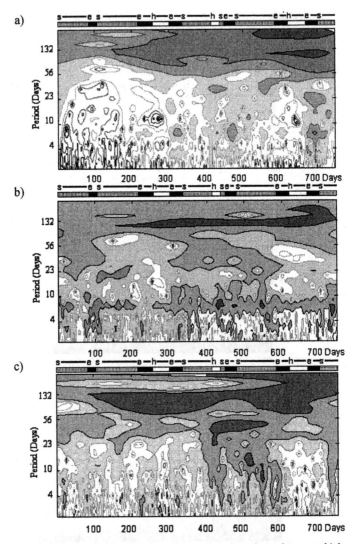

Fig.4. The wavelet power spectrum of logs series. a) logs into the web server, b) logs of the university administration, c) logs of teachers, (e – exams, h – holidays, s – semester). The grey area indicates the local maximum. The calculations have been carried out using computer program published in [12], (Wavelet software was provided by C. Torrence and G. Compo, and is available at URL: http://paos.colorado.edu/research/wavelets/").

2.2. Dynamics Analysis

For identification of dynamic properties of different group of users the nonlinear methods of data analysis have been used [7], [8], [9].

Reconstruction of attractor in a certain embedding dimension has been carried out with using the stroboscope coordination. In this method the subsequent coordinations of attractor points have been calculated based on the subsequent samples distance of time delay τ. The time delay is multiplication of time distance between the samples Δt [7]. The attractor reconstruction can not be automated. The choice of proper quantity of time delay τ has an important impact on reconstruction [7], [8]. In Fig.5 the reconstruction of the attractor from www logs series and autocorrelation function of www logs have been presented. The value of autocorrelation function decreases with the increase of τ, that suggests that data has been generated by deterministic chaos process [7], [8], [9].

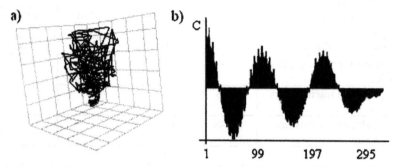

Fig. 5. The attractor reconstruction and autocorrelation function. a) The attractor reconstruction from www logs series, d) Autocorrelation function of www logs series.

The identification of nature (deterministic chaos, periodic or stochastic) of analyzed data can be estimated with using the Hurst exponent. For the signals of stochastic character $H=0.5$. The border point N^* between area, where the $H>0.5$ and area, where $H=0.5$ corresponds with the boundary of the natural period of analyzed system.
For experimental data correlation dimension D_2 based on the Grassberger – Procaccia method [8] and largest Lyapunov exponent based on the Wolf [13] algorithm can be calculated. Correlation dimension is the measure of number of degree of freedom of the system but the largest Lyapunov exponent (L) identifies the nature of data. A positive value of largest Lyapunov exponent indicates that in the considered system the deterministic chaos appears. The time of stability loss in the system can be estimated by value of $1/L$.
In the Table 1 the results of non-linear analysis have been presented.
The identification of correlation between the time series of e-learning server requests can be calculated with using the correlation coefficient (C) [14]. When $|C|$ is close to 1, the analyzed time series are correlated. When the large and low values in both series appear at the same time, then $C>0$; but when large values in first series meet low values in other series, then $C<0$. When C is close to zero, then the time series are not correlated.

Table 1. Results of nonlinear analysis

	Pages	Teachers	Administration	Unit
Time of autocorrelation disappearance	35	47	31	days
Hurst Exponent	0.93	0.812	0.839	
Border point N^*	140	130	130	days
Correlation Dimension	2.25	5.25	5.5	
Largest Lyapunov Exponent	0.105	0.0685	0.0698	1 bit/days
Time of stability loss	9.5	14.6	14.3	days
Correlation www pages with:	-	0.3	0.49	
Correlation teachers logs with:	0.3	-	0.5	
Correlation administration logs with:	0.49	0.5	-	

Results of calculation (presented in the Table 1) of time periods, in which the autocorrelation disappears, show that the shortest period appears in time series of administration logs and is equal to 31 days. This value corresponds with monthly cycle of Dean Office working time. We can observe the similar length of time period of autocorrelation disappearance in the time series of www logs. In this case the time period is equal to 35 days. The largest time period appears in time series of teachers' logs and is equal to 47 days. The obtained values of Hurst exponent and largest Lyapunov exponent show that all analyzed series have the character of deterministic chaos. The largest value of Hurst exponent has been obtained for time series of www logs. The natural periods of all analyzed series obtained from R/S analysis are similar to semester.

The correlation dimension obtained for attractors reconstructed from analyzed time series shows that the attractors reconstructed from administration workers and teachers' logs have the most complex structure. In case of www logs the obtained correlation dimension equal to 2.25 suggests that changes of number of www logs can be modelled by low dimensional model.

The analyses of largest Lyapunov exponent allow us to estimate the time interval in which the system remains stable. In the result of analyses we may conclude that changes of www logs are the most unstable process. In this case the number of www logs can be predicted within one week. In case of administration workers and teachers' logs the number of logs can be predicted within two weeks.

In the table 1 the results of calculating of correlation coefficient between the data series are presented. All calculated coefficients are positive – it means that the increases and decreases of logs numbers occur in the same time in both series. The lowers correlation appears between the www and administration workers logs.

3 Conclusion

Analyses carried out in the paper show that proposed methods are useful to analyse dynamics of e-learning system.

The values obtained from Hurst exponent and largest Lyapunov exponent show that all analyzed series have the character of deterministic chaos.

The Fourier analysis allows us to identify the: annual, semester, weekly, 3.5 daily and 2.3 daily dominant frequencies of the system. The 7 days cycle seems to correspond to the weekly cycle of administration work, but remaining 3.5 and 2.3 days cycles are connected with changing of log numbers within the week. The wavelet analysis allow us to identify the time periods in which we can find the changes of log numbers with the frequency identified in Fourier analysis. The 7 days cycle of changes of number of administration workers'logs is present in the entire time of system working time. In the teachers' logs the appearance of 3.5 days cycle is correlated with time of exams. In the www logs the 7 days cycle is visible too. The intensity of appearance of such cycle increases during the students'examination time and disappears during the summer holidays and semesters.

The administration workers, teachers and www logs are correlated in such a way that the increases and decreases of logs numbers occur in the same time in all series. The lowest correlation appears between the www and administration workers logs.

The LMS system activity is the result of two main processes: educational and administrative activities. The carried out analyses show that activities of users reach the highest values always at the end of exams period but not within the semester. This suggests that activities of teachers and students seem to be dominated by their administrative works.

References

1. Higher School of Finance and Management in Bialystok internet site www.wsfiz.edu.pl
2. System 'Recto' documentation.
3. Regulation of The Higher School Chancellor of June 2003, Nr RA/4301/15/2003 with attachments 1-3.
4. Analog 5.91beta1 – www.analog.cx, 1sth April 2005
5. S. Turner, *Analog 6.0: How the web works, system documentation*, www.analog.cx/docs/webworks.html, 19 December 2004.
6. S.Haigh, J. Megarity, *Measuring Web Site Usage: Log File Analysis*, www.collectionscanada.ca/9/1/p1-256-e.html, 4th August 1998.
7. J. Awrejcewicz, R. Mosdorf, Analiza numeryczna wybranych zagadnie dynamiki chaotycznej. WNT Warszawa, 2003.
8. H.G. Schuster. Chaos deterministyczny – wprowadzenie, Wydawnictwo Naukowe PWN, Warszawa 1993.
9. G.L. Baker, J.P. Gollub. Wstęp do dynamiki układów chaotycznych, Wydawnictwo Naukowe PWN, Warszawa 1998.
10. J.T. Białosiewicz, Falki i aproksymacje, WNT, Warszawa, 2000.
11. C. Torrence, G. P. Compo, A Practical Guide to Wavelet Analysis. Bulletin of the American Meteorological Society, Vol. 79, No. 1, 1998.

12. C. Torrence, G. P. Compo, A Practical Guide to Wavelet Analysis, With signifi-
    cance and confidence testing. http://paos.colorado.edu/research/wavelets/
13. A. Wolf, J.B. Swift, H.L. Swinney, H.L. and J.A. Vastano, Determining
    Lyapunov Exponent from a Time series, Phisica-D, 16 (1985) 285-317.

Can a Negative Selection Detect an Extremely few Non-self among Enormous Amount of Self Cells?

Akira Imada

Brest State Technical University
Moskowskaja 267, 224017 Brest, Republic of Belarus
akira@bsty.by

Abstract. We have had lots of reports in which they asserted a negative selection algorithm successfully distinguished non-self cells from self cells, especially in a context of "network intrusion detection" where self patterns are assumed to represent normal transactions while non-self patterns represent anomaly. Furthermore they went on to assert a negative selection gives us an advantage that we use only a set of self cells as training samples. This would be really an advantage since we usually don't know what do anomaly patterns look like until they complete an intrusion when it's too late. We, however, suspect, more or less, its applicability to a real system. This paper gives it a consideration to one of the latest such approaches.

1 Introduction

A sultan has granted a commoner a chance to marry one of his 100 daughters by presenting the daughters one at a time letting him know her dowry that had been defined previously. The commoner must immediately decide whether to accept or reject her and he is not allowed to return to an already rejected daughter. The sultan will allow the marriage only if the commoner picks the daughter with the highest dowry. --- "Sultan's Dowry Problem" [1]

In real world, we have a problem in which we can easily access to any one of the possible candidate solutions, most likely not but still have a few chance to be the true one, which we don't know in advance.

The ultimate extreme of such a problem is sometimes called *a-needle-in-a-haystack* problem (see Fig. 1). One of such a needle, originally proposed by Hinton & Nowlan [1], is exactly the one configuration of 20-bit binary string,

---

[1] According to the author(s) of the web-page of Cunningham & Cunningham, Inc. (http://c2.com) the problem was probably first stated in Martin Gardner's Mathematical Recreations column in the February 1960 issue of The Scientific American. To explore the problem more in detail, see, e.g., http://mathworld.wolfram.com. We thank Mariusz Rybnik at University Paris XII for suggesting that the problem is reminiscent of our context.

hence the search space of which is made up of 2^{20} points and only one point is the target to be searched for. Therefore, no information such as how close is a currently searching point to the needle.

Yet another problem, *a-tiny-flat-island-in-a-huge-lake* — this is a problem we once came across when we had explored a fitness landscape defined on all the possible synaptic weight values of a fully-connected spiking neurons to give them a function of associative memory [2]. To simplify it we formalized the problem in more general form as follows.

Testfunction 1 (A tiny flat island in a huge lake) [2] *Find an algorithm to locate a point in the region A all of whose coordinates are in $[-a, a]$ ($a < 1$) in an universe of the n-dimensional hypercube all of whose coordinate x_i lie in $[-1, 1]$ ($i = 1, \bullet \ ; n$).*

Many researchers in artificial immune system community have suggested us that the problem might be easy if we use the concept of negative selection. To simply put, the negative selection is an evolutionary selection mechanism by which immune system trains itself only using *self cells* as training samples, so that it can recognize *non-self cells* afterwards.

The simplest option is to test a set of samples one by one, as many as possible, to know whether each of those samples is the true solution or not. If we have a good luck, then our goal is attained. However, should we rather be more than lucky? As a trial, we train the system in parallel using those samples during the procedure, regardless of whichever the real solution might be found or not as a result. Then even if we are unlucky, we can at least expect that the system will recognize the true solution later after the training easier than before.

In this paper, we approach the problem from this view point. Or rather more in general, we take it a pattern classification problem, under the constraint that we have two classes one of which includes an extremely few patterns while the other includes an almost infinite number of patterns. Thus, we might as well

Fig. 1. A fictitious sketch of fitness landscape of *a-needle-in-a-haystack*. The haystack here is drawn as a two-dimensional flat plane of fitness zero.

---

[2] It is not necessarily to be said for the top of the island to be "flat", but the originally this was a test-bed for evolutionary computations, and the fitness of the island region is one, and zero in a lake region. That is why.

take it a task of discrimination of a few of non-self cells as anomaly patterns
from enormous amount of self cells which represent normal patterns.

One of such latest approaches among others is by Zhou Ji and Dasgupata [3].
They wrote

> The idea of negative selection was from T cell development process in
> the thymus. If a T cell recognizes self cells, it is eliminated before deploy-
> ment for immune functionality. In an analogous manner, the negative
> selection algorithm generates the detector set by eliminating any detec-
> tor candidates that match self samples. It is thus used as an anomaly
> detection mechanism with the advantage that only the negative (normal)
> training data are needed.

Recalling our universe is n-dimensional Euclidean space, let us check two algorithms they proposed: one is to generate detectors of constant sized hyper-spheres
and the other is to generate variable sized hyper-spheres. They concluded that
detectors which detect anomaly patterns are successfully created just by training
with normal patterns.

When we think of a network intrusion detection, we usually don't know what do
anomaly patterns look like in advance. Hence this feature of training with only
normal patterns is really advantageous. Our concern then is what if the number
of non-self cells is extremely smaller than the number of self cells, which is of
usual cases when we think of a network intrusion detection. In order to explore
this issue, we apply their algorithms to *a-tiny-island-in-a-huge-lake* mentioned
above. We can control the difficulty of the task by changing the value of a,
as well as the dimension of the universe. The ultimate case is when all of the
coordinates of the target points shrink to zero, and this is the problem known
as *a-needle-in-a-haystack*.

2 Algorithm

So far lots of algorithms to distinguish non-self patterns from self patterns have
been proposed. The goal of these algorithms is to create detectors which cover
non-self space as much as possible. Here, in this paper, we concentrate on the algorithm called *"Augmented Negative Selection Algorithm with Variable-Coverage
Detectors"* proposed in 2004 by Zhou Ji and Dasgupata [3], as well as its simpler
version in which detector size is constant instead of variable, also proposed by
the same authors in the same article. The followings are these two algorithms
that we paraphrased the original ones with the semantics being intact. Firstly,
the simpler version is:

Algorithm 1 (Constant-sized Detector Generation) *After setting (i) N_t,
the number of training samples; (ii) r_d, the radius of detector; and (iii) N_d, the
total number of detectors:*

1. *Create N_s samples of self cells at random.*
2. *Create a hyper-sphere which has the radius r_d and whose center locates at random in $[-1, 1]$. This is a candidate detector to detect non-self cells.*
3. *If this-hyper sphere does not contain any sample self cells, then put it as a detector in D, the detector's repertoire. Otherwise delete the hyper-sphere.*
4. *Repeat 2-3 until we find N_d detectors.*

This algorithm, in our humble opinion, does not contain the concept of negative selection or whatever in an immune system metaphor neither, if not at all. The second one is:

Algorithm 2 (Variable-sized Detector Generation) *After setting (i) N_t, the number of training samples; (ii) r_s, the radius of self cells; (iii) c_0, expected coverage, i.e., the degree to how much those created detectors cover non-self cells; (iv) c_{max}, the upper bound of self coverage; and (v) N_d, the maximum number of detectors:*

1. *Empty D, the detector's repertoire.*
2. *Try to find a point $\mathbf{x} = (x_1, \cdots, x_n) \in [-1, 1]^n$ which is not contained by any of the valid detectors so far created, unless the number of those trials exceeds $1/(1 - c_0)$. If no such $\mathbf{x}$ is found, then terminate the run.* [3]
3. *If r, the distance between $\mathbf{x}$ and its closest self sell in the training sample, is larger than the radius r_s, i.e., if the candidate doesn't include any of the sample self cells, then add the sphere whose center is $\mathbf{x}$ and radius is r to D as a new valid detector.*
4. *If no such $\mathbf{x}$ can be found within the consecutive trials of $1/(1 - c_{max})$ time, then terminate the run.* [4] *Otherwise repeat 2 and 3, until we find a total of N_d detectors.*

We do not think this algorithm strongly reflects an immune system either, despite the title of the original paper indicates it. However at least the title holds true in the sense that detectors are chosen by trying to match them to the self strings and if a detector matches then it is discarded, otherwise it is kept. This is, above all, what we call a natural selection algorithm.

3 Evaluation of How it Works

We use a measure originally proposed by Lopes et al. [4] in which four quantities, i.e., (i) true-positive, (ii) true-negative, (iii) false positive, and (iv) false negative are used. Here we assume positive sample is non-self and negative sample is self, since detectors are designed to detect non-self cells. Hence, these four terms are

---

[3] This is because when we have sampled m points and only one point was not covered, the expected coverage is $1 - 1/m$. Hence the necessary number of tries to ensure expected coverage c_0 is $m = 1/(1 - c_0)$.
[4] See also the footnote above replacing c_0 with c_{max}.

defined in the sence that (i) t_p (true positive) — true declaration of positive sample, i.e., non-self declared as non-self (ii) f_p (false positive) — false declaration of positive sample, i.e., self declared as non-self (iii) t_n (true negative) — true declaration of negative sample, i.e., self declared as self (iv) f_n (false negative) — false declaration of negative sample, i.e., non-self declared as self. Under these definitions $d_r = t_p/(t_p + f_n)$ implies detection rate, and $f_a = f_p/(t_n + f_p)$ implies false alarm rate.

4   Experiment, Results, and Discussion

As a preliminary experiment, we tried a random search for the needle in the 20-dimensional haystack by creating 5000 candidate strings at random, and checking, one by one, if each of the sample is the needle or not. We assume we have only one needle which principally we don't know where. The result is shown in Fig. 2, and we found it is still not such a difficult problem if we use a standard PC found everywhere nowadays.

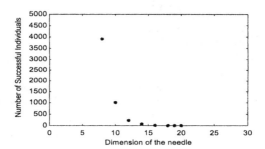

Fig. 2. The number of happened-to-be-the-needle out of 5000 random creations of the candidate.

Taking this random search as our *placebo* experiment, what will happen if we exploit one of the lately reported more sophisticate methods? We now assume the whole universe is n-dimensional hyper-cube $[0, 1]^n$ as mentioned already; any point all of whose coordinates lies in $[(0.5 - a), (0.5 + a)]$ $(0 < a < 0.5)$ is non-self cell, whilst other points in the universe are self cells [5] ; and all the self cells are hyper-sphere whose radius is r_s.

---

[5] We modify our Testfunction-1 for the sake of simplicity of coding in this way, which keeps the problem equivalent to the original one.

4.1   A 2-dimensional version of an-island-in-a-lake

First of all, in order for our eyes to be able to observe the behavior of the algorithms, our experiment is performed on a 2-dimensional space, that is, we set $n = 2$. We employ a set of 500 randomly selected points in the self region as the training samples, and 1000 points randomly chosen from entire space is the test data. The reason of these settings is to enable us to compare our results with those in the original proposition [3].

Both the regions claimed normal and abnormal when r_s is set to 0.1 are shown in Fig. 3. The location of the self points in the training sample and the created detectors when we set $r_s = 0.1$ which is the value recommended by the original proposition [3] are shown in Fig. 3. So far so good. However, our goal is to rec-

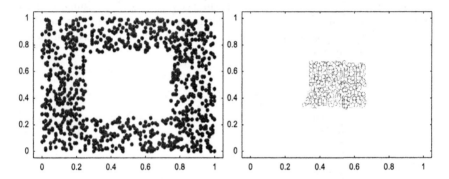

Fig. 3. A set of five hundred self-points employed as training samples (Left),and a set of five hundreds detectors created by the Algorithm-1 with $a = 0.25$ and $r_s = 0.1$ (Right) from an experiment in 2-dimensional space.

ognize non-self patterns from extremely tiny region. Hence the next experiment is a dependency on the value of a. Fig. 4 shows the number of required trials to find the pre-defined number of detectors, which is 500 here, and the number of successes when those 500 detectors tried to detect the 500 non-self samples. Both are plotted as a function of value of a using the Algorithm-1 with $r_s = 0.1$ to create the detectors. As we can see in the Figure, the difficulty of the task becomes harder exponentially as a becomes smaller, and therefore we know this algorithm would not work if the region to be searched for is extremely tiny.

4.2   A 20-dimensional version of an-island-in-a-lake

Next of our interest is what happens when we increase dimensionality. All we found was it becomes much more difficult than in the case $n = 2$. What we

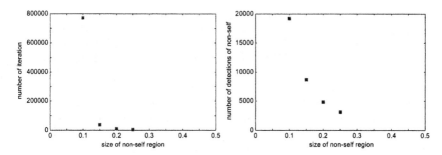

Fig. 4. The number of iteration required to find 500 successful detectors (Left), and
the number of successes when 500 detectors tried to detect 500 non-self samples, that
is, the number of successes out of 25000 events (Right). Both are as a function of value
of a when we experimented with the Algorithm-1 with $r_s = 0.1$ in 2-dimensional space.

found, for example, is even if we increase the number of training sample of self
patterns from 1000 to 10000, the distribution of the coordinates of samples is
very sparse when $n = 20$. If the algorithm worked well, the detector would be
supposed to locate only in the non-self region, such as Fig. 5 (Right) which is
from a result of 2-dimensional experiment for comparison purpose, while the
result in 20-dimensional experiment, as shown in Fig. 5 (Left), was not in that
way. We can see in the figure that the coordinates of the whole detectors are

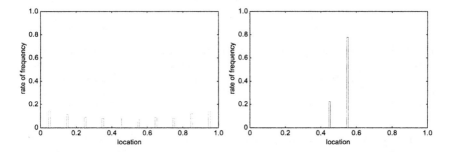

Fig. 5. The distribution of all the coordinates of the detectors for an experiment with
$n = 20$ (Left), and the distribution when $n = 2$ for the purpose of comparison (Right).

almost uniformly distributed, which means a failure to find a set of successful
detectors.

Then, we give it a consideration of how will the Algorithm-2 (Variable Sized

Detector) improve the situation. In an experiment in 20-dimensional space where the Algorithm-2 creates certain number of detectors with 1000 training samples of self patterns. Non-self region in this experiment was $[0.495, 0.505]^{20}$ and radius of self was set to 0.1. As a result of a run under $c_0 = 0.99$, a total of 96 detectors are created.

First, we studied how *true-positive* and *false-positive* rate are influenced by dimensionality. As shown in Fig. 6 (Left), the perfect situation when $n = 2$ abruptly deteriorates even $n = 3$. Alas!

Next, we ran the algorithm for $n = 5$, 15, 20, and 25 to study a dependency of the degree to how successfully the detector will be created on the dimension of search space. The number of detectors created is somehow similar in each dimension, ranging from 91 to 96. In Fig. 5 (Right), we show detection-rate and false-alarm-rate as a function of dimensionality. Though not satisfactorily, we see somewhat of a successful result, at least as for detection-rate.

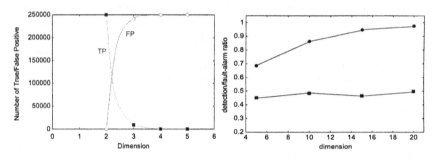

Fig. 6. (Left) True-positive and False-positive as a function of dimensionality. (Right) Detection-rate shown with circles and false-alarm-rate shown with rectangles as a function of dimensionality in a series of experiments where the Algorithm-2 creates certain number of detectors from 91 to 96 with 1000 training samples of self patterns.

Further, we will explore different parameter values with the goal being to learn the limit of how small non-self region and how large the dimensionality under which the algorithm can detect non-self points successfully. Then we will experiment by lowering the value c_0 which is 99.99% and 99% in the original version. Those results are not shown here since our experiments have sometimes reversed our expectations so far.

5   Conclusion

We have obtained the similar results with the experiments by Zhou Ji and Dasgupata [3] only on the condition that the domain of non-sell is not so small and dimension is 2.

Usually, however, in the real world problem, anomaly patterns are extremely fewer than the normal ones. As such, our concern is on an extreme case. Unfortunately, we have not so far observed any satisfactory results under this extreme situation. In fact, Zhou Ji and Dasgupata [3] wrote

> As an exception, the algorithm may also terminate when it fails to sample any non-self point after many repetitions. That implies that the self region covers almost the entire space. It may happen when the self samples are randomly distributed over the space, or the chosen self-radius is too big.

And as they went on to write concerning another experiment in the same paper [3] "One of the three types of IRIS data is considered as normal data, while the other two are considered abnormal," the number of normal and abnormal is usually comparable in such experiments.

We are exploring a number of other different approaches to the same target, that is, *a-tiny-flat-island-in-a-huge-lake* or its binary version *a-needle-in-a-haystack*. What we have tried so far are experiments by means of

- Negative selection of binary detectors with r-contiguous matching (See [5]);
- Immuno-fuzzy approach (See [6]);
- Evolving a set of fuzzy rules (See [7]);
- Fuzzy neural network approach (See [8]);

and so on..., to detect a *tiny-island* or a *needle*.

Though still a lot of experiments have been resistant to be positively analyzed, this series of works is not to show a counter example for an assertion, but to call for challenges. The objective is to detect anomaly phenomena which take place only occasionally and hence we don't know what does it look like, while we have enormous amount of daily normal phenomena. As far as we know, this is still an open issue and we are trying to find approaches. We hope this paper will evoke interests in this problem in our community. The challenge is awaiting us.

References

1. G. E. Hinton and S. J. Nowlan (1987) "How Learning can Guide Evolution." Complex Systems, 1, pp. 495-502.
2. A. Imada (2004) "How a Peak on a Completely-flatland-elsewhere can be Searched for? -- A Fitness Landscape of Associative Memory by Spiking Neurons." Proceedings of Advanced Computer Systems and Computer Information Systems and Industrial Management Applications, Vol.2, pp. 171-150.
3. Zhou Ji and D. Dasgupata (2004) "Augmented Negative Selection Algorithm with Variable-Coverage Detectors." Proceedings of the Congress on Evolutionary Computation, pp. 1081-1088.

4. H. S. Lopes, M. S. Coutinho, and W. C. Lima (1997) "An Evolutionary Approach to Simulate Cognitive Feedback Learning in Medical Domain." Genetic Algorithms and Fuzzy Logic Systems, World Scientific, pp. 193–207.

5. A. Imada (2005) "Can a Negative Selection Detect Unique Non-self Cell in an Infinitely Large Number of Self Cells?" Proceedings of the International Conference on Pattern Recognition and Information Processing, pp. 127–131.

6. A. Imada (2005) "Can an Immuno-fuzzy Approach Detect Only a Few Non-self Cells Existed in an Enormous Amount of Self Cells?" Proceedings of the International Workshop on Intelligent Data Acquisition and Advanced Computing Systems: Technology and Applications, pp. 74–77.

7. A. Imada (2005) "Can a Fuzzy Rule Look for a Needle in a Haystack?" Proceedings of the Turkish Symposium on Artificial Intelligence and Neural Networks, pp. 63–70.

8. A. Imada (2005) "Can a Fuzzy Rule Extraction Find an Extremely Tiny Non-self Region?" Proceedings of the International Workshop on Artificial Neural Networks and Intelligent Information Processing, pp. 35–41.

An Average Length of Computations of Normalized Probabilistic Algorithms

Joanna Karbowska-Chilińska

Technical University of Bialystok, Faculty of Computer Science

asia@chilan.com

Abstract: In this paper we establish average length of computations of normalized probabilistic algorithm. The main problem is to verify whether the transformation of the program M into its normal form $\overline{M}$, with only one loop preserves average length of computations. We show that this transformation does not significantly influence on program M behaviour and preserves the order of the function which describes average complexity of the algorithm .

1 Introduction

Iterative probabilistic algorithms are used for modelling algorithmic situations, which suit Markov Chains model [1]. They are used in practice e.g. in co-ordinating distributed computer networks, message routing or graphs and geometric algorithms.

If we consider e.g. a program in the form M: *while γ do while δ do K* and m_{in}, m_{out}, m_M denotes respectively average number of internal loop iterations, external loop iterations and the whole program M iterations then it may happen that $m_M \neq m_{out} \cdot m_{in}$. In this case we cannot use structural construction of the program M in order to estimate average length of its complexity. We decide to transform program M to the normal form.

The plan of the paper is as follows: in Section 2 we shall give basic knowledge about iterative probabilistic program. In Section 3 we shall describe how to transform program to the normal form. We shall formulate the lemma about property of program in normal form. Next, we shall write a conclusion concerning the average length computation of a program and its normal form. Section 4 contains description how calculate the average length of computation any probabilistic program. In Section 5 we shall transform real situation description into a probabilistic algorithm and we shall estimate average length of its computation by means of the fundamental matrix of the program in the normal form. On the other hand we shall compare this result with result received on the basis of experiment. Section 6 contains summary of the results presented in the paper and some directions for further work.

2 Probabilistic Programs

In this section we give basic knowledge about iterative probabilistic program which is interpreted for every variable x_i in finite universe U_i.

The formal syntax and semantics definitions of the abstract algorithmic language L_p describing probabilistic programs are given in [2, 6].

We start with short L_p language description.

Syntax

Probabilistic programs are understood as iterative programs which are built by using a standard deterministic instructions as below:

$x_i := a$, *begin ... end*, *if ... then ... else ...*, *while ... do ...*,

and two probabilistic constructions:

$x_i := random$, where *random* is a random generator function with a given probability distribution $\rho: U_i \to [0,1]$,

either$_p$ ... or ... where the first part is chosen with the probability p and the latter part with the probability $(1-p)$ correspondingly.

Semantics

Probabilistic programs are interpreted in probabilistic structures $\langle \Im, \rho \rangle$ where $\Im = \langle U, V, F, R \rangle$. The set U is universe which is defined as $U = U_1 \cup ... \cup U_h$ where U_i denotes universe given for x_i variable which is from the set individual variables V, F is the set of functors, R is the set of predicates.

$M(x_1, x_2, ..., x_h)$ (or shortly M) denotes the program with h variables. The set of all valuations is represented by $W_h = \{\omega_1, \omega_2, ..., \omega_N\}$ where $N = |U_1 \times U_2 \times ... \times U_h|$. Each valuation we get on input with a probability determined by an initial distribution $\mu: W_h \to [0,1]$. M program execution leads to a new final distribution μ'. This fact we denote as $\mu' = M_{\langle \Im, \rho \rangle}(\mu)$.

We can effectively determine a transition matrix M for every program M, which is interpreted in structure $\langle \Im, \rho \rangle$ on the basis of the following lemma [2]:

Lemma 2.1

For every program M interpreted in structure $\langle \Im, \rho \rangle$ and for the initial distribution μ, we can effectively construct the matrix $M = [m_{ij}]_{i,j=1...N}$ such as the final distribution μ' is calculated as below:

$$\mu' = \mu \bullet M.$$

An element m_{ij} of matrix M corresponds to the probability that ω_j is the output valuation after M is finished if input valuation ω_i appears with the probability 1.

$\square$

The ways of the matrix M construction for all type of program constructions are described in [1,6].

Remark: Let $\{x_1, ..., x_l\}$ be a subset of $\{x_1, ..., x_h\}$. Each distribution $\mu : W_h \to [0,1]$ can be treated as a distribution $\bar{\mu}$ defined on W_l in the following way:

for each valuation $\omega \in W_l$ we define $W_h(\omega) = \{v \in W_h: \omega(x_i) = v(x_i) \ \ i=1,...,l\}$ and $\bar{\mu}(\omega) = \sum_{v \in W_h(\omega)} \mu(v)$. We shall often write $\mu : W_l \to [0,1]$ instead of $\bar{\mu} : W_l \to [0,1]$.

By M_γ^1 we denote the matrix after the first step program iteration M: *while γ do K.*

The matrix M_γ^1 is equivalent to the program matrix: *if γ then K* and M_γ^1 corresponds to the absorbing Markov Chain matrix [2, 6].

We can treat probabilistic programs with at least one nonlooping and the final valuation on the basis described above as an absorbing Markov Chain.

We can use the absorbing Markov Chain theory [3, 4] to calculate basic characteristic of probabilistic program e.g. average number of steps *while* loop or number of entries in a given temporary state.

3 Normal form of a probabilistic program

L_p syntax allows to use some *while* loops in the program structure [2,6] e.g. compound several loops or nested *while* loops, etc... .

In this section we shall use the fact that one can transform every probabilistic program into a form which contains single occurrence of *while* loop [7,9].

Definition 3.1 (cf.[7])

A program M is in the normal form iff:

$$M : begin \; M_1; \; while \; \gamma \; do \; M_2 \; end;$$

where M_1 and M_2 are programs without loops.

□

Let $v = M_\Im(v_0)$ denotes final valuation after execution M program from an initial valuation v_0.

Lemma 3.1 (cf.[7])

For every deterministic program $M(x_1,...,x_h)$ in any structure $\Im$ exists program $\overline{M}(x_1,...,x_h,z_1,...,z_l)$ in the normal form and following condition is satisfied:

$v = M_\Im(v_0)$ iff $\overline{v} = \overline{M}_\Im(v_0)$ and $\overline{v}(x_i) = v(x_i)$ for $i = 1,...,h$.

□

Further, we show that in the case where $M(x_1,...,x_h)$ is a probabilistic program and $\overline{M}(x_1,...,x_h,z_1,...,z_l)$ is corresponding program in the normal form, probabilities appearance of final valuations in these programs are the same. It means that for every initial distribution μ program M and $\overline{M}$ execution leads to final distribution $\eta = M_{<\Im,p>}(\mu)$ and $\overline{\eta} = \overline{M}_{<\Im,p>}(\mu)$ such as $\eta = \overline{\eta}$.

The program $\overline{M}$ mentioned above can be determined effectively by use of the procedure based on rules given in [7,9].

Construction of the program $\overline{M}$ is inductive with respect to the algorithmic constructions of the program M. We build the program in normal form corresponding to the algorithm with n constructions by use an assumption that we can build the program $\overline{M}$ for a program with less than n algorithmic constructions. For example, we assume that the program in the following form: M: *begin K_1; K_2 end* contains n algorithmic constructions. Each of programs K_1; K_2 has less than n constructions. We transform each of them by using suitable rules [7, 9] depending on structure of given program. Each transformation reduces the number of loops and adds auxiliary variable z_i to the set V of the program M. This variable is chosen from the set $V=\{x_1, x_2, x_k,..\}$ in such way, that $z_i=x_t$ where t denotes the smallest number which has not appeared as index of the program variables yet. In this way programs K_1 and K_2 are reduced to the form:

$\overline{K}_1 : begin\ M_1;\ while\ \gamma\ do\ M_2;\ end;\ \ \overline{K}_2 : begin\ N_1;\ while\ \delta\ do\ N_2;\ end;$ where programs: M_1, M_2, N_1, N_2 are without loops. Next we make last transformation using appropriate transformation rule [7]. The final result is follows:

$\overline{M} : begin$
   $z:=a;\ M_1$
   $while\ (\gamma \wedge (z = a)) \vee (\delta \wedge (z = b)) \vee (\neg\gamma \wedge (z = a))\ do$
      $if\ \gamma \wedge (z = a)\ then\ M_2$
            $else\ if(\neg\gamma \wedge (z = a))\ then\ begin\ N_1;\ z:=b;\ end$
            $else\ N_2\ ;$
   $end;$

We need some definitions in order to describe arbitrary program computations and its normal form.

Definition 3.2
Configuration (a state of the computation) of a program $K(x_1, ..., x_r)$ in data structure $\langle \mathfrak{S}, \rho \rangle$ we shall mean the following triple:

$$s_K=\langle\{K_0, K_1, K_2,...,K_m\},\{\omega(x_1),...,\omega(x_r)\}, p\rangle$$

where $K_0,...,K_m$ are finite number of subprograms, which will be running in the order as they were written here, $\omega(x_1),...,\omega(x_r)$ is current valuation of variables occurring in the program $K(x_1, ..., x_r)$, p denotes probability of occurring this valuation.

□

Definition 3.3
Direct succession is a binary relation $\overset{\langle\mathfrak{S},\rho\rangle}{\to}$ determined in the set of all configurations in $\mathfrak{S}$ structure:

$\langle\{x_i:=\tau, K_1, K_2,...,K_m\},\omega, p\rangle \overset{\langle\mathfrak{S},\rho\rangle}{\to} \langle\{K_1, K_2,...,K_m\},\omega', p\rangle,$
   if $\omega(x)= \omega'(x)$ for $x_i\neq x$ and $\omega'(x_i)=\tau_\mathfrak{S}(\omega)$

$\langle\{x_i:= random, K_1, K_2,...,K_m\},\omega, p\rangle \overset{\langle\mathfrak{S},\rho\rangle}{\to} \langle\{K_1, K_2,...,K_m\},\omega', p\cdot q_i\rangle,$
   if $\omega(x)= \omega'(x)$ for $x_i\neq x$ and $\omega'(x_i)=a_{i\mathfrak{S}}(\omega)$
and q_i denotes probability assignment element a_i to variable x_i

$\langle\{if\ \wp\ then\ K'\ else\ K''\ fi, K_1,...,K_m\},\omega, p\rangle \overset{\langle\mathfrak{S},\rho\rangle}{\to} \langle\{K', K_1,...,K_m\},\omega, p\rangle,$
   if $\langle\mathfrak{S}, \rho\rangle, \omega\models \wp$

$\langle\{if\ \wp\ then\ K'\ else\ K''\ fi, K_1,...,K_m\},\omega, p\rangle \overset{\langle\mathfrak{S},\rho\rangle}{\to} \langle\{K'', K_1,...,K_m\},\omega, p\rangle,$
   if $\langle\mathfrak{S}, \rho\rangle, \omega\models \neg\wp$

$\langle\{either_q\ K'\ or\ K''\ ro, K_1, K_2,...,K_m\},\omega, p\rangle \overset{\langle\mathfrak{S},\rho\rangle}{\to} \langle\{K', K_1,...,K_m\},\omega, p\cdot q\rangle$

$\langle\{either_q\ K'\ or\ K''\ ro, K_1, K_2,...,K_m\},\omega, p\rangle \overset{\langle\mathfrak{S},\rho\rangle}{\to} \langle\{K'', K_1,...,K_m\},\omega, p\cdot(1-q)\rangle$

$$\langle\{begin\ K';\ K''\ end,\ K_1,\ K_2,...,K_m\ \},\omega, p\rangle \xrightarrow{\langle\Im,\rho\rangle} \langle\{K',K'',\ K_1,...,K_m\},\omega, p\rangle$$

$$\langle\{while\ \wp\ do\ K'\ od,\ K_1,...,K_m\},\omega, p\rangle \xrightarrow{\langle\Im,\rho\rangle} \langle\{K',\ while\ \wp\ do\ K'\ od,\ K_1,...,K_m\},\omega, p\rangle$$
$$if\ \langle\Im,\ \rho\rangle,\ \omega\models \wp$$

$$\langle\{while\ \wp\ do\ K'\ od,\ K_1,...,K_m\},\omega, p\rangle \xrightarrow{\langle\Im,\rho\rangle} \langle\{K_1,...,K_m\},\omega, p\rangle\ if\ \langle\Im,\ \rho\rangle,\ \omega\models \neg\wp$$

$\square$

Definition 3.4

By computation of the program K (scenario) in structure $\langle\Im, \rho\rangle$ at initial valuation ω^0 and at initial probability p^0 we shall mean the sequence s_K such, as:
1) the first element of this sequence is $s_K^0 = \langle K, \omega^0, p^0\rangle$
2) if i-th element of the sequence s_K is determined and:

   a) configuration $Konf$ such as $s_K^i \xrightarrow{\langle\Im,\rho\rangle} Konf$ exists, then $(i+1)$-the element of the sequence s_K is denoted and $s_K^{i+1} \overset{def}{=} Konf$

   b) otherwise the element s_K^{i+1} is not denoted and $s_K^i = \langle\varnothing, \omega, \rho\rangle$ is the last element of the sequence, $\varnothing$ is empty sequence of programs.

$\square$

If sequence s_K is finite then the number of its elements will be called the length of K computation and denoted by $|s_K|$.
The set of all scenarios of the program K at initial distribution μ is denoted by $S_{K,\mu}$.

Let us assume $K(x_1,...,x_r)$ is any program with k-loops and $\overline{K}(x_1,...,x_r,z_1,...,z_{k-1})$ denotes corresponding program with one loop, which is built by use $k-1$ times suitable transformations rules.

Lemma 3.2

For every scenario $s_K \in S_{K,\mu}$ in the form:
$$s_K^0 = \langle K, \omega^0(x_1),...,\omega^0(x_r), p^0\rangle,..., s_K^l = \langle\varnothing, \omega^l(x_1),...,\omega^l(x_r), p^l\rangle,$$
we may uniquely assign scenario $s_{\overline{K}} \in S_{\overline{K},\mu}$:
$$s_{\overline{K}}^0 = \left\langle \overline{K}, \overline{\omega}^0(x_1),...,\overline{\omega}^0(x_r), \overline{\omega}^0(z_1),...,\overline{\omega}^0(z_{k-1}), \overline{p}^0\right\rangle,...,$$
$$...,s_{\overline{K}}^m = \left\langle\varnothing, \overline{\omega}^m(x_1),...,\overline{\omega}^m(x_r), \overline{\omega}^m(z_1),...,\overline{\omega}^m(z_{k-1}), \overline{p}^m\right\rangle\ assuming$$
that $\omega^0(x_i) = \overline{\omega}^0(x_i),\quad i = 1,...,r$ and $p^0 = \overline{p}^0$ such as:

A. $\omega^l(x_i) = \overline{\omega}^m(x_i)\quad i = 1,...,r$

B. $p^l = \overline{p}^m$

and the following dependency holds between the lengths of scenarios:
$$|s_K| \leq |s_{\overline{K}}| \leq C \cdot |s_K|\quad C \leq 3^{k-1} \tag{1}$$

$\square$

Speaking informally the transformation program $K(x_1, \ldots, x_r)$ to the normal form $\overline{K}(x_1, \ldots, x_r, z_1, \ldots, z_{k-1})$ preserves valuations on the set of $x_1, \ldots, x_r$ and probability appearance of these valuations.

It is easy to check that each scenario $s_{\overline{K}} \in S_{\overline{K},\mu}$ maps to some scenarios of $s_K \in S_{K,\mu}$. Considering this fact and the lemma 3.2 the mapping: $f : s_K \to s_{\overline{K}}$ is an injection and a surjection.

As a corollary of the lemma 3.2 we can formulate the following remark.

Let us assume, that $p(s_K)$ denotes execution probability of scenario s_K. $|S|$ and $|\overline{S}|$ denote average length of computation of program K and $\overline{K}$ respectively, and they are defined in the following way:

$$|S| = \sum_{s_K \in S_{K\mu}} p(s_K) \cdot |s_K|, \quad |\overline{S}| = \sum_{s_{\overline{K}} \in S_{\overline{K}\mu}} p(s_{\overline{K}}) \cdot |s_{\overline{K}}|.$$

Remark: If program $\overline{K}$ is a result of transformation program K to the normal form, then the following dependency takes place between average length of their computations:

$$|S| \le |\overline{S}| \le C_1 \cdot |S| \quad C_1 \le 3^{k-1} \tag{2}$$

Therefore, average length of the program $\overline{K}$ computation is longer than the average length of program K computation. The order of the functions describing these two quantities is the same. We use normal form to estimate the average number of program K repetitions.

4 Average length of computation of a probabilistic program

We focus our attention on the calculation of the average number of repetitions (average length of computation) of any probabilistic program M. Depending on the structure of the program we shall consider some cases.

A general idea: a program M is in the form *while γ do K* where K has no looping states and has no loops .

In this case we use the theory of absorbing Markov Chains [3, 4]. The canonical matrix M_γ^1 looks as follows:

$$M_\gamma^1 = \begin{pmatrix} T & R \\ 0 & I \end{pmatrix} \tag{3}$$

T- denotes submatrix, where its elements denote probability of transitions from nonfinal valuations to nonfinal valuations,

R- denotes submatrix, where its elements denote transitions from nonfinal valuations to final valuations,

I- denotes identify submatrix, where its elements denote transitions from final valuations to final valuations.

We can calculate the vector of average number of repetitions of the program M: *while γ do K* using the following dependency [6]:

$$m = F \bullet e \qquad (4)$$

where $F = (I-T)^{-1}$ and e is one column of ones.

The value m_i is the average number of subprograms executions, under condition that the execution of program M begins in a nonfinal valuation ω_i.

When a program M is in the form *while γ do K* where K contains some loops then we may consider two methods calculating of the average length of computation.

Method I: the program is considered as Markov Chain.

First, we build the transition matrix M of the corresponding chain. Next, we establish average absorbing time of this chain [4]. This value corresponds to average length of computation of the program M.

Method II: the probabilistic program M is transformed to the equivalent normal form with one *while* loop.

We use strategy described in the general idea to count the average number of steps.

In Section 3 we analyzed method II cost.

Example 4.1. Let M denote the following program:

M: begin
    while ((x≠c) and (x≠d)) do x:=random;
    while x≠d do x:=random;
  end;

$U=\{b, c, d\}$ is the universe, $\rho(b)=1/4$, $\rho(c)=1/2$, $\rho(d)=1/4$ is the random distribution. Calculation of the average length of M computation is our goal.

a) the solution on the basis of method I

The following Markov Chain corresponds to the program M:

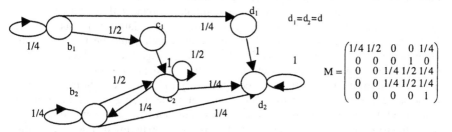

Fig. 4.1. Matrix M of the Markov Chain

We received a vector m_1 where its elements are average number of program M steps using the expression (4). The interpretation of the vector is following: when we start a computation of the program M from states $\omega_1=b_1$ or $\omega_2=c_1$, $\omega_3=b_2$ or $\omega_4=c_2$, we stop after 14/3, 5, 4, 4 steps respectively.

b) the solution on the basis of method II

On the basis of transitions rules, we obtain the normal form of the program $\overline{M}$.

begin
  z:=a;
  while ((z=a) and (x≠c) and (x≠d)) or ((z=b) and (x≠d)) or ((z=a) and (x≠b)) do

if ((z=a) *and* (x≠c) *and* (x≠d)) *then* x:=random
  else if ((z=a) *and* (x≠b)) *then* z:=b;
    else x:=random;
end;

The set of all possible valuations of the program $\overline{M}$ contains 6 elements: $W_h=\{\omega_1$ =(b, b), ω_2 =(b, c), ω_3 =(a, b), ω_4 =(a, c), ω_5 =(a, d), ω_6 =(b, d)\} (generally ω_i=(z, x) for i=1...6).

We can check [6] that after one iteration of the program $\overline{M}$ we can construct matrix as below :

$$\overline{M}_\gamma^1 = \begin{pmatrix} 1/4 & 1/2 & 0 & 0 & 0 & 1/4 \\ 1/4 & 1/2 & 0 & 0 & 0 & 1/4 \\ 0 & 0 & 1/4 & 1/2 & 1/4 & 0 \\ 0 & 1 & 0 & 0 & 0 & 0 \\ 0 & 0 & 0 & 0 & 0 & 1 \\ 0 & 0 & 0 & 0 & 0 & 1 \end{pmatrix}$$

We calculate the vector $\overline{m}$ where its elements corresponds the average numbers of program $\overline{M}$ steps.

valuation	ω_1	ω_2	ω_3	ω_4	ω_5
Average number of steps	4	4	5	5	1

5 Average length of computation of a simplified version of a probabilistic process

Real stochastic processes are modelled using iterative probabilistic processes [1]. In this section first we give a description of the following real situation, concerning of use CSMA/CD protocol in Ethernet network.

Let us assume, that we observe some computers connected to network by a common cable. When a computer tries to transmit a data frame, its network interface card listens to the signal on the cable which could be transmitted by other nodes. This may be achieved by monitoring voltage level on the cable. Data is only sent when no signal is detected and the physical medium is idle. If two network interface cards installed in computers try to simultaneously transmit data at the same time a collision will occur. After that, nodes taking part in the collision wait random period of time before they attempt to retransmit data. The retransmission attempt of single frame is repeated maximum16 times. After this number of attempts the transmitter gives up transmission and logs an error.

First, we shall describe simple version of the real situation described above using probabilistic algorithm. The object of our description will be situation when any computer tries to transmit data to other node in network. We assume that a retransmission attempt of single frame is repeated maximum 3 times.

By the variable LS, we shall denote a state corresponding to the following situation: LS=1 means that the cable is busy and our computer is still listening to the moment when the cable will be idle (LS=0). We assume that the cable is idle twice frequently than busy. The transmission can be started provided that LS=0. The variable CL will describe whether during the transmission other computer also starts transmission. If CL=1 we have collision, otherwise if CL=0 data is transmitted. We assume that collision may not occur twice frequently than it may occur. By T we denote auxiliary variable which has values belonging to the set {0,1}. T=1 denotes transmission success. The variable TEST is the number of attempts and it takes following values: 0,1,2.

Above description leads to the following probabilistic algorithm M :

```
M: while (TEST<3) and (T=0) do
      begin
      LS:=random_LS; while LS=1 do LS:=random_LS;
      if LS=0 then begin CL:=random_CL;
                        if CL=0 then T:=1 ; TEST:=TEST+1;
              end;
   end;
```

We propose transformation the program M to the normal form $\overline{M}$ and use method II described in section 4 in order to determine average length of M computation.

```
M̄ : begin
      Z:=0;while ((TEST<3) and (T=0) and (Z=0))or (Z=1) do
         if ((TEST<3) and (T=0) and (Z=0)) then begin LS:=random_LS; Z:=1; end
         else if LS=1 then LS:=random_LS
            else begin
                     CL:=random_CL; if CL=0 then T:=1 ;TEST:=TEST+1; Z:=0;
                end;
   end;
```

The set of all possible valuations can generally be represented as $\omega_i=(Z, T, TEST, CL, LS)$ for $i=1,...,49$. For example, valuations can be enumerated as follows: $\omega_1=(0,0,0,0,0),\omega_2=(0,0,0,0,1),\omega_3=(0,0,0,1,0),...,\omega_{13}=(1,0,0,0,0),...,\omega_{25}=(1,1,0,0,0),$ $\omega_{26}=(1,1,0,0,1),...,\omega_{37}=(0,1,0,0,0),...,\omega_{48}=(0,1,2,1,1),\omega_{49}=(...,...,3,...,...).$ Valuations from ω_{37} to ω_{49} are final.

We create matrix $\overline{M}^1$ which corresponds to one step of program $\overline{M}$. Next, we calculate average number of steps of $\overline{M}$. These values correspond to the average length of process which transmits data according to the state in which we began process. For example, if this process was started in state ω_1, it stops after 8,444 iterations. If we take assumption that one repetition of loop executes in one unit of time, then average number of loop repetitions is average transmission time of data frame.

The algorithms $\overline{M}$ and M were implemented in C language and the were executed 1000000 times. The pseudorandom number generator Mersenne Twisters from GNU Scientific Library [8] was used.

For each computation from the state ω_1 the number of repeating loops was established and the average value was determined. This "experimental" average number of loop repetitions of program $\overline{M}$ equals $m_{\overline{M}} = 8,448$. The corresponding "theoretical" number of loop repetitions described in this section is 8,444. We obtained in "experiment" $m_M = 6,337$ as average number of repetitions of the whole program M. The $m_{\overline{M}}$ to m_M ratio equals to 1,331.

Transformation of M to the normal form in this experiment extends average length of computation by about 33 percents.

6   Final remarks

The determination of average length of probabilistic program computation which contains a few loops was the main goal of this paper.
We discussed two solutions of this problem. The first method is popular (a program is treated as Markov Chain), so we focused our attention on transformation of a program to the normal form with only one loop. The operation of transformation preserves the final valuations and probabilities of probabilistic algorithms. Basing on the fact that the orders of the functions describing the average length of programs computations are the same, we use the normal form of the program to estimate average length of program computation with some loops.
In our future work we shall compare these two methods. The results will be used in the case of the probabilistic algorithms with continuous time parameter.

Acknowledgments: This work was supported by Bialystok University of Technology under grant S/WI/1/03.

References

1   Borowska A., Dańko W., Karbowska-Chilińska J.: Probabilistic Algorithms as a Tool for Modelling Stochastic Processes, Proceedings of the conference CISIM 2004, 14-16 June, 2004, Ełk, Poland.
2   Dańko W.: The Set of Probabilistic Algorithmic Formulas Valid in a Finite Structure is Decidable with Respect to its Diagram, Fundamenta Informaticae, vol. 19 (3-4), pp. 417-431, 1993.
3   Feller W.: An Introduction to Probability Theory, PWN, Warsaw 1977.
4   Iosifescu M.: Finite Markov Processes and Their Applications, John Wiley & Sons, New York, London 1988.
5   Karbowska-Chilińska J.: An Average Length of Computations of Probabilistic Algorithm of the Basis of the Theorem of Normal Form of Programs, Proceedings of the conference CISIM 2005, 30.VI-3.VII, 2005, Ełk, Poland.
6   Koszelew J.: The Methods for Verification Properties of Probabilistic Programs, Ph. D. thesis IPI PAN Warsaw, 2000.
7   Mirkowska G., Salwicki A.: Algorithmic Logic, D. Reidel Publ. Co. & PWN Warsaw, 1987.
8   Matsumoto M., Nishimura T.: Mersenne Twister: A 623-dimensionally Equidistributed Uniform Pseudorandom Number Generator, ACM Trans. on Modeling and Computer Simulation Vol. 8, No. 1, January 1998, p.3-30.
9   Stapp L.: The Normal Form Theorem for Probabilistic Programs, University of Warsaw, 1979 (not public manuscript).

A Marine Environment Simulator for Testing Ship Control Systems in Dangerous Situations

Andrzej Lebkowski, Krzysztof Dziedzicki, Marcin Tobiasz, Roman
Smierzchalski, Miroslaw Tomera

Gdynia Maritime University, Gdynia, Poland, drow@atol.wsm.gdynia.pl

Abstract. The article presents a simulator for testing the operation of automatic
systems controlling ship's motion in situations threatening with collision, at the
presence of poor hydro-and-meteorological conditions. The goal of the presented system is to support the navigator in decision making, with possible full
replacement of his work in the future. Discussed is a method of determining a
safe trajectory for the ship, and controlling its motion along this trajectory. The
marine environment simulator presents navigational situations in a 3D graphical
mode.

1 Introduction

Modern marine transport requires preserving dates of delivery to harbours located all
over the world, irrespective of weather conditions and volumes of transported cargo.
In case of passenger transport, an additional requirement should be taken into account
which is providing passengers with adequate level of comfort. On the other hand,
there is a tendency to reduce ship operation costs, and realisation of this task may
unintentionally involve threats to human life and natural environment. Losing transported cargo is also possible. That is why securing safety of sailing is one of more
important issues in present-time marine navigation.
Among all causes of sea accidents, navigational errors compose a relatively big group
[1, 2]. Out of fifteen biggest ships lost in years 2003-2004, as many as nine cases
referred to collision or stranding [2]. A method leading to the reduction of sea acci-
dent risk may be introducing solutions that support the navigator in decision making
in the situations threatening with collisions.
The article presents a simulator used for verifying the operation of automatic systems
controlling ship's motion at sea. Analysed is the operation of the system in the situation threatening with collision, and in the presence of unfavourable hydro-and-
meteorological conditions. The developed simulator presents navigational situations
using 3D graphics.

2 The marine ship control system

An essential issue concerning sea navigation is securing high safety of sailing. One of
conditions to be met for proper realisation of this task is keeping a safe distance at
which the objects sailing at sea pass each other. Determining the sailing trajectory,
which consists of a series of turning points for the ship, should also take into account

economic criteria, important from the ship owner's point of view. These criteria include: trajectory length, time needed for covering it, changes in ship's speed along particular trajectory segments, and number of manoeuvres to be executed by the ship. During the navigation along the already determined trajectory, a necessity for its change may occur. Possible trajectory changes should take into account the effect of all navigational constraints on the safety of sailing. These navigational constraints can be either of static or of dynamic nature. The static constraints include lands, water lanes, restricted traffic areas, navigational buoys, and lighthouses. The dynamic constraints have the form of moving vessels, and/or the areas of unfavourable weather conditions.

Controlling the own ship can be executed by the PFSS (Path Finder and Ship Steering) system. Due to fact that it combines two techniques in its operation, which are evolutionary algorithms and the theory of fuzzy sets, the system will bear the name of a hybrid system for own ship control. The optimal trajectory of the own ship is determined using an evolutionary algorithm (AE) presented in detail in [3],[4],[5]. The realisation of the already determined trajectory is executed by a trajectory controller, described in [4],[5],[6]. The adopted structure of own ship control in a collision situation is shown in Fig. 1.

The optimal own ship trajectory is determined at three levels of control. At the first level, on the basis of known location of the starting and target harbours the global passing trajectory is determined, using the evolutionary algorithm and taking into account the navigational constraints. This task is executed by the GR (Global Route) subsystem of the PFSS system.

Taking into account the dynamics of the own ship and the existing hydro-and-meteorological conditions, on the basis of the trajectory determined by the GR subsystem, control parameters are determined for the real trajectory of the own ship. The process is supervised by the second control level of the PFSS system, the task of which is to control ship's motion along the trajectory. At this level, the fuzzy trajectory controller is used. This controller uses, as the reference, a virtual ship moving along the trajectory determined by the GR subsystem. The trajectory controller making use of the virtual ship allows controlling the motion of the own ship along the trajectory segments linking consecutive turning points. In the vicinity of the turning points the virtual ship, followed then by the real object, moves along assumed semicircles. The radii of the semicircles are determined in separate procedures of the trajectory controller, taking into account manoeuvring characteristics of the own ship. The developed trajectory controller consists of two separate fuzzy controllers of Mamdami type, namely the course controller and the speed controller. During the operation of these controllers, the deflection from the assumed course and the speed of the own ship along the assumed global trajectory are controlled and corrected in real time. The knowledge bases of the above discussed fuzzy controllers make use of expert's knowledge.

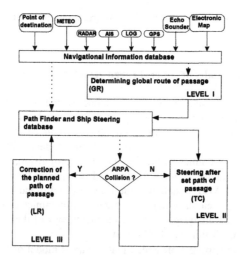

Fig. 1. The structure of own ship control with the aid of PFSS system in a collision situation.

The third level of the own ship control in the PFSS system is activated in cases of
collision threat signalled by the ARPA (Automatic Radar Plotting Aids) system.
ARPA delivers processed data from the radar system on current positions and speed
parameters of other object moving in the vicinity of the own ship. These data are also
compared with those received, via radio, from AIS (Automatic Identification System). The vicinity of the own ship is defined as the area surrounding the ship within
the range of radar observation. In practice, the range of this area is dictated by technical characteristics of the radars and can extend up to 120 sea miles. In cases when the
safety zone, defined by the navigator around the own ship, is intruded by another
ship, or the trajectory of the own ship crosses that of another moving object, ARPA
generates a collision alarm signal. When this situation takes place, the alarm signal
initiates the operation of an evolutionary algorithm, which makes corrections in the
global trajectory already determined for the own ship. The evolutionary algorithm
introduces new turning points, or corrects the location of the already existing points
in order to maintain the optimal passing trajectory for the own ship. Correction of the
global passing trajectory is done for the line segments between the current virtual ship
position, being the source of the collision alarm, and the crossing point of the trajectory with the horizon of observation, defined by the navigator. This trajectory part
bears the name of a local passing trajectory of the own ship. This trajectory consists
of a sequence of line segments of constant course and speed, and depends on the data
delivered by ARPA on the navigational environment. The third level of the own ship
control in PFSS was given the name of the LR (Local Route) subsystem..

3 Modelling dynamic environment for safe ship control system

In order to verify the operation of PFSS, the 3D graphical simulator of navigational
environment was developed. Its role is to map the behaviour of the own ship moving
against the static and dynamic navigational constraints. The developed simulator
allows modelling various navigational situations, with further verification of opera-

tion of the own ship control system. The programme was written in the object technique making use of C++.

3.1 Mathematical model of general cargo vessel B-481

A basic component of the simulator is the model of the own ship. It is expected to map truly and precisely dynamic characteristics of the real vessel. The simulator uses a mathematical model of a general cargo vessel of roll on/roll off type, bearing a shipyard symbol B-481 [7]. A general scheme of the model is given in Fig. 2.

The model includes dynamics of the hull and main propulsion, consisting of a single adjustable blade propeller, a blade rudder, and two lateral thrusters, one at the bow and one at the stern. Also modelled is the effect of hydro-and-meteorological disturbances (wind, waves, sea currents), and changes in dynamics caused by shallow water. The model allows analysing dynamic characteristics of the own ship for two operating states: ballasted ship and 100% load.

The equations composing the presented mathematical model of the B–481 vessel are solved using a method based on the Runge-Kutta algorithm, presented in [9].

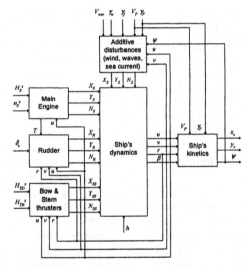

Fig. 2. Structure of the mathematical model of the own ship: $H^z{}_S$ – assumed pitch of the main propulsion adjustable blade propeller, $n^z{}_S$– assumed rotations of the main propulsion propeller, T – thrust of the main propulsion propeller, δ_z – assumed deflection of the blade rudder, $H^z{}_{TD}$ – assumed propeller pitch of the bow thruster , $H^z{}_{TR}$ – assumed propeller pitch of the stern thruster, V_{wsr}, χ_w – average speed and direction of the real wind, γ_f – direction of sea waves, V_p, γ_p – speed and direction of sea current, h – depth of the sailing region, u – ship's longitudinal speed, v – ship's transverse speed, r – ship's angular speed, β - drift angle, x_s, y_s – position coordinates, ψ - ship's course, X, Y, N – forces and moments acting on ship's hull, [7]

3.2 Modelling navigational environment

The developed simulator of the marine environment allows modelling various navigational situations.

The dynamic objects, modelled in the simulator, are moving vessels and areas of unfavourable weather conditions, including cyclones. A cyclone is defined as the area of an assumed radius, moving at an assumed speed in an assumed direction. The weather conditions observed in the centre of the cyclone are assumed the worst, and improving with increased distance from the cyclone centre.

The trajectories of other approaching ships consist of sequences of line segments with fixed courses and speeds, and are not subject to modifications. Dynamic characteristics of the approaching ships are not determined nor modelled, only their kinetics is taken into consideration.

The model of hydro-and-meteorological disturbances includes forces from sea currents and wind. Data on atmospheric conditions are generated in the simulator and taken into account when the system of equations comprising the mathematical model of the own ship is solved. Current values of particular parameters are generated in a random way, smoothness of their changes being preserved.

Modelled were also other static components of the marine environment, having the form of navigational buoys, lighthouses, and fishing nets. The simulator takes into account the effect of shallow water, modelled in the form of polygons with attributed depths. It was preliminarily assumed that the simulator would allow the object to move in the marine environment, integral part of which is the coast-line making the constraints for ships' motion. Land configuration is randomly generated, preserving an assumed contour of the coast-line.

4 Operation of the simulator and simulation tests

Parameters of motion of the dynamic objects and the positions of static objects, including land contours and shallow water regions, are initialised once when the programme is starter.

During the operation of the programme the information is cyclically exchanged between the mathematical model of the ship and the graphic environment. Changes in ship's position, course and/or speed are visualized in the displayed graphics. The simulator user can control the ship and particular parameters of its operation There is also a possibility to observe the vicinity of the ship. The navigating window of the simulator is shown in Fig. 3.

In order to model navigational situations, twenty 3D silhouettes were implemented of various types of vessels (tankers, bulk cargo ships, passenger ferries, sailing vessels, and yachts) essential from the point of view of MPDM regulations. Some silhouettes available in the simulator are shown in Fig. 4.

The simulator user can observe changes in weather situation and sea state, presented in 3D graphical technique. The length and height of waves are changed according to Pedersen scale, while atmospheric conditions are determined using the Beaufort scale, for which the visibility ranges have been determined. Different meteorological conditions are shown in Fig. 4.

Fig. 3. PFSS simulator navigating window

Static elements, modelled in the simulator, that compose the navigational situation are shown in Fig. 5.

The radar screen with the ARPA system implemented in the simulator is shown in Fig. 6. In presented situation the own ship encounters two ships. The second of them is causing the collision risk. The lands and the shallow water which is marked by the buoys are the additional constraints for given situation. The developed manoeuvre which makes possible to avoid the collision is visible on the fig. 7. The correction of the global route of passage is marked by the dotted line. The achieved trajectory of the own ship is marked by the solid line.

Behavoiur of own ship is described by the set of the parameters presented in the chapter 3.1. The most important of them are presented on fig. 8. During realisation of the developed manoeuvre the ship was under influence of disturbances like the wind, the sea strem etc. The graphical charts which describing those disturbances are visible on fig. 9.

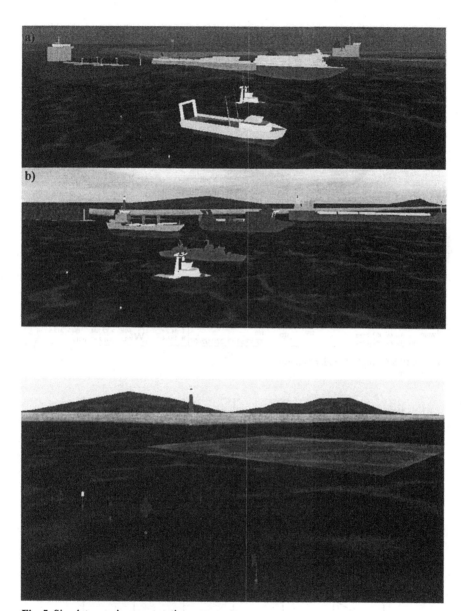

Fig. 5. Simulator environment static components

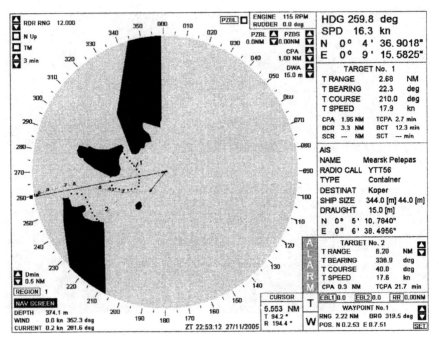

Fig. 6. PFSS simulator radar window

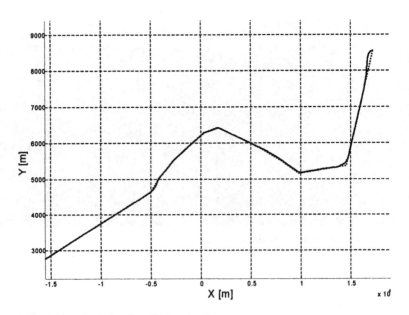

Fig. 7. The achieved solution for collision situation

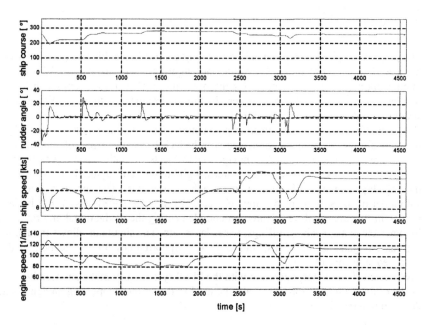

Fig. 8. The main parameters of the move of the own ship during realisation of the developed
manoeuvre

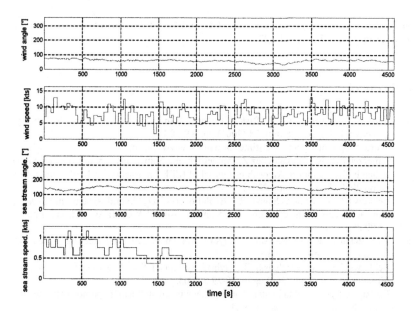

Fig. 9. The disturbances during realisation of the developed manoeuvre

5 Conclusions

The presented hybrid PFSS system for safe ship control in a collision situation, making use of computer techniques: evolutionary algorithms and fuzzy control for determining optimal passing trajectory for the own ship, makes a novel approach to the problem of avoiding collisions at sea, in the environment with navigational constraints of static and dynamic nature.

The simulator models basic dynamic parameters of the marine environment. Taken into account are phenomena connected with bad visibility, the effect of shallow water, and/or the presence of other navigational objects of static (lands, water lanes, navigational buoys, restricted traffic areas, lighthouses) and dynamic nature (other moving ships and areas of unfavourable weather conditions). The applied mathematical model of the ship maps dynamic characteristics of the B-481 vessel. Further activities in this area will be oriented on complementing the navigational environment by other elements, such as: offings, water lanes, etc. The simulator allows modelling various navigational situations, thus providing opportunities for verification of the proposed ship control system.

The presented simulator, operating with the PFSS system, may make an effective tool for learning sea navigation. It can also be used as the system supporting navigators in decision making at sea.

6 Acknowledgement

This work was supported by the State Committee for Scientific Research in Poland, under grant No. 3-T11A-003-27.

References

1. Soares C. G., Teixeira A.P.: Risk assessment in maritime transportation, Reliability. Engineering and System Safety 74 (2001) pp.299-309
2. World Shipbuilding and Maritime Casualties. www.isl.org.
3. Śmierzchalski R., Michalewicz Z.: Modelling of a Ship Trajectory in Collision Situations at Sea by Evolutionary Algorithm. Journal of IEEE Transaction on Evolutionary Computation 2000 No.3 Vol.4, pp.227-241.
4. Łebkowski A., Śmierzchalski R.: Evolutionary-fuzzy hybrid system of steering the moveable object in dynamic environment. MCMCWC, IFAC Girona Spain, 17-19.09.2003.
5. Śmierzchalski R., Łebkowski A.: Hybrid system of safe ship steering at sea MMAR Międzyzdroje Poland, 2003.
6. Łebkowski A., Śmierzchalski R.: Hybrid System of Safe Ship Steering in a Collision Situation at Sea. KAEiOG Łagów 26-29.5.2003.
7. Galbas J.: Synteza układu sterowania precyzyjnego statkiem za pomocą sterów strumieniowych, PhD Thesis, Gdańsk 1988.
8. Teukolsky S.A., Vetterling W.T., Flannery B.P.: Numerical Recipes in C The Art of Scientific Computing. Cambridge University Press 2002.

Image Enhancement and Image Half-toning Using Fluid Particles Physics Dynamics

Kurosh Madani

Image, Signal and intelligent Systems Laboratory (LISSI / EA 3956), PARIS XII Univesity,
Senart-Fontainebleau Institute of Technology, Bât.A, Av. Pierre Point,
F-77127 Lieusaint, France
madani@univ-paris12.fr

Abstract. Fluid particles physics and related theories have been sources of inspiration for a large number of powerful computational techniques. A class of these powerful techniques, particularly efficient in the case of degraded images reconstruction, is the class of stochastic algorithms. Among them, especially, "simulated annealing" based approaches, inspired from particles thermodynamics, show several attractive features. However, the reconstruction of degraded images using iterative stochastic processes requires a large number of operations and is very time consumer. This paper deals with image enhancement and restoration approach based on particles interaction in a 2-D fluid. Several models have been presented. Implementation compromises of the presented approaches have been discussed. Simulation results validating issued techniques have been reported.

1 Introduction

Physics and related phenomena have been and remain central motivations for developing theories in mathematics. Especially, probability theory and issued probabilistic techniques have contributed in formalization of a wide range of areas in physics among which are: thermodynamics, fluids mechanics and solid state physics. If these areas, as other areas of physics, have upgraded from mathematics, since the middle of last century they have been sources of inspiration for a large number of computational powerful techniques. A significant example is the increasing importance, since their introduction by Metropolis and Ulam [1], of Monte-Carlo algorithms for solving computational problems in high dimensional spaces.
A class of these algorithms, called "simulated annealing", has been derived from Metropolis algorithm by Kirkpatrick [2] and [3] leaded to powerful tools to obtain near optimal solution to NP (non polynomial) complex optimization problems. Another class of applications called "stochastic relaxation" have been reported by Geman & Geman [4], for which a number of applications in image processing have been described by [5] showing the possibility of parallelization of these algorithms. Finally, in [6], Carnevali et al. show the equivalence between a physical system (modeled in the frame of the Ising model) and image restoration problem and have proposed a powerful iterative stochastic relaxation based algorithm for picture half-toning and picture smoothing (filtering) problems [6].
Several interests contribute to appeal of such approaches: the first advantage of such techniques is related to the fact that they don't need any prior hypothesis on nature of

information to be processed. So, in the area of image restoration, one doesn't need any prior knowledge concerning the image to be restored. The second reward comes from local interaction in such approaches offering a natural parallelization possibility. Another advantage is related to the fact that a same "cost function minimization" process is used for both half-toning and smoothing operations. So, firstly a multi-level image (degraded one) is converted on a half-toned image and secondly, the obtained half-toned image is smoothed or restored. Finally, the binary nature of half-toned image offers possibility to restore degraded multi-level images using binary images restoration techniques, which are quicker comparing to the multi-level image processing techniques.

However, generally, the reconstruction of degraded pictures with iterative stochastic processes needs a large number of operations leading to very time consummator computation procedures [13]. Three approaches could be combined to reduce the processing time. The first one consists on simplifying the algorithm in order to reach an acceptable execution time. The second one consists on finding acceptable compromises in order to reach convergence conditions (which generally are based on infinite dynamics and asymptotical conditions [7]) in a finite dynamics setting. Finally, the last one consists on using a well adapted (dedicated) computer or processor architecture [8]. In fact, taking into account the local character of the information in a picture, several authors have suggested to operate in a parallel way ([9], [10], [11], [12]).

This paper deals with image enhancement and image half-toning using fluid particles physics issued techniques. The next section of the present paper will first introduce a simple image noises filtering algorithm inspired from "magnetic spins" theory in order to set up the background (philosophy) of such kind of models. Then, the original Carnevali's algorithm, a more complex model which uses the Metropolis updating dynamics, will be presented. Finally, the same section will discuss a modified version of this algorithm using a different updating dynamics (Glauber dynamics). The section 3 will discuss the implementation compromises. The two updating dynamics (Metropolis's one and Glauber's one) will be compared to point out compromises leading to a reasonable implementation of Carnevali's algorithm for image enhancement and restoration. The section 4 will present and discuss the implementation aspects. Simulation results validating those compromises will be reported in this section. Finally, the last section will conclude the present article giving some perspectives.

2 Image and 2-D Fluid Particles System

One of the famous models dealing with thermo-dynamical particles interaction is the Ising model. Issued from statistical physics, this model asserts that macroscopic state of a fluid results from probabilistic (statistical) features of local interactions of particles composing the fluid. A particle is supposed on the one hand, to interact with other particles and on the other hand to interact with external forces (fields). So, a given particle of such system will interact with its neighbors in some neighborhood (the nearest particles). In this case, one can associate an energy function to such particles which will depend on the one hand to some external interaction (external field), and on the other hand, to internal interactions (in particles local neighborhood). Fig.1 gives a schematic of 2-D particles interaction neighborhood.

Neighborhood

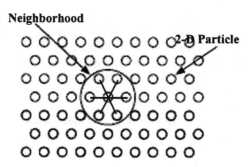

Fig. 1. General bloc diagram of 2-D system of fluid particles.

By analogy to the fluid particles system, an image could be assimilated to a 2-D thermodynamically modeled system where each image's pixel is a 2-D particle interacting with other particles (other pixels). In this way and based on the above-mentioned analogy between an image and a fluid system, the perceptible aspect (visible aspect) of an image could be assimilated to a particular "state" of that 2-D fluid system, which depends on thermo-dynamical conditions (as the thermo-dynamical state of the matter which could be gas, liquid or solid). As for a fluid particles system, an "energy function" (called also "cost function") could be associated to a pixel. The pixel's energy could be defined on the basis of local features of the image (pixels local interaction) or on the basis of global characteristics (pixels interaction with some external force).

2.1 Image Noises Filtering Modeled as 2-D Magnetic Spins Interaction

Image pixels (i.e. particles of this 2-D system) are supposed to change their "magnetic spin's" state, which takes two different values (polarization): "spin-up" (i.e. "1") or "spin-down" (i.e. "0"). Each pixel interacts with its four neighbors (localized at east, west, north and sought of the considered pixel). The interaction is assumed to be local only (no external magnetic field disturbs the system). The energy associated to a pixel depends to its magnetic state as well as to magnetic states of its neighbors. It is defined as the average of states of interacting particles. Finally, the state updating dynamics is a simplified "Fermi-Dirac" dynamics given by relation (1) where E_b – black pixel energy, E_w – white pixel energy, T – system's temperature (supposed to be a positive value).

$$P_b = \frac{e^{-E_b/T}}{e^{-E_b/T} + e^{-E_w/T}} \tag{1}$$

The principle of noise removal is based on the following principle: the noisy image is assimilated to the state of a 2-D fluid particles system in "high temperature". So, the cooling (decreasing the temperature) of such 2-D fluid particles system will lead to noise elimination from the image. However, the cooling process should be repeated successively in order to stabilize the system's final state. Fig.2 gives example of successive cooling-heating decreasing stress process conducting to noise removal. Fig.3 give simulation results relative to noise filtering of the noisy image using a dynamics based on successive "decreasing thermal chocks". The system starts from high temperature state (corresponding to the noisy image). Then a cooling-heating decreasing stress (thermal chock) is applied to the system several times (until reaching a low temperature gradient).

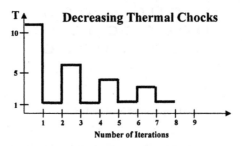

Fig. 2. Successive cooling-heating decreasing thermal shocks diagram.

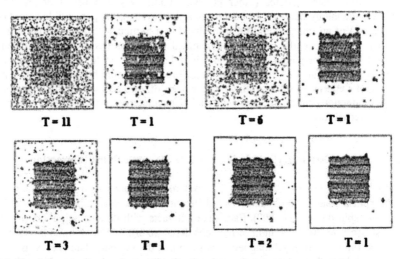

Fig. 3. Simulation results showing cooling-heating decreasing stress successive steps.

2.2 Carnevali's Algorithm

Inspired, as the above-presented noise removal simple approach, from Ising's theory, the Carnevalli & al. algorithm (introduced in [6]) assimilates also each image's pixel to a particle in a 2-D thermodynamically modeled system. Carnevali & al. show the equivalence between the 2-D Ising model and image low level processing. They gave the energy functions corresponding to image smoothing (noise filtering) and image half-toning. The image half-toning consists on encoding a multilevel (grey level) image in order to obtain a binary image in which grey levels are represented by some spatial (2-D) density of binary states (for example, a spatial density of "1" in a given region of the half-toned image). Let focus this case. The following notation will be used:

- $a_{i,j}$: pixel of the multilevel image, with $a_{i,j} \in [-1, +1]$
- $b_{i,j}$: corresponding pixel of the half-toned image
- $V_{i,j,k,l}$: some kernel with the following properties:

$$V_{i,j,k,l} \geq 0 \text{ and } \sum_k \sum_l V_{i,j,k,l} = 1$$

The energy function (particle interaction) could be written as relation (2), where $\lambda = 2$, $\hat{a}_{i,j} = \sum_k \sum_l V_{i,j,k,l} \, a_{k,l}$ and $I_{i,j,k,l} = \sum_n \sum_m V_{i,j,n,m} \, V_{n,m,k,l}$.

$$E = -\frac{1}{\lambda} \sum_i \sum_j \hat{a}_{i,j} \, b_{i,j} + \frac{1}{\lambda} \sum_{i_1} \sum_{j_1} \sum_{i_2} \sum_{j_2} I_{i_2,j_1,i_2,j_2} \, b_{i_1,j_1} \, b_{i_2,j_2} \qquad (2)$$

To update the pixel's value, original Carnevali's algorithm uses the Metropolis dynamics which samples the system's states according to the Boltzmann's distribution. In the "Metropolis" updating rule (updating dynamics), the new value of the pixel is decided according to the relation (3), where T – control parameter (called also "temperature"), X_i^n – the i-th particle's state at discrete time n, E – the system's energy value, P(.) – probability function. $P\left(X_i^{n+1} \leftarrow \overline{X_i^n}\right)$ signifies the probability to replace the pixel's value by the complementary binary value of the pixel's actual value.

$$\begin{cases} \textit{If } E' < E : X_i^{n+1} = \overline{X_i^n} \\[2mm] \textit{If } E' < E : X_i^{n+1} \leftarrow RND\,(X,T)\, \textit{with} : P\left(X_i^{n+1} \leftarrow \overline{X_i^n}\right) = Z\,e^{\frac{E'-E}{T}} \end{cases} \qquad (3)$$

Glauber decision dynamics is another alternative rule to decide the state changes. This second updating rule, called "Glauber" decision rule, operates according to the relation (4) where $P\left(X_i^{n+1} \leftarrow \text{"0"}\right)$ signifies the probability to assign value "0" to the i-th particle's state (i.e. probability for replacing its actual state's value by "0"). In this updating rule, in all cases, the new value of the pixel (state) is determined randomly. The relation (4) corresponds to the probability to have a "0" as new value of i-th pixel in the image. As in the case of the Metropolis dynamics, the state transition probability depends on the one hand, to the pixel's energy and on the other hand to the T control parameter.

$$\begin{cases} P\left(X_i^{n+1} \leftarrow \text{"0"}\right) = \dfrac{1}{1 + \exp\left(\dfrac{-E_i}{T}\right)} \\[4mm] \forall E : \\[2mm] P\left(X_i^{n+1} \leftarrow \text{"1"}\right) = 1 - P\left(X_i^{n+1} \leftarrow 0\right) \end{cases} \qquad (4)$$

Several points of the original Carnevali's algorithm make this algorithm and issued image processing techniques unrealizable (not easy to implement). Among the most important ones are the following:

- in the original version of the algorithm the image pixels values belong to the con-

tinuous interval [-1 , +1].
- in the same way, the energy is also encoded supposing an infinite precision (all possible values belonging to the continuous interval [-1 , +1]).
- concerning the update dynamics (Metropolis dynamics), the convergence is insured only asymptotically. In the reality, the processing time is a chief condition to make a technique usable.

Taking into account the above presented discussion, the implementation of the algorithm requires modification of the original algorithm. However, the modification of the original algorithm should be completed by a number of heuristic compromises in order to establish the convergence conditions.

2.3 Model Modification

As the Carnevali's model, the proposed modified model is also based on 2-D particles interactions physical process. However, several aspects are completely different from the Carnavali's model. The modified points are:
- all used values in the new model are integers with finite number of bits (number, which should be determined),
- all $V_{i,j,k,l}$ are supposed to be constants and identical,
- the value of λ parameter in relation (2) is supposed to be 1,
- the parameter T is also supposed to be an integer.

The first consequence of the above-considered corrective hypothesis is related to the energy value, which will become also integer and not normalized. However, as in the Carnevali's (original) version of this algorithm the simulated annealing control parameter T is a real, so, such hypothesis is equivalent to a measurement gauge (standard) modification for this control parameter.

According to the above mentioned hypothesis (relative to the algorithm's modifications), and considering the fact that in the Carnevali's process the neighborhood doesn't change, the energy variation will be given by the relation (5) with : $b_{i,j} \in \{0 , 1\}$ and $\Delta b_{i,j} \in \{-1 , 0 , 1\}$. The decision dynamics could be the Metropolis (as in the case of Carnevali's original version) or the Glauber's one.

$$\Delta E = E - E' = -\hat{a}_{i0,j0} \, \Delta b_{i,j} + I \sum_{k \neq i_0} \sum_{l \neq j_0} b_{i,j} \, \Delta b_{i,j} \tag{5}$$

3 Implementation Compromises

As a first compromise, we have considered a 256 levels input image. That means that each pixel of the input image is coded with 8 bits only. The second point concerns the interaction neighborhood. Two neighborhoods could be considered: "4 nearest cells" neighborhood and "8 nearest cells" neighborhood. However, the choice of the first connection topology doesn't lead to the most appropriated solution because of the weak number of interacting cells in such connection topology.

The next constraint is related to the convergence conditions: that could be seen as the number of necessary iterations to have an acceptable result. Three points will hold sway the compromise: the first one is the temperature control parameter range of variations, the second one, is the resemblance criteria between the multileveled and half-toed images, and the last one is the choice of an appropriated updating dynamic. These three points are not independent from each other. For example, an acceptable resemblance criterion will depend on the one hand, to the choice of an appropriated updating dynamic, and on the other hand to the number of iterations before stooping the processing as well as to the temperature control parameter evolution.

The T control parameter's evolution has been performed using the following simple heuristic $T_k = T_{k-1} - 1$ where T_k are integers. The starting value of T_k is also an integer and $T_{FINAL} = 1$ (minimum value of T_k) stops the processing. The main advantage of such dynamic is it's implementation facility.

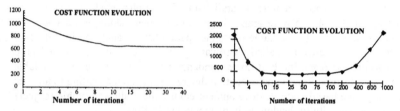

Fig. 4. Energy function (cost function) evolution using Metropolis (left) and Glauber's (right) updating dynamics.

Concerning the update dynamic, Fig.4 shows examples of simulated cost function evolution in the case of the Metropolis and Glauber updating dynamics respectively. The process interruption condition (stop condition) corresponded to T parameter value reaching the magnitude $T_{FINAL} = 1$; for the starting value of T parameter (T_0) a set of values, varying from 1 to 1000, have been considered. One can remark that there is a range where the cost functions reaches some minimum value. This result leads to following conclusions: an acceptable resemblance could be obtained with 30 to 70 iterations. The starting value of the temperature control parameter could then be chosen in a finite range: $30 < T_0 < 50$.

An acceptable neighborhood around a pixel is a 3 by 3 (i.e. the pixel and its 8 neighbors). In this case, the local energy (E) associated to a given pixel of the input multilevel image at a given value of T control parameter will satisfy the following condition: $0 < E < 8\alpha$, where α– maximum possible value of the pixel grey level (256 with the considered compromises discussed in previous section). If ΔE denotes the energy variation during a step of the process, then according to the modified algorithm, the range of variations of ΔE will satisfy the following condition: $\Delta E < 2^{12}$ (i.e. about 4000).

4 DSP Processors Based Parallel Implementation

The implementation has been based on a "large grain" parallelization: consisting on dividing the image in several sub-images and processing each sub-image by a dedicated unit. As the most recurrent operation is the "multiplication" operation, a DSP architecture becomes a pertinent choice for hardware implementation of the presented technique. However, the number of processing units (here DSP) is depending to the available hardware architecture (offering only a limited number of processors). That's why the implementation strategy should be optimized from the point of view of algorithm to hardware transfer methodology.

4.1 Implementation Methodology

The implementation has been performed using Algorithm to Architecture Adaptation (A^3) methodology ([14], [15], [16], [17]), an algorithm-to-hardware optimizer designed by INRIA (Institut National de Recherche en Informatique et Automatique). In this methodology, the implementation is seen as a set of graph transformations. Firstly a graph theory based software description of the algorithm is performed leading to some potential (required) parallelism of its implementation: a software execution graph, called 'software graph' is generated. Then, taking into account the hardware architecture, the available (possible) parallelism is analyzed leading to a graph description of hardware called 'hardware graph'. The above mentioned graphs are transformed to reach the best correspondence between software and available hardware architecture. Finally, an execution diagram is generated leading to an executable 'C' language based code. A development environment allows graphic (object) based description possibility leading to implementation facility.

In our case, the hardware implementation is based on four TMS 320C40 DSP processors ([16] [17]). As the used DSP processor is a 32 bits processor, we have organized the memory register in the following way:

- bits 0 and 1 are dedicated to the changes announcement.
- bits 2 to 14 correspond to the ΔE_T.
- bits 15 indicates if the pixel belongs to a marked region of the image.
- bits 16 to 23 are dedicated to the storage of the multilevel input image pixel value.
- bits 31 indicates that the level of the output image pixel (0 for black and 1 for white).
- others bits are dedicated to the pixel's position in the image.

At the beginning of the process, the bit 15 is set down to 0, and the bit 31 set up to 1 (which indicates that the initial output image is a black image). The figure 6 represents the execution micro-actions bloc diagram issued from A^3 optimization methodology and corresponding tool. It leads to the fully digital parallel hardware implementation of the algorithm. C1 to C4 are four DSP processors. The input image is divided into four sub-images with a single pixel overlap region. Each DSP unit processes one sub-image. The result of each unit is collected by the manager processor ('root ' in the Figure 5, which is also a DSP processor) and communicated to the main computer (a Pentium 100 PC).

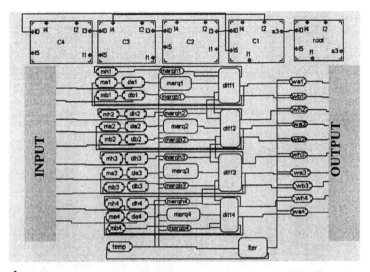

Fig. 5. A^3 methodology issued implementation micro-actions execution bloc diagram.

4.2 Experimental Results and Performances Measurement

Figures 6 shows examples of the image half-toning obtained from our parallel hardware implementation. One can remark that the output binary images reproduce the gray levels of the original multilevel image. The Table 1 summarizes the experimental results relative to the performance evaluation of the system. This table gives the execution time, the speed-up indicator and the efficiency indicator when the system (PC computer) operates without additional DSP, with one additional DSP, with 2 additional DSP, with 3 additional DSP and with 4 additional DSP. The speed-up indicator represents the time gain obtained under a given degree of parallelization (number of additional devices, here additional DSP). The efficiency indicator, depending to both speed-up indicator and parallelization degree, is computed using the relation (6).

$$\text{Eff.} = \frac{(\text{Speed} - \text{Up}) \times 100}{\text{Parallelization deg ree} + 1} \tag{6}$$

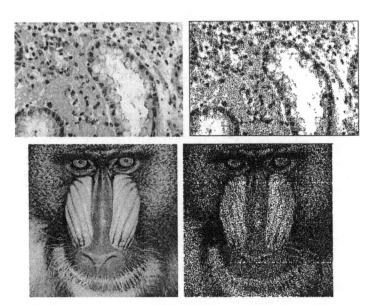

Fig. 6. Experimental results of image half-toning using hardware implementation showing original multilevel input images (left) and half-toned binary images (right).

Table 1. Experimental results relative to the performance evaluation of the system.

Degree of parallelization	Execution Time (s)	Speed-Up	Efficiency (%)
PC Computer only	7. 58	---------	---------
PC + 1 DSP	4.03	1.88	94.3
PC + 2 DSP	2.73	2.77	92.5
PC + 3 DSP	2.11	3.59	89.8
PC + 4 DSP	1.71	4.43	88.6

One can remark that this indicator decreases with parallelization degree. The reason is related to the increase of number of communications (here communication time between DSP processors) when the number of used processors increases. In other words, when one increases the number of processing units, it is not always possible to reach computational speed proportionally to the processor's number incensement. Moreover, in case where inappropriate processor architecture is used, the incensement of the number processors could conduct to a lowest performance comparing to a single processor computational time.

5   Conclusion

Two simulated annealing based algorithms, inspired from fluid particles physics, for image processing have been presented and discussed. The first one enhancing degraded image and the second encoding color images in half-toned representation. The main advantage of such approach is related to the fact that in they don't need any prior hypothesis on nature of information to be restored. However, iterative stochastic processes require a large number of operations and are still out of real time. To improve the execution time of such stochastic iterative algorithms, a DSP based fully digital implementation has been studied, discussed and validated. The implementation architecture has been optimized to reach acceptable computational complexity taking into account the available hardware and using A^3 methodology. Another approach to reduce the processing time is hybridization of simulated annealing and artificial neural network (ANN) models where a partial simulated annealing issued image is restored using an ANN [18].

ACKNOWLEDGEMENTS

I would like acknowledge Dr. Nabil Mesbah who worked during several years with me on this project in the frame of his Ph.D. research work. The DSP based hardware implementation has been realized thank to collaboration between our Institute and the Institut National de Recherche en Informatique et en Automatique (INRIA). The author wish thanks Dr. Yves Sorel research director from INRIA for valuable help and fruitful collaboration.

References

1. Metropolis N., S. Ulam S., Measuring Utility by a Single-Response Sequential Method, J. of Am. Statistical Assn. 44, (1949).
2. Kirkpatrick S., Gelatt S. D., Vecchi M.P., Optimization by simulated annealing, Science 8-67, (1983).
3. Kirkpatrick S., Optimization by simulated annealing: Quantitative studies, J. of Statistical Phys. 34, 975, (1984).
4. Geman S., Geman D., Stochastic relaxation, Gibbs distribution and Bayesian restoration of images, IEEE Trans. PAMI, Vol. 3, 1984, pp 721-741, (1984).
5. Murray D.W., Kashko A., Buxton H., A parallel approach to the picture restoration algorithm of Geman and Geman, Image Vision Computing Vol. 4, N¡ 6, 1986, pp. 133-142, (1986).
6. Carnevalli P., Coletti L., Patarnello S., Image processing by simulated annealing, IBM J. of Res. and Dev. Vol 29 N¡ 6, Nov. 1985, pp. 569-579, (1985).
7. Derin H., Won C.S., "A parallel image segmentation algorithm using relaxation with varying neighborhood and its mapping to array processors," Comput. Vision, Graphic Image processing. Vol 44, (1987).
8. Aarts S., De Bont F., Habers E., "Parallel implementation of statistical coding algorithms", The VLSI Journal. Vol 4, (1986).
9. Moldovan D.I., "Parallel processing: from application to systems," Mogan Kafman San Mateo Inc. Calif. (1993).

10. Charot F., "Architecturess parallèles pour traitement d'images," Technique et Science Informatique. Vol 13, N°3, (1994).
11. Madani K., Mesbah N., Discussion on a massively parallel implementation of simulated annealing algorithms for image processing, International Symposium on Intelligent Systems and advanced manufacturing, Unconventional Imaging for Industrial Inspection, Philadelphia, Pennsylvania, USA, (1995).
12. Madani K., From Parallelization To Hybrid Neural Based Implementation of simulated annealing based image processing, J. of Neuro-Computers: development and application, N°5-6, Russian Academy of Sciences, Moscow, pp. 79-91. 2002.
13. Mitra D., Romeo F., Sangiovanni-Vicentelli A., "Convergence and finite-time behavior of simulated annealing", Proc. of 24-th Conf. on Decision & Control, (1985).
14. Lavarenne C., Sorel Y., "Spécifications, optimisation des performances et génération d'exécutifs pour application temps réel embarquée multi-processeur avec SynDex" CNES International Symposium Les Saintes Maries de la Mer, France, (1992).
15. Lavarenne C., Sorel Y., "Performance optimization of multiprocessor real-time application by graph transformations", Parallel Comp., Grenoble, France, (1993).
16. Lavarenne C., Sorel Y., T. Grandpierre, " Modèle d'exécutif distribué temps réel pour SynDex, " INRIA, France, (1998).
17. Mesbah N., "Image Half-toning and simulated annealing techniques: algorithm adaptation and parallel implementation", Ph. D. thesis report, University PARIS XII, Sénart Institute of Technology, Sénart, France, (1999).
18. Madani K., "From Particles Interaction Physics to Image Enhancement and Image Reconstruction and Enhancement", in *Image Analysis, Computer Graphics, Security Systems and Artificial Intelligence Applications*, Ed.: K. Saeed, R. Mosdorf, J. Pejas, O-P. Hilmola and Z. Sosnowski, ISBN 83-87256-86-2, pp. 119-143, 2005.

Tandem Models with Blocking in the Computer Subnetworks Performance Analysis

Walenty Oniszczuk[1]

[1]Bialystok University of Technology, Faculty of Computer Science,
15-351 Bialystok, Wiejska 45A, Poland
walenty@ii.pb.bialystok.pl

Abstract. A new algorithm for computing main measures of effectiveness in a special type of a tandem model with finite capacity of buffer is presented. In such a model, the finite capacity buffer is located between two multi-channel nodes, where tasks are processed. This type of model provides realistic and objective foundation for performance evaluation in the discrete flow systems such as information systems, computer networks, etc. For instant, in the tandem model with finite capacity of buffer, if the buffer is full, the blocking mechanisms restricts the arrival of any new processes and the newly generated tasks are blocked in an input node until the transmission process is resumed.

1 Introduction

In the mathematical models of discrete flow systems, which are effective and realistic tools for performance analysis of wide class systems such as transportation networks, flexible manufacturing systems, or telecommunication subnetworks, tandem models with finite capacity of buffer and blocking mechanisms are often used [1, 6, 13, 14, 22].
Over a period of years, many publications have been written related to the analysis and application of tandem models however, but there is still a great interest to the systems with limitations on the capacity of buffers under different blocking mechanisms [2, 3, 4, 8, 16, 21]. The blocking mechanism restricts the total intensity of input streams by forcing certain limitations on the blocking and synchronization mechanisms [5, 9, 20].
This paper provides a mathematical study of a special type of a tandem model with finite capacity of a buffer. In this type of model, the buffer is located beetween two multi-channel nodes (tandem configuration is shown in Fig. 1). As it is shown in Fig. 1, the tandem has an input node with N parallel service lines and the other, output node consists of c parallel service lines. In the tandem model, all these service lines in the output node have a common waiting buffer with finite capacity which is equal to m. If the buffer is full (blocking), we might experience a storage problem with the newly generated tasks. In this document, blocked tasks are located temporarily on the input node. In this scenario, if the buffer has any free space, the transmission process to the service center is immediately resumed.
In this paper, the all-possible states of the tandem have been defined, that allows the calculation of steady-state probabilities and main measures of the effectiveness. In addition, a number of algorithms are presented allowing calculation of some parame-

ters such as blocking probability, mean response time in the output node, blocking time, the percentage of buffers filling, tandem throughput etc.

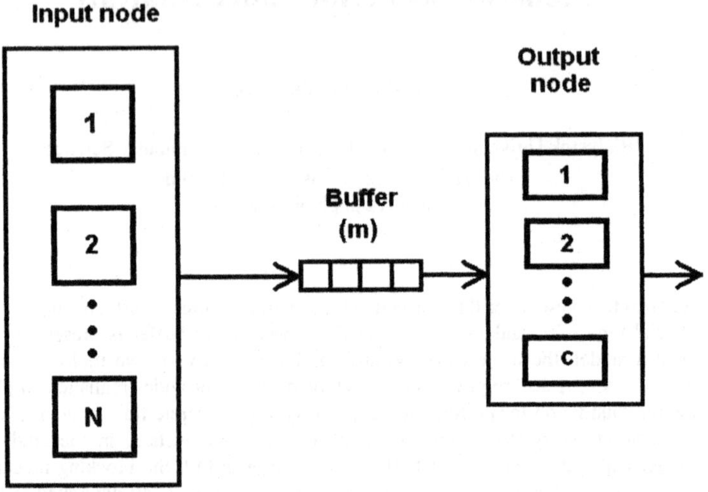

Fig. 1. Tandem configuration with blocking

2 Exact analysis of the mathematical model

Let us consider the tandem model with the finite capacity of buffer as presented in Fig. 1. The general assumptions for this model are:

- the input node has N parallel service lines,
- any input line generates tasks independently and arrival process is exponentially distributed and depicted with parameter $\lambda = 1/a$ (where a is the mean inter-arrival time),
- c parallel service lines on the output node are available,
- each service time in the output node is exponentially distributed with the mean value $s = 1/\mu$ (where μ is the mean service rate),
- the capacity of buffer is finite, say, of size m.

The state diagram for the presented tandem has the following structure:

$$H_0 \xleftarrow{\mu_1} \xrightarrow{\lambda_0} H_1 \dots H_{c+m} \dots H_{N+c+m-1} \xleftarrow{\mu_{N+c+m}} \xrightarrow{\lambda_{N+c+m-1}} H_{N+c+m}$$

For this model, the possible states are:

H_0 – idle tandem (empty buffer and output node),

H_1 – one task in process at any service line in the output node, empty buffer,

. . .

H_c – c tasks in the process, empty buffer,

H_{c+1} – c tasks in the process, one task in the buffer,

. . .

H_{c+m} – c tasks in the process, m tasks in the queue (the buffer is full),

$H_{c+m+1} - c$ tasks in the process, m tasks in the queue (the buffer is full),
a newly generated task is blocked in the input node,

$H_{c+m+2} - c$ tasks in the process, m tasks in the queue (the buffer is full),
two tasks are blocked in the input node,

...

$H_{N+c+m} - c$ tasks in the output node, m tasks in the buffer, N tasks are
blocked in the input node.

Now, we will determine the effective task rates in the tandem:

$$\lambda_0 = \lambda_1 = ... = \lambda_k = N \cdot \lambda \qquad \text{for} \quad 0 \le k \le c+m \tag{1}$$

$$\lambda_k = (N+c+m-k) \cdot \lambda \qquad \text{for} \quad c+m+1 \le k \le N+c+m .$$

and the service rates in the output node:

$$\mu_1 = \mu, \quad \mu_2 = 2 \cdot \mu, \quad ..., \quad \mu_i = i \cdot \mu, \quad ..., \quad \mu_c = ... = \mu_{N+c+m} = c \cdot \mu . \tag{2}$$

Based on queuing theory [3, 12, 14], before we evaluate the main measurements of effectiveness, we must calculate all the probabilities of states p_k $(k = 0, ... , N+c+m)$ in the statistical equilibrium.

The steady-state probability p_k can be interpreted as the probability of finding k tasks in the tandem at an arbitrary point of time after the process has reached statistical equilibrium.

The set of equations to get the steady-state solution for p_k [12], may be written as:

$$0 = -(\lambda_k + \mu_k) p_k + \mu_{k+1} p_{k+1} + \lambda_{k-1} p_{k-1} \qquad \text{for} \quad k=1, 2, 3, ... , N+m+c-1 \tag{3}$$

$$0 = -\lambda_0 p_0 + \mu_1 p_1 \qquad \text{for} \quad k=0$$

$$0 = \lambda_{N+c+m-1} p_{N+c+m-1} - \mu_{N+c+m} p_{N+c+m} \qquad \text{for} \quad k=N+c+m .$$

These equations may be solved recursively, by the first writing of the equivalent equation relating p_1 with p_0 :

$$p_1 = \frac{\lambda_0}{\mu_1} p_0 . \tag{4}$$

similarly for p_k :

$$p_k = \frac{\lambda_0 \cdot \lambda_1 \cdot \lambda_2 \cdots \lambda_{k-1}}{\mu_1 \cdot \mu_2 \cdot \mu_3 \cdots \mu_k} p_0 . \tag{5}$$

or equivalently:

$$p_k = \frac{N\lambda \cdot N\lambda \cdots N\lambda}{\mu \cdot 2\mu \cdots k\mu} \cdot p_0 = \frac{N^k}{k!} \rho^k \cdot p_0 \qquad \text{for} \quad 0 \le k \le c \tag{6}$$

$$p_k = \frac{N\lambda \cdot N\lambda \cdots N\lambda}{\mu \cdot 2\mu \cdots c\mu \cdot c\mu \cdots c\mu} \cdot p_0 = \frac{N^k \cdot c^c}{c! \cdot c^k} \rho^k \cdot p_0 \qquad \text{for} \quad c < k \le c+m$$

$$p_k = \frac{N\lambda \cdot N\lambda \cdots (N+c+m-k)\lambda}{\mu \cdot 2\mu \cdots c\mu \cdot c\mu \cdots c\mu} \cdot p_0 = \frac{N^{c+m} c^c N!}{c^k (N+c+m-k)! c!} \rho^k \cdot p_0$$

$$\text{for } c+m < k \leq N+c+m \quad \text{and where } \rho = \frac{\lambda}{\mu} \, .$$

Where p_0 is found by the commonly-used way from $\sum_{k=0}^{N+c+m} p_k = 1$, as

$$p_0 = [\sum_{k=0}^{c} \frac{N^k}{k!}\rho^k + \frac{c^c}{c!} \sum_{k=c+1}^{c+m} \frac{N^k}{c^k}\rho^k + \frac{N^{c+m}c^c N!}{c!} \sum_{k=c+m+1}^{N+c+m} \frac{\rho^k}{c^k(N+c+m-k)!}]^{-1} \, . \, (7)$$

Now, we can derive measurements of effectiveness for the tandem network with finite capacity of buffers using steady-state probabilities given by Equation 6 in the following manner:

1. Idle tandem probability:

$$P_{idle} = [\sum_{k=0}^{c} \frac{N^k}{k!}\rho^k + \frac{c^c}{c!} \sum_{k=c+1}^{c+m} \frac{N^k}{c^k}\rho^k + \frac{N^{c+m}c^c N!}{c!} \sum_{k=c+m+1}^{N+c+m} \frac{\rho^k}{c^k(N+c+m-k)!}]^{-1}$$

$$(8)$$

2. Blocking probability p_{bl}:

$$p_{bl} = p_{c+m+1} + \ldots + p_{c+m+N} = p_0 \cdot \frac{N^{c+m}c^c N!}{c!} \sum_{k=c+m+1}^{N+c+m} \frac{\rho^k}{c^k(N+c+m-k)!} \, . \, (9)$$

3. The average number of tasks in the buffer v:

$$v = 1 \cdot p_{c+1} + \ldots + (m-1) \cdot p_{c+m-1} + m \cdot p_{c+m} + m \cdot p_{c+m+1} + \ldots + m \cdot p_{c+m+N} =$$

$$= \sum_{k=c+1}^{c+m} (k-c) \cdot p_k + m \cdot \sum_{k=c+m+1}^{c+m+N} p_k =$$

$$= p_0 \cdot \frac{c^c}{c!} \sum_{k=c+1}^{c+m} \frac{(k-c) \cdot N^k}{c^k}\rho^k + m \cdot p_0 \cdot \frac{N^{c+m}c^c N!}{c!} \sum_{k=c+m+1}^{N+c+m} \frac{\rho^k}{c^k(N+c+m-k)!} \, .$$

$$(10)$$

4. The average number of blocked tasks in the input node n_{bl}:

$$n_{bl} = 1 \cdot p_{c+m+1} + 2 \cdot p_{c+m+2} + \ldots + N \cdot p_{N+c+m} =$$

$$= \sum_{k=c+m+1}^{c+m+N} (k-c-m) \cdot p_k = \frac{N^{c+m}c^c N!}{c!} \sum_{k=c+m+1}^{N+c+m} \frac{(k-c-m) \cdot \rho^k}{c^k(N+c+m-k)!} \, . \quad (11)$$

5. The average number of tasks in the both: the buffer and the output node n:

$$n = 1 \cdot p_1 + 2 \cdot p_2 + \ldots + (c+m-1) \cdot p_{c+m-1} + (c+m) \cdot p_{c+m} + \ldots + (c+m) \cdot p_{c+m+N} =$$

$$= \sum_{k=1}^{c+m} k \cdot p_k + (c+m) \cdot \sum_{k=c+m+1}^{N+c+m} p_k =$$

$$= p_0 \cdot \left[\sum_{k=1}^{c} \frac{k \cdot N^k}{k!} \rho^k + \frac{c^c}{c!} \sum_{k=c+1}^{c+m} \frac{k \cdot N^k}{c^k} \rho^k + \right.$$
$$\left. + (c+m) \cdot \frac{N^{c+m} c^c N!}{c!} \sum_{k=c+m+1}^{N+c+m} \frac{\rho^k}{c^k (N+c+m-k)!} \right] \tag{12}$$

6. The average number of non-blocked tasks on the input node l_1:

$$l_1 = N \cdot p_0 + ... + N \cdot p_{c+m} + (N-1) \cdot p_{c+m+1} + ... + (N - i) \cdot p_{c+m+i} + ... + 0 \cdot p_{c+m+N} =$$

$$= N \cdot \sum_{k=0}^{c+m} p_k + \sum_{k=c+m+1}^{N+c+m} (N+c+m-k) \cdot p_k = \tag{13}$$

$$= p_0 \left[\sum_{k=0}^{c} \frac{N^{k+1}}{k!} \rho^k + \frac{c^c}{c!} \sum_{k=c+1}^{c+m} \frac{N^{k+1}}{c^k} \rho^k + \frac{N^{c+m} c^c N!}{c!} \sum_{k=c+m+1}^{N+c+m} \frac{(N+c+m-k) \cdot \rho^k}{c^k (N+c+m-k)!} \right]$$

7. The average number of tasks on the service lines in the output node l_2:

$$l_2 = 0 \cdot p_0 + 1 \cdot p_1 + ... + c \cdot p_c + c \cdot p_{c+1} + ... + c \cdot p_{c+m+N} =$$

$$= \sum_{k=0}^{c} k \cdot p_k + c \cdot \sum_{k=c+1}^{N+c+m} p_k =$$

$$= p_0 \left[\sum_{k=0}^{c} \frac{k \cdot N^k}{k!} \rho^k + \frac{c^{c+1}}{c!} \sum_{k=c+1}^{c+m} \frac{N^k}{c^k} \rho^k \right.$$
$$\left. + \frac{N^{c+m} c^{c+1} N!}{c!} \sum_{k=c+m+1}^{N+c+m} \frac{\rho^k}{c^k (N+c+m-k)!} \right] \tag{14}$$

8. The mean rate of arrivals into the output node Λ:

$$\Lambda = N \cdot \lambda \cdot p_0 + ... + N \cdot \lambda \cdot p_{c+m} + (N-1) \cdot \lambda \cdot p_{c+m+1} + ... + (N-k) \cdot \lambda \cdot p_{c+m+k} +$$
$$... + 0 \cdot \lambda \cdot p_{c+m+N} =$$

$$= N \cdot \lambda \cdot \sum_{k=0}^{c+m} p_k + \lambda \cdot \sum_{k=c+m+1}^{N+c+m} (N+c+m-k) \cdot p_k =$$

$$= p_0 \cdot \lambda \cdot \left[\sum_{k=0}^{c} \frac{N^{k+1}}{k!} \rho^k + \frac{c^c}{c!} \sum_{k=c+1}^{c+m} \frac{N^{k+1}}{c^k} \rho^k + \right.$$
$$\left. + \frac{N^{c+m} c^c N!}{c!} \sum_{k=c+m+1}^{N+c+m} \frac{(N+c+m-k) \cdot \rho^k}{c^k (N+c+m-k)!} \right] \tag{15}$$

9. The mean response time of the output node (waiting + service times) q:

$$q = \frac{n}{\Lambda} . \tag{16}$$

10. The mean waiting time in the buffer w :

$$w = \frac{v}{\Lambda} . \tag{17}$$

11. The mean blocking time of tasks in the input node t_{bl} :

$$t_{bl} = \frac{n_{bl}}{\Lambda} \quad .$$

(18)

12. The mean delay time in the tandem t_d :

$$t_d = \frac{1}{\lambda} + t_{bl} + w + \frac{1}{\mu} \quad .$$

(19)

13. Tandem throughput σ :

$$\sigma = \frac{N}{t_d} \quad .$$

(20)

3 Numerical example

In this section, the results of the tandem examination (configuration as on Fig. 1) are presented. To demonstrate the analysis of tandem with blocking, the following configuration parameters are chosen, for the input node: $N = 28$ with $a=1/\lambda$ that changes within a range from 10.0 to 80.0 time units with the step which is equal to 5 (for studying model with the different coefficient of the utility). The output node contents $c = 6$ parallel service channels, and the service time $s = 4.0$ time units. The buffer has finite capacity (size) $m = 12$.

For the above model with a finite buffer capacity, the following results were obtained, where the most part of them are presented on the Fig. 2, 3 and Tables 1, 2.

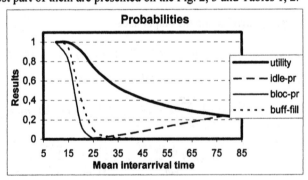

Fig. 2. The probability factors (parameters), where *utility* is the utilization factor, *idle-pr* is the probability of the idle output node, *bloc-pr* is the blocking probability of the input node and *buff-fill* is the filling co-efficient of the tandem buffer

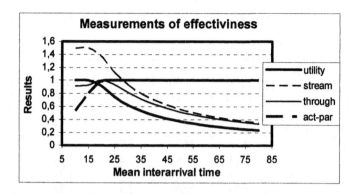

Fig. 3. The parameters related to the mean number of tasks: *utility* is the utilization factor, *stream* is the mean rate of tasks arrival into the output node, *through* is the tandem throughput co-efficient, *act-par* is the relation co-efficient (the average number of non-blocked tasks to N)

Table 1. The main measurements of the effectiveness: a comparison of the mean time parameters

a	Mean time				Utility
	q	w	t_{bl}	t_d	
10	12.00	8.00	8.67	30.66	1.000
15	11.57	7.57	3.70	30.27	0.998
20	7.58	3.58	0.42	28.00	0.914
25	5.04	1.04	0.02	30.06	0.746
30	4.39	0.39	0.00	34.39	0.622
35	4.18	0.18	0.00	39.18	0.533
40	4.09	0.09	0.00	44.09	0.467
45	4.05	0.05	0.00	49.05	0.415
50	4.03	0.03	0.00	54.03	0.373
55	4.02	0.02	0.00	59.02	0.339
60	4.01	0.01	0.00	64.01	0.311
65	4.01	0.01	0.00	69.01	0.287
70	4.01	0.01	0.00	74.01	0.267
75	4.00	0.00	0.00	79.00	0.249
80	4.00	0.00	0.00	84.00	0.233

Table 2. The main measurements of the effectiveness: a comparison of the mean number of tasks

a	Mean number of tasks					Utility
	n_{bl}	v	l_1	l_2	n	
10	13.00	12.00	15.00	6.00	18.00	1.000
15	5.54	11.34	22.46	5.99	17.33	0.998
20	0.57	4.91	27.43	5.49	10.40	0.914
25	0.02	1.16	27.98	4.48	5.64	0.746
30	0.00	0.37	28.00	3.73	4.10	0.622
35	0.00	0.14	28.00	3.20	3.34	0.533
40	0.00	0.07	28.00	2.80	2.87	0.467
45	0.00	0.03	28.00	2.49	2.52	0.415
50	0.00	0.02	28.00	2.24	2.26	0.373
55	0.00	0.01	28.00	2.04	2.05	0.339
60	0.00	0.01	28.00	1.86	1.87	0.311
65	0.00	0.00	28.00	1.72	1.72	0.287
70	0.00	0.00	28.00	1.60	1.60	0.267
75	0.00	0.00	28.00	1.49	1.49	0.249
80	0.00	0.00	28.00	1.40	1.40	0.233

4 Conclusions

In this paper, a new approach to the exact analysis for a special type of tandem with a finite buffer capacity is proposed. For this kind of the tandem model the exact steady-state solution is provided and studied based on the main performance measurements as functions of the tandem topology and given input parameters.

Acknowledgements: This work was supported by the Bialystok University of Technology under grant W/WI/7/03.

References

1. Akyildiz I.F.: Mean Value Analysis for Blocking Queuing Networks. IEEE Transaction on Software Engineering 14(4) (1988) 418-428
2. Balsamo S., De Nitto Persone V.: Closed queueing networks with finite capacities: blocking types, product-form solution and performance indices. Performance Evaluation 12(2) (1991) 85-102
3. Balsamo S., De Nito Persone V., Onvural R.: Analysis of Queueing Networks with Blocking. Kluwer Academic Publishers, Boston (2001)
4. Badrah A., Czachórski T., Domańska J., Fourneau J.-M.,Quessette F.: Performance evaluation of multistage interconnection networks with blocking – discrete and continuous time Markov models. Archiwum Informatyki Teoretycznej i Stosowanej 14(2) (2002) 145-162
5. Boucherie R.J., van Dijk N.M.: On the arrival theorem for product form queueing networks with blocking. Performance Evaluation 29(3) (1997) 155-176
6. Clo M.C.: MVA for product-form cyclic queueing networks with blocking. Annals of Operations Research 79 (1998) 83-96

7. Economou A., Fakinos D.: Product form stationary distributions for queueing networks with blocking and rerouting. Queueing Systems 30(3/4) (1998) 251-260

8. Gomez-Corral A.: A Tandem Queue with Blocking and Markovian Arrival process. Queueing Systems 41(4) (2002) 343-370

9. Kaufman J.S., Rege K.M.: Blocking in a shared resource environment with batched arrival processes. Performance Evaluation 24 (1996) 249-263

10. Kouvatsos D., Awan I.: Entropy maximization and open queueing networks with priorities and blocking. Performance Evaluation 51(2-4) (2003) 191-227

11. Martin J.B.: Large Tandem Queueing Networks with Blocking. Queueing Systems 41(1/2) (2002) 45-72

12. Oniszczuk W.: Metody modelowania. Wydawnictwa Politechniki Białostockiej, Białystok (1995)

13. Onvural R.: Survey of closed queuing networks with blocking. Computer Survey 22(2) (1990) 83-121

14. Perros H.G.: Queuing Networks with Blocking. Exact and Approximate Solution. Oxford University Press, New York (1994)

15. Pinsky E., Conway A.D.: Mean-value analysis of multi-facility blocking models with state-dependent arrivals. Performance Evaluation 24 (1996) 303-309

16. Ramesh S., Perros H.G.: A two-level queueing network model with blocking and non-blocking messages. Annals of Operations Research 93(1/4) (2000) 357-372

17. Sereno M.: Mean value analysis of product form solution queueing networks with repetitive service blocking. Performance Evaluation 36-37 (1999) 19-33

18. Stasiak M., Głąbowski M.: A simple approximation of the link model with reservation by a one-dimensional Markov chain. Performance Evaluation 40 (2000) 195-208

19. Strelen J.Ch., Bärk B., Becker J., Jonas V.: Analysis of queueing networks with blocking using a new aggregation technique. Annals of Operations Research 79 (1998) 121-142

20. Tolio T., Gershwin S.B.: Throughput estimation in cyclic queueing networks with blocking. Annals of Operations Research 79 (1998) 207-229

21. Zhuang L., Buzacott J.A., Liu X-G.: Approximate mean value performance analysis of cyclic queueing networks with production blocking. Queueing Systems 16 (1994) 139-165

22. Zhuang L.: Acceptance instant distributions in product-form closed queueing networks with blocking. Performance Evaluation 26 (1996) 133-144

Interchangeable Strategies in Games without Side Payments on the Base of Uncertain Information on Resources

Henryk Piech, Aleksandra Ptak, Marcin Machura

Technical University of Czestochowa, Institute of Mathematics and Informatics
Dabrowskiego Street, 73, 42-200 Czestochowa, Poland,
hpiech@adm.pcz.czest.pl

Abstract. The test of use of elements modern theory of utility was undertaken to solving the corporate problems connected from distributing the supplies. Interchangeable strategy treats to patent medicines accumulating supplies and administering them. The utility function permits to estimate players preferences or simply their need. The problem of using of the utility function is not the issue the explicitly determined owing to fact, that there is possibility of manipulating of utility parameters. Therefore selection of these parameters in such way to optimize the quality (the satisfaction) of reached compromise is the purpose of the proposed methodology. The considering the possible divisions of supplies is one of aspects of optimization. Another aspect it is the optimal selection, with point of sight of quality compromise, levels of parameters of utility function. It is possible to take into consideration both aspects thanks for using Solvers which algorithms, in many original modifications, were introduced in work "Applied Interval Analysis" (authors: Jaulin L., Kieffer M., Didrit O., Walter E.). This fuzzy or interval character of parameters of the utility function or level of supplies is comfortable, approximate to reality, and also elastic with point of sight of optimization the form of interpretation of input data.

1 Introduction

As a rule in cooperative games, it is possible to attribute to every coalition a specific value determining a payment which the coalition is able to obtain. The payment shared among coalitions should be solved in this problem by taking into consideration a so-called transitive usefulness or the possibility to make a withdrawal [1]. However, side payments are not always possible. Every coalition can also share out a sum of initial resources using a cooperative game which is not characterized by the best attainable payment but a whole sequence of possibilities to obtain payment vectors (usefulness) of individual speculators from this coalition. The payment vectors result from the possibilities to share resources.

The aim of this paper is to investigate the possibilities of distribution of fixed (or limited) resources according to needs expressed by means of the usefulness function. The parameters of the usefulness function are almost always estimated quantities and they can be, and even should be, presented in the fuzzy form [15, 23]. It not only makes their optimal selection in a given range possible but it also brings closer the precise characterizing of needs and compromises corresponding to real and rational conditions. The structure of the publication permits the presentation of both the strategy of "fuzzy" arguments and examples of functions with parameters in the range of fuzziness and optimization of selected parameters [17]. Examples based on speculations on the stock exchange where we have limited financial resources, allow to expressively show the principles of creating and optimization of the usefulness function. The principle of choosing best compromise for all the speculators gives a framework to implement algorithms taking its assumptions into consideration in conditions of technological, economic or ecological competition [22].

2 Conventions of creating usefulness function

The usefulness function feature is sensitive to changes of parameters relating to the quality and convenient for interpreting the value range of the function [5]. Exemplifying forms of such a function are:

$$U(w,a) = \sqrt{w} - a \tag{1}$$

$$U(w1,w2,w3) = \sqrt{(1 + a1 * w1)(1 + a2 * w2)(1 + a3 * w3)} - 1 \tag{2}$$

where: U – values of payments, w and wi – values of resources, a and ai – deterministic constants or their fuzzy equivalents.

Value ranges of the membership function fluctuate, as a rule, from a few to a dozen or so also taking on negatives. It happens that they are limited by the maximum quantity from among the resources (wi).
Table 1 presents the exemplifying resources. Each speculator (four of them are in this example) can point to which level of usefulness satisfies him (Table 2). Relying on this information, it is possible to determine optimal constants ai in formula 2.

Table 1.

4	7	5	poziomy zasobów

Table 2.

3	5	4	4	zadane wartości funkcji użyteczności
1 gracz	2 gracz	3 gracz	4 gracz	

An estimation of optimal values of the constants can be done by means of the Solver. Table 3 shows the obtained results.

Table 3. Values of constants a

a1	a2	a3
-0.041	1.687	4.686

The real consumption of resources by individual speculators amounts to:

Table 4. Real consumption of resources

w1	w2	w3	
0.370742	1.842483	0.724964	1 speculator
2.125802	2.283603	2.315661	2 speculator
0.237468	2.088095	1.092017	3 speculator
0.047473	1.087654	1.784038	4 speculator
resources1	resources2	resources3	

The use of the Solver guarantees satisfaction of conditions from tables 1 and 2 with
the accuracy: 0.002126

The other convention assumes various parameters (constants) in the application functions of different speculators:

$$U1(w1,w2,w3) = \frac{}{\sqrt{(1 + a1(1) * w1(1))(1 + a2(1) * w2(1))(1 + a3(1) * w3(1))} - 1} \tag{3}$$

$$U2(w1,w2,w3) = \frac{}{\sqrt{(1 + a1(2) * w1(2))(1 + a2(2) * w2(2))(1 + a3(2) * w3(2))} - 1}$$

....

$$Un(w1,w2,w3) = \frac{}{\sqrt{(1 + a1(n) * w1(n))(1 + a2(n) * w2(n))(1 + a3(n) * w3(n))} - 1}$$

In this case, by satisfying the conditions presented in tables 1 and 2, one obtains the
following optimal constants and levels of resources for all speculators:

Table 5.Table 6. Estimation of weights and consumption of resources

a1	a2	a3	w1	w2	w3	coalitionist
0.271	1.841	4.794	0.718	1.682	0.474	1 speculator
2.239	0.729	0.730	2.354	2.010	1.819	2 speculator
-0.595	5.126	2.166	0.573	2.060	1.053	3 speculator
-0.833	2.545	4.533	0.354	1.247	1.654	4 speculator

2.49E-10- estimated error of constants ai
0.000228- estimated error of the distribution level of resources wi

3 Fuzzy presentation forms of parameters and values of usefulness function

If the real values of parameters (for example - distribution levels of resources) of the
usefulness function are controlled or the range of their variability is set, then the use
of fuzzy strategies to record their level is purposeful. It can be an interval of parame-

ter values (with the equal level of membership function $\mu(x)$ – Figure 1a) or a set distribution of belonging at a concrete interval of parameter values (Figure 1b, c).

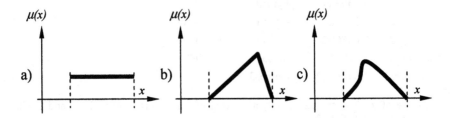

Fig. 1. 1a, b and c. Fuzziness of continuous parameters of usefulness function with various shapes of membership function

Discretization of parameters does not bring any changes into the classic form of transition from continuity to discreet forms that can be presented in a reduced method as in Figures 2a, b and c.

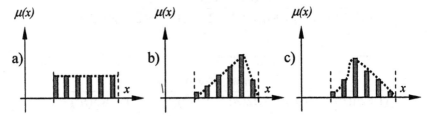

Fig. 2. a, b and c. Fuzziness of discrete parameters of usefulness function with various shapes of membership function

Fuzziness of the distribution level of resources for each of the four speculators can be shown in the following way (Figure 3a and b):

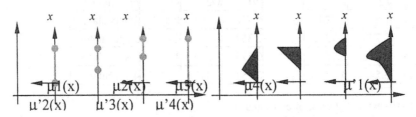

Fig. 3. 3a and b. Fuzzy strategy describing distribution of resources x among speculators

An exemplifying situation with the set fuzzy interval of values of the usefulness function is analyzed below. The purpose of the analysis is to estimate the distribution level for optimal usefulness levels.

Table 7. Table 8. Lower and upper fuzziness limits of usefulness function [Udi, Ugi]

3	6
5	8
4	5
4	6

The optimal solution, as it can be expected, concentrates round the lower limit of the usefulness function. Calculations were done for the parameters of the usefulness function described in Table 3. The solution after the realization of 1000 iterations was obtained with the accuracy of 1.78E-06. Table 9 illustrates the solution.

Table 9. Optimal values of usefulness function selected from interval given in Tables 7 and 8

3.015879
5.000001
4.006435
4.000001

Table 10. Allocation of resources for optimal values of usefulness function

w1	w2	w3	
0.902	1.754	0.689	1 speculator
2.413	1.973	1.756	2 speculator
0.286	2.042	1.004	3 speculator
0.399	1.231	1.550	4 speculator
4.000	7.000	5.000	<sums of re-sources

Let us now allow fuzziness of the distribution of resources which can be set to be given perhaps with the aid of graphs of isolevels (level lines) corresponding with the [min, opt, max] values (Figure 4).

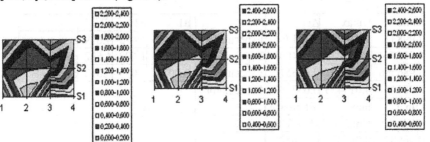

Fig. 4. Graphs of distribution fuzziness of resources according to Tables 10(opt), 11(min), 12(max)

Table 11. Table 12. Distribution fuzziness of resources (upper and lower limits)

w1	w2	w3	
0.880	1.740	0.650	1 speculator
2.360	1.970	1.730	2 speculator
0.250	2.020	1.000	3 speculator
0.360	1.200	1.490	4 speculator
3.850	6.930	4.870	<sums

w1	w2	w3	
0.920	1.770	0.712	1 speculator
2.440	1.990	1.780	2 speculator
0.290	2.110	1.020	3 speculator
0.420	1.263	1.590	4 speculator
4.070	7.133	5.102	<sums

The result of fuzziness at the distribution levels of resources is fuzziness of the usefulness function (Table 13). The usefulness function is now identical for individual speculators.

Table 13. Fuzzy values of usefulness function depending on fuzziness levels of resources (Table 11 and 12) relating to individual speculators

Umin	Umax	ΔU	
2.917612	3.078356	0.160744	1 speculator
4.963431	5.052160	0.088729	2 speculator
3.980514	4.102911	0.122397	3 speculator
3.876972	4.099116	0.222144	4 speculator
min resources	max resources	differences	
Umin - Ut	Umax-Ut	Umax -Umin	
0.261471	0.332543	0.071073	

Ut in Tables 13 and 14 determines the set level of the usefulness function values. If constants $[\underline{a}, a]$ are subjected to fuzziness then the usefulness functions $[\underline{U}, \overline{U}] = [Umin, Umax]$ will also be subjected to fuzziness.

Table 14. Table 15. Fuzziness of usefulness function resulting from fuzziness of constant parameters a ($[\underline{a}, a]$)

Umin	Umax	ΔU	
2.998327	3.030092	0.031765	1 speculator
4.963744	5.027838	0.064095	2 speculator
3.986556	4.02307	0.036514	3 speculator
3.981481	4.015423	0.033943	4 speculator
min a	max a	difference	
Umin-Ut	Umax-Ut	Uopt-Ut	
0.069893	0.096423	0.02653	

a1	a2	a3	
-0.0426	1.673	4.679	amin
-0.0398	1.698	4.692	amax
0.0028	0.025	0.013	amax-amin

Minimization of the dispersion (variation) of distribution levels also influences the usefulness function values. Table 16 illustrates the results of such activities.

Table 16. Levelling of distribution dispersion of resources

0.995	1.746	1.244	mean value
0.000347	1.94E-05	0.010634	standard deviation
resources 1	resources 2	resources 3	

The analysis shows that a satisfactory solution fulfilling a few criteria is not always possible:

- set level of the usefulness function $((Ut-Up)>=0$, Table 19), *(criterion 1)*
- no exceeding of resources $((wit-wip)>=0$, Table 17), *(criterion 2)*
- minimal dispersion of resources (min(s. d. (wi), Table 16 and 20) *(criterion 3)*

Table 17. Allocation scale of resources

w1t-w1p	w2t-w2p	w3t-w3p		sum
0.02184	0.014126	0.022209	differences	0.058175

Table 18. Values of constants in function of usefulness *(2)*

a1	a2	a3
-0.06675	1.675416	4.681322

Table 19. Corruption degree of usefulness function in search process of optimal solution by means of the Solver fulfilling *criterion 2 and 3*

Up	Ut	Up-Ut	
3.982737	3	0.982737	1 speculator
4.026576	5	-0.97342	2 speculator
3.998027	4	-0.00197	3 speculator
4.000132	4	0.000132	4 speculator

Divergence of the usefulness functions (in modular sense): **1,958267**

Table 20. Effect of dispersion minimization of resources with reference to individual speculators; (min(s. d. (wi))

w1p	w2p	w3p	
0.995	1.746	1.233	1 speculator
0.995	1.746	1.259	2 speculator
0.995	1.746	1.242	3 speculator
0.994	1.746	1.243	4 speculator
3.978	6.986	4.978	
w1t	w2t	w3t	
4	7	5	

The fulfilment of *criterion 2* and *criterion 3* leads to the corruption of *criterion 1* (Table 19). Keeping *criterion 1* validity leads to unsatisfiability of the other criteria [26]: *criterion 1* and *criterion 2* (in this example, of course). However, it is possible even in this example to obtain a chance of fulfilment of all three criteria (Table 24, 25 and 26) by a change of set requirements (e.g. standardizing the level of the usefulness function, Table 21 and 22).

Table 21. Compatibility of assumptions and practical use of resources

3.978	6.987	4.961	w1p,w2p,w3p
4	7	5	w1t,w2t,w3t

Table 22. Differences between assumptions and practical allocation of resources

w1t-w1p	w2t-w2pw	w3t-w3p		
0.021894	0.012667	0.039313	differences	0.073873

Table 23. Optimal values of constants *a* by fulfilment of *criteria 1, 2* and *3*

a1	a2	a3
-0.06547	1.675947	4.681515

Table 24. Standardized requirements as to usefulness for all speculators

Up	Ut	Up-Ut	
3.993073	4	-0.00693	1 speculator
3.997657	4	-0.00234	2 speculator
4.007438	4	0.007438	3 speculator
3.997942	4	-0.00206	4 speculator

Table 25. Minimal level keeping dispersion of resources

0,995	1,747	1,240	mean value
0.007208	0.000331	0.00346	0.011- summary standard deviation
resources 1	resources 2	resources 3	

Table 26. Standardized dispersion of resources by standardized level of usefulness of speculators

wp1	wp2	wp3	
0.994	1.747	1.237	1 speculator
1.004	1.746	1.241	2 speculator
0.994	1.747	1.245	3 speculator
0.986	1.747	1.239	4 speculator
3.978	6.987	4.961	
w1t	w2t	w3t	
4	7	5	

4 Conclusions

The selected examples of fuzziness presentations of independent parameters and the analysis of the influence on fuzziness of dependent quality parameters, relating to quality, lead to the following conclusions:

Exchangeable strategies (without side payments) often lead to a collision of interests that is reflected in difficulties in obtaining optimal solutions satisfying all parties (speculators) and fulfilling all the criteria. It is noticeable in the example with various requirements as regards to usefulness (Table 19) and in the tendency to standardize the level of distribution of resources (Table 20).

The standardization of treatment of all speculators is conducive to find optimal solutions but they do not always lead to honest or fair solutions.

Differentiation in treatment of speculators through the change of the usefulness function form, the change of the distribution principle and in consequence through differentiation of the allocation levels of resources is a step towards fair solutions taking into consideration even nuances in speculators' evaluation.

Fuzziness is a form close to real conditions and, at the same time, it gives greater ranges of optimization in a theoretically infinite set of criteria. However, this flexibility can lead to phenomena from the borderland of manipulation, so it has to be controlled and limited to the selection of rational and necessary criteria for a concrete problem.

References

1. Aumann R.: Survey of repeated games. In Essays in Game Theory and Mathematical Economics in Honor of Oskar Morgenstern, Institute Mannheim, Vein, 1981
2. Bamos A.: On Pseudo-Games. Annals of Mathematical Statistics No. 39, 1968
3. Binmore K., Kirman P., Tani P.: Frontiers and Game Theory. MIT Press, 1993
4. Conway J. H.: On number and Games. Academic Press, 1976
5. Czogała E., Perdycz W.: Elements and methods in fuzzy sets theory. PWN, Warsaw, 1985 (in Polish)
6. Ellison G.: Learning with One Rational Player. MIT Press, 1994
7. Fudenber D., Tirole J.: Game Theory. MIT Press, 1991
8. Fundenberg D., Kreps D.: Lectures on Learning and Equilibrium in Strategic Form Games. Core Lecture Series, 1990
9. Harsanyj J., Selten R.: A General Theory of Equilibrium Selection in Games. MIT Press, 1988.
10. Harsanyj J.: Games with Randomly Disturbed Payoffs. International Journal of Game Theory, No. 2, 1973
11. Hofbauer J.: Stability for Best Response Dynamic. University of Viena, 1995
12. Isaacs R.: Differential games. Wiley, 1965
13. J.F.Nash: Non cooperative games. Ann. Math., 2, pp. 296-295, 1951
14. J.Nash: Equilibrium points in N- persons games. National Academy of Sciences, 36, pp. 48-49, 1950
15. Lachwa A.: Fuzzy world of files, numbers, relations, facts, rules and decisions. Akademicka Oficyna Wydawnicza Exit, Warsaw 2001 (in Polish)
16. Loeve M.: Probability Theory. Berlin Springer Verlag, 1978
17. Luce D., Raiffa H.: Games and Decisions. PWN, Warsaw, 1996 (in Polish)
18. Nachbar J.: Evolutionary Selection Dynamic in Games. International Journal of Games Theory, No. 19, 1990

19. Nachbar J.: Prediction, Optimization and Learning in Repeated Games. Econometrica, 1995
20. Owen G.: Theory of Games. PWN, Warsaw, 1982 (in Polish)
21. Ozyildirim S.: A discrete dynamic game approach. Computers Math. Applic., 32 (5), pp. 43-56, 1996
22. Papadimitriou C.H.: Games against nature. J. Comp. System Sci., 31, pp. 288-301, 1985
23. Piegat A.: Fuzzy modelling and controlling. Akademicka Oficyna Wydawnicza Exit, Warsaw 2003 (in Polish)
24. Shapley L.: Some Topics in Two-Person Games. In Advances in Game Theory, Princeton University Press, 1964
25. Straffin P.D.: Theory of Games. Wydawnictwo Naukowe Scholar, Warsaw 2001 (in Polish)
26. Syslo M., Deo N., Kowalik J.: Discrete optimisation algorithms. PWN, Warsaw 1995 (in Polish)
27. Vavock V: Aggregating Strategies. Conference on Computational Learning Theory, 1990
28. Wetzeel A.: Evaluation of the effectiveness of genetic algorithms in combinatorial optimization. University of Pittsburgh, 1983
29. Zadeh L. A.: Fuzzy limitations calculus; design and systems; methodological problems. Ossolineum 1980 (in Polish)

Properties of Morphological Operators Applied to Analysis of ECG Signals

Krzysztof Piekarski[1], Pawel Tadejko[2], Waldemar Rakowski[2]

[1] Technical University of Bialystok, Institute of Mathematics and Physics,
15-351 Bialystok, Wiejska 45A,
Poland, kp@csk.pl
[2] Technical University of Bialystok, Faculty of Computer Science,
15-351 Bialystok, Wiejska 45A,
Poland, {ptad@ii, W.Rakowski@}.pb.bialystok.pl

Abstract. In this paper, we evaluate a multiscale-filtering scheme based on the mathematical morphological theory. We show that opening and closing a signal with a gray scale operator can change the original signal in many ways depending on the shape and size of structuring element (SE). Within this framework, the problem of choosing an appropriate structuring element in ECG signal pre-processing is studied. Some theoretical results for morphological operators applied to analysis of ECG signals are derived. In order to obtain a measure of the performance of different structuring elements, we propose new filtering scheme and evaluate some tests with signals from MIT/BIH database.

1 Introduction

In the paper we investigate the problem of automatic detection of 1D signal characteristic features paying our attention to biomedical signals and in particular to ECG signals. Usually a signal is initially transformed before any detection is possible. A few approaches for such transformation are known [8] and we apply so called morphological filters based on morphological operators. We study properties of such operators for a given class of signals and present numerical results of QRS detection from real ECG signals contained in the MIT/BIH Database [7]. Theoretical results concern continuous signals with at most one extreme value. Although ECG signal is more complex but locally it often fulfils the above requirements. It is shown that under certain assumptions some of morphological operators do not change the original signal. A rectangular structuring element is subjected to theoretical considerations. Numerical part is realized with help of Matlab environment. We propose various combinations of morphological filters and conduct experiments for different structuring elements. Their usefulness for QRS detection is compared. It turns out that in some cases results of detection are significantly better than without morphological filters.

In morphological filtering [10], each signal is viewed as a set, and its geometrical features are modified by morphologically convolving the signal with a structuring element, which is another set of simple shape and size. By varying the structuring element we can extract different types of information from the signal.

2 Mathematical Morphology

Morphological filters are nonlinear signal transformations that locally modify geometric features of signals. They stem from the basic operations of a set-theoretical
method for signal analysis, called mathematical morphology, which was introduced
by Serra [6].
In the sequel we use definitions of grey-level morphology basic operators in the same
form as in [1]. Let us recall that *erosion* Θ of a function $f : R \rightarrow R$ by a structuring
element $b : R \rightarrow R$ can be defined as

$$(f \Theta b)(s) = \min_{x}\{f(s+x) - b(x) : (s+x) \in D_f \wedge x \in D_b\} \tag{1}$$

where $D_f = \operatorname{supp} f$, $D_b = \operatorname{supp} b$. In a similar way, *dilation* $\oplus$ is an operator
given by

$$(f \oplus b)(s) = \max_{x}\{f(s-x) + b(x) : (s-x) \in D_f \wedge x \in D_b\} \tag{2}$$

Two other operators: *closing* $\bullet$ and *opening* $\circ$ are defined with help of (1) and (2),
i.e.

$$f \bullet b = (f \oplus b) \Theta b, \quad f \circ b = (f \Theta b) \oplus b \tag{3}$$

2.1 Properties of Morphological Operators

It is easy to check that

$$f \bullet b = (f^c \circ \hat{b})^c, \quad f \circ b = (f^c \bullet \hat{b})^c \quad \text{(duality)} \tag{4}$$

where $f^c = -f$ and $\hat{b}(x) = b(-x) \ \forall x \in R$. We have also [2]

$$(f \circ b) \circ b = f \circ b, \quad (f \bullet b) \bullet b = f \bullet b \quad \text{(idempotency)}. \tag{5}$$

Assume that

$$D_f = \langle x_f; x_f + \Delta_f \rangle, \quad D_b = \langle x_b; x_b + \Delta_b \rangle \text{ for } \Delta_f > \Delta_b > 0. \tag{6}$$

From the numerical point of view it is important to know what are supports of functions modified by above morphological operations. We have

Lemma 1 *If (6) holds then*

$$D_{f \Theta b} = \langle x_f - x_b - \Delta_b; x_f + \Delta_f - x_b \rangle, \tag{7}$$

$$D_{f \oplus b} = \langle x_f + x_b; x_f + \Delta_f + x_b + \Delta_b \rangle, \tag{8}$$

$$D_{f \bullet b} = \langle x_f - \Delta_b; x_f + \Delta_f + \Delta_b \rangle, \tag{9}$$

$$D_{f \circ b} = \langle x_f - \Delta_b; x_f + \Delta_f + \Delta_b \rangle. \tag{10}$$

Proof: From (1) and (6) we obtain that for erosion $x_f \leq s + x \leq x_f + \Delta_f$ and $x_b \leq x \leq x_b + \Delta_b$. The smallest possible value for s is $x_f - x_b - \Delta_b$ and the biggest is $x_f + \Delta_f - x_b$ so we get (7). In the same way from (2) and (6) support for dilation given by (8) is obtained. To get (9) it is sufficient to apply (7) not for a function f but for $f \oplus b$ so $x_f + x_b \leq s + x \leq x_f + \Delta_f + x_b + \Delta_b$ thus $x_f - \Delta_b \leq s \leq x_f + \Delta_f + \Delta_b$. Similarly, the equation (10) is the result of application of (8) to a function $f \ominus b$. Q.E.D.

In next lemma it is proved that under certain conditions opening and closing do not change original signal f.

Lemma 2 *Let* $f \in C(R)$, $D_1 = \langle x_f; x_f + \Delta_1 \rangle$, $D_2 = \langle x_f + \Delta_1; x_f + \Delta_1 + \Delta_2 \rangle$, $D_f = \mathrm{supp}\, f = D_1 \cup D_2$, $b(x) \equiv b = const.$ *on* D_b *given by (4)* , $\Delta_1 > \Delta_b > 0$, $\Delta_2 > \Delta_b$.

(a) If $f|_{D_1}$ *is non-decreasing and* $f|_{D_2}$ *is non-increasing then exists* $x_0 \in (x_f + \Delta_1 - \Delta_b; x_f + \Delta_1)$ *such that*

$$(f \bullet b)|_{D_1 \cup D_2} \equiv f, \quad (f \circ b)|_{D_1 \cup D_2 \setminus (x_0; x_0 + \Delta_b)} \equiv f. \tag{11}$$

(b) If $f|_{D_1}$ *is non-increasing and* $f|_{D_2}$ *is non-decreasing then exists* $x_0 \in (x_f + \Delta_1 - \Delta_b; x_f + \Delta_1)$ *such that*

$$(f \bullet b)|_{D_1 \cup D_2 \setminus (x_0; x_0 + \Delta_b)} \equiv f, \quad (f \circ b)|_{D_1 \cup D_2} \equiv f. \tag{12}$$

Proof: (a) Consider a function f satisfying assumptions of the lemma. Let $g(x) = f(x + \Delta_b) - f(x)$. Obviously $g(x)$ is continuous, $g(x_f + \Delta_1 - \Delta_b) = f(x_f + \Delta_1) - f(x_f + \Delta_1 - \Delta_b) \geq 0$ and $g(x_f + \Delta_1) = f(x_f + \Delta_1 + \Delta_b) - f(x_f + \Delta_1) \leq 0$ hence from the Darboux theorem we obtain that there exists $x_0 \in \langle x_f + \Delta_1 - \Delta_b; x_f + \Delta_1 \rangle$ such that $f(x_0) = f(x_0 + \Delta_b)$. Let us denote $\Delta_f = \Delta_1 + \Delta_2$. It is easy to verify that

$$(f \ominus b)(s) = \begin{cases} f(x_f) - b, & s \in \langle x_f - x_b - \Delta_b; x_f - x_b \rangle \\ f(s + x_b) - b, & s \in \langle x_f - x_b; x_0 - x_b \rangle \\ f(s + x_b + \Delta_b) - b, & s \in \langle x_0 - x_b; x_f + \Delta_f - x_b - \Delta_b) \\ f(x_f + \Delta_f) - b, & s \in \langle x_f + \Delta_f - x_b - \Delta_b; x_f + \Delta_f - x_b \rangle \end{cases} \tag{13}$$

and similarly

$$(f \oplus b)(s) = \begin{cases} f(s - x_b) + b, & s \in \langle x_f + x_b; x_f + \Delta_1 + x_b) \\ f(x_f + \Delta_f) + b, & s \in \langle x_f + \Delta_1 + x_b; x_f + \Delta_1 + x_b + \Delta_b) \\ f(s - x_b - \Delta_b) + b, & s \in \langle x_f + \Delta_1 + x_b + \Delta_b; x_f + \Delta_f + x_b + \Delta_b\rangle \end{cases} \tag{14}$$

Let $D_3 = \langle x_f + x_b; x_f + \Delta_1 + x_b\rangle$, $D_4 = \langle x_f + \Delta_1 + x_b; x_f + \Delta_f + x_b + \Delta_b\rangle$. Function $(f \oplus b)|_{D_3}$ is non-decreasing and $(f \oplus b)|_{D_4}$ is non-increasing thus we can apply (13) for closing:

$$(f \bullet b)(s) = \begin{cases} (f \oplus b)(x_f + x_b), & s \in \langle x_f - \Delta_b; x_f) \\ (f \oplus b)(s + x_b), & s \in \langle x_f; x_0 - x_b) \\ (f \oplus b)(s + x_b + \Delta_b), & s \in \langle x_0 - x_b; x_f + \Delta_f) \\ (f \oplus b)(x_f + \Delta_f + x_b + \Delta_b), & s \in \langle x_f + \Delta_f; x_f + \Delta_f + \Delta_b\rangle \end{cases} \tag{15}$$

with $x_0 \in \langle x_f + \Delta_1 + x_b - \Delta_b; x_f + \Delta_1 + x_b\rangle$. From (14) we see that it is possible to take $x_0 = x_f + \Delta_1 + x_b$. Then by (14) and (15) we obtain (17) so $(f \bullet b)|_{D_1 \cup D_2} \equiv f$.

Let now $D_5 = \langle x_f - \Delta_b; x_0 - x_b\rangle$, $D_6 = \langle x_0 - x_b; x_f + \Delta_f - x_b\rangle$. Function $(f \ominus b)|_{D_5}$ is non-decreasing and $(f \ominus b)|_{D_6}$ is non-increasing thus from (14) we get expression for opening:

$$(f \circ b)(s) = \begin{cases} (f \ominus b)(s - x_b) + b, & s \in \langle x_f - \Delta_b; x_0) \\ (f \ominus b)(x_0 - x_b) + b, & s \in \langle x_0; x_0 + \Delta_b) \\ (f \ominus b)(s - x_b - \Delta_b) + b, & s \in \langle x_0 + \Delta_b; x_f + \Delta_f + \Delta_b\rangle \end{cases} \tag{16}$$

By (13) we come to equality $(f \circ b)|_{D_1 \cup D_2 \setminus (x_0; x_0 + \Delta_b)} \equiv f$.

(b) If f satisfies the assumptions of lemma then f^c fulfils requirements of part *(a)*. Moreover, $\hat{b}$ in (4) is a structuring element of the same shape and width but different beginning as b. From *(a)* we see that $(f^c \bullet \hat{b})|_{D_1 \cup D_2} \equiv f^c$ and by (4) we get $(f \circ b)|_{D_1 \cup D_2} \equiv f$. Applying (4) for the other duality property we arrive to conclusion that $(f \bullet b)|_{D_1 \cup D_2 \setminus (x_0; x_0 + \Delta_b)} \equiv f$ Q.E.D.

From Lemma 2 we easily get

Corollary 1 *Let assumptions of Lemma 2 be satisfied and $f(x_f) = f(x_f + \Delta_f) = 0$.*
(a) If $f|_{D_1}$ is non-decreasing and $f|_{D_2}$ is non-increasing then $f \bullet b \equiv f$ $\forall x \in R$.
(b) If $f|_{D_1}$ is non-increasing and $f|_{D_2}$ is non-decreasing then $f \circ b \equiv f$ $\forall x \in R$.

Let us take two possibly different structuring elements b_1 and b_2 of the type considered so far. Define one more morphological operation © as follows:

$$f©(b_1, b_2) = 1/2[(f \circ b_1) \bullet b_2 + (f \bullet b_2) \circ b_1]. \tag{17}$$

The operation given by (17) we call in the sequel CUMFB (Commonly Used Morphological Filter Block). In paragraph 3 we apply CUMFB to ECG signal pre-processing. Now let us derive some properties of $\copyright$. We can formulate

Lemma 3 *(a) If* $f \bullet b_2 = f$ *and* $(f \circ b_1) \bullet b_2 = f \circ b_1$ *then* $f\copyright(b_1, b_2) = f \circ b_1$ *and*

$$\underbrace{(...(f\copyright(b_1,b_2))\copyright(b_1,b_2))...)\copyright(b_1,b_2)}_{n \text{ times}} = f \circ b_1 \qquad (18)$$

(b) If $f \circ b_1 = f$ *and* $(f \bullet b_2) \circ b_1 = f \bullet b_2$ *then* $f\copyright(b_1, b_2) = f \bullet b_2$ *and*

$$\underbrace{(...(f\copyright(b_1,b_2))\copyright(b_1,b_2))...)\copyright(b_1,b_2)}_{n \text{ times}} = f \bullet b_2 \qquad (19)$$

Proof: Equality $f\copyright(b_1, b_2) = f \circ b_1$ comes immediately. From (17) and idempotency given by (5) we have

$$(f\copyright(b_1,b_2))\copyright(b_1,b_2) = (f \circ b_1)\copyright(b_1,b_2) = \qquad (20)$$
$$= 1/2[((f \circ b_1) \circ b_1) \bullet b_2 + ((f \circ b_1) \bullet b_2) \circ b_1] =$$
$$= 1/2[(f \circ b_1) \bullet b_2 + (f \circ b_1) \circ b_1] = 1/2[f \circ b_1 + f \circ b_1] = f \circ b$$

and hence (18) holds. Part *(b)* of the lemma can be proved in the same way. Q.E.D.

Remark 1 *Let us notice that if function* f *satisfies assumptions of Corollary 1 then the same we can say about* $f \circ b$ *and* $f \bullet b$ *so in this case we have a fulfilment of demands of Lemma 3.*

3 Experimental Studies

Detecting QRS complexes in the ECG [8] is one of the most important tasks that need to be performed. Most of the algorithms usually use three stages to process the ECG signal: 1) noise suppression and background normalization, 2) signal transformation and filtering, and 3) QRS detection. The annotated ECG records available from the MIT/BIH (Massachusetts Institute of Technology and Beth Israel Hospital) arrhythmia database [7] have been used for the experiments and evaluation of different classifiers in this study. The morphological filter pre-processing stages and beat detection algorithm were implemented using the MATLAB programming environment.
A structuring element is characterized by its shape, width, and height. Its width, or length, is largely determined by the duration of the major waves and the sampling rate. Denoting the duration of one of the waves as T sec, and the sampling rate as S Hz, the number of samples that correspond to a wave is $T \times S$. The values of the structuring element determine the shape of the output waveform.

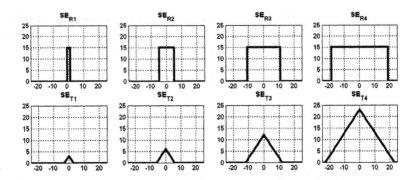

Fig. 1. Shape of structuring element used to evaluate morphological filtering. Rectangles: SE_{R1}, SE_{R2}, SE_{R3}, SE_{R4} - vectors has a length of 3, 10, 22, 38 samples and triangles: SE_{T1}, SE_{T2}, SE_{T3}, SE_{T4} - a length of 5, 11, 23, 45 samples.

Falsely detected beats FP (false positive) and undetected beats FN (false negative) are used to rate sensitivity of QRS detection in our experimental filtering schemes.

3.1 Simple morphological filtering

In this section, we study the influence of morphological opening and closing on shape of ECG signals. In Lemma 2 we proved, that when duration of structuring element is smaller than the each peak or pit of ECG signal, opening and closing do not change original signal. We show below that our theoretical consideration from paragraph 2 let us to formulate some basic criteria to build filtering scheme.

Since the opening and closing operations are intended to remove impulses, the structuring element must be designed so that the filtering process does not remove the important waves in the ECG signal. We have employed different size of structuring elements for the opening and closing operations, and we see that our theoretical speculations were confirmed. If the data are opened (Fig. 2, b), c), d)) by rectangular structuring element then the operation removes peaks and if the data are closed (Fig. 2, f), g), h)) then pits are removed. We see that longer structuring element has bigger impact on the shape of output waveform. Results for triangular structuring element are very similar.

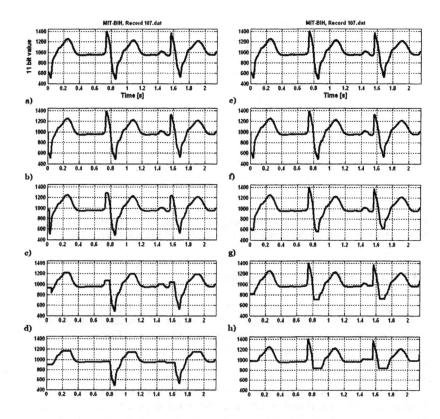

Fig. 2. Results of filtering record sample 107 from MIT/BIH database. Original signal (top), operation opening with structuring elements: a): SE_{R1}, b) SE_{R2}, c) SE_{R3}, d) SE_{R4}, operation closing with structuring elements: e): SE_{R1}, f) SE_{R2}, g) SE_{R3}, h) SE_{R4}.

3.2 Noise suppression and background normalization

Morphological filtering is performed by processing the data in the second stage in few steps. Processing the data through a sequence of opening and closing operations performs impulsive noise suppression. The ECG signal, as well as any baseline drift, is estimated by processing the data using an opening operation followed by a closing operation. Processing the data using a closing operation followed by an opening operation forms a second estimate of the signal. The result from this step is the average of the two estimates. We described this pre-processing in Lemma 3 and it was called CUFMB.

Background normalization is performed by estimating the drift in the background and subtracting it from the incoming data. Estimation follows in the same way like described above but we used two structuring elements. For opening operation structuring element has size of L and for closing size of $2L$.

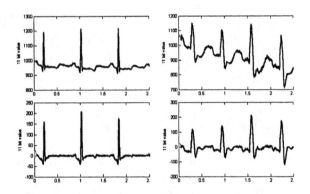

Fig. 3. Effects of noise suppression and background normalization performed for samples from MIT/BIH. Original signals (top), from left: records 100 and 109, and filtered (bottom).

3.3 More complex morphological filtering

Many applications of mathematical morphology use only a single structuring element. In some cases, this may not produce the best results. Combination of morphological elementary operations (multiscale filtering) as well as the utilization of two or more structuring elements (multiple SE) can improve the performance of morphology based filtering.

In this paper the results of computations for sequence of morphological operations were presented. We use one SE for Erosion, one for Dilation and two different SE for Opening and Closing. Based on obtained results we propose for filtering a dedicated block including consecutive stages: noise suppression, performed n-times background normalization (both operations described in paragraph 3.2), dilation, closing, and dilation, called below - Multistage Morphological Filtering (MMF).

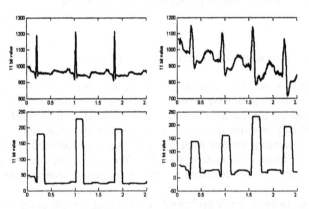

Fig. 4. Effects of MMF performed for samples from MIT/BIH. Original signal (top), from left: records 100 and 109, and filtered (bottom).

In addition to illustrating the impact of using multiple and multiscale techniques we have shown effects of our work with MMF block.

Table 1. Results of QRS detection. Values of FP and FN, w/o and with MMF block.

MIT/BIH record	FP w/o MMF	FP w. MMF	FN w/o MMF	FN w. MMF
100	371	1	0	1
109	356	31	0	0

We are interested in identifying beats during the first 10 minutes of signal from MIT/BIH database. The objective of this investigation is to determine the impact of applying MMF on the classification QRS in ECG signal. The criteria of assessment of performance was build based on the algorithm presented in Friesen's paper [9]. Algorithm called AF1 belongs to class of mixed amplitude and first derivative of QRS detection algorithms.

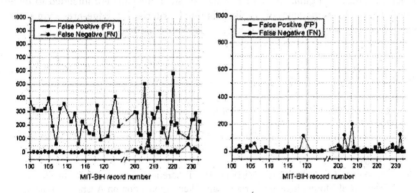

Fig. 5. Results of QRS detection, w/o pre-processing (left) and filtered by MMF block (right).

The experiments show that MMF block construction, has very big impact for characteristic of output signal (Fig. 4. bottom). Despite the fact that MIT/BIH database consist of wide spectrum of ECG signals we obtained similar results for all data. Figure 5 shows level of QRS detection (exactly false positive and false negative ratio) performed on all ECG signals from database produced by MMF block. It is easily seen that this combination of elementary operations got better results in QRS detection (Fig. 5. right).

4 Results and discussion

In the past, many approaches have been proposed for edge-preserving signal smoothing [3]. It has been proven that as belonging to nonlinear filtering techniques - morphological dilation and erosion satisfy the causality and the additive semigroup property required by multiscale analysis for signals of any dimension with local maxima and local minima as singular points [4] [5].

We introduce an edge-controlled enhancing functional for signal processing, based on mathematical morphology filtering. Multistage morphological filtering are presented for fast and effective smoothing. This operation preserves peak amplitudes and used for ECG signal enhancement for further processing, like QRS detection.

5 Conclusion

Dilations, erosions, opening and closing, the basic nonlinear convolutions of morphological signal processing, can be combined in many ways to create more complex morphological operators that can solve a broad variety of problems in signal and image analysis and nonlinear filtering.

In this paper, we have considered the signal processing aspects of mathematical morphology operators, especially the shape and size of SE and multistage filtering that are important relative to their application in ECG signals processing

We have derived results for morphological operators applied to the given class of functions and rectangular SE. Other shapes of such elements are intended to be analysed [11]. Developments of finding optimal criteria for edge-preserving signal smoothing based on MMF are currently under investigation.

References

1. Gonzalez, R.C., Woods, R.E.: Digital Image Processing. 2nd ed. Prentice Hall, New Jersey (2001)
2. Leymarie, F., Levine M.D.: Curvature Morphology. Tech. Rep. TR-CIM-88-26, Computer Vision and Robotics Laboratory, McGill University, Montreal, Quebec, Canada (1988)
3. Chu-Song, C., Ja-Ling, W., Yi-Ping, H.: Theoretical Aspects of Vertically Invariant Gray-Level Morphological Operators and Their Application on Adaptive Signal and Image Filtering, IEEE Transaction on Signal Processing, Vol. 47, no. 4, (April 1999)
4. Chu, C. H., Delp, E. J.: Impulsive noise suppression and background normalization of electrocardiogram signals using morphological operators, IEEE Transaction on Biomedical Engineering, Vol. 36, no. 2 (February 1989)
5. Sun, P., Wu, Q. H., Weindling, A. M., Finkelstein, A., Ibrahim, K.: An Improved Morphological Approach to Background Normalization of ECG Signals, Transaction on Biomedical Engineering, Vol. 50, no. 1 (January 2003)
6. Serra, I.: Image Analysis and Mathematical Morphology, New York Academic, 1982
7. MIT/BIH Arrhythmia Database: The MIT/BIH arrhythmia database CD-ROM, Harvard-MIT Division of Health Sciences and Technology (1992)
8. Köhler B-U., Hennig C, Orglmeister R.: The Principles of Software QRS Detection, IEEE Engineering in Medicine and Biology (January/Febraury 2002)
9. Friesen G. M., Jannett T. C., Jadallah M. A., Yates S. L., Quint S. R., Nagle H. T.: A Comparison of the Noise Sensitivity of Nine QRS Detection Algorithms, IEEE Transaction on Biomedical Engineering, Vol. 37, no. 1 (January 1990)
10. Maragos P.: Morphological Signal and Image Processing, CRC Press LLC (2000)
11. Tadejko P, Rakowski W.: Matlab Simulink in modeling morphological filters for electrocardiogram signal processing, Simulation in Research and Expansion, XIII Science Work-shop, PTSK (2005)

Input's Significance Evaluation in a Multi Input-Variable System

Izabela Rejer

University of Szczecin, Faculty of Economics and Management
Mickiewicza 64/66, 71-101 Szczecin, Poland
i_rejer@uoo.univ.szczecin.pl

Abstract. One of the most important problems that can be met during a process of modeling of a real system is a problem of insufficient data points. This problem is often discussed in the modeling literature, however, so far no satisfactory solution has been proposed. The aim of this article is to present a method for evaluating the importance of model's inputs which helps to overcome mentioned problem. The proposed method is an enhanced version of the method of local walking models, introduced two years ago. The practical applicability of the proposed method will be demonstrated via the example of evaluating the significance of 150 potential input variables of the prognostic model of an unemployment rate.

1 Introduction

"A multi-dimensional system" is a name which is commonly attributed to systems placed in an input space consisted of at least 20-30 potential input variables. Before building a model of such a big system it is necessary to find out which of its potential input variables are the most important for its behavior. The whole pool of methods used for evaluating the significance of input variables can be divided into three main groups:
- methods based on analyzing linear dependencies existing in the examined system, e.g.: principal component analysis (PCA) [1, 4, 9], linear discrimnant analysis (LDA) [1, 2, 9], independent component analysis [4], methods based on linear regression and correlation [1] etc.,
- methods based on analyzing non-linear two-dimensional dependencies existing in the examined system, e.g.: neural networks (especially perceptron and radial ones) [9, 3, 8], non-linear regression [1], fuzzy curves [8, 5] etc.,
- methods based on analyzing non-linear multi-dimensional dependencies existing in the examined system, e.g.: non-linear independent component analysis (NICA) [4], non-linear discriminant analysis (NDA), sensitivity analysis [13], hierarchical method [6, 12], genetic algorithms (GA) [2] etc.

Naturally, the most reliable results of inputs significance can be obtained when the methods that belong to the last group are applied in the significance evaluation process. The reason for this is that these methods simultaneously analyze a large number of input variables and are not limited to linear dependencies. However, methods from this group have also two shortcomings limiting their usefulness for real multi-dimensional systems; a large group of them have very heavy data requirements, often impossible to meet in most real systems (e.g. sensitivity analysis, NICA, NDA), and the others require a construction of a huge set of non-linear auxiliary models, which is a time consuming process, especially when a system is described by a large number of input variables (GA, step-by-step method).

The aim of this article is to present a method which weaken these shortcomings, that is, which can be applied even when the number of input variables existing in the analyzed system exceeds the number of its data points and which limits the number of non-linear auxiliary models that have to be built during the modeling process.

2   Theoretical background of the local walking models method

There is a well known method used to determine the significance of input variables in a linear system. The main idea of it is to analyze and compare the slope coefficients of a system's linear model. According to this method this input variable is regarded as the most significant which is related to the slope coefficient of the largest absolute value (naturally, all input variables have to be normalized to the same interval). The explanation of this rule is very simple – a large value of a slope coefficient means that even very small changes in the input variable, corresponding to this coefficient, result in very large changes in the output variable.

Figure 1 illustrates the approach discussed above via a system consisting of two input variables: $x1$ and $x2$, described by the equation: $y = x1 + 5x2$. Figure 1a shows the whole 3D model of the system and figures 1b and 1c show the slopes of the model's surface in its 2D subspaces: $x1$-y and $x2$-y. As it can be noticed, the slope of the model's surface towards the axis $x2$ is much greater than the slope towards the axis $x1$. This indicates that the variable $x2$ is much more important than the variable $x1$.

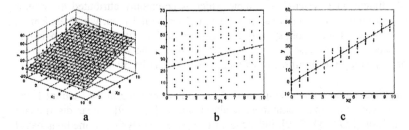

a   b   c

Fig. 1. An example of inputs' significance evaluation in a linear system

The method of local walking models modifies the method described above so that it could be used for linear approximation of a non-linear system. Naturally, it is apparent that in most cases a non-linear system cannot be described by a single linear model because it might cause too drastic reduction of information (fig. 2a). However, the negative impact of linear approximation can be significantly reduced when, instead of one linear model, a set of linear local models is applied (fig. 2b).

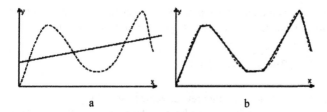

Fig. 2. Approximation of a non-linear system by one linear model (a) and by a set of linear models (b)

3   Standard version of the local walking models method

The method of local walking models is based on segmental-linear approximation but it differs slightly from the classic one, shown in the fig. 2b. In the classic approximation, consecutive linear models are built using separate subsets of data. This, however, requires a large data set, especially when the rate of system's non-linearity is very high. In order to lessen this requirement, consecutive models, in the local walking models approach, are built by shifting the modelling window across very small fixed amount of data. In this way, each local model covers some of the data points which are used also in other models. As a result more linear models can be built and a better rate of approximation can be obtained [10, 11]. Figure 3 displays the process of constructing succeeding linear models in a two-input non-linear system.

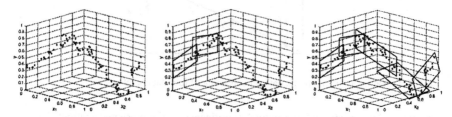

Fig. 3. A process of constructing succeeding linear models in a two-input system

The approximation of a non-linear multi-dimensional system by a series of local multi-dimensional linear models can be stated by the following set of equations:

$$y = a_{1,0} + a_{1,1}x_1 + a_{1,2}x_2 + \ldots + a_{1,n}x_n \qquad t \in (1,k) \tag{1}$$

$$y = a_{2,0} + a_{2,1}x_1 + a_{2,2}x_2 + \ldots + a_{2,n}x_n \qquad t \in (1+i, k+i)$$

$$\ldots\ldots\ldots\ldots\ldots \qquad\qquad \ldots\ldots\ldots\ldots\ldots$$

$$y = a_{m,0} + a_{m,1}x_1 + a_{m,2}x_2 + \ldots + a_{m,n}x_n \qquad t \in (1+(m-1)i, (m-1)i+k),$$

where: n - number of variables, m - number of linear local models, k - number of data in single local model, i - size of the shifting, t - consecutive number of data point, $t \in (1\ldots z)$, z - number of data in the whole system, y - output variable, $x_1 \ldots x_n$ - input variables, $a_0 \ldots a_m$ - vectors of slope coefficients of local models.

Linear approximation of a given data set is a process aimed at finding a linear model which minimizes the total distance between all data points and the model (fig. 4):

$$\min\left(\sum_{i=1}^{n}\left|y_{Ri} - y_{Ti}\right|\right), \tag{2}$$

where: y_{Ri} - real value of variable y_i, y_{Tli} - theoretical value of variable y_i.

In general, equation 1 is very difficult to solve because there is no analytic method which can be used to calculate a minimum value of a ruthless multi-dimensional function. Therefore, a common approach taken in order to find parameters of a linear model, is to replace the ruthless function by a square function:

$$\min\left(\sum_{i=1}^{n}\left(y_{Ri} - y_{Ti}\right)^{2}\right). \tag{3}$$

This is often a good solution because it allows calculating the derivative of the distance function in a direct way. Unfortunately, it has also a negative effect – it causes a decrease in approximation precision. The reason for this is that the square function does not treat all data in the same way but it pays little attention to the data points which are close to the model and much more attention to the data points lying in further distances from the model.

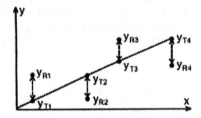

Fig. 4. Linear approximation of a data set consisting of four data points

As previously mentioned, the inputs' significance in the presented method is evaluated on the basis of the models' parameters. Therefore it is very important to establish these parameters with the highest possible precision. Hence, the models' parameters should be estimated by minimizing the ruthless, not the square, function. However, as the minimum value of the ruthless multi-dimensional function cannot be calculated in an analytic way, another approach to deal with this task has to be taken.

A well-known tool which works on the basis of minimizing a function, not in an analytic but in a numeric way, is an Artificial Neural Network (ANN). The ANN tries to find the optimal value of the error function iteratively adding very small corrections to the network parameters. Therefore the ANNs performance may be aimed not only at minimizing of the square error but also at minimizing of the absolute error [4][6].

Naturally, the iterative process of changing ANN's parameters always consumes a lot of time. Hence, mostly it is not advisable to use ANN for linear approximation. The majority of scientists would accept the decrease in precision rather than the elongated modelling time. However, the truth is that both goals (precise results and short time) may be obtained simultaneously, simply by joining two methods, the ANN, and the method based on minimization of equation 3, which is popularly called the Least Square Method (LMS).

Based on the above considerations the parameters of each linear local model are calculated, in the local walking models method, in two steps. In the first step the rough values of the parameters are evaluated using LMS. Next, these rough values are used as the starting parameters of a Linear Neural Network (LNN), which works with them further in order to obtain a more precise linear approximation.

When the approximation, described by equation 1, is done, the inputs' significance is established by calculating the arithmetic averages of the vectors of regression coefficients:

$$S_{xi} = \frac{1}{m}\sum_{j=1}^{m}\left|a_{ij}\right|, \tag{4}$$

where: S_{xi} - global significance of the input variable x_i, a_{ij} - coefficient of input variable x_i of j linear local model (equation 1).

S_{xi} is a relative measure that gives information about the order of priority of input variables in the analyzed system. Obviously, the calculation of the S_{xi} coefficients has to be based on the whole set of m slope coefficients. Therefore, before calculating S_{xi}, variables that, due to high correlation, have been eliminated from the process of building of any of the linear local models, have to incorporate right slope coefficients. Since, a high linear correlation of two variables means that both influence the analyzed output variable in a very similar (if not an identical) way, the variable eliminated from the model adopts the coefficient of the variable which was present in the model.

4 Enhanced version of local walking models method

The approach described above has one serious limitation - it cannot be applied in systems in which number of potential input variables is equal or greater than number of data points. This is a result of an overfitting phenomena, which can appear when the number of data points used in the modeling process is not significantly bigger than the dimension of the input vector. Therefore, in order to build a set of correct (non-overfitted) local linear models, each model has to be based on data set containing much more data points than input variables.

This indicates that in systems in which the dimension of an input vector is equal or bigger than number of data points there is no possibility to build a set of models (or even one model) containing all potential input variables. In systems like this, the whole input space has to be divided into subspaces of such a size which will allow to build a set of non-overfitted linear local models. Naturally, to preserve the reliable results of inputs significance evaluation, the subspaces should contain adequately large number of input variables. Obviously, in a general case it is difficult to establish the best ratio between the number of data points and the number of input variables existed in each subspace – so far the best experimental results have been obtained when the value of this ratio was set between 4 and 5.

It is important to remember that the best results of the inputs significance analyzes can be obtained when each input variable is analyzed in regard to all other input variables. Therefore, when the decomposition process is performed, it is not enough to place each variable in one subspace. Instead of that, each variable should be included to such number of subspaces to be analyzed at least once with any other variable.

Figure 5 illustrates an algorithm which is used in proposed approach for a decomposition of an input space. The exemplary system (presented in this figure), described by 50 potential input variables is divided into 10 subspaces of 20 variables. As it can be noticed each input variable is connected to all other input variables, what means it will be analyzed in regard to all of them.

<table>
<tr><td>model 1</td><td>- inputs:</td><td>1-10 and 11-20</td></tr>
<tr><td>model 2</td><td>- inputs:</td><td>1-10 and 21-30</td></tr>
<tr><td>model 3</td><td>- inputs:</td><td>1-10 and 31-40</td></tr>
<tr><td>model 4</td><td>- inputs:</td><td>1-10 and 41-50</td></tr>
<tr><td>model 5</td><td>- inputs:</td><td>11-20 and 21-30</td></tr>
<tr><td>model 6</td><td>- inputs:</td><td>11-20 and 31-40</td></tr>
<tr><td>model 7</td><td>- inputs:</td><td>11-20 and 41-50</td></tr>
<tr><td>model 8</td><td>- inputs:</td><td>21-30 and 31-40</td></tr>
<tr><td>model 9</td><td>- inputs:</td><td>21-30 and 41-50</td></tr>
<tr><td>model 10</td><td>- inputs:</td><td>31-40 and 41-50</td></tr>
</table>

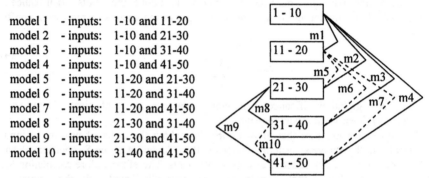

Fig. 5. The algorithm of decomposition of the input space of the analyzed system

When the decomposition algorithm, illustrated in the figure 5, is applied in the process of investigating the significance of input variables, the S_{xi} coefficients are calculated as the arithmetic averages of the vectors of slope coefficients of the models from all subspaces:

$$S_{xi} = \frac{1}{m*s} \sum_{j=1}^{m*s} |a_{ij}|,$$

(5)

where: s - number of subspaces.

5 Prognostic model of an unemployment rate

The method described in section 4 was used to choose input variables which should be introduced to a prognostic model of an unemployment rate. The survey was based on monthly data, provided by the Polish Statistic Department, describing the analyzed system's behavior in years: 1992-2001. Data from the first eight years was used in a modeling process while data from the last two years was used to verify the prognostic capabilities of the created model. The output variable of the model was the unemployment rate in a next month $y(k+1)$ and the set of potential input variables consisted of:

- 24 basic macroeconomic factors (minimal salaries, rate of rediscount, personal income tax, money supply etc.), denoted as: $x_i(k)$,
- 5 time delays of each factor, denoted as: $x_i(k-1)$, $x_i(k-2)$, $x_i(k-3)$, $x_i(k-4)$, $x_i(k-5)$,
- the unemployment rate in a present month $y(k)$ and its 5 time delays: $y(k-1)$, $y(k-2)$, $y(k-3)$, $y(k-4)$, $y(k-5)$.

Since, there were 150 potential input variables and only 90 data points, a set of input subspaces had to be created to carry out inputs' significance analyzes:

- in order to keep the ratio between the number of data points and the number of input variables in the interval <4, 5>, the number of input variables in each subspace was set to 20 (ratio=4.5);
- in order to analyze each variable in regard to all other variables, number of subspaces was set to 105.

The parameters of each linear local models' set, created over each input subspace, were set as follows:

- the size of shifting was set to 1,
- the amount of data in each local model was set to double number of input subspace dimension (40).

The estimation of the models coefficients was performed in two steps. First, the coefficients of all 5355 local linear models were evaluated with LSM. Then, all coefficients were readjusted with LNN. The process of adjusting models parameters was performed on the PC computer with processor Pentium IV 2,4 GHz and 512MB of memory and lasted about five hours.

After the modeling process, equation 5 was used to establish the ranking of importance of the potential input variables. The short version of this ranking, containing only the most and the least important variables, is presented in the table 1. As it can be noticed, the results from the table 1 are in agreement with the common sense knowledge. According to them, the biggest influence on the unemployment rate in a month *(k+1)* have variables representing unemployment rate in previous months.

In order to verify the results of the ranking of importance from table 1, a prognostic model of the analyzed system was built. The modeling process was performed it two steps.

1. In the first step the non-linear correlation of input variables was tested and some variables were removed from the ranking.
2. In the second step an inductive approach was used to choose which of the remaining input variables should be introduced to succeeding non-linear models of the analyzed system.

The non-linear correlation between all 22350 pair of input variables was evaluated on the basis of equation 6 [14]. As a result, 40 input variables, highly correlated with other variables (in more than 98%) were removed from the further survey. The short version of a new ranking of importance is presented in the table 2.

Table 1. The ranking of importance of potential input variables

No.	Variable	S_x		No.	Variable	S_x
1	unemployment rate (k)	0,88	...	145	government income (k-1)	0,09
2	unemployment rate (k-1)	0,78	...	146	personal tax (k-5)	0,09
3	unemployment rate (k-2)	0,72	...	147	government outcome (k-2)	0,08
4	unemployment rate (k-3)	0,68	...	148	number of quarter (k-3)	0,08
5	number of inhabitants (k-2)	0,68	...	149	number of quarter (k-4)	0,08
6	number of inhabitants (k-1)	0,66	...	150	number of graduates (k-3)	0,07

Table 2. The ranking of importance after removing 40 variables of the highest values of the non-linear correlation coefficient

No.	Variable	S_x		No.	Variable	S_x
1	unemployment rate (k)	0,88	...	105	import (k-2)	0,09
2	unemployment rate (k-2)	0,72	...	106	import (k-1)	0,09
3	number of inhabitants (k-2)	0,68	...	107	government income (k-1)	0,09
4	average salaries (k-2)	0,57	...	108	personal tax (k-5)	0,09
5	money supply (k-1)	0,52	...	109	government outcome (k)	0,08
6	unemployment rate (k-4)	0,51	...	110	number of graduates (k-3)	0,07

$$nlc_{x1x2} = \sqrt{1 - \frac{\sum_{i=1}^{z}(x_{R1i} - x_{T1i})^2}{\sum_{i=1}^{z}(x_{R1i} - x_{A1})^2}}, \qquad (6)$$

where: nlc_{xy} - coefficient of non-linear correlation between variables x_1 and x_2, x_{R1i} - real value of variable x_1, x_{T1i} - theoretical value of variable x_1, calculated on the basis of neural models, x_{A1} - arithmetic average of variable x_1.

The results of the ranking from the table 2 were used in the process of building a five input model of the analyzed system. The modeling process was performed in steps according to the error descent criterion. In each step one variable from the ranking of importance was added to the model and the model's error was evaluated. If the new added variable caused a drop of the model's error, it was regarded as an important one and was left in the model. On the other hand, if the new added variable caused an increase of the model's error, it was skipped in the current modeling step.

The models' performance was compared not only on the basis of the training data (monthly data from years: 1992-1999) but also on the basis of their prediction capabilities (estimated on monthly data from years 2000-2001). Both model's errors, the training error and the prediction error, were calculated according to the following equation:

$$E = \frac{1}{z}\sum_{i=1}^{z}|y_{Ri} - y_{Ti}|, \qquad (7)$$

where: E - model's error, z - number of data points (90 for training error and 24 for prediction error), y_{Ti} - real value of output variable, y_{Ri} - theoretical value of output variable.

Non-linear neural networks of following parameters were used as a modeling tool [3, 7]: flow of signals: one-way, architecture of connections between layers: all to all, hidden layers: 1 hidden layer with 4-5 sigmoid neurons, output layer: 1 linear neuron, training method: backpropagation algorithm with momentum and changing learning rates, training aim: to minimize the average absolute error, training time: 100000 epoch, number of training repetitions per each model: 10, testing method: 16-cross-fold validation.

Models of the unemployment rate in a *(k+1)* period built during succeeding steps of the modeling process were as follows:

- one-input model – input: *unemployment rate (k)*; training error: 3.27%; prediction error: 3.09%,
- two-input model – inputs: *unemployment rate (k), unemployment rate (k-2)*; training error: 2.79%; prediction error: 2.41%,
- three-input model – inputs: *unemployment rate (k), unemployment rate (k-2), number of inhabitants (k-2)*; training error: 2.11%; prediction error: 2.17%,
- first four-input model – inputs: *unemployment rate (k), unemployment rate (k-2), number of inhabitants (k-2), average salaries (k-2)*; training error: 2.36%; as the variable *average salaries (k-2)* did not caused the drop of the model's error, it was skipped in this modeling step;
- second four-input model – inputs: *unemployment rate (k), unemployment rate (k-2), number of inhabitants (k-2), money supply (k-1)*; training error: 1.92%; prediction error: 2.10%,
- first five-input model – inputs: *unemployment rate (k), unemployment rate (k-2), number of inhabitants (k-2), money supply (k-1), average salaries (k-2)*; training error: 2,18%; once again the variable *average salaries (k-2)* did not caused the drop of the model's error, so it was not introduced to the final five-input model,
- second five-input model – inputs: *unemployment rate (k), unemployment rate (k-2), number of inhabitants (k-2), money supply (k-1), unemployment rate (k-4)*; training error: 1.40%; prediction error: 1.98%.

6 Conclusion

The aim of this article was to present a method of evaluating the significance of potential input variables in real multi-dimensional systems. As it was underlined in section 4, the main benefit of this method is that it can be applied when the number of data points describing the analyzed system is very limited – even when it is smaller than the number of potential input variables. Another important feature of the proposed method is that it allows to examine the biggest possible subspaces of the analyzed system, which means only a very few information of the system behavior is lost. When multi-dimensional systems are analyzed, it is no sensible to examine their input variables only with regard to the output variable without referring to other input variables. Such approach causes too high reduction of information, the more input variables are analyzed together, the more precise results of input's significance can be obtained.

As it was presented in the article, the proposed method is not only the theoretical construction but it also gives reliable results when applied in real systems. The application of this method for evaluating the significance of potential input variables of a prognostic model of the unemployment rate allowed to build the model of a very high precision of predictions (the prediction error of the final five-input model was smaller than 2%). Moreover, as it was mentioned in the article such significant result was obtained in a very reasonable time. If, instead of creating the ranking of importance, all possible five-input models were compared, it would cost considerably greater amount of time, because $6*10^8$ non-linear neural models would have to be built to deal with this task.

References

1. Aczel, A. D.: Complete Business Statistics, Richard D. Irwin Inc., Sydney (1993)
2. Back, B. B.: Choosing Bankruptcy Predictors Using Discriminant Analysis, Logit Analisis, and Genetic Algorithms, Turku Centre for Computer Science Technical Report No 40, (1996)
3. Demuth, H., Beale, M.: Neural Network Toolbox User's Guide, The Math Works Inc., Natick MA USA (2000)
4. Lee, T.: Independent Component Analysis - Theory and Applications, Kluwer Academic Publishers, Boston (2001)
5. Lin, Y., Cunningham, G. A.: A New Approach to Fuzzy-Neural System Modeling, IEEE Transaction on Fuzzy Systems, vol. 3, no. 2 (1995)
6. Liu, H., Motoda, H.: Feature selection for knowledge discovery and data mining, Kluwer Academic Publishers, USA (1998)
7. Masters, T.: Practical Neural Networks Recipes in C++, Academic Press Inc (1993)
8. Piegat, A.: Fuzzy Modeling and Control, Physica-Verlag, New York (1999)
9. Reed, R. D., Marks, II R. J.: Neural Smithing – Supervised Learning in Feedforward Artificial Neural Networks, The MIT Press, Massachusetts (1999)
10. Rejer, I.: A method of investigating a significance of input variables in non-linear high-dimensional systems, Artificial Intelligence and Security in Computing Systems, Proceedings on 9th International Conference, ACS'2002, pp. 73-80, Kluwer Academic Publisher, London (2003)
11. Rejer, I.: A method of modeling a multi-dimensional system via artificial intelligence methods on the example of an unemployment in Poland, The Publishing House of the Szczecin University, Szczecin (2003)
12. Sugeno, M., Yasukawa, T.: A Fuzzy-Logic-Based Approach to Qualitative Modeling, IEEE Transaction on Fuzzy Systems vol. 1, no. 1 (1993)
13. Sung, A. H.: Ranking importance of input parameters of neural networks, Expert Systems with Applications 15, pp. 405-411 (1998)
14. Zelias A.: Statistic methods, Polish Economic Publisher, Warszawa (2000)

Calculating the Fractal Dimension of River Basins, Comparison of Several Methods

Adam Szustalewicz [1], Andreas Vassilopoulos [2]

[1] Institute of Computer Science, University of Wroclaw, Poland
asz@ii.uni.wroc.pl
[2] Remote Sensing Laboratory, Geology Department, University of Athens, Greece
Vassilopoulos@geol.uoa.gr

Abstract. A new program was prepared for approximate calculation of the fractal dimension of natural objects. The program takes care to fulfill demand of the fractal theory about the minimal covering of the measured object. Three other programs are being presented for comparison and the results obtained by all of them on the same data sets are described

Keywords. fractal, fractal dimension, Box-Counting Dimension, minimal covering

1 Introduction

Erosion problems require investigation of the river shapes complexity. Curves representing rivers on maps vary in form. They are more or less complicated (see Figs. 1, 2) and fractal methods might be quite appropriate to measure how wrinkly these curves are. The calculation of the fractal dimension of such objects is perfectly suitable to such problems.

Real data – like river branches – are usually prepared in form of maps in different scales. The graphical resolution of such data is bounded to one pixel only and all theoretical assumptions about covering the measured object with arbitrary small squares can not be fulfilled.

Section 2 presents shortly assumptions of the fractal theory, numerical algorithms for approximate calculation of fractal dimension of given objects and problems arising in practice.

Section 3 describes four programs and their variants applied to calculations.

Section 4 presents data sets. Four of them are natural – maps of different scales and one artificial – the generated fractal.

Sections 5 and 6 contain a description of obtained results and some remarks about fractal dimension of the same object, but given in maps different scales.

2 The concept of the fractal dimension

2.1 Box-Counting Dimension

One of the most widely used dimensions is the Box-counting dimension [2], [7]. Let us recall its definition formulated for objects located on a plane.

Definition. *Suppose, for given* $\varepsilon > 0$ *the measured object is covered with sets of diameter at most* ε. *Let* $N(\varepsilon)$ *be the smallest number of such sets needed for covering the whole object. The lower and upper box-counting dimension of the object are defined respectively as the limits*

$$\underline{d} = \lim_{\varepsilon \to 0} \frac{\log(N(\varepsilon))}{\log(1/\varepsilon)} \quad and \quad \overline{d} = \overline{\lim_{\varepsilon \to 0}} \frac{\log(N(\varepsilon))}{\log(1/\varepsilon)}.$$

If both the limits are equal then we refer their common value as the **Box-Counting Dimension** *of considered object and denote by* d :

$$d = \lim_{\varepsilon \to 0} \frac{\log(N(\varepsilon))}{\log(1/\varepsilon)}. \tag{1}$$

There are several other definitions of $N(\varepsilon)$ which can be used in definition of box-counting dimension formulated above. For instance, $N(\varepsilon)$ can be defined as

1. *the smallest number of closed balls of radius* ε *that cover the object;*
2. *the smallest number of squares of side equal to* ε *that cover the object;*
3. *the number of* ε *- mesh squares that intersect the object;*
4. *the smallest number of sets of diameter at most* ε *that cover the object.*

Definitions listed above are the most convenient for particular applications. The easiest is definition 3 which permits to cover the measured object with regular square grid. It appears most often in implemented algorithms.

2.2 The numerical approximation of fractal dimension

Numerical methods for calculating approximate values of d relay on the fact that formula (1) can be rewritten for small ε in equivalent form as

$$\log(N(\varepsilon)) \approx d \, \log(1/\varepsilon) + const. \tag{2}$$

Formula (2) suggests the existence of a linear dependence between the variables $y = \log(N(\varepsilon))$ and $x = \log(1/\varepsilon)$. Thus, the idea for calculating a number close to d is realized by constructing the linear regression between x and y in form $y = a + bx$ and taking the slope b of this line as the approximation of d.

The numerical algorithm for calculating b proceeds in three steps:

1. construct a sequence of coverings of the measured object with equal squares for the finite sequence of different side lengths $\{\varepsilon_j\}$,

2. evaluate the linear regression line $y = a + bx$ taking
$$y_j = \log(N(\varepsilon_j)) \text{ and } x_j = \log(1/\varepsilon_j),$$

3. calculate the slope b of this regression.

This slope b is the numerical approximation of the Box-Counting Dimension of the measured object.

2.3 The problems arising in practice

Practical problems are connected with the fact that in graphical representations of real data their graphical resolution is limited to one pixel only and employment of very small values of ε is impossible. There are several questions:

1. How to construct the sequence $\{\varepsilon_j\}$?

2. How to estimate the best value of slope b? Basing on all available data pairs $\{(\varepsilon_j, N(\varepsilon_j))\}$ $(j = 1,...,j_{max})$, or on a chosen subset of pairs only, for instance a subset of the smallest ε_j?

3. Are the four definitions of $N(\varepsilon)$, cited in section 2.1, really equivalent in practical cases, when applying of arbitrary small ε_j is impossible?

4. What about the property of minimal coverage – demand of the theory – can it improve obtained results?

5. How to ensure that for every considered ε the number $N(\varepsilon)$ of squares needed for covering the object is the minimal one?

Some answers can be found in the short presentation of applied programs in the next section, some – in description of results at the end of paper.

3 Applied programs and their derivatives

There are four main programs:

1. HARFA (Harmonic and Fractal Image Analyzer) is a program written in Borland Pascal and implemented in the Institute of Physical and Applied Chemistry, Brno University of Technology [4]. We use a demo version of the actually existing HARFA 5.0.

2. PATZEK is a Matlab function written by T. W. Patzek from U. C. Berkeley in 2002 [5]. The main procedure and some interesting results of measured coastlines of some countries can be found in Patzek's teaching materials. The rest can be obtained after a contact with the author.

3. SASAKI is a program written in Object Pascal (Borland Delphi 6) by Hirouki Sasaki [6]. User has some possibilities to edit some calculated values during the run of the program. The program may be obtained after a contact with the author.
4. RIVER is an original program written in Matlab by the first author. Program takes care to fulfill the demand of the theory about minimal covering. RIVER realizes minimal coverings for such geometrical figures as segments, rectangles and circles [8].

We will apply all programs (their variants) to measure the fractal dimensions of objects given in binary maps. All variants realize calculation of the approximate value of fractal dimension accordingly to the steps described in section 2.2.

In programs HARFA, PATZEK and SASAKI the entire data image is covered with a sequence of regular square grids with side lengths $\{\varepsilon_j\}$ counted in pixels.

Now more details of the programs and how we have used them.

3.1 HARFA and its possibilities

HARFA is a big program realizing various problems in three general domains: Harmonic analysis, Fractal analysis and Filtration. Every data image must be a square of length being a power of 2 from 32 to 2048 pixels. From the possibilities of the program we used only the option of Fractal analysis by the box-counting methods.

3.1.1 Estimators of the fractal dimension ('C', 'D', 'C+', 'D+')

Applied lengths ε_j change from 2 (pixels) to $\varepsilon_{\max}$ pixels, where $\varepsilon_{\max}$ is close to one-third of the side length of the data image (over 700 pixels for large data).

User can select the number of used grids in two variants:

*   *continuous variant* – all possible grids with side lengths ε_j $\{\varepsilon_j : 2 \leq \varepsilon_j \leq \varepsilon_{\max}\}$ are used. This variant is called HARFAC,
*   *discrete variant* – at most 30 different grids can be chosen. The chosen sides of grids should be almost uniformly distributed between 2 and $\varepsilon_{\max}$ pixels. This variant is called HARFAD.

In all chosen variants, program HARFA can give two different estimates of the fractal dimension. They are obtained by counting in a different way the slope of the exhibited regression.

One estimator, denoted in the following by 'C' or 'D' (depending on the variants HARFAC or HARFAD) represents the overall slope of the graphed regression.

The other, denoted in the following by 'C+' or 'D+' (depending on the variants HARFAC or HARFAD) is evaluated in a more complicated way:

Let m be a natural number (authors suggest $m = 20$). HARFA permits to observe what are the slopes of linear regression lines constructed for all possible subsets of m successive points $\{(\log(1/\varepsilon_j), \log(N(\varepsilon_j)))\}$. The most often appearing slopes $\{ b_i^* \}$ are chosen and the maximal value of them is taken as the second estimator of the fractal dimension.

3.2 PATZEK

This program obtains the slope of linear regression line between $\log(N(\varepsilon))$ and $\log(1/\varepsilon)$ based on five data points only. The points are calculated by dividing both sides of the considered image (the binary array) into about 4, 8, 16, 32 and 64 equal parts. About, because there are no restrictions (as in HARFA) about the form of powers of 2 for side lengths. There were no problem with the accuracy in considered data sets because accordingly the demand of HARFA – all data images were squares with lengths of power of 2. We will denote the obtained value as 'P'.

3.3 SASAKI

The applied lengths ε_j are defined as all powers of 2 and should be smaller than the half of the longer side of the image. The slope of the calculated linear regression line for all prepared pairs $\{(\log(1/\varepsilon_j) , \log(N(\varepsilon_j)))\}$ will be denoted as 'S'.

The program gives the user possibilities to delete some points from the displayed regression. The slope calculated for the remaining points is usually the slope of the "best fit linear regression line" and will be denoted as 'S+'.

3.4 RIVER

RIVER is an attempt to fulfill the demand of the theory about the minimal covering of the measured object. The program is prepared for working with objects presented in rectangular binary images. The implemented algorithm proceeds in five steps:

1. Program cuts out from the given data image the smallest rectangle containing the object and works on it only.

2. The values $\{\varepsilon_j : j = 1,2,..., k\}$ have the form of all powers of 2 or 3, being less than the half of the greater side of the rectangle cut out from the image and containing the object.

3. For every length ε_j the minimal(?) number $N(\varepsilon_j)$ of squares needed to cover the object is calculated. The position of every succeeding square is selected individually, starting from edges and external columns or rows of the rectangular image. *It can be proved that $N(\varepsilon_j)$ are the minimal numbers for figures like segments, rectangles, circles* [8].

4. Now, from the set of all prepared pairs $\{(\varepsilon_j, N(\varepsilon_j))\}$ ($j = 1,2,..., k$), six particular subsets are chosen. *The rules of this selection form the ground of the algorithm. The principles of the choice of these particular subjects were established in former experiments – not described here.*

These particular six subsets are now applied for the construction of six regression lines for the analyzed data. In such a way six new values of slopes $\{b_i\}$ ($i = 1,2,...,6$) are obtained. (These six slopes appeared in the past experiments [8] as the best approximations of fractal dimension for all considered test-figures.)

5. The mean of these six values $\{b_i\}$ is taken as the approximation of the fractal dimension d of the measured object and will be denoted as 'R'.

Now we proceed to calculate the fractal dimensions of the produced data.

4 Data

All programs presented in the previous section are applied to calculate the fractal dimensions of five objects. Four of objects are natural – geographical data, the last object is an artificial one – a fractal.
The first three objects are original maps of the greatest river of Sifnos, Greece. The maps were created in scales 1:25.000, 1:50.000 and 1:100.000 (Figs. 1, 2).

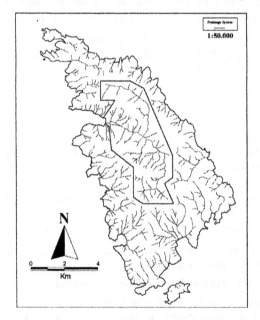

Fig. 1. Drainage system of the Sifnos Island with one river chosen

The fourth object is the coastline of Greece (Fig. 3) an image downloaded from internet [9].
The fifth object is a mathematical one: the fractal Sierpinski Triangle (Fig. 4) generated by a suitable program.
All objects were prepared for calculations in the following way:

Every object was placed into a sufficiently large square binary image with lengths equal to the power of two – accordingly to demand of HARFA. Then every object was rotated, flipped and shifted to different places of its image in twelve different manners. This way, for every object, 12 different binary images were obtained and programs will consider all of them.
Now we describe the considered objects in more detail.

4.1 The river-basin in the Sifnos Island

Sifnos is one of Greek Islands of the western Cyclades and lies about 80 nautical miles from Pireus. The island has an area of 74 sq. kilometers and a shoreline of 70 km.

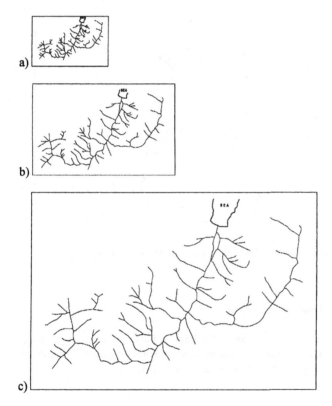

Fig. 2. The parts of three maps with the chosen river of Sifnos. The scales and sizes of the maps are: a) 1:100.000, 139×304, b) 1:50.000, 369×585, c) 1:25.000, 774×1148
At our disposal were three maps of Sifnos prepared in different scales: 1:25.000, 1:50.000 and 1:100.000 created in GIS (Geographical Informatics System MapInfo) in the Remote Sensing Laboratory, Geology Department, University of Athens [3].

Because of the different scales of the maps, their image arrays are different in size, and consequence, the pixel representation of the drawn objects is less for maps in smaller scales. It means that the whole of the branches are present in every map, but each one's shape is less accurate in a map of smaller scale. Let us compare the shapes of river branches presented below in sizes proportional to the map scales.

The GIS creates the maps on the basis of the digital data stored in vector format. A very interesting feature of these maps is that **each map contains all details of the river branches which are known for the system.**

The percentage of black pixels in these three images equals to: a) 3.57%, b) 1.90%, and c) 0.95%. Can it be expected that a river on a map of smaller scale will have a larger fractal dimension than the same river on a map of greater scale?

4.2 The coastline of Greece

The binary map of the coastline of Greece was taken from [9].

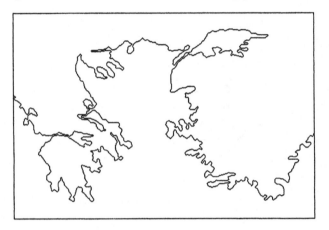

Fig. 3. The coastline of Greece. The size of the image array: 339×508

4.3 The fractal Sierpinski Triangle

Sierpinski Triangle is the attractor of the Iterated Function System [1] which consists of three contractive affine transformations. A sequence of generated points creates the fractal, as the number of points increases - see Fig. 4.

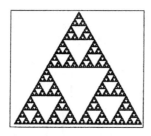

Fig. 4. The fractal Sierpinski Triangle. The size of the image array: 311×361

The present figure was generated by a Matlab function; altogether 10^8 points were generated. It is known that the fractal dimension of Sierpinski Triangle equals $d = 1.5849625...$

5 Results

As it was described at the beginning of section 4, every object was prepared for calculations in form of 12 binary square images. On every image the object was shifted to different places, was rotated or flipped. Thus, every program calculated fractal dimensions of 12 different images (theoretically of the same fractal dimension) and we can present now distributions of obtained results.

Variants HARFAD, HARFAD+, HARFAC, HARFAC+, PATZEK, SASAKI, SASAKI+ obtained usually different values of the prepared 12 images with the same object, and confidence intervals can be presented.

Shifting or rotating of the object does not matter for RIVER and results for all 12 images of the same object are equal. But RIVER uses six, usually different values $\{b_i\}$ of slopes calculated from the special subsets of data pairs (sect. 3.4) and puts their mean as the output value for the dimension d. Thus, we plot for RIVER the confidence intervals obtained on the basis of these 6 values.

All the results will be presented now in Fig. 5 in the form of *95% confidence intervals for calculated fractal dimension* plotted for all objects and all applied programs.

The confidence intervals, connected with results of variants, are drawn over the names of measured objects. In the top of figure are letters (or letters with +) identifying the names of applied variants: D (HARFAD), D+ (HARFAD+), C (HARFAC), C+ (HARFAC+), P (PATZEK), S (SASAKI), S+ (SASAKI+), R (RIVER).

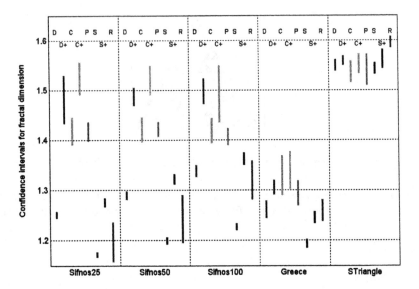

Fig. 5. Confidence intervals for fractal dimension. Letters in the top D, D+, C, C+, P, S, S+, R
identify names of programs and their variants

Horizontal axis contains five intervals, each one for successive object:
- Sifnos25, Sifnos50, Sifnos100 – maps in different scales of the river,
- Greece – the coastline of Greece,
- STriangle – fractal Sierpinski Triangle.

Now a few about obtained results.
- Only fractal dimension $d = 1.5849625...$ of Sierpinski Triangle is known
  precisely. The value closest to d is obtained by RIVER.
- Variant 'S+' has in all cases the best fit linear regression line obtained by
  removing the "worst" data points ($\log(1/\varepsilon_j)$, $\log(N(\varepsilon_j))$) manually.
  This fact suggests that maybe the best results are results close to values obtained by 'S+'. As we see – results obtained by 'D' and 'R' for all measured
  objects have this feature.
- There are two groups of results obtained for the river in maps of different
  scales. The first group of dimensions calculated by 'D', 'S', 'S+' and 'R' is
  growing up. The second group, calculated by 'D+', 'C', 'C+', 'P' contains
  values close to each other for all three scales.

6 Discussion and Final Remarks

- For the mathematical object – Sierpinski Triangle all programs yield similar
  values of the sought fractal dimension. The best is RIVER.
- Values obtained for natural objects are different in limits up to 15-20% of
  the estimated dimension.

- Very interesting are the two main tendencies which can be observed for objects of different scales. There are four variants which yield values close to each other: 'D+', 'C', 'C+' and 'P'. Four other variants: 'D', 'S', 'S+' and 'R' obtained results growing up for objects in maps of smaller scales. Which is the correct tendency?

We may use some arguments for or against results of some variants:

- 'D+', 'C+' obtain probably overestimated results because in both cases the maximal slope from the most often appearing linear regression lines is chosen.
- Results of 'S+' are obtained after additional data correction. Selecting and deleting "the worst points" ($\log(1/\varepsilon_j)$, $\log(N(\varepsilon_j))$) can be an improving action when user knows the theoretical value of dimension. Generally, after not too many and carefully performed corrections, the obtained result can be really better.
- 'R' obtains good results for objects as complicated as fractals and for simple figures like circles or segments. We hope that its results, obtained for all the considered objects, should be good as well. Long confidence intervals obtained for 'R' follow from fact, that the six slopes from calculations – not the output results – were used to them (sec. 3.4).

Thus, in our opinion, the growing tendency of fractal dimensions of rivers in maps of decreasing scales is the correct tendency.

References

1. Barnsley, M., Fractals everywhere, Academic Press, Boston, 1993
2. Falconer, K., Fractal geometry, Mathematical Foundations and Applications, Wiley, New York (1999)
3. Gournelos, Th., Evelpidou, N., Vassilopoulos A., Developing an Erosion risk map using soft computing methods (case study at Sifnos island), Natural Hazards, Vol. 31, No 1. Kluwer Academic Publishers, January (2004), 39-61
4. Zmeskal, O., Nezadal, M., Buchnicek, M., Bzatek, T. Harmonic and Fractal Image Analyzer, Brno (2005), http://www.fch.vutbr.cz/lectures/imagesci (HARFA 5.0)
5. Patzek, Tad. W., E240 Lecture materials, http://patzek.berkeley.edu/indexold.html the main page, http://petroleum.berkeley.edu/patzek/e240/Lecture04Materials.htm Coastline.m
6. Sasaki, H., Fractal analysis system for Windows, http://cse.naro.affrc.go.jp/sasaki/index-e.html
7. Szustalewicz, A., Numerical problems with evaluating the fractal dimension or real data, in Ed. Pejaś J., Piegat A., Enhanced Methods in Computer Security, Biometric and Artificial Intelligence Systems, Kluwer Academic Publishers, Springer (2005) 273-283
8. Szustalewicz, A., Choosing best subsets for calculation of fractal dimension by the box-counting method, manuscript (in preparation)
9. http://polymer.bu.edu/pub/OGAF/pc/EXAMPLES.ZIP

Automatic Management of Tele-Interpretation Knowledge in a Wearable Diagnostic Device

Ryszard Tadeusiewicz[1], Piotr Augustyniak[1]

Department of Automatics, Biocybernetic Laboratory AGH University of Science and Technology Krakow, Poland rtad|august@agh.edu.pl

Abstract: This paper presents the aspects of remote management of interpretation knowledge embedded in a wearable health monitor based on vital signs. Expected high autonomy of a wearable device and the reliable interpretation intelligence requiring computation power are opposite requisites. The presented concept of programmable recorder assumes high flexibility of the remote device, however only certain aspects of adaptation were implemented up to today. The device programmability is implemented on the software platform and applied to the processing and transmission functions with the aim of continuous optimization of resources use towards the best diagnosis quality. The prototype was designed as an ECG-oriented monitor, but the application of spread intelligence-based monitors extends beyond the traditional long term ECG recording and covers the area of exercise, emergency and elderly people surveillance in various combinations.

Keywords: Ambient intelligence, Ubiquitous computing, Telemedicine, Home care, Remote control, Signal analysis

1 Introduction

The telemedicine based on remote acquisition of various vital signs [4] [10] opens wide application area ranging from the equipment for clinical use to the home care devices [5], [9]. Several telediagnostic services commercialized recently in US and Europe, offer the continuous monitoring of cardiac risk people. Such services typically use closed wireless networks of star topology. The interpretive intelligence aiming at derivation of diagnostic features from recorded time series is implemented in the recorder or in the supervising server. Both approaches have serious limitations. The *central intelligence* model uses the communication channel continuously to report raw signals and needs the uninterrupted carrier availability which makes the transmission cost very high. The *spread intelligence* model assumes that the capturing device interprets

the signal and issues an alert message in case of abnormalities. Although
the *spread* interpretation *intelligence* reduces the communication costs, the
diagnosis quality is affected due to resources limitation typical to a wearable
computer. Other alternatives, like a triggered acquisition method typical for
the ECG event recorders, suffer from poor reliability since a manually operated
device risks to miss an event when the patient in pain is unable to start the
capture session.

Our research aims at combining the advantages of both interpretive intelligence models. This could be achieved by extending the adaptivity of spread
interpretation procedures and complementing the remote interpretation by
server-side analysis with result-dependent task sharing. The consequence of
such extensions is the event-dependent report content and reporting frequency.
The operating principle of interpretation task sharing follows generalized relations between human cardiologists.

The design of remotely controlled interpretive device includes three essential prerequisites:

- the automatic interpretation is supervised by the experienced staff with
  support of technically unlimited knowledge base with respect to the context of previous results.
- the signal is interpreted in real time and conditionally transmitted without
  delay, so any medical intervention necessary may start immediately.
- the recorder is marketed as low-cost general-purpose interpretive device
  and remotely personalized accordingly to the patient status and diagnostic
  goals.

Two dimensions named here: '*levels*' and '*aspects*' of adaptation are high-
lighted in this paper. They are discussed in details throughout chapter 2 in
context of processing and throughout chapter 3 in context of data representation. In chapter 4 an experimental biosignal recording device and the result
of the in-field tests are presented. Conclusions, perspectives and final remarks
are summarized in chapter 5.

2 Adaptivity of the Hardware and the Software

In a typical star-shaped topology of distributed surveillance network (fig. 1)
patient-side wearable recorders are supervised and controlled by a central node
server archiving the captured information as signals and data. Assuming both
device types are equipped with signal interpretation software, optimization of
the task sharing between them affects directly the remote power consumption
and the costs of digital communication. One of the principles of our design
is the continuous adjustment of this balance, as the interpretation goals and
priorities vary with time and patient. Considering many factors known before
the examination begins, but also relying on directly preceding diagnostic results, the task sharing accustoms the general-purpose recorder to a particular
case.

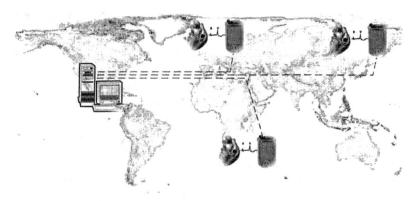

Fig. 1. Typical topology of surveillance network using wireless digital communication

New concept of adaptive vital signs recorder for ubiquitous health care emerges from the above remarks. Our proposal joins the artificial intelligence approach to both cooperating device types and the generalized tasks sharing rules practiced by human medics. It is assumed that the automatic interpretation task is partly performed by the remote device and than complemented by a software thread running on the supervising server. For the transmission, intermediate results are prioritized accordingly to the changes of diagnostic goals and current patient state. The adaptivity concerns also the communication data format, so the actual report content and frequency are negotiated between the supervising server and each remote monitor independently. This is a distributed optimization process considering multiple criteria such as diagnosis quality, transmission channel use and power consumption.

2.1 Adaptation Levels

Adaptation levels are used to describe the extent and technical measures used for modification of remote recorder functionality. Three *adaptation levels* combine hardware and software solutions are ordered by potential flexibility:

- modification of interpretation parameters,
- modification of the software structure and scope by means of dynamically linked libraries,
- modification of the hardware structure and functionality with use of analog and digital reprogrammable circuitry.

2.2 Adaptation Aspects

Adaptation aspects are used to describe the medical application range that the remote device may cover due to its adaptivity. Our current viewpoint allows to enumerate several *adaptation aspects*, however the list would be completed by future users:

- acquisition and interpretation of many different vital signs (ECG, EMG, EOG, blood pressure, phonocardiography, uterine contraction and other signals from the human and his surrounding) up to the number of channels available in the hardware and with their proper sampling characteristics.
- cooperation with the supervising server as a transparent recorder, in a partial autonomy with optimized interpretation task share or as an independent remote device performing full signal interpretation.
- operation in a continuous surveillance mode or as an event monitor triggered manually or by given physiological event with an optional pre-trigger,
- continuous adaptation of the interpretation depth following the patient status and the diagnosis goals.

3 Adaptive Data Formats

A side effect of remote intelligence flexibility, however very interesting in the resources optimization aspect, is the multitude of output data formats ranging from the raw electrogram to the sparse medical parameters (e.g. heart rate). The modifiable communication protocol helps avoiding the unnecessary data transmission and impacts both the power consumption and the wireless channel use and consequently reduces the monitoring costs to the acceptable level. Basic interpretation result consisting of few universal diagnostic parameters is reported continuously and more detailed reports for short time intervals are issued on demand. Every occurrence or suspicion of any abnormality is reported with a more detailed representation of less processed data accordingly to the limitation of interpretation capacity by available resources. For difficult but rare events of short-time duration, the report includes a corresponding strip of raw signal. The machine description of the electrocardiogram contains all meta-information interfacing the non-assisted signal interpretation routines and the semi-automatic or manual diagnostic decision making. The flexible transmission formatting algorithm includes the result of our previous studies on cardiologist's relations. The report formatting procedure can be remotely reprogrammed upon request, because the goal of accurate reproduction of the expert reasoning process in a computer algorithm may be achieved by several approaches differing in the final data set contributing to the optimal ECG description.

3.1 Expert-Machine Learning

The computer algorithm calculates parameters d being a quantitative description of the waveform in the n-dimensional diagnostic domain $\mathbf{D}^n$. The

parameters are well defined on physiological background, but not always easy
to derive properly from the unknown signal.

$$d \in \mathbf{D}^n : d \rightarrow w_1 \cdot f_1(s) \otimes w_2 \cdot f_2(s) \otimes, \ldots, \otimes w_n \cdot f_n(s) \tag{1}$$

where f_i are heuristic signal transforms and w_i are corresponding weighting
functions. This approach is commonly used in the ECG-dedicated hardware-
embedded procedures for bedside interpretive recorders. Usually during the
tests of newly developed interpretation software the results are calculated
for a limited database (learning set), verified, and used for corrections of
computation coefficients.

3.2 Matching Pursuit

The procedure compares the current record with a set of dictionary functions
$g_{\gamma 0} \in \mathbf{S}$ known beforehand. Amplitude and scale normalization are used to
suppress most of extracardiac variability sources. The matching coefficients
R^n estimate how far the signal f could be explained by a given pattern set.
The decomposition procedure starts with the best fitted pattern

$$f = (f, g_{\gamma 0})g_{\gamma 0} + R^1 f \tag{2}$$

and the residual signal R is recursively processed up to the desired number of
coefficients n:

$$R^i f = (R^i f, g_{\gamma i})g_{\gamma i} + R^{i+1} f. \tag{3}$$

The procedure yields the signal represented by a set of matching coefficients R^i
over the dictionary functions $g_{\gamma i}$ and the remaining sequence $R^n f$ representing
all unexplained signal components:

$$f = \sum_{i=0}^{n-1}(R^i f, g_{\gamma i})g_{\gamma i} + R^n f. \tag{4}$$

The inverse of *unexplained energy* is the estimate of matching quality (or
dictionary adequacy). The construction of appropriate dictionary resulting in
explanation of principal diagnostic features with use of minimum number of
coefficients is a very challenging and still unresolved issue.

3.3 Extension of Compression Algorithms

ECG data compression techniques do not have a common mathematical expression and are usually classified in three major categories:

- direct data compression (e.g. AZTEC, SAPA, CORTES, delta coding, approximate Ziv-Lempel etc.)
- transform coding (e.g. Karhunen-Loeve Transform, Discrete Cosine Transform, wavelets etc.)

- parameter extraction methods (e.g. linear prediction, vector quantization, neural networks etc.)

Since the expectation of maximum signal fidelity at a minimum data rate is very similar to those of signal compression, specialized data reduction algorithms may be adapted to the computation of machine ECG description. Main assumption of such adaptation is no necessity to accurate data reconstruction. This approach is already commercialized for management of digital multimedia as the MPEG-7 standard. However, in case of medical record the diagnostic meaning of the signal have to be preserved with maximum care. Therefore, the unchanged content is completed by a preceding data fingerprint containing the description of most representative features from the user's viewpoint. Some ECG-dedicated compression methods use pre-calculated rough estimate of local signal importance and the compression applies a non-uniform data loss strategy compromising high reduction rate at high fidelity of medical contents [2].

3.4 Syntactic Description of the Electrogram

The syntactic description of the electrogram consists of words composed of symbols x_i belonging to the finite alphabet.

$$\mathbf{V} = \{x_1...x_n\} \tag{5}$$

The alphabet includes tokens referring to the waveform shapes expected in the signal as well as the features of signal derived automatically. Tokens are grouped to symbols using a grammar $G_A = (V_N, V_N, S_{out}, S_{in})$ accordingly to its syntactic and semantic rules.

$$X \rightarrow a, for X \in V_N \ and \ a \in V_N \cup V_T \tag{6}$$

$$Y_1 = f_1(X_{11}, \ldots, X_{1n1}, Y_1, \ldots, Y_n)$$

$$\vdots \tag{7}$$

$$Y_n = f_n(X_{n1}, \ldots, X_{nnn}, Y_1, \ldots, Y_n)$$

where X_{ij} are symbol attributes and f_i represent semantic procedures. Definition of semantic rules is based on the cardiologist's reasoning and thus high adequacy of signal representation can be well combined with algorithms flexibility [3], [11], [12].

4 Experimental Recorder for Cardiology - Design and Tests

A portable ECG recorder was developed in our Laboratory in collaboration with cardiology researchers. The design includes a limited subset of the prerequisites considered above for an adaptive remote monitoring device. The prototype meet the following criteria:

- provides three simultaneous multi-purpose channels sampled at up to 200 Hz,
- supports cooperation with a GSM modem for on-line wireless transmission of recorded signal or with the PDA as the source of data for interpretation,
- guarantees autonomous operation for at least 24 hours of operating.

The recorder was designed for medical experiments. For the maximum flexibility and hardware-independence of the interpretation process, all the algorithm was implemented in a cooperating PDA. The recorder does not contain reprogrammable hardware, but the basic set of remote configuration commands offers high flexibility of acquisition parameters.

The recorder was developed with use of the popular *MicroConverter* [1] circuit integrating analog to digital converters, serial communication interfaces, internal flash memory and a '51-type processing kernel running at 2,7V. The design follows the general guidelines for real-time portable devices where the speed and the power management are both critical. Moreover, during all the development process the requirements of international standards for medical devices and electromagnetic compatibility [6], [7], [8] were carefully observed. The diagram of the recorder's circuitry is displayed in figure 2.

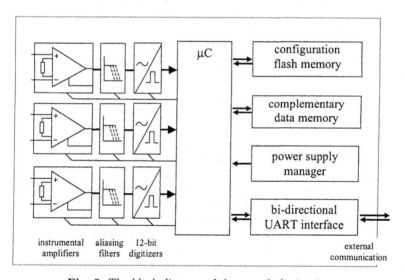

Fig. 2. The block diagram of the recorder's circuitry

The analog circuitry repeats the same architecture in each recording channel and uses micropower (230 μW) instrumental amplifiers with rail-to-rail input and output signal swing. The digitizers embedded in the *MicroConverter* chip guarantee 12-bits resolution. The effective input voltage range is adjustable from $\pm$2mV to $\pm$16mV in order to cover wide area of applications.

The use of the bi-directional UART interface enables a direct connection to a PDA computer or to a mobile telephone for independent wireless communication. The communication channel transfers the captured data and signals to the supervising server as well as textual messages and configuration data in the opposite direction.

The prototype features a complementary memory lasting for data storage (ca. 12 minutes) or data buffer depending on the recording mode or for a closed-loop buffer of user-defined length for the pre-trigger data. The internal non-volatile memory stores the recorder's configuration and maintains the device status, the data organization and other settings in case of power failure.

Extensive tests were performed in order to confirm the recorder's ability to deliver a medically meaningful signal representation. The electrical tests were performed in a specialized laboratory complying with TUV/ISO measurements standards. We applied typical testing procedure for ECG long-term recorders. Electrical tests of the transmission channel were limited to the electromagnetic compatibility (EMC) and interference immunity issues. Main results of these measurements are displayed in table 1.

Table 1. Selected results of recorders electrical tests

parameter	value	conditions
bandwidth	0.03 ÷ 100Hz	-3 dB
1 LSB linearity range	-1.87 ÷ 1.83 mV	2mV range
voltage noise (ref. to input)	8.3 μV	0.1 ÷ 10 Hz
CMRR	92 dB	DC ÷ 100 Hz (worst case)
channel crosstalk	-77 dB	DC ÷ 100 Hz (worst case)

First part of tests concerned the use of remote recorder in the independent transmission mode. The support of the following functions was found operating exactly as intended: scheduled acquisition to the memory; scheduled acquisition and transmission over a GSM telephone in various conditions; acquisition and transmission initiated remotely over a GSM telephone; changing of the configuration memory contents over a GSM telephone. The complimentary set of embedded functions manage the recorder's operation in some unlucky situations. The test results confirm the correct support of transmission break, multiple connection retries, data stream redirection etc. The power supply monitoring enables the data-safe shutdown and wake-up with reporting to the supervising server, however sudden power failure (battery disconnection) occurs too fast to be serviced correctly.

Second part of tests concerned the recorder's configuration with a PDA-based interpretation module. In this configuration the adaptivity is significantly extended and includes adjustment of all processing parameters, on-line modification of communication protocol and reconfiguration of processing routines architecture. The applied PDA uses Pocket Windows operating system that is compatible with Microsoft Windows platform for desktop PCs and provides easy software development and interfacing with standard peripherals. The software architecture consists of a static process management and communication control kernel and of a set of randomly-linked basic interpretation routines. Depending on the medical need, each routine implemented as a dynamic function library can be adjusted remotely with a vector of interpretation parameters, linked, unlinked or replaced by an alternative routine from the basic set or by the code provided by the supervising server (fig. 3).

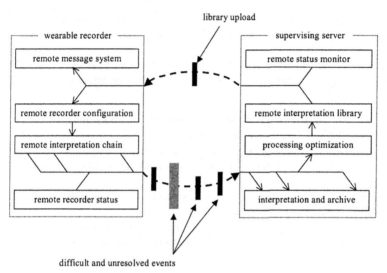

Fig. 3. Cooperation of the remote monitor and the supervising server aiming at optimization of diagnosis quality, transmission channel use and power consumption

5 Conclusions and Perspectives

The wireless physiological monitor for medical experiments was prototyped successfully and fulfills the intended application area in environmental cardiology. The recorder implements main principles of adaptivity and automatic management of teleinterpretation knowledge proposed in this paper. Its principal advantage is the flexibility of automated interpretation very close to the process performed by human medics. The area of application may be thus easily extended to open networks providing various medical surveillance services and having a considerable impact to the health care in the future. The novelty of our approach opens an unexploited area of medical telediagnostics. Certain new aspects are listed below, but many others may emerge in an everyday clinical practice:

- adaptive contents of patient status description varying from a general overview to a detailed report dependent on the result severity assessed by the software or on the extent of matching to a specific diagnostic goal,
- extended adjustability of monitoring and auto-alerting parameters, accordingly to the patient-specific signal, during the initial recording phase and anytime thereafter.
- real-time reconfiguration of interpretive intelligence in pursuit of any unexpected event and completion of the resources-limited remote interpretation by the supervising server software or with intervention of human experts.

Except for the laboratory testing, the recorder was already evaluated in two research projects aiming at muscle fatigue assessment and stress influence on domestic animals.

Although main scientific and engineering goals were achieved, the design and testing of the wearable diagnostic device revealed some issues for future consideration:

- improved compatibility of the interpretive software running on the remote device and on the supervising server,
- investigation of human interpretation process and required reporting format adaptation in context of previous diagnostic results and examination goals.
- supervising of several remote monitors and management of patient's data archive by a multi-threaded software.
- use of interactive communication channel for patient messages interchange (e.g. instructions in case of technical troubles, medical risk or medication intake).

6 Acknowledgment

This work was supported by Polish State Committee for Scientific Research grant no: 3T11E 001 27

References

1. ANALOG DEVICES http://www.analog.com/ microconverters
2. Augustyniak P. "Adaptive Discrete ECG Representation - Comparing Variable Depth Decimation and Continuous Non-Uniform Sampling" IEEE Computers in Cardiology 29, 165-168, Memphis 2002.
3. Augustyniak P. "Automatic Understanding of ECG Signal" Springer, IIPWM Conference, pp. 599-602, Zakopane 2004.
4. Chiarugi F. et al. "Real-time Cardiac Monitoring over a Regional Health Network: Preliminary Results from Initial Field Testing" IEEE Computers in Cardiology 29, 347-350, Memphis 2002.

5. Gouaux F., et al. "Ambient Intelligence and Pervasive Systems for the Monitoring of Citizens at Cardiac Risk: New Solutions from the EPI-MEDICS Project" IEEE Computers in Cardiology 29, 289-292, Memphis 2002.
6. IEC 60601-2-25 "Medical electrical equipment: Particular requirements for the safety of electrocardiographs" ed. 1999.
7. IEC 60601-2-27 "Medical electrical equipment: Particular requirements for the safety electrocardiographic monitoring equipments" ed. 1994.
8. IEC 60601-2-47 "Medical electrical equipment: Particular requirements for the safety, including essential performance, of ambulatory electrocardiographic systems" ed. 2001.
9. Maglaveras N., et al. "Using Contact Centers in Telemanagement and Home Care of Congestive Heart Failure Patients: The CHS Experience" IEEE Computers in Cardiology 29, 281-284, Memphis 2002.
10. Nelwan S.P., van Dam T.B., Klootwijk P. and Meil SH. "Ubiquitous Mobile Access to Real-time Patient Monitoring Data" IEEE Computers in Cardiology 29, pp. 557-560, Memphis 2002.
11. Papakonstantinou G., Skordolakis E., Gritzali F. "An attribute grammar for QRS detection. Pattern Recognition" vol. 19, 297-303, 1986.
12. Tadeusiewicz R. "Automatic Understanding of Signals" Springer, IIPWM Conference, pp. 591-598, Zakopane 2004.

Evaluation of Clusters Quality in Artificial Immune Clustering System - SArIS

Sławomir T. Wierzchoń[1, 2], Urszula Kużelewska[1]

[1] Department of Computer Science, Białystok Technical University
15-351 Białystok, ul. Wiejska 45ª
uk@ii.pb.bialystok.pl
[2] Institute of Computer Science, Polish Academy of Sciences,
01-237 Warszawa, ul. Ordona 21
stw@ipipan.waw.pl

Abstract. This paper presents evaluation of the clustering results of SArIS – clustering algorithm based on immune systems theory. The partitionings of 2- and multi-dimensional data are evaluated in comparison to results obtained by other grouping methods – k-means and hierarchical. To assess compactness and separation of groups there were calculated values of clustering validity index – CDbw and its components.

1 Introduction

A typical approach to clustering a set X of objects into $k \geq 2$ clusters is to apply a criterion function that maps a set C of all partitions of X into the set of non-negative reals $\mathbf{R}$. Unfortunately, the size of the set C is of order $O(n^k)$, where $n = |X|$ stands for the number of objects, cf. [1]. Thus it is impossible to simply check all partitionings and select the best one. When X is a subset of m-dimensional Euclidean space, i.e. each object from the set X can be described by m-dimensional vector of measurements, a hill-climbing algorithm is used to find a good grouping. In this case the criterion function takes a form

$$J(\mathbf{U},\mathbf{C}) = \sum_{j=1}^{k} \sum_{i=1}^{n} (u_{ij})^{\alpha} d^{\beta}(\mathbf{x}_i, \mathbf{c}_j), \alpha \geq 1, \beta = 2 \tag{1}$$

where $\mathbf{C} = [\mathbf{c}_1, \ldots, \mathbf{c}_k]_{m \times k}$ is a matrix of prototype parameters (typically: cluster centers), $\mathbf{U} = [u_{ij}]_{n \times k}$ is a partition matrix, $\mathbf{x}_i$ stands for the vector describing i-th object from X, and $d(\mathbf{x}_i, \mathbf{c}_j)$ is a measure of a distance (usually: Euclidean) from $\mathbf{x}_i$ to the j-th cluster prototype. The quantity u_{ij} measures the degree of membership of i-th object to j-th cluster. If $u_{ij} \in \{0, 1\}$ for all values of i, j we say that $\mathbf{U}$ represents hard partition, and if $u_{ij} \in [0, 1]$ – $\mathbf{U}$ is a fuzzy partition matrix provided that: (a) for all i: $\sum_{j=1,\ldots,k} u_{ij} = 1$, and (b) for all j: $0 < \sum_{i=1,\ldots,n} u_{ij} < n$ (consult [2] for details).
Under such a setting we search for the minimal value of the index $J(\mathbf{U}, \mathbf{C})$ over the set U of all the matrices satisfying the conditions (a) and (b) mentioned above. Unfortunately, the optimization approach, although conceptually elegant, has a number of drawbacks (cf. e.g.[3]): (i) the result strongly depends on the initial guess of centroids (or assignments), (ii) computed local optimum is known to be a far cry from the global one, (iii) it is not obvious what a good k to use, (iv) the process is sensitive

with respect to outliers, (v) the algorithm lacks scalability, (vi) only numerical attributes are covered, and finally (vii) resulting clusters can be unbalanced (in some cases even empty). To overcome the drawbacks (i), (ii) and (vii) a number of biologically inspired metaheuristics was examined like evolutionary strategies or genetic algorithms – see e.g.[1], [3] and [4] for a short overview and some propositions. As concluded in [4], "... GGA[2] will always provide good partitions by settling in one of the most (in many cases the most) desirable extrema and never in an extremum representing a degenerate partition. It is ideal for testing an objective function for which no calculus based (or other approach) exists. If the data partitions or clusters produced by the genetic clustering approach are 'good', faster approaches to optimizing the objective function can be developed".

In this paper, a new algorithm based on the immune system metaphor is proposed not only to overcome the drawbacks (i), (ii) and (vii) but also to overcome the most difficult aspect of the clustering problem, i.e. the choice of the proper number of clusters. To test how efficient our algorithm is, we compare the quality of generated clusterings with the groupings generated by two "classical" clustering algorithms: *k-means* and *hierarchical*.

2 Validation of clustering

The process of validation and evaluation of a clustering algorithm can be performed "manually" by an expert, or by an automated procedure. As noted in [1], most of these methods are relatively informal. Manual methods are mainly concerned with such issues like: cluster interpretability, and cluster visualization, while "automated" procedures involve plotting assumed quality criterion against the number of groups. We simply plot the value of such a criterion for $k = 1, 2, 3, ...$ and look for large jumps to determine the appropriate number of groups. A reader interested with these topics is referred to [3] (sect. 10.2), [5] or [1].

Recently proposed *CDbw* index, [6], measures (a) the separation of the clusters, and (b) their compactness. The compactness of the data set is measured by the intra-cluster density, denoted *intraDen*, which is equal to the average density within clusters, whereas the separation, denoted *Sep*, takes into account both the distances between the closest clusters and the inter-cluster density, *interDen*, measured as the average density in the region among clusters. This way, for a given clustering c, $CDbw(c) = intraDen(c) \cdot Sep(c)$. *CDbw* exhibits no trends with regards to the number of clusters and is independent on the clustering algorithm used. As stated in [6], it "always indicate the optimal input parameters for the algorithm used in each case". Further, "CDbw handles efficiently arbitrary shaped clusters since its definition is based on multi-representative points describing the structure of clusters". These multi-representatives are generated according to the ext procedure: In the first iteration, the point farthest from the mean of the cluster under consideration is chosen as the first scattered point. In each subsequent iteration, a point form the cluster is chosen that is farthest from the previously chosen scattered points.

---

[2] GGA is a shorthand of "genetically guided algorithm".

3 The immune clustering algorithm - SArIS

SArIS is a slightly modified version of the immune based algorithm proposed already in [7]. Its aim is to recover the "natural" structure within a set of antigens (i.e. a training set) by producing a set of antibodies. We assume that both antigens and antibodies are represented as *m*-dimensional vectors, and components of these vectors belong to the unit interval. Each antibody can be viewed as summarization of a group of similar antigens what corresponds to the idea of cross-reactive immune memory (consult [8] for details).

1. Load and normalize a set of antigens, $Ag = \{ag_1, ..., ag_m\}$, $ag_i \in [0, 1]^n$
2. Generate randomly a set of antibodies, $Ab = \{ab_1, ..., ab_p\}$, $ab_j \in [0, 1]^n$
3. Calculate initial *NAT* value.
4. Determine connections in the set *Ab*, by joining each two antibodies ab_i, $ab_j \in Ab$, such that $d(ab_i, ab_j) < NAT$
5. At every iteration
   5.1. Calculate stimulation level of all antibodies as the distance from all training points located not further than $A_{aff} \cdot NAT$.
   5.2. Remove the least effective cells *Ab*.
   5.3. Remove a number of *Ab* cells participating in recognition of the same antigen, and save the best matched cells, or these cells, which uniquely recognize other antigen.
   5.4. Calculate new value of the *NAT*.
   5.5. Re-connect cells in the network.
   5.6. Leave the algorithm if the stopping condition is true.
   5.7. Execute cloning.
   5.8. Mutate the clones.
   5.9. Add the best clones to the set *Ab*.

Fig. 1. Pseudo-code of the *SArIS* algorithm

Here similarity between two immune cells is measured in terms of Euclidean distance between these cells. Further, two sufficiently similar antibodies are joined by a link; this way a graphical structure emerges from a set of competing antibodies, and separate components of this graph correspond to the clusters in the set of antigens. The process of graph creation mimics formation of so-called immune network, originally proposed by Jerne (again, consult [8] for details).

More precisely, when antigens are presented to the network, the antibodies become stimulated and the level of stimulation of each antibody depends on: (a) its ability to recognize particular antigens (called *affinity* and measured by Euclidean distance between two cells), and (b) its affinity to neighbouring cells in the immune network. High affinity to antigens increases stimulation level of a given antibody, while high affinity to neighbouring antibodies decreases this level. This mechanism prevents formation of too dense clusters in the graphical structure.

According to the clonal selection theory (described in [8]), only the most stimulated cells survive. They are further subjected cloning (with the rate proportional to the stimulation level) and mutation (with the rate inversely proportional to stimulation level). Most efficient mutants are added to the set of antibodies what increases diversity of the immune repertoire. Figure 1 shows pseudo-code of the immune algorithm.

One of the most important parameter of the system is *NAT* (*Network Affinity Threshold*), originally proposed in [9]. It determines the granularity of the emerging network and its overall connectivity. The algorithm adaptively modifies the *NAT* value by calculating in each iteration the average length of all edges between the nodes.
The papers [7], [10] offer more detailed description of the presented algorithm.

4 Experiments

To examine cluster quality of resulting immune partitioning, a number of experiments was performed using 2- and multi-dimensional datasets. The entire immune algorithm was compared with two classical algorithms: *k-means*, [1], and *hierarchical complete*, [11]. Apart visual evaluation of partitioning, validity indices such as *interDen*, *intraDen*, *sep*, and *CDbw* were computed. As mentioned in Section 2, these indices may be useful in determining proper number of clusters for non-automatic clustering algorithms *k-means* and *hierarchical*. Thus, plots of the values of these indices against the number of clusters were also analysed.
To calculate the *CDbw* index, and its components, we need a part of training data called their representatives. For the algorithms *k-means* and *hierarchical* the representatives were determined in the way described in [6], since both the algorithm cluster entire data. In case of *SArIS*, the final partitioning is imposed by the set of antibodies which cannot be identified with training data and the number of antibodies is considerably lesser than the number of antigens. The set of antibodies stands for representatives used to calculate the indices.
Below the results for four data sets, called *spherical4Class*, *spherical6Class*, *iris*, and *wines*, respectively are reported. The set *spherical6Class*, taken from [12] and shown in the right part of Fig. 2, is a 2-dimensional set of 300 points representing six different classes. Similarly, the set *spherical4Class*, shown in the left part of Fig. 2, is a slight modification of previous data set; it consists of 200 points representing four well separated classes. The sets *iris* and *wines*, available from [13], are well known multidimensional sets; their 2-dimensional projections are displayed on Fig. 3.

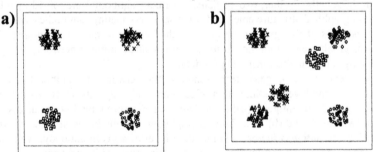

Fig. 2. Twodimensional data sets: *spherical4Class* (a) and *spherical6Class* (b)

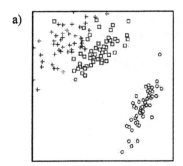
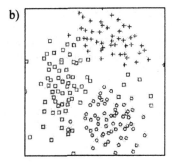

Fig. 3. Sammon's mapping of multi-dimensional datasets (a) iris, (b) wines

In case of *spherical4Class* data set all the algorithms easily predict correct number of clusters. Plots of the values of *interDen*, *intraDen*, *sep* and *CDbw* indices against the number of clusters for *k-means* algorithm are presented in Fig. 4. For hierarchical algorithm these plots are almost identical, thus we do not reproduce them. For hierarchical algorithm these plots are almost identical, thus we do not reproduce them.

The maximal values of *intraDen*, *sep* and *CDbw* and minimal of *interDen* appear when data are clustered in 4 groups. The number of clusters recovered by *SArIS* also equals 4 (for parameters $s=2.0$, $A_{aff}=0.4$ and *init_pop*=10).

To get a better insight how these algorithms behave, the quality of partitioning created by these algorithms when the number of clusters equals 4 is presented in Table 1.

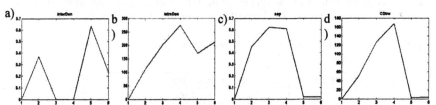

Fig. 4. Dependence of (a) *interDen*, (b) *intraDen*, (c) *sep*, and (d) *CDbw* indices on the number of clusters ($c=2, ..., 6$) for the *k-means* algorithm on *spherical4Class* dataset. Optimal values of indices appear for $c=4$

Table 1. Comparison of clustering result of the algorithms *k-means*, *hierarchical* and *SArIS* for *spherical4Class* dataset

Algorithm		interDen	intraDen	sep	CDbw
k-means (c=4)		0.00	274.45	0.610	167.65
hierarchical (c=4)		0.00	287.27	0.608	174.60
SArIS	n=55	0.00	294.86	0.610	179.92
	n=68	0.00	297.84	0.611	182.06
	n=71	0.00	295.77	0.609	180.12

The value of *interDen* is 0.00 for all the methods, but *intraDen*, *sep* and *CDbw* reach maximum for *SArIS* result. Notice that *SArIS* is a probabilistic algorithm – that is why we present results obtained in three different runs resulting in different memory size:

55, 68 and 71 cells. Remarkably, in all three runs of *SArIS* we obtain clusters of better quality than clusters produced by the two "classical" algorithms.

Figure 5 shows plots of the values of *interDen, intraDen, sep* and *CDbw* indices against the number of clusters obtained when *k-means* algorithm was run on *spherical6Class* dataset.

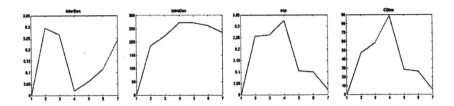

Fig. 5. Dependence of (a) *interDen*, (b) *intraDen*, (c) *sep*, (d) *CDbw* on the number of clusters (*c*=2..7) for algorithm *k-means* on *spherical6Class* dataset. Optimal values of indices appear for *c*=4

The plots of dependence of the indices values for non-automatic methods suggest the proper number of cluster is 4 (see Fig. 4) - the maximal values of *intraDen, sep* and *CDbw* and minimal of *interDen* appear when data are clustered in 4 groups. On the contrary, *SArIS* (for parameters *s*=2.0, A_{aff} =0.4 and *init_pop*=10), correctly determines proper number of clusters.

Table 2 contains values of the quality indices for three tested algorithms when the number of clusters equals 6. The highest quality results is generated by *SArIS*.

Table 2. Comparison of clustering result of the algorithms *k-means*, *hierarchical* and *SArIS* for *spherical6Class* dataset

Algorithm		interDen	intraDen	sep	CDbw
k-means (*c*=6)		0.164	203.90	0.105	21.48
hierarchical (*c*=6)		0.114	271.43	0.099	26.99
SArIS	*n*=93	0.160	290.25	0.108	31.27
	n=98	0.114	286.25	0.098	28.15
	n=102	0.142	290.30	0.107	31.16

Next dataset (*iris* – see Fig. 3a) is a four-dimensional set containing three convex clusters. Each clusters consists of 50 points, and only one of them is separable from the others. Plots of dependence of the quality indices against the number of clusters for *k-means* algorithm are shown on Fig. 6. From these plots it follows that the data should be divided into two separate classes. On the contrary to *SArIS* produces proper number of 3 clusters (for parameters *s*=1.6, A_{aff}=0.3 and *init_pop*=10).

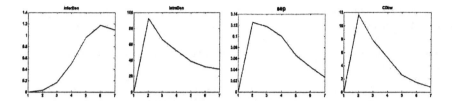

Fig. 6. Dependence of (a) *interDen*, (b) *intraDen*, (c) *sep*, (d) *CDbw* on the number of clusters (*c*=2..7) for algorithm *k-means* on *iris* dataset. Optimal values of the indices appear for *c*=2

Table 3 contains the quality indices when partitioning *iris* data by *k-means*, hierarchical and *SArIS* algorithm for *c*=3 clusters.

Table 3. Comparison of clustering result of the algorithms *k-means*, *hierarchical* and *SArIS* for *iris* dataset

Algorithm		interDen	intraDen	sep	CDbw
k-means (*c*=3)		0.167	66.22	0.118	7.81
hierarchical (*c*=3)		0.222	69.66	0.153	10.67
SArIS	*n*=78	0.366	116.91	0.176	20.58
	n=83	0.302	115.27	0.162	18.73
	n=103	0.140	128.99	0.113	14.62

The best clusters (*CDbw*=20) of very good separability (*sep*=0.176) are generated by *SArIS* in case of *n*=78. Another run of *SArIS* (*n*=103) produces very dense clusters (*intraDen*=129) with almost empty space between these clusters (*interDen*=0.14).

A thirteen-dimensional set of *wines* (see Fig. 3b) contains three overlapping clusters containing 59, 70 and 47 points, respectively. Plots of dependence of the quality indices against the number of clusters for *k-means* method are shown on Fig. 7. Again, this method suggest wrong number of clusters, i.e. *c* = 2, while *SArIS* is able to split the set in 3 correct groups (for parameters *s*=1.4, A_{aff}=0.7 and *init_pop*=10).

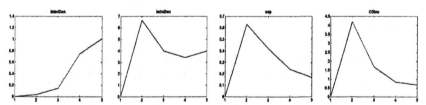

Fig. 7. Dependence of (a) *interDen*, (b) *intraDen*, (c) *sep*, (d) *CDbw* on the number of clusters (*c*=2..5) for algorithm *k-means* on *wines* dataset. Optimal values of the indices appear for *c*=2.

Table 4 presents clusters quality of the examined methods on *wines* dataset expressed by indices *interDen*, *intraDen*, *sep* and *CDbw*. The algorithm *k-means* creates partitioning of lowest density between clusters (*interDen*=0.189), the *hierarchical* method produces groups extremely separated (*sep*=0.36), however *SArIS* produces partitioning characterised by significantly greater values of *intraDen* (134.08) and *CDbw* (17.55) indices.

Table 4. Comparison of clustering result of the algorithms *k-means*, *hierarchical* and *SArIS* for *wines* dataset

Algorithm		interDen	intraDen	sep	CDbw
k-means (c=3)		0.189	52.55	0.146	7.68
hierarchical (c=3)		0.26	5.44	0.36	1.98
SArIS	n=243	0.354	134.08	0.13	17.55

5 Conclusions

Coping with 2-dimesional data allows visual verification of clustering results. However, when data dimensionality exceeds 3, we may need to use cluster validity indices to evaluate results of a clustering algorithm. Recently proposed index *CDbw*, 6, is inclined to identify compact and well-separated clusters of arbitrary shape.

Clustering validity indices are also used to determine the proper number of clusters. Clustering algorithms must be run several times on the same dataset for different number of groups to split. Then the plot of dependence of the index value against the number of clusters is examined. This technique is time-consuming (particularly in case of the massive datasets) and the plots not always suggest proper answer. This phenomenon is caused by the limitations and assumptions underlying chosen validity index. Most of such indices is predisposed to cope with convex groups and they are usually data-dependent. Therefore automatic algorithms dominate parametric methods in situations, when we do not own any knowledge about the number of groups.

In this paper an attempt to compare the quality of two classical algorithms: *k-means* and *hierarchical* with a new one – *SArIS* has been proposed. The quality is measured by four indices mentioned in Sect. 2. In almost all described experiments *SArIS* was able to generate proper partitioning with most dense and highly separable clusters.

References

1. Everitt, B. S.: Cluster Analysis. 3rd Edition. Edward Arnolds. London (1993)
2. Bezdek, J.C.: Pattern Recognition with Fuzzy Objective Functions. Plenum Press. New York (1981)
3. Berkhin, P.: Survey of clustering data mining techniques. Technical Report, Accrue Software, San Jose CA (2002)
4. Hall, L.O., Ozyrut, B., Bezdek, J.C.: Clustering with genetically optimized approach. IEEE Trans. on Evolutionary Computation 3 (1999) 103-112
5. Halkidi, M. et all: On clustering validation techniques. Journal of Intelligent Information Systems 17 (2-3) (2001) 107-145
6. Halkidi, M., Vazirgiannis, M.: Clustering validity assessment using multi representatives. Proceedings of SETN Conference. Thessaloniki Greece (2002)
7. Wierzchoń, S.T., Kużelewska, U.: Stable clusters formation in an Artificial Immune System. Proc. of 1st Intern. Conference on Artificial Immune Systems (2002) 68-75
8. de Castro, L. N., Timmis, J. I.: Artificial Immune Systems: A New Computational Intelligence Approach. Springer-Verlag (2002)

9. Timmis, J.: Artificial immune systems: A novel data analysis technique inspired by the immune network theory. PhD thesis, Department of Computer Science, University of Wales, Aberystwyth. Ceredigion Wales August (2000)
10. Wierzchoń, S.T., Kużelewska, U.: ImmuNet: A new technique of data exploration based on Artificial Immune Networks. Proceeding of VII Conference KAEiOG (2004)
11. Johnson, S.C.: Hierarchical clustering schemes. Psychometrika 2 (1967) 241-254
12. Bandyopadhyay, S., Maulik, U.: Genetic clustering for automatic evolution of clusters and application to image classification. Pattern Recognition 35 (2002) 1197-1208
13. Newman, D.J., Hettich, S., Blake, Merz, C.L.: UCI Repository of machine learning databases url = http://www.ics.uci.edu/~mlearn/MLRepository.html (1998)

Convergence Analysis of the Boundary Geometry Identification Obtained by Genetic Algorithms in the PIES

Eugeniusz Zieniuk[1], Krzysztof Szerszeń[2], Agnieszka Bołtuć[3]

University of Finance and Management in Bialystok, Faculty of Engineering
Grunwaldzka 1 st, 19-300 Elk, Poland
[1] e-mail: ezieniuk@ii.uwb.edu.pl, [2] kszerszen@ii.uwb.edu.pl,
[3] aboltuc@ii.uwb.edu.pl

Abstract. The paper presents an approach to 3D boundary identification carried our by the Parametric Integral Equation System (PIES) and Genetic Algorithm (GA). The aim of this study was to evaluate the influence of the number and arrangement of measurement points on result of identification process. The enclosed example provides a detailed description of the problem, for chosen geometry and different number of measured points.

1 Introduction

The simulation of practical problems often leads to solve boundary value problems. In general, they can be classified into two major groups: forward problems (analysis) [2,11] and inverse problems (synthesis) [1,4]. The inverse problems are ill-posed [7] and may be solved by new computational methods which are the subject of many researches and publications. In the synthesis problems it is necessary to determine, for example, the shape of the domain, boundary conditions or domain parameters determine on the basis of the measurement values obtained at some chosen points of a real domain or boundary of the problem considered.

Known numerical methods such as: the Finite Element Method (FEM) [11] and the Boundary Element Method (BEM) [2] are used to solve these optimizations. Hence the effectiveness of obtaining the solution will depend to a large extend on the ease of carrying out the modification of boundary geometry. FEM and BEM method do not offer such a possibility and any modification of the boundary requires its renewed discretization of the domain (FEM) or the boundary (BEM).

Therefore the classical Boundary Integral Equation (BIE) [2] was analytical modified in our own researches. The main aim of that modification was the separation of simultaneous approximation of the boundary geometry and boundary functions. As a result of analytical modification of BIE a new Parametric Integral Equation System (PIES) was proposed. This approach allows to eliminate traditional discretization the domain and boundary and provides continuous description of 3D boundary geometry by surface patches. In this paper the boundary geometry is described by Bézier patches [9] of third degree, which are defined in a normalized form by posing a small number of Bézier control points.

The purpose of this paper is to apply and analyze the effectiveness of the PIES for the identification of 3D smooth boundaries in inverse boundary value problems. The problem is reduced to a reconstruction of unknown part of the boundary based on comparison known empirical values with values obtained as a result of numerical solving of 3D analysis problem for given boundary. The proposed approach has been developed as a combination of genetic algorithm (GA) and the PIES, where the PIES is responsible for solving forward boundary problems, and GA for identification process.

The coupling of PIES and GA turns out an effective way [10] of 3D boundary identification. In the case of presented paper we try to answer the question: if and what influence on identification process have the number and arrangement of measurement points. Experimental results for chosen 3D geometry are presented and analyzed for different number of identified points.

2 The definition of 3D boundary in PIES

The PIES for 3D boundary-value problems is obtained by extending the tested concept for 2D problems as an analytical modification of the BIE [8]. The PIES for boundary problems described by Laplace's equation takes the following explicit form [9]

$$0.5u_l(v,w) = \sum_{j=1}^{n} \int_{v_{j-1}}^{v_j} \int_{w_{j-1}}^{w_j} \left\{ \overline{U}_{lj}^*(v_1,w_1,v,w)p_j(v,w) - \overline{P}_{lj}^*(v_1,w_1,v,w)u_j(v,w) \right\} J_j(v,w)dvdw \cdot \quad (1)$$

The boundary definition in PIES system can be defined by various parametric representations of surfaces used in computer graphics. The geometry described by means of six Bézier surfaces [6] and shown in Fig. 1 is used in presented identification analysis.

a)   b)   c)

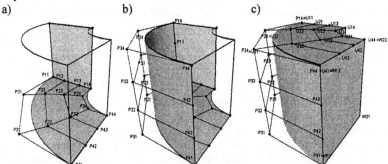

Fig.1. Further stages of defining 3D boundary geometry by means of Bézier control points: a) b) Bézier surfaces of the third   degree for non-linear fragments of the boundary geometry, c) final definition of the whole boundary geometry by 6 patches

The boundary declaration is reduced to define a minimal number of control points (16 for individual surface). We can join several patches together to form a closed surface. This approach creates the tool for modelling the given geometry with continuous conditions and reduces the total number of input data. This declaration is much more simpler that in FEM or BEM methods. The information about the defined boundary is included in the kernels $\bar{U}_{lj}^{*}(v_1,w_1,v,w)$, $\bar{P}^{*}_{lj}(v_1,w_1,v,w)$ from equation (1) in the following form

$$\bar{U}_{lj}^{*}(v_1,w_1,v,w)=\frac{1}{4\pi}\frac{1}{[\eta_1^2+\eta_2^2+\eta_3^2]^{0.5}}, \ \bar{P}^{*}_{lj}(v_1,w_1,v,w)=\frac{1}{4\pi}\frac{\eta_1 r_1^{(j)}(v,w)+\eta_2 r_2^{(j)}(v,w)+\eta_3 r_3^{(j)}(v,w)}{[\eta_1^2+\eta_2^2+\eta_3^2]^{1.5}} \quad (2)$$

by insertion Bézier patches, expressed by mathematical formula $P(v,w)$ in the following relations

$$\eta_1 = P_l^{(1)}(v_1,w_1)-P_j^{(1)}(v,w), \ \eta_2 = P_l^{(2)}(v_1,w_1)-P_j^{(2)}(v,w), \ \eta_3 = P_l^{(3)}(v_1,w_1)-P_j^{(3)}(v,w). \quad (3)$$

Hence only control points of individual Bézier patches are needed to model 3D boundary geometry and the number of these points is reduced to minimum.

3 The formulation of the identification problem

The presented identification problem focuses on reconstruction of the unknown shape of the boundary based on known empirical values, obtained in some measurement points. The identified boundary, shown in Fig. 1, is built by Bézier patches. Only control points are posed to their definition. Consequently, the identification of the boundary geometry is reduced to Bézier control points identification. As a result of the performed identification coordinates of searched corner points were obtained. In order to verify the reliability of the procedure of boundary identification a forward problem is solved by PIES and numerical values at measurement points are compared with experimental ones. The problem can be formulated as the minimalization of the difference between the measured and computed values at selected domain points, which is expressed as

$$fitness = \frac{\sum_{i=1}^{N}\left|u_i^{*}-u_i^{x}\right|}{N}, \quad (4)$$

where u_i^{x} are experimental values of measurement points in the domain , u_i^{*} are numerical values obtained by the PIES for identified boundary geometry, N – number of measurement points. The performed optimization function (4) is also the fitness function with minimum of implemented genetic algorithm, when $u_i^{*}=u_i^{x}$, for every $i=1,...,N$.

The identification process, shown in Fig.2, is steered by genetic algorithm.

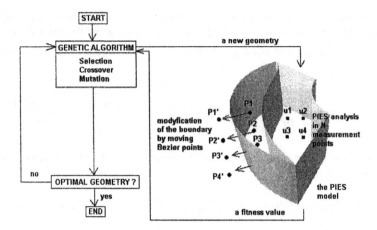

Fig. 2. Scheme of GA identification of the 3D boundary in PIES

Applied binary-coded GA is based on GALib software library [3,5] with genetic operators and parameters presented in Table 1.

Table 1. Used parameters of GA

gene length	16 bits
selection	roulette wheel
crossover	one point crossover
crossover rate	0.6
mutation	bit flip mutation
mutation rate	0.03
population size	25

The chromosome consists the coordinates of identified Bézier points.

4 Testing example

The investigated problem concentrates on the identification of an unknown part of boundary geometry $B_1 = \Gamma_1 + \Gamma_2 + \Gamma_3$ shown in Fig. 3 for stationary heat flow with known, constant part of the boundary B_2. Considered boundary geometry is modeled by means of six Bézier patches. Identification of an unknown part of the boundary reduces to determine the shape of Bezier patches $\Gamma_1, \Gamma_2, \Gamma_3$ described by control points with coordinates presented below.

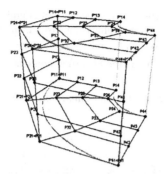

Fig. 3. Control points of identified part of the boundary

$$
\Gamma_1 = \begin{bmatrix}
P_{11}(0,8,0) & P_{12}(1.66,8,0) & P_{13}(3.33,8,0) & P_{14}(5,8,0) \\
P_{21}(x_1,y_1,0) & P_{22}(\tfrac{1}{3}(x_1+5),\tfrac{1}{3}(y_1+6.33),0) & P_{23}(\tfrac{2}{3}(x_1+5),\tfrac{2}{3}(y_1+6.33),0) & P_{24}(5,6.33,0) \\
P_{31}(x_2,y_2,0) & P_{32}(\tfrac{1}{3}(x_2+6.33),\tfrac{1}{3}(y_2+5),0) & P_{33}(\tfrac{2}{3}(x_2+6.33),\tfrac{2}{3}(y_2+5),0) & P_{34}(6.33,5,0) \\
P_{41}(8,0,0) & P_{42}(8,1.66,0) & P_{43}(8,3.33,0) & P_{44}(8,5,0)
\end{bmatrix}
$$

$$
\Gamma_2 = \begin{bmatrix}
P'_{11}(0,8,0) & P'_{12}(0,8,1.66) & P'_{13}(0,8,3.33) & P'_{14}(5,8,5) \\
P'_{21}(x_1,y_1,0) & P'_{22}(x_1,y_1,1.66) & P'_{23}(x_1,y_1,3.33) & P'_{24}(x_1,y_1,5) \\
P'_{31}(x_2,y_2,0) & P'_{32}(x_2,y_2,1.66) & P'_{33}(x_2,y_2,3.33) & P'_{34}(x_2,y_2,5) \\
P'_{41}(8,0,0) & P'_{42}(8,0,1.66) & P'_{43}(8,0,3.33) & P'_{44}(8,0,0)
\end{bmatrix}
$$

$$
\Gamma_3 = \begin{bmatrix}
P''_{11}(0,8,5) & P''_{12}(1.66,8,5) & P''_{13}(3.33,8,5) & P''_{14}(5,8,5) \\
P''_{21}(x_1,y_1,5) & P''_{22}(\tfrac{1}{3}(x_1+5),\tfrac{1}{3}(y_1+6.33),5) & P''_{23}(\tfrac{2}{3}(x_1+5),\tfrac{2}{3}(y_1+6.33),5) & P''_{24}(5,6.33,5) \\
P''_{31}(x_2,y_2,5) & P''_{32}(\tfrac{1}{3}(x_2+6.33),\tfrac{1}{3}(y_2+5),5) & P''_{33}(\tfrac{2}{3}(x_2+6.33),\tfrac{2}{3}(y_2+5),5) & P''_{34}(6.33,5,5) \\
P''_{41}(8,0,5) & P''_{42}(8,1.66,5) & P''_{43}(8,3.33,5) & P''_{44}(8,5,5)
\end{bmatrix}
$$

(5)

To simplify the identification process only 2 coordinates $x_1, y_1, (x_2, y_2) = const$ and
4 coordinates x_1, y_1, x_2, y_2 of selected control points, are searched by GA. These
coordinates allow to significantly change the shape of the identified boundary. The
initial guess for the identification process is provided by assuming the coordinates of
the control point from the following range

$$
x_i \in \left(x_{i(MIN)}, x_{i(MAX)}\right), y_i \in \left(y_{i(MIN)}, Y_{i(MAX)}\right), \; i = 1,2
\qquad (6)
$$

The identification quality is measured as the difference between the identified and
original points related to a range of possible GA's values, defined by

$$
E = \sum_{i=1}^{M} \left(\frac{\left|x_i^* - x_i\right|}{\left|x_{i(MAX)} - x_{i(MIN)}\right|} + \frac{\left|y_i^* - y_i\right|}{\left|y_{i(MAX)} - y_{i(MIN)}\right|} \right),
\qquad (7)
$$

where x_i^*, y_i^* -coordinates of original Bézier points and $M = 1,2$.

In order to verify the reliability of the procedure of boundary identification a forward problem was solved and numerical values at measurement points were compared with experimental ones. The unknown boundary B_1 is assumed to be maintained at constant temperature $u = 0$, while on the identified boundary B_2 a constant temperature $u = 100$ was set.

Sample identification process of 4 coordinates x_1, y_1, x_2, y_2 steered by GA is presented in Fig. 4.

a)   b)

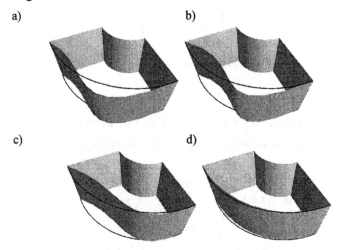

c)   d)

Fig. 4. The boundary geometry identification: a) geometry from initial population, b), c) the next stages of identification processes d) the final geometry

Detailed researches related with influence of the number of measurement points on identification process were performed, 3, 6, 9 and 12 points in the domain of considered boundary geometry were taken into consideration.

Results obtained after first 50 iterations with the population consists of 25 chromosomes are presented in Table 2.

Table 2. Input data and results from chosen identification processes

Number of measurement points u_i^*	Two identified points Average error of co-ordinates*	Four identified points Average error of co-ordinates*
3	5.253%	13.452%
6	3.624%	11.498%
9	2.524%	7.832%
12	2.343%	6.031%

(*- results obtained by GA with 25 chromosomes and after 50 iterations, and repeated 15 times)

The progress of evolving function E (7) can be seen in the Fig. 5.

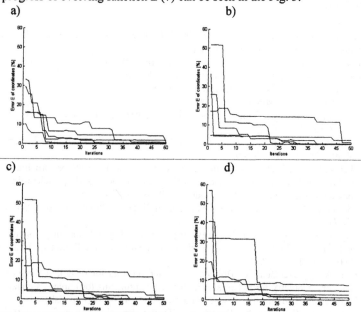

Fig. 5. Some values of E obtained for identified geometry for : a) 3, b) 6, c) 9 and
d) 12 measured $u_i^{\bullet}$ values

As can be seen the number of identified coordinates of control points has great influence on accuracy of obtained results. But we can also observe, that more accurate results are obtained when the number of measurement points increases.

5 Conclusions

The proposed method used in this paper is the simplest method giving at the same time, accurate results. Paper presents some examples of boundary geometry identification with different number of identified and measurement points. Using the calculations from a number of other numerical examples analyzed by the authors, it appears, the most accurate results are obtained when number of measurement points is larger than 9. After that number there is some stability of solutions. We can also observe, that accuracy of obtained results depends on the number of identified coordinates. Therefore second conclusion is that: if the number of identified points increasing than the number of measurement points should be larger.

References

1. Beck, J. V., Blackwell B., St. Clair, Jr. C. R.:Inverse Heat Conduction: Ill-posed Problems. Wiley-Interscience, New York (1985)
2. Brebbia, C.A., Telles, J.C.F., Wrobel, L.C.: Boundary element techniques, theory and applications in engineering. Springer, New York (1984)
3. Goldberg, D. E.: Genetic Algorithms in Search, Optimization, and Machine Learning, Reading. MA: Addison-Wesley (1989)
4. Liu, G.R., Han, X.: Computational inverse techniques in non-destructive evaluation. CRC Press LLC (2003)
5. Massachusetts Institute of Technology: GALib C++ Genetic Algorithms Library. Version 2.4, http://lancet.mit.edu/ga/.
6. Mortenson, M.: Mathematics for Computer Graphics Applications: An Introduction to the Mathematics and Geometry of Cad/Cam, Geometric Modeling, Scientific Visualization, and Other CG Applications. Industrial Press (1999)
7. Tikhonov, A.N., Arsenin, V.Y.: Solution of Ill-posed Problems. John Wiley & Sons (1977)
8. Zieniuk, E.: A new integral identity for potential polygonal domain problems described by parametric linear functions. Engineering Analysis with Boundary Elements, Vol. 26/10, (2002), 897-904
9. Zieniuk, E., Szerszeń, K., Bołtuć, A.: Bézier surfaces for modeling three-dimentional boundary geometry for potential boundary-value problems for Laplace's equation. PTSK Symulacja w badaniach i rozwoju, Kraków (2004), 447-454 (in polish)
10. Zieniuk, E., Szerszeń, K., Bołtuć, A.: 3D boundary shape identification in boundary-value problems using the Parametric Integral Equation System with the aid of genetic algorithms. Image Analysis, Computer Graphics, Security Systems and Artificial Intelligence Applications, Vol. I, WSFiZ Press, Białystok, (2005), 43-51
11. Zienkiewicz, O.C.: The Finite Element Methods. McGraw-Hill, London (1977)

INDEX